The New Politics of Sinn Féin

T0341761

The New Politics
of Sinn Féin

Kevin Bean

LIVERPOOL UNIVERSITY PRESS

First published 2007 by
Liverpool University Press
4 Cambridge Street
Liverpool, L69 7ZU

British Library Cataloguing-in-Publication Data
A British Library CIP Record is available

ISBN 978-1-84631-144-4 cased
ISBN 978-1-84631-146-8 limp

Typeset in Apollo by Koinonia, Bury
Printed and bound by CPI Group (UK) Ltd, Croydon, CR0 4YY

In memory of my mother, Madge McGowan

Contents

Acknowledgements

This book began as a response to the many questions raised by developments in Provisional Republican politics since the early 1990s. In particular, it attempts to define the nature of those changes and to suggest some reasons why they have taken the form that they have. This process of change has been a complex and convoluted one. It has produced tens of thousands of column inches and scores of books that attempt to explain a pattern of events that few outside the inner circle of the Provisional leadership (and possibly not many even there) could have predicted when Republicans began to 'engage' with the British government in the late 1980s.

My own contribution to this enterprise rests on the work of others who have written about the peace process and Republicanism over the last twenty years. My debt to them is apparent in how I have thought and written about these issues. This project would not have been completed without the help and cooperation of three groups of people. The first group comprises activists, politicians, civil servants and others who were either involved in the events and the processes that I describe or who closely observed them. They were generous with their time and recollections as well as being unfailingly helpful in terms of my requests for interviews and other assistance. Without their full cooperation this account would have contained even more limitations and weaknesses. I wish to thank: David Adams, Patricia Campbell, Tony Catney, Brian Feeney, Phillip Ferguson, Jim Gibney, Sir David Goodall, Tomás Gorman, Tommy Gorman, Claire Hackett, Pauline Hadaway, Tom Hartley, Brendan Hughes, the late John Kelly, Jake Jackson, Bobby Lavery, Sir Gerry Loughran, Tommy and Traolach Lyons, Bernadette McAliskey, John McAnulty, Eamonn MacDermott, Dr Anthony McIntyre, Tommy McKearney, Mickey McMullen, Donncha Mac Niallais, Kevin McQuillen, Danny Morrison, Sir Richard Needham, Ruairí Ó Brádaigh, Eoin Ó Broin, Siobhan Ó Dhuibhir, Malachi O'Doherty, Dr Dara O'Hagan, Dr Felim Ó hAdhmaill, Richard O'Rawe, Liam Ó Ruairc, Glen Phillips, Gerard Rice and Matt Treacy, as well as various current and former members of the Provisional Republican movement.

Secondly, a number of colleagues and friends, connected to the Institute of Irish Studies, the University of Liverpool and to other institutions, have helped to clarify my ideas through discussion, reading draft chapters and offering sound advice. I am indebted to Professor Marianne Elliott, Dr Colin Irwin, Dr Ian McKeane, Dr Pat Nugent, Dr Maria Power, Dr Frank Shovlin, Dr Diane Urquhart, Linda Christensen, Dorothy Lynch, Harvey Cox, Dr Michael Huggins, Professor Richard English, John Shaw, Dr Peter Shirlow, Professor Jonathan Tonge, Geraldine Maguire, Liam Ó Ruairc, Dr Mark Hayes, Peter Day, David Elliott, Dr Kevin MacNamara, Dr Rogelio Alonso, Bernadette Dyer, Pauline Hadaway, Deirdre McGuire, Bernadette Bean and Teresa Bean for their help and support.

Lastly, I wish also to acknowledge the assistance of the staff in the University of Liverpool Library, the Belfast Central Newspaper Library and the British Library, London. Special thanks should also be given to Yvonne Murphy and Dr Kris Brown of the Northern Ireland Political Collection in the Linen Hall Library, Belfast for helping me through the maze of sources and pointing me towards some fruitful areas of research. I am also grateful to everyone at Belfast Exposed Photographic Gallery for their help, not only in obtaining the cover photographs, but also in providing me with new insights into life in the city through their exhibitions, photographic archive and publications. Anthony Cond and his colleagues at Liverpool University Press were efficient and helpful during the long process of editing and production. Their hard work was vital in turning the manuscript into the finished article. Finally, many thanks are owed to my family and friends for their support in numerous ways during the research and writing. Without their help it would not have been completed.

List of Abbreviations

ACE	Action for Community Employment
ANC	African National Congress
CRJ	Community Restorative Justice
DUP	Democratic Unionist Party
EU	European Union
GLC	Greater London Council
INLA	Irish National Liberation Army
IRA	Irish Republican Army
LCI	Labour Committee on Ireland
MEP	Member of the European Parliament
MLA	Member of the Legislative Assembly
MP	Member of Parliament (UK)
NGOs	Non-governmental Organizations
PLO	Palestine Liberation Organization
PSNI	Police Service of Northern Ireland
PUP	Progressive Unionist Party
SDLP	Social Democratic and Labour Party
TD	Teachta Dála/Member of the Dáil
TUAS	Tactical Use of Armed Struggle/Totally Unarmed Strategy
UDA	Ulster Defence Association
USDT	Upper Springfield Development Trust

Introduction

They moved through Washington as smoothly as sharks in warm water...
Whatever they were, or had been, they were politicians to their fingertips,
wholly at ease in their surroundings.[1]

Where British cultural symbols are involved in public life, equivalent
Irish cultural symbols should be given equal prominence. Statues of Irish
Republican icons placed at Stormont will make it more welcoming for nation-
alists.[2]

From Loughgall to Stormont

On 10 May 2007, the Sinn Féin weekly newspaper *An Phoblacht* carried
a front page photograph of a smiling Ian Paisley and Martin McGuinness
at the swearing-in of Northern Ireland's new devolved executive. Tucked
away at the top of the same page was the strapline: 'Huge Crowds Pay
Tribute to Loughgall Martyrs', referring to a Republican commemoration
for eight IRA volunteers killed by the SAS in May 1987. The juxtaposi-
tion of the two events was commented on by supporters and critics of the
Provisionals as symbolizing the distance that the Provisional movement
had travelled in the last twenty years. To the Provisionals' unrepentant
Republican opponents, the new devolved executive 'solidified English
rule' and was a betrayal of the cause for which the Loughgall volunteers
had died.[3] For Martin McGuinness, the distance between Loughgall and
the assembly at Stormont was not just a question of time. Speaking at the
commemoration, he argued that the journey undertaken 'by the Republican struggle ... [had opened] up ... a democratic and peaceful path
towards Irish unity and independence'.[4]

1 Former British Ambassador to the USA Sir Christopher Meyer describing Provisional
  leaders Gerry Adams and Martin McGuinness in Washington, DC. See Meyer, 2005,
  113.
2 Sinn Féin Assemblyman Paul Butler, quoted in 'SF calls for equality at Stormont', 10
  May 2007, http://www.u.tv/newsroom/indepth.asp?pt=n&id==82142.
3 'Paisley and Adams join to solidify English rule', *Saoirse*, April 2007.
4 Martin McGuinness quoted in P. Whelan, 'Huge crowds pay tribute to Loughgall
  Martyrs', *An Phoblacht*, 10 May 2007.

It is easy to contrast the statesmanlike rhetoric of 2007 with the militant language of 1987. In 2007, the Provisionals' 'primary political objective is to deliver Irish reunification and a genuine process of national reconciliation on the island': in 1987, Republicans were 'committed to the armed struggle … [as] the only means by which the British government can be forced to break its stranglehold on political progress and peace'.[5] Given that the initial contacts of the peace process were already underway before Loughgall, the conversion of the Provisionals from militant revolutionaries into constitutional nationalists is already passing from the realm of contemporary politics into that of history. It is an accomplished fact for a political generation whose members are too young to remember the Troubles: to them, veteran Provisionals are simply middle-aged politicians appealing for votes.

It is also an accomplished fact of political life for many commentators and analysts who have long accepted without question that the Provisionals are a constitutional party. The Irish and British governments have publicly accepted the Provisionals' *bona fides* since 1997, and as the pictures prove, in 2007 a smiling Ian Paisley was now prepared to go into government with what he had once described as 'the terrorists of IRA/Sinn Féin'.[6] There was a valedictory tone in the speeches and the commentaries: to many, a 'formal line' had been drawn 'under decades of hostility and strife' to create 'a deal that is going to stick'.[7] The historic and unprecedented meeting between Gerry Adams and Ian Paisley in March 2007 likewise carried the 'subliminal but unambiguous message' that 'after 3,700 deaths, the Troubles are over and the real politics can begin'.[8] Behind the political rhetoric and the media hyperbole a number of questions remained, about what would constitute the future 'real politics' in the region, and just as importantly about what had brought the region to this historic crossroads. Many of the questions that had been central to the politics of the peace process remained relevant to the brave new world of Northern Irish politics; they had not really been addressed, much less answered.[9]

One of the most important of these concerned the nature of the Provisional movement and its transformation into a mainstream political party

5   Martin McGuinness quoted in P. Whelan, 'Huge crowds pay tribute to Loughgall Martyrs': 'Loughgall Martyrs', *An Phoblacht/Republican News* May 14th 1987.
6   I. Paisley, 'Election Platform', *Newsletter*, 4 May 2005.
7   A. Cowell and E. Quinn, 'Home rule returns to Northern Ireland', *International Herald Tribune*, 9 May 2007.
8   D. McKittrick, 'Two worlds come together to broker a new era of hope', *The Independent*, 27 March 2007.
9   For one view of the unanswered questions about the Provisional movement, see Alonso, 2007, 1–6.

'ready for government North and South'.[10] This process of change and the creation of what became known as New Sinn Féin were central to many of the narratives of Northern Irish politics since the 1980s.[11] For the Irish and British governments, as well as Unionist politicians, separating the style from the substance of Provisionalism had been essential to their understanding of political progress. Although the two governments had understood that the Provisional leadership was trying to 'get off the hook of violence' from the late 1980s, and that by 1993 had effectively accepted that there could be 'no reunification without the consent of a majority in Northern Ireland', the management of these changes was of necessity a long and complex process.[12]

Understanding this as a management process that succeeded through the personal efforts of Tony Blair and Bertie Ahern and the good offices of influential external parties, such as the USA, is a convincing narrative, but does not fully explain the pattern of events.[13] Likewise, while the 'remarkable political skill' of the IRA leadership in executing a volte-face 'few Irish political leaders have ever had to attempt' is widely accepted, this emphasis on the subjective understates the impact of fundamental changes in the wider political environment on the development of the Provisional movement.[14]

A feature of many assessments of Irish Republicanism and indeed of Northern Irish politics in general is to focus on their historically deter-mined and exceptionalist characteristics. From the beginning of the Troubles, Northern Ireland has frequently been described as a place apart whose contemporary communal conflict is simply the latest episode in an endemic quarrel of the type that the rest of Europe abandoned in the seventeenth century. Similarly, Provisionalism has been interpreted as the product of a powerful Republican tradition shaped by an eternal dialectic between careerism and principle. This form of historical determinism enables analysts and critics to see New Sinn Féin's original sin of parlia-mentary politics more clearly by using the mirror of Clann na Poblachta and Fianna Fáil.[15]

A closer examination shows the substance of Provisional ideology in

10 'Ready for government North and South' (editorial), *An Phoblacht*, 3 May 2007.
11 Maillot, 2005, 1–6.
12 G. FitzGerald, 'Wise leaders who learned difficult lessons', *The Irish Times*, 3 February 2007.
13 D. Ó Ceallaigh, Irish Ambassador to the UK, speaking at the Institute of Irish Studies, University of Liverpool, 6 February 2007.
14 G. FitzGerald, 'Wise leaders who learned difficult lessons', *The Irish Times*, 3 February 2007.
15 White, 2006, 151.

a rather different light. Instead of a continuous tradition, what emerges is a much more malleable and pragmatic form of politics shaped by a wide range of social forces and ideological influences. Above all, it is as a product of its time and place rather than as an unthinking replication of hallowed tradition that the trajectory of Provisionalism can be best understood. From its founding moment, the environment that shaped the movement extended beyond the streets of West Belfast and the villages of East Tyrone to guerrilla campaigns in Latin America and civil rights activism in the USA. This eclecticism and pragmatism has been a hallmark of Provisional Republicanism, along with its susceptibility to the pull of powerful external ideological forces. As one leading Provisional strategist described it:

> *The exigencies of survival meant that Republicans couldn't allow themselves to be constrained by principle* ... Life is complex, circumstances change ... and as in nature, it is those who can adapt who survive. In fact, to use and exploit the system in a considered way, both in its contradictions or whatever advantages it offers to achieve one's ultimate aims is often to do the revolutionary thing. This, to me, is the story of the peace process. [Emphasis added][16]

Danny Morrison's assessment of Provisional politics makes it even more difficult to track the changes in the movement's ideology and draws us back to the perennial question: 'What is Irish Republicanism?' Republican critics of the Provisionals could point to an almost theological sense of tradition that conferred moral and judicial legitimacy on them as 'the legitimate government of Ireland'.[17] Others attempted to establish the full extent of the Provisionals' betrayal by comparing their current politics with previous positions.[18] If the lack of a developed theoretical tradition militated against a clear definition of Republican ideology, wider changes in the political and ideological landscape during the last quarter of the twentieth century had an even more significant impact on the politics of the Provisionals.

The politics of a changing world

The relatively stable Cold War world was swept away by far-reaching changes that had a fundamental impact on all political and ideological projects. The ideological decline of the left, the defeat of national

16 D. Morrison, 'Paisley just a blip in the ongoing peace process', *Daily Ireland*, 8 February 2006.

17 See speech at a Republican Sinn Féin Easter Commemoration quoted in 'Editorial', The Plough: E-mail Newsletter of the Irish Republican Socialist Party, vol. 4, no. 12, 19 April 2007, http://www.theplough.netfirms.com/.

18 For an example of this frequently used argument, see 'Oops! Did I say that?', *The*

liberation movements and the apparent triumph of neoliberalism resulted paradoxically in the emergence of new hybrid forms of politics that combined a culture of contentment with a sense of deep-seated crisis.[19] Many of these changes were identified with the collapse of the USSR, but it is now clear that the causes and effects were much wider than that. In particular, the political projects of the left that were rooted in the universalist values of the Enlightenment were increasingly challenged by new forms of particularism. It was in this radically altered political climate that what became the ideological project of New Sinn Féin first emerged.

Whilst some analysts have accurately compared the Provisionals' political trajectory to that of other movements that have capitulated and accommodated themselves to the status quo, the Provisionals have also been influenced by the dominant strands of 'identity politics' within Northern Ireland itself.[20] These ideological forms have become the dominant consensus, reflected in British government attempts to stabilize and normalize politics and society within the region. As the framing ideology for all aspects of life, the 'politics of identity' give the state the 'responsibility to recognize, respect and protect the "cultural identities" of Northern Ireland's two communities'. This meant that politics is 'no longer concerned with grand visions about who should run society … Rather it is obsessed … with striking a careful balance between two apparently volatile communities', strengthening a politics of grievance and communal recognition.[21] The Provisionals did not simply absorb these particularist politics through a form of ideological osmosis. The politics of identity were cognate with the strong elements of ethno-political and cultural nationalism already present within Republicanism.

The ideological collapse of the left into forms of particularism also exerted a direct influence on those Provisionals who had most closely identified with radical projects in the 1970s and 1980s. However, the most important factor was the increasing engagement between the British state and the nationalist community that shaped the context for the Republican political project through community activism, electoral politics and local government during the 1980s and 1990s. These interactions not only resulted in numerous contacts that drew nationalists into a closer working relationship with the state in its various forms; they also directly and indirectly determined the political and social agenda within the nationalist

Sovereign Nation, February/March 2006.

19 D. O'Brien, 'What shapes how we vote', *The Irish Times*, 31 July 2006.

20 K. Allen, 'The Death of Radical Republicanism', *International Socialism*, Issue 114, Spring 2007, 51–56.

21 All quotations from B. O'Neill , 'Riots for recognition', *spiked politics*, 14 September 2005, http://www.spiked-online.com.

community and so subtly altered the ideological and political framework of Provisional politics.

This interaction between the state and the nationalist community was so significant politically because of the state's predominant role in the political economy of Northern Ireland. The British state's interventionist social and economic policy was a vital part of its normalization strategy, which was designed to defeat the IRA and contain Sinn Féin's political challenge in the 1980s. One of the paradoxes of this strategy was that it actually strengthened the Provisional movement's position within its base areas and facilitated a process of institutionalization. As part of the ballot-paper-and-armalite strategy, Republicans had developed a strong organizational structure within the nationalist community. This was further consolidated as a structure of power by the access to resources that it gained as a result of strengthening its contacts with the state. Community organizations and political structures that had started out as agencies of revolutionary mobilization became gatekeepers between the state and the nationalist community, as well as acting as transmission belts for the Provisional movement.

The result was that by the early 1990s the Provisional movement's position within the nationalist community had some of the characteristics of a state power. That power, however, was reliant both directly and indirectly on access to British state resources, as well as its role as a mediator between the state and the 'resistance community'. Even before the peace process, members of what the Provisionals defined as 'the broad Republican community' were acting as partners in the state's community strategy, and even though they believed that they were subverting it, in practice it was the state that was subverting and transforming their revolutionary strategy.

Most importantly, from the late 1980s onwards, key parts of the Republican political agenda were concerned with making demands directed towards the state. Issues of discrimination and the allocation of resources became the stuff of everyday politics, and Provisional politicians ensured that their community got its fair share. While theoretically wishing to overthrow the state, the practice was to bargain and mobilize to pressurize it. Republicans were essentially functioning within an ideological framework and political context defined by the state. The peace process and the resulting political settlement merely formalized what had been a growing structural relationship between the nationalist community, the Provisional movement and the British state since the 1980s.

In this context, it may appear to Republican critics that the Provisionals have joined the long list of Irish people who have taken English gold and been bought off by the state. However, the British state is much more powerful than that, and its power resides in its ability to shape the social and political context within which opponents conduct their challenge and people live their lives. In a period of demobilization and depoliticization, this power is greatly enhanced.

These issues, and their implications for the future of Northern Ireland in general and Republican politics in particular, are addressed in the following chapters. The analytical model that is employed is not a crude one that suggests a simplistic relationship between an economic and social base, and an ideological superstructure. There is not a simple input–output model for ideological development. The interaction between economy, state and civil society is complex: structures of political and social power are frequently contradictory, with hazy boundaries and fluid forms.

In the contemporary world, the state appears able to determine both the political and the social context in which challengers operate, and thus shapes the nature of their politics. However, its power is constrained to a certain extent by those same opponents: both as a structure of social power and as an instrument for the construction and the maintenance of an ideological hegemony, it must take these oppositional groups into account.[22] Thus the functioning of the state and the forms of its ideology are, to some extent, also shaped by this engagement with opponents.

My broad aim is to understand the contradictory structures of power and ideological forms that have emerged as a result of nearly forty years of conflict in Northern Ireland. These forms and structures will continue to exert influence over the politics of a post-conflict society. The rapid pace of social and economic change along with other aspects of the normalization process will not quickly transform Northern Ireland into a slightly more edgy version of either Surrey or Dublin 4.[23] A society whose politics and consociational institutions are structured around communal division will ensure that the politics of Provisionalism, like those of most other political actors in the region, will follow the patterns laid down during the peace process, and will continue to revolve around resource allocation and the recognition of identities.

A subsidiary theme is to rescue Northern Ireland, and Republican politics in particular, from the enormous condescension of exceptionalism by locating and understanding the new politics of Sinn Féin within a much broader framework than the narrow ground of Northern Ireland. Likewise, this account of the Provisionals' political development is critical of those contemporary forms of historical determinism that portray human beings

22 Hobsbawm, 2007, 25.
23 L. Ó Ruairc, 'The agreed truth and the real truth: the new Northern Ireland', *Variant*, 29, Summer 2007.

as merely the passive carriers of ideologies, rather than conscious agents attempting to understand and act on the world as they interpret it.

...and back to Loughgall

The book is not a detailed blow-by-blow account of the peace process, or a narrative of the ideological evolution of New Sinn Féin. Such accounts already exist and that story does not need retelling.[24] Likewise, Republican critics of the New Sinn Féin project have proven themselves adept at close reading of the collected works of Gerry Adams and highlighting the shifts in position over the last twenty years. What this book does attempt is to understand the patterns of thought and the structures of meaning that underpin New Sinn Féin.

To do this, the book is divided into two linked groups of chapters. One group (Part I), organized around the theme of 'community', discusses the emergence of the Provisionals as a structure of power within the nationalist community. It focuses on their origins within a mass movement of the nationalist working class and rural poor in the early 1970s, and their attempts to establish communal hegemony through the discourse of the resistance community. This part also discusses how the development of Provisionalism was shaped by the wider structures of nationalist civil society and its interaction with the various structures of the British state. These chapters conclude by considering the contemporary impact these Provisional structures of power have on the hybrid social structures of the 'new Northern Ireland'.

Part II focuses on the ideological origins of New Sinn Féin. It situates Provisionalism in a global political context and shows that its politics are comparable to other ideological projects that have undergone a similar transformation since the late 1980s. These chapters consider the tension between the universal and the particular within Republicanism, and how this is reflected in specific aspects of the contemporary Provisional project. They trace how politics in Northern Ireland are increasingly structured by forms of consociationalism and communal resource allocation by the state, and how this has shaped the New Sinn Féin project. In particular, these sections discuss the impact that identity politics have had on Republican theory and practice in the 1990s and 2000s. These chapters also assess Republicanism's declining sense of agency and historical subjectivity as they are reflected in the changing nature of the Provisionals' politics of transition. These changes have directly influenced Sinn Féin's

---

24 For an example of what have become the best standard accounts, see Moloney, 2007 and English, 2003.

peace process strategy and its willingness to participate in the devolved government of Northern Ireland as part of an historic compromise with Unionism.

Another look at Loughgall will illustrate the impact of these ideological changes on the political and social life of the nationalist community. In May 1987, *An Phoblacht/Republican News* argued:

> Republicans do not complain about the way in which the British forces carried out their operation. Centuries of British terror have taught us to expect it. The illegitimacy of the forces which carried out the Loughgall killings is not simply in their actions there but in their very presence in our country. It has always been and always will be illegitimate and unacceptable.[25]

On 23 August 2004, it was reported that relatives of one of the IRA members killed at Loughgall had had a 'very useful 'meeting with the Police Service of Northern Ireland's (PSNI) Chief Constable. One family member commented afterwards: 'It clarified a number of issues we wanted dealt with and we will move on from there... We are just a family trying to get to the truth about what happened to my brother.' The police spokesperson described the encounter in similar terms: 'It was a useful meeting with an open two-way discussion. The Kellys raised a number of issues with the Chief Constable. He in turn offered his assessment of the decision to deploy the army against what he termed a dangerous gang.'[26]

These two reports, seventeen years apart, are a small but significant illustration of the shift in Republican thinking that has occurred over that period. The first is defiant and unapologetic in support of the armed campaign, arguing that the 'murder' and illegitimacy of the security forces actions at Loughgall lay not only in the act of premeditated killing by the SAS, but in their its presence as a foreign occupation force in Northern Ireland. The second proceeded from a different premise entirely. The statements of the relatives and the police echoed each other and seemed almost to reflect in their language and therapeutic tone a joint search for truth as part of a process of reconciliation. The relatives did question the police force's ability to deliver the truth, not because of any illegitimacy on the part of the state but because the PSNI was not deemed sufficiently independent. In 1987, Republicans were engaged in an exchange of fire with the police: now they are engaged in an exchange of opinion as part of the search for truth and consensus. Such has been the ideological transformation of Provisional Republicanism. Such is the focus of this book.

---

25 'Loughgall Martyrs', *An Phoblacht/Republican News*, 14 May 1987.
26 S. O'Neill, 'IRA man's family calls Orde meeting "useful"', *Irish News*, 24 August 2004.

Part I

Defining the Community

Introduction to Part I

The history of Provisionalism can be summarized as one of a long retreat from the highpoint of the early 1970s to the current pragmatic adaptation to the status quo. As the insurrectionary wave that had produced the Provisionals began to recede after 1974, they were forced to manoeuvre for nearly twenty years to avoid obvious military and political defeat. However, by the 1990s Republicans were eventually compelled to yield and through the peace process arrive at their current position of accommodation with the British state in Northern Ireland.

The chapters in Part I discuss the development of Provisional Republicanism as a political organization and a structure of power in the 1980s and 1990s. The central theme is an outline of the processes that transformed the Republican movement from an anti-state insurgency with claims to revolutionary leadership to a potential partner in governing the state it was pledged to destroy. Political sociologists have explained similar political transformations and incorporation as following an iron law of oligarchy.[1] Theories of institutionalization explain how social movement organizations 'become players in the conventional political process, thereby losing their initial character as challengers to the status quo and the forces in power.'[2] So powerful are these forces that it has been suggested that in the future, 'contentious politics' in capitalist societies might be domesticated and 'institutionalized into ordinary politics, as were the strike and the demonstration in the nineteenth century.'[3]

These arguments alert us to the significance of the political environment, the 'external factors and forces that channel and mitigate protest', and the determining power of the state to shape political challengers within these patterns of change.[4] The political environment in which the Provisionals function should be understood in as broad a way as possible, to include not only other political actors but also the social and economic determinants that ultimately structure political life.

1 Michels, 1959.
2 Rucht, 1999, 153.
3 Tarrow, 1994, 9.
4 Rucht, 1999, 153–154; Michels, 1959.

Thus, to understand how this process changed the ideological and political practice of the Republican movement we need to assess the impact of conscious state strategies acting in conjunction with processes of social and economic change. The operative term here is 'conscious', as both British governments and Republicans do not passively reflect the social and economic currents around them, but devise strategies in an attempt to shape them to their own advantage.

Combining this understanding with an awareness of the importance of the strategic choices available, it is possible to assess the degree to which the evolution of the Provisionals, like other social movement organizations, is 'shaped more by interactions with other actors than by processes internal to a movement'.[5] What emerges is a more complex dialectic between the British state and Republicanism mediated by and through these other independent variables, such as the economy and the development of civil society in nationalist areas. Consequently, both parties to the conflict made their own history, but not under conditions of their own choosing.

If the relationship defined by the British state marks one boundary for the development of the Provisionals, then the civil society of the nationalist community defines the other. The crisis of the Northern Irish state in the early 1970s produced a favourable political opportunity structure for the emergence of the Provisionals: however, it was the associative networks of nationalist civil society that 'provide the material, symbolic and human resources that facilitate activism in militant nationalism', and proved decisive in the mobilization of support for Republicanism among sections of the nationalist population.[6] These spontaneous origins as a 'working-class organization based in the ghetto areas of the cities and in the poorer rural areas' gave Republicanism the ideologically eclectic and pragmatic character that continues to be its hallmark in the twenty-first century.[7] If we wish to understand the future trajectory of Provisionalism we need to understand the complexities of this relationship between movement and community.

Borrowing terminology from the theory of the state, it is possible to define contemporary Republicanism as a structure of power. Furthermore, we can classify this structure in terms of the degrees of consent and coercion that define the relationship between Provisionalism and the nationalist community. Shifts in the balance between these elements of consent and coercion indicate the patterns and mechanisms of the institutionalization

5 Oliver and Myers, 2003, 19.
6 Casquette, 2001, 240–241.
7 'Northern Ireland: Future Terrorist Trends (the Glover Report)', quoted in Cronin, 1980, 342.

process, as well as showing the nature of political authority and legitimacy within Provisionalism. The extent to which Republicans were able to establish a certain hegemony from the 1970s onwards may point to a degree of consent within sections of the nationalist population. However, how this position was consolidated and maintained thereafter might reveal more about the degree of coercion employed and thus the nature of the movement's social power.

From their founding moment, the Provisionals deployed the language of community as part of an attempt to establish a wider hegemony and mobilize support for the armed struggle in their base areas. Republicans themselves defined this relationship with 'the base', as they termed it, by developing the concept of the 'resistance community'. The development of electoral politics in the 1980s marked a shift from the revolutionary legitimation of the 'resistance community' to the representational mandates of community politics. Republican purists argued that electoralism was the means whereby Sinn Féin, like Fianna Fáil before it, was incorporated into establishment politics. While electoral politics did bring the Provisionals into greater contact with the state, they were a symptom of deeper processes: other, more important, dynamics were at work within the nationalist population.

Social and economic change in the 1980s and 1990s, both independent of and mediated through the state, combined with conscious British state strategy to alter the terrain on which the battle was to be conducted. The mechanisms and structures for pragmatic adaptation lay within the changing nature of civil society within the nationalist community itself. One key area for this engagement and for the development of new forms of political structures was the community sector. Mediating between the state and the community, these organizations began to reformulate community politics as lobbying for resources, acting as conduits for funding and channels of influence within this micro-society. The framing of politics in this way aided the transformation of Republicanism from revolutionary nationalism to a pressure group operating within the moral economy of the British state. Other by-products of this process were the increased institutionalization of this sector and a strengthening of the Provisionals' political influence and social power within the nationalist community.

The results of this process of engagement were uneven, reflecting the tension between consent and coercion within Republicanism. Those aspects of Provisional politics that rested on consent reflected the incorporation of Republicans into 'normal' liberal democratic politics. However, significant elements of social power remained, reflecting Provisionalism's origins within the resistance community. Ultimately, this hegemony gave the movement something of the character of a pseudo-state, resting as it did on the coercive power of the armed body of the IRA and Republican influence in the structures of this micro-society.

This power was tolerated by the British state within certain limits, and indeed aspects of state strategy acted to strengthen and consolidate these developments. The peace process and the operation of the new political dispensation after the Good Friday Agreement only acted to further this pattern. To the state, the Provisionals were people it could do business with, and they remained indispensable in the management of conflict. The toleration of a Republican pseudo-state within limits that did not challenge the authority of the 'real' state remains an acceptable if messy compromise. To their Republican critics, the Provisionals were acting in a de facto partnership with the British state to control the nationalist population. They defined the Republican movement as a structure of power dominating the community, which is 'almost fascist in attitude towards their own people and afraid of losing control ... it is the power of fear.'[8]

The existing organizational culture and structure – which is rooted in the military needs of the armed struggle and the conspiratorial tradition – facilitated this development: the ethos of the army predominated in the party.[9] Thus the new forms of Provisionalism grew from within the old: there was no obvious break, but instead an organic evolution in the soil of nationalist civil society and watered by British state strategy since the 1980s. In this way, the organizational forms of contemporary Provisionalism are the products of forces external and internal to Republicanism.

Consequently, Provisionalism remained a hybrid movement whose structures look backwards to armed struggle and forwards to constitutional politics. The contradictions between the ballot paper and the armalite had long been recognized by Republicans.[10] However, for much of the peace process these structural problems were 'parked' or fudged, tensions over decommissioning and criminality notwithstanding. It remains to be seen whether, in the latest forms of post-Belfast Agreement politics, these contradictions can be resolved, or whether the process of institutionalization has preserved Provisionalism's contradictory structure of power as an ineradicable and necessary feature of Northern Ireland's political and social life.

---

8 John Kelly, former leading Provisional activist and Sinn Féin MLA, interview, 23 July 23 2005.

9 Anthony McIntyre, former Republican prisoner and political activist, interview, 23 August 2005.

10 Danny Morrison, former senior Republican strategist, interview, 5 January 2004.

Chapter 1

Shaping the Terrain: Economy, State and Civil Society

The majority of the population live in clustered housing estates where sectarianism ... extortion, poor health and paramilitaries are too ordinary to raise any comment. These conditions have attracted vast sums of money to Northern Ireland, but the beneficiaries are not on the housing estates. Those who manage the money [and] apportion it ... are part of a vast public sector who depend on outside money. In the leafy Victorian suburbs, those who live outside the conflicts fought in the housing estates ... are on benefits just as much as those on the 'bru'.[1]

The thirty-year war between the Republican movement and the British state has primarily been considered as a military and political conflict: in comparison to these main battlefields, social and economic factors have been relegated to peripheral roles. In particular, the terrain of civil society and its relationship with the state has rarely been theorized as a decisive factor in the conflict in Northern Ireland.[2]

The power of the contemporary state is often characterized by the degree to which it can successfully create and reproduce political and social hegemony, a type of power that rests on complex forms of consent as opposed to simple coercion.[3] In post-Gramscian theorization, for example, this dominant consensus is produced by a multifaceted interaction between the state in all its forms and 'independent' civil society.[4]

The very term 'civil society' is itself problematic in political theory. Some readings in the 1990s saw civil society as an intermediate layer standing apart from, and independent of, the state, providing a transcendent element that could ensure democratization in societies undergoing transition, such as in Eastern Europe and Southern Africa. Many hoped that after the Belfast Agreement such a form of civil society could develop

---

1 P. Morgan-Barnes, 'How the peace and reconciliation money is spent: an opera for our place and times', quoted in *Linen Hall Library Events Guide,* June–August 2006.
2 Cochrane, 2002, ix–x.
3 Hobsbawm, 2000, 31–40.
4 The following arguments are influenced by the typologies suggested in Bertramsen *et al.,* 1991, 196–210.

in Northern Ireland as a means of weakening communal and sectarian division.[5]

Others define civil society as a site of contestation for hegemonic power between the state and potential challengers. When defined as a realm of social interaction, autonomous from both economy and state, that stands between the private sphere and the state, civil society can been seen as vital to political mobilization in providing the:

> terrain where social movements organize and mobilize ... [and] diffuse their values and world views ... [forming] an intermediary sphere between social movements and political power, a sphere that does not so much lie outside political power bur rather penetrates it deeply.[6]

The crucial arena for this process of penetration lies in the 'soft' structures of state power. While the direct military and political functions of the state make it potentially the most powerful actor in the Northern Irish conflict, it would be wrong to assess its role simply in terms of formal state structures, armed bodies of men or even financial resources. As a structure of power the state exerts a wide ideological and cultural influence over these 'autonomous' forms of civil society. In Northern Ireland this relationship has proved to be significant in shaping the political and social environment. In this way even oppositional forms of politics in the region are ultimately determined by the state in its various guises.

The definition of state power needs to be widened beyond its traditional forms to include the penumbra of para-state structures and intermediate layers surrounding the core state that are drawn into its orbit as it attempts to shape civil society. It is in this flexible architecture, with its ill-defined boundaries between the state and civil society, that the machineries for the construction of consent are located. Such an understanding more accurately reflects the changing complexities of the relationship between the British state, the economy and civil society in Northern Ireland than a simple focus on repression and social control.

The economy of paradox, 1985–2005

The pace and pattern of social and economic change in Northern Ireland was profound in the last quarter of the twentieth century. The social and political environment of the early twenty-first century is unrecognizable in comparison with the 1980s, let alone with the beginnings of the Troubles in the late 1960s. These structural changes have had significant effects on society at all levels: a powerful combination of external and

5 Guelke, 2003, 61–78.
6 Casquette, 1996, 211–212.

internal forces has shaped the new realities of life in nationalist communities and their reflection in the shifting framework of political life.

However, this process has received little attention in the literature of political economy where 'there have been few analyses of what local reforms and global economic, social and technological shifts have meant with regard to the transformation of interests and identities' in the region.[7] Even before the radical reconfiguration of international capitalism in the 1970s and 1980s, which 'buffeted Northern Ireland with considerable force', it has been convincingly argued that:

> capitalism ... has created an intricate sequence of hierarchies that oversee the allocation of material and figurative resources in the province. The manner in which these seemingly distinct systems of privilege interact generates many of the nuances and dynamics of contemporary Northern Irish society.[8]

In this way it is more accurate to locate contemporary Northern Ireland within the mainstream of late twentieth-century western European societies rather than defining it as peripheral and uniquely backward.[9] Thus paradoxically, the really unique features of this society can only be fully understood as part of a wider international pattern rather than simply as the product of a singular Northern Irish exceptionalism. As Giddens has argued, in the broader context of the 'global shakeout' of the 1990s Northern Ireland 'looks, in a certain sense, typical rather than unusual'.[10]

Northern Ireland's social and economic landscape is a product of the declining structures of traditional industrial capitalism and the new currents of post-industrialism. Globally, this 'postmodern economy' has been defined as a 'sea change in the surface appearance of capitalism', which saw a shift from economic and social organization based on mass production to more 'flexible' systems of production and the rise of new service industries in the advanced capitalist economies.[11]

In the 1990s and 2000s this transformation was frequently defined in terms of an inexorable process of globalization that intimately connected the 'local' to the 'global' through the medium of transnational companies and the hegemony of popular consumerist culture. These changing patterns are evident throughout Northern Ireland, with a particular concentration in the Greater Belfast region.[12]

---

7 Shirlow and Murtagh, 2006, 99.
8 Coulter, 1999, 5.
9 Wichert, 1999, 180.
10 Giddens, 1995, 9.
11 Harvey, 1989, 189.
12 See, for example, *Laganside Corporation Annual Report and Accounts 2003–2004* (Belfast, 2004), 2, which highlights the momentum behind Belfast's continuing regeneration.

These processes have given the region's economy some uneven and contradictory features. The continued decline of traditional manufacturing occurs alongside growth in the public sector, retailing and other service employment. The economic power of the public sector and the strengthening of the more consumptionist elements of this late capitalist economy within retailing, urban regeneration and the cultural industries has 'conferred considerable affluence upon a broad section of Northern Irish society'.[13] As Shirlow has perceptively argued in relation to the Belfast city region: 'There are new patterns of consumption and an attempted re-imaging of city life in an effort by the British state to uphold middle-class lifestyles and to present Northern Ireland as a normalizing place.'[14]

Other examples of this tendency towards normalization include high levels of retail spending, strong patterns of leisure consumption and a buoyant housing market throughout the region. Combined with increasing levels of owner-occupation (encouraged by earlier right-to-buy legislation) and higher levels of employment, these factors illustrate the increased consumer confidence that makes 'Ulster ... currently the UK's fastest-growing region.'[15]

Belfast's economic development during the 1990s and 2000s was a visible embodiment of these changes, largely resting upon 'the growing purchasing power of the province's professional and business classes'.[16] The re-development of central areas of Belfast through the Laganside and associated projects since the late 1980s, and the instrumentalist deployment of culture and heritage tourism as tools for economic regeneration in the Cathedral and Titanic quarters, give the city centre the prosperous appearance and feel of any contemporary provincial European city.[17]

Beyond the central district, the physical appearance of much of the city has changed radically since the late 1970s due both to public sector housing development and, in the 1990s, increasing private sector involvement.[18] The impact of the built environment on the social psychology of urban populations has been established as a significant factor in political life.[19] The social and economic life of many citizens in the 2000s now takes place in a built environment that is physically distinct and culturally

---

13 Coulter, 1999, 66.

14 Shirlow and Murtagh, 2006, 99.

15 'Reasons to be cheerful' (editorial), *Guardian*, 9 December 2004; N. Mathiason, 'Why the south-east is so last century', *Observer*, 18 December 2005.

16 Coulter, 1999, 66

17 'Reasons to be cheerful' (editorial), *Guardian*, 9 December 2004; T. Templeton, 'Why Belfast is the best place to be young', *Observer*, 23 November 2004.

18 For changing patterns of housing tenure in Belfast, see Boal, 1995, 52

19 R. Solnit,'Democracy should be exercised regularly, on foot', *Guardian*, 6 July 2006.

different from the terrain of the Troubles.[20]

In the 1990s and 2000s, the peace process strengthened these tendencies towards integration into the new economy. By the early 1990s, these economic forces had developed an independent dynamic, giving the region's society and economy something of the contradictory character and unsteady equilibrium of contemporary capitalism, with all that implies for existing political and social relationships.

These patterns reproduce a form of dual economy, with a polarization between those with skills and the means to mobility, and the increasingly marginalized poor within declining labour markets.[21] These contradictions of poverty and prosperity remain the defining characteristics of the political economy of Northern Ireland. Some critics point to the role of the state in maintaining this social inequality and producing a risk-averse 'BMW syndrome'. This cushions local business and supports a comfortable middle-class lifestyle for some professionals and senior public sector employees. This has a similar impact across the social scale, because 'Northern Ireland is the only part of the United Kingdom where the average wage in public administration is higher than the average wage in manufacturing'.[22]

Others rightly pointed to the negative features of this 'economy of paradox' by arguing that this rebranding merely puts lipstick on the gorilla, and fails to engage with the real problems of poverty and sectarian division.[23] The region remains one of the most unequal societies in the developed world. The scale of poverty is a reflection of widening income inequalities that are considerably greater than those in the UK. According to a recent comprehensive survey, 'more than 185,000 households are poor and over half a million people live in poor households ... and over a third (37.4 per cent) of all this society's children are being brought up in poverty'.[24]

While the unemployment rate has fallen since 1985, when 21 per cent of the workforce drew unemployment benefit, much of the expansion has been in low-quality, low-paid jobs.[25] Northern Ireland's average income

20 For examples of the wider social and political significance of the changing urban environment, see Duncan, 2003; Hils, 2004; and Allen and Kelly, 2003.

21 Murtagh, 2001, 439–440.

22 M. O'Muilleoir, 'Northern Ireland – an engine with very few moving parts', Ireland-click.com, 14 January 2002; J. Arnold, 'Can Northern Ireland compete?', BBC News Northern Ireland, 20 June 2003, http://news.bbc.co.uk/go/pr/fr/-/1/hi/business/2983694.stm.

23 Neill, 1995.

24 Patsios and Tomlinson, 2003, 43–44.

25 Shirlow and Shuttleworth, 1999, 27–46.

still remains near the bottom of UK regions.[26] Other indicators of poverty are the lowest working age economic activity rate of all UK regions, and a disproportionate number of the unemployed disguising real levels of unemployment by drawing other benefits, such as long-term sickness benefit.[27]

Thus despite economic growth, these supposedly 'new' times did not end social inequalities or class tensions.[28] They did, however, shift the dominant discursive framework away from traditional conceptions of class by fuelling moral panics around the threat of the excluded, alienated underclass, and by forging new social divisions within the working population between the disadvantaged, the marginalized and the insecure, and the privileged.[29]

The nature and extent of poverty and social exclusion have obvious political implications for both policy-makers and political actors. These social changes and political preoccupations increasingly found their own specific echoes in late twentieth-century Northern Ireland. Overlying the established sectarian faultlines in Northern Irish society, another set of unspoken assumptions and a new politics of fear developed. These reflect the concerns of the comfortable but insecure classes and focus on the issues of crime and public disorder that have become so familiar as symbols of uncertainty and threat in developed societies.[30] In the 1980s, the rise of Sinn Féin as an electoral force was explained in terms of social alienation and urban deprivation. Contemporary discussion of 'loyalist alienation' and rioting for recognition since 1998 has touched on similar themes.[31] It is a mark of the discursive shift within the new politics of Provisionalism that Republicans, too, increasingly use similar symbolic fears to mobilize voters and consolidate support in their community.[32]

---

26 Gaffkin and Morrissey, 1987, 136–159; and J. Arnold, 'Can Northern Ireland compete?', BBC News Northern Ireland, 20 June 2003, http://news.bbc.co.uk/go/pr/fr/-/1/hi/business/2983694.stm.

27 Department of Enterprise, Trade and Investment, 'Northern Ireland Economic Performance Report 2005' (Belfast, 2006), and M. O'Muilleoir, 'Northern Ireland – an engine with very few moving parts', 14 January 2002, http://irelandclick.com.

28 Giddens, 1995.

29 Hutton, 1994.

30 For examples of moral panics, see O'Connell and Greenfield, 2006.

31 S. Howe, 'Loyalism's rage against the fading light of Britishness', *Guardian*, 10 October 2005.

32 'Residents of a Poleglass estate at their wit's [sic] end as vandals tear up neighbourhood', *Liberty* (Colin Sinn Féin newsletter), May 2006; G. Burns, 'Councillor appeals for alcopops ban', *Andersonstown News*, 22 July 2006.

Shaping the terrain

Post-industrial Northern Ireland, with its fragmented working class, preponderance of service industries and flexible working practices, could be described as an almost textbook example of this post-Fordist economy, except for one decisive feature: the predominant political and socio-economic role played by the British state. Denigrated as a 'workhouse economy' in the 1980s and for much of the 1990s, the state played, and indeed continues to play, the decisive role in the region's economic and social life.[33] However, the paradox is that the relatively interventionist role of the state in Northern Ireland has acted to strengthen many of the 'flexible' features associated with the reconfigured economies, rather than merely signifying the inertia of corporatism. The politics of the peace process have furthered these social and economic patterns. Despite, or perhaps because, of the increased sectarian segregation and communalization of political life in Northern Ireland since 1998, 'the economy has and continues to be an instrument for political contestation and social control … [it is an arena] which can be mobilized by the British state as an instrument of political and social control.'[34]

Proportionately, the state was more significant in Northern Ireland than in the UK. After thirteen years of direct rule, in 1985 public expenditure accounted for 70 per cent of Northern Ireland's GDP (gross domestic product) and some 45 per cent of the workforce was employed in the public sector. When the public and private sectors were combined, around 70 per cent of the workforce was employed in services in this period. Despite the growth of new economic sectors and the changing composition of the state's security apparatus, after 1998 some 40 per cent of employment in Northern Ireland is still provided by the British state.[35]

State intervention is evidenced directly through high levels of public expenditure and transfer payments (such as social security benefits), and indirectly through support for business development and investment. The headline figure of £4 billion usually cited for the British 'subvention' does not take into account both discretionary and non-discretionary expenditure: when these are added together the figure for British transfers is nearer £10 billion, which further increases the overwhelming economic and political weight of the state in the region's life.

Alongside this overt role, which includes a range of direct and indirect interventionist measures, the state and its agencies provides practical and financial assistance to private companies, thus generating employment

33 Teague, 1987, 8.
34 Shirlow, 1997a, 133.
35 Coulter, 1999, 65.

and profits in Northern Ireland's private sector. The recent growth in private sector investment fuelling Belfast's regeneration has been largely underpinned by pump-priming and strategic support by the state.[36]

The proposals for the modernization and rationalization of government functions and structures emerging from the review of public administration that was launched in 2002 highlight the public sector's continued importance.[37] The reduction in the numbers of government departments and local authorities, and the continued transfer of state functions via partnership arrangements to the quasi-independent 'third sector' of voluntary and community organizations, actually *increases* the relative political and social significance of the state in Northern Ireland.

If anything, the stop–go politics of the post-Good Friday Agreement period and the hiatus of continued direct rule in the 2000s acted to strengthen these roles and to increase the state's ability to shape the economic and social terrain that underpins local political life. The state's continued dominance in the life of the region is illustrated by the framing of Northern Irish politics as communal positioning and bargaining for resources allocated by the state. This economic and social weight reinforced the political significance of the British government as a political arbiter and a dispenser of patronage to supplicant political entrepreneurs mediating on behalf of 'their' communities. The alleged request for £30 million by UDA (Ulster Defence Association) leaders in 2006 in return for disbanding is perhaps just an extreme example of this style of political bargaining.[38] The political manoeuvring involving the British and Irish governments and Northern Ireland's political parties during the summer of 2006 around the issue of the restoration of devolved institutions further illustrated that power.[39]

The origins of the state's role lay in a deliberate policy orientation that was described as 'the third arm of the British government's strategy ... the ... economic and social war against violence'.[40] Successive British governments since the 1960s have formulated policies that recognize, with varying degrees of emphasis, the relationships between high levels of unemployment, social deprivation, communal conflict and anti-state violence: in doing so, these interventionist economic and social policies had a significant impact on shaping Northern Irish society and politics.[41]

36 Needham, 1998, 267–270.
37 Knox and Carmichael, 2005; Morrow, 2005.
38 H. McDonald, 'UDA wants handout of £30m to disband', *Observer*, 16 July 2006.
39 Doyle, 'Academic selection issue rests with north's politicians – Blair', *Irish News*, 13 July 2006.
40 Needham, 1998, 1.
41 Gaffkin and Morrissey, 1990, 63–95.

However, it was not until the 1980s that the full strategic value of the economic instrument was fully recognized.[42] During this period, a basic policy framework was established that continued in essentials for the following twenty years. One Secretary of State for Northern Ireland defined its significance as follows:

> We all know that better security and economic policies are interlinked. There is no future for Northern Ireland as an economic wasteland, no future for Northern Ireland through terrorism and no future in a political vacuum; we need action on all fronts.[43]

The unique political conditions in the region and the significance of the state as an economic and social actor determined that economic policy inevitably had strategic and political implications and objectives that were different to those in the rest of the United Kingdom. Rhetorically, economic policy was framed using the language of normalization and was designed to provide the conditions and the confidence for local business to invest. However, these policies also had a specifically *political* purpose of countering Republican arguments and undermining the Provisionals' base of support:

> Arguments about a failed state could only be answered if you could see that the state was starting to succeed in terms of social and economic progress. Of course, [Gerry] Adams … didn't want that because … the more economic success began to show through, he would lose control of his own community because they were not reliant on him and his advice centres … if people had jobs they would start to become independent.[44]

The politics of prosperity

Counter-insurgency merged with mainstream urban, social and economic policy concerns during this period. British social and economic strategy developed as an ad hoc mixture, closely reflecting (and in turn influencing) policy models for dealing with social disorder, alienation and social exclusion already operating in post-industrial cities in Britain and the USA.[45] These 'shared visioning' models of urban planning, employed in racially-divided Detroit and Baltimore, or in riot-torn Brixton and Liverpool 8, were based on the use of community development and economic regeneration as

42 Neumann, 2003, 179–188.

43 Quoted in Gaffkin and Morrissey, 1990, 62.

44 Sir Richard Needham, former Parliamentary Under-Secretary of State (Northern Ireland Office) 1985–1992, interview, 25 July 2005.

45 Sir Gerard Loughran, former Permanent Secretary in the Department for Economic Development (Northern Ireland) 1991–2000, interview, 16 August 2005.

motivators for social cohesion and progress. The Heseltine model, as developed in other areas of the UK, was very influential in Northern Ireland, according to some readings of British social and economic strategy.[46] In many ways these urban policies were to establish the foundations of the later, post-1998 'reinvention of urban Ulster as normal, placeless and able to hold its own in a competitive global economy'.[47]

British objectives were broadly focussed on attempting to restore 'prosperity, pride and normality' using 'familiar UK models of urban regeneration', with a central focus on 'rebuilding Belfast', the cockpit of the Troubles.[48] For example, the Belfast Urban Plan of 1989, reflecting the shift from manufacturing to service industries, focused on the development of retailing, leisure and tourism as key elements in the city's transformation to a post-industrial economy. Spearheaded by the Laganside Corporation, the local equivalent of Britain's urban development corporations, the project echoed developments like Salford Quays and London's Docklands, with its emphasis on city-centre regeneration, riverside reclamation and 'yuppification'.

Informed by the trickle-down theory of urban development, in which the regenerated city engenders economic activity and enterprise, the Belfast Urban Plan was designed to place the city within a contemporary post-industrial, post-Fordist framework. Urban regeneration could also serve a political project beyond mere rebuilding, just as it had in Detroit, Baltimore and Toxteth.

On a micro-level,

> it could be argued that the image of a tribal city could be ameliorated if the residential part of Inner Belfast became less visibly divided into the two sectarian blocs by the inclusion of 'Yuppie' settlements, which act to 'neutralise' more sections of the urban core.[49]

Likewise, 'an improvement in the fortunes of the city centre' might well become a:

> factor in building a shared sense of civic pride, security and enjoyment among people whose attitudes, shaped by separated experience, may well be mutually antagonistic ... radiating a sense of citizenship outward to a divided population.[50]

Retail development and job-creation programmes that encouraged young people into the nascent shared space of the city centre were central to

46 Ibid.
47 Murtagh, 2001, 432.
48 Hadaway, 2001, 40.
49 Gaffikin and Morrissey, 1990, 133.
50 Hadaway, 2001, 40.

this approach.[51] It was argued that 'the key thing was to make Northern Ireland become normal and, in making it normal, the challenge for the IRA was to destabilize it without the blame being cast on their shoulders'.[52]

Similar themes of normalization were reflected in social policy at both the macro- and micro-levels, across the region and in specifically targeted areas. For example, social and economic policy initiatives such as Making Belfast Work (1988) looked beyond directly economic impacts, emphasising the importance of harnessing the 'goodwill and enthusiasm of all the community'.[53] This regeneration not only dramatically altered the physical appearance of the city as a whole, but also provided a new social context and environment in which people lived and acted politically.

These initiatives had a particular focus on the regeneration of 'Republican' West Belfast, containing as it did 'concentrations of both violence and deprivation' that were seen as key battlegrounds in the struggle for the hearts and minds of the nationalist population.[54] Republicans were keenly aware of the political implications of these strategies. It was argued, usually by reference to Brigadier Kitson's counter-insurgency doctrine, that the British had been attempting 'to make inroads into the nationalist community through the medium of "community relations" and the promotion of community groups that the state could liaise with since the early 1970s'.[55] These economic policies were seen as a part of an integrated British approach linking a range of policies (from housing and planning through to education and employment) as part of a unified strategy to control the nationalist population and defeat Republicanism.[56]

Much of the actual policy implementation appeared to rest on older traditions of state intervention drawn from earlier regimes. For example, at the height of the Thatcherite period, when the minimalist state was the order of the day in the rest of the UK, a senior minister could argue that 'Thatcherism didn't exist in Northern Ireland... It was the one part of the United Kingdom where Keynesianism was still rampant'.[57] Others, however, have argued that this emphasis overstates the coherence of the political agenda and underplays the degree to which this Keynesianism coexisted with Thatcherite practice: there was 'no feather-bedding, and

---

51 Sir Richard Needham, interview, 25 July 2005.
52 Ibid.
53 Gaffikin and Morrissey, 1990, 140.
54 Ibid.
55 F. Ó hAdhmaill, former republican prisoner and community activist, interview, 31 August 2005.
56 Sinn Féin, 'Report of Internal Conference on Community Politics', May 1991.
57 Lord Prior quoted in Neumann, 2003, 37.

Northern Ireland was not spared the impact of Thatcherism'.[58]

This suggests that much contemporary discussion about British strategy is a *post hoc* rationalization, giving an impression of a coherence that was not necessarily apparent at the time.[59] While there is evidence of a degree of coordination and shared purpose, implementation in the Northern Irish context was often erratic, being subject to a variety of contradictory influences, causing analysts who posit a polycentric theory to doubt the existence of a unified rational state actor.[60]

Baiting the hooks?

British attempts to influence nationalist civil society in the 1980s were not initially directed at the Provisionals as such. The dominant assessment remained that the Republicans were 'a fanatical party and that rational negotiations were not possible ... there was absolutely no thought at that time that the Provisionals could be brought into any kind of political settlement.'[61]

Rather than attempting to draw the Provisionals into mainstream politics by developing partnerships with community groups identified with Republicanism, the strategy aimed to push these groups to the margins. The controversy over political vetting and cuts in British government funding to community groups in the late 1980s was a reflection of this approach. It reflected a deeper centralization of policy-making in the 1980s under direct rule, which focussed on the centre (both politically and geographically), denied and excluded Republican and loyalist interests and 'crudely constructed [working class areas] as violent, unreliable and inaccessible'.[62] West Belfast was central to the successful operation of this strategy in the 1980s and 1990s. To both the British government and the Provisionals, West Belfast symbolized a 'conjunction of political/military resistance, deprivation and discrimination': militarily and politically it was the cockpit of the conflict in Northern Ireland.[63]

Consequently, from 1988 onwards the British government's Making Belfast Work project imbued programmes of economic and social development, education and training, health and environmental action with

58 Sir Gerard Loughran, interview, 16 August 2005.
59 Ibid.
60 Sir Richard Needham, interview, 25 July 2005.
61 Sir David Goodall, former Deputy Secretary Cabinet Office 1982–1984, interview, 26 July 2005.
62 Murtagh, 2001, 434.
63 Gaffikin and Morrissey, 1990, 146.

an explicitly political rationale and direction.[64] Here, the general aims
of community regeneration were appended to a specific political agenda
informed by the belief that economic and social progress made political
accommodation easier. Republicanism would be therefore be undermined
by providing, for example:

> the SDLP and their leader with the proof they required to show their people
> that cooperation with a British government could bring results, and that
> economic and social improvement could bring opportunities denied them
> by violence and deprivation. We also observed that the IRA were finding
> that a bomb in Derry brought a very much stronger reaction from their
> own community that one in Belfast city centre, and if we could halt the
> bombs in the north-west it would become more difficult to justify destroying
> 'economic' targets elsewhere.[65]

In this way, the British government at both the macro-level and the micro-
level joined the internal battle for hegemony within the Catholic community.
On one side were Sinn Féin's advice centres, Republican-inspired initiatives
like the black taxi service, and the network of community, cultural and
social groups that constituted Republican civil society. On the other side
were the SDLP and the Catholic Church, using traditional parochial and
Catholic social networks and linking with local businesses to develop an
alternative focus for both economic and social action, and politics.

In this campaign of normalization, the role of the Belfast action teams
between 1988 and 1995 in building links on the ground was regarded as
significant by government and Republicans alike. The action teams were
civil servants who liaised at a local level with community groups and other
elements of nationalist civil society. As Sir Richard Needham argued:

> It was a vital part of our strategy to talk to and underpin those who lived
> in terrorist-dominated areas; it gave us access to them and opportunities to
> wean them away from violence... We were able to support discreetly those
> antagonistic to republicanism.[66]

This contest for legitimacy was not as direct as the potential dual power that
had existed in the early 1970s, but the Provisionals' community politics
could still be said to implicitly pose a challenge to the authority of the
state on another front. The action teams worked within clear guidelines
and were designed to cross-fertilize a number of policy areas that would
develop and strengthen the legitimacy of the state within the nationalist population. The model was that of a partnership that empowered

---

64   Ibid.
65   Needham, 1998, 196.
66   Needham, 1998, 190.

communities with a light touch from the state: as one insider argued, 'if the initiative had been seen as simply counter-insurgency we would not have got a response.'[67]

The micro-management of the action teams aimed to create 'mini-areas of authority and administration' that used funding and resource allocation to demonstrate government commitment to the areas and acted as an alternative pole of attraction and centre of power to that of the Provisionals.[68] Some believed that this process could be the basis for wider political engagement, moving from conflict management and 'keeping the lid on the cauldron' to a political process that mobilized nationalist civil society to 'give back power to local authorities and local communities.'[69] Republicans, both as individuals and as an organized political group, were an integral part of this civil society. Increasingly during the late 1980s and 1990s they were drawn into closer contact with the state through the operation of these British economic and social strategies. This approach combined a range of incentives and political benefits with security containment and 'structures that forced the protagonists to debate with [government] ... [it was hoped that from] that they will get around the table to broaden the discussion'.[70]

Interestingly, this line of reasoning paralleled that of Republicans who believed that their armed campaign would close down the range of British policy options and would ultimately force direct negotiations with the Provisionals.[71] Certainly, key aspects of the form and the style of the peace process were to emerge from contacts of this type between the Provisionals and the British state.

An example of this combination of political strategy and social policy in the early 1990s was the Springvale project in West Belfast. Springvale and other projects like it throughout Northern Ireland explicitly connected the British government's use of economic and social opportunity to the political end of undermining support for the IRA. As Richard Needham described Republican participation in the project: 'Without their goodwill we would have found progress hard if not impossible... the bait caught the herring.'[72]

This project presented Republican politicians with a dilemma: whether to boycott it as an inadequate British initiative or, as elected representatives,

67 Sir Gerard Loughran, interview, 16 August 2005.
68 Sir Richard Needham, interview, 25 July 2005.
69 Ibid.
70 Ibid.
71 Danny Morrison, interview, 5 January 2004.
72 Needham, 1998, 206–207, describing his strategy for the Springvale project in 1990.

contribute to a development that benefited their community. For British ministers, Republican involvement was significant in that it opened up further contradictions within the ballot paper and armalite strategy, between an IRA bombing campaign that destroyed jobs and Sinn Féin demands for greater investment in West Belfast.

British government economic and social policy in West Belfast, with its motivation of 'drawing them [the Republican movement] into the net' and making Sinn Fein a 'part of that very different part-public, part-private partnership which was the essence of our long-term solution', would appear to confirm the view that the state had a deeply-considered and carefully-calculated strategy to use regeneration as a means of ensnaring the Republican movement within conventional politics.[73] Likewise, it presupposed that the Republican leadership would be easily netted by the lure of funding and employment for west Belfast.[74] A more realistic assessment, perhaps, is to assume that both parties were aware of the others' motives and that in the case of the Republicans, any hooks that were being taken had been swallowed long before 1990.[75]

Fair employment and the politics of equality

The British government's power to define the ideological as well as the political and social framework for other actors in Northern Ireland is illustrated by the impact of the Fair Employment Act of 1989. In particular, Republicans and other community activists were increasingly operating in an environment closely shaped by this legislation and the wider British policy agenda that created it.

The legislation drew together a number of threads from the British social policy agenda that had emerged during the 1980s, as well as reflecting some of the initiatives of the Anglo–Irish Agreement of 1985. However, there were also significant departures from previous practice that were to have a fundamental impact on the political outlook of the nationalist population in general. This impact can be seen in what was to become known in the 1990s as 'the equality agenda', which focussed on gaining equality and parity of esteem for the nationalist population within Northern Ireland. This emphasis on immediate practical and achievable policy aims meant that the long-term project of reunification receded.

Perhaps the most significant feature of the Fair Employment Act was

---

73 Needham, 1998, 207–208.

74 However, Needham himself appears to contradict that impression by his references to Republican scepticism about British motives; ibid.

75 See Sinn Fein, 'Report of Internal Conference on Community Politics', May 1991.

its explicit enshrining of the discourse of communal conflict in legislative form. This was in marked contrast to previous policy frameworks, which had emphasized that discrimination was an individual issue rather than a structural product of collective discrimination. It was also radically different from the Thatcherite emphasis on individualism then dominant in Britain.

Drawing on the dominant British discourse that defined the Northern Ireland conflict as an internal one between the two traditions of nationalism and unionism, the legislation's underlying premise was that inequality between the the two traditions was the source of legitimate grievance and therefore needed to be addressed as a prerequisite for political stability.

This structural analysis of inequality enshrined in the act was congenial to the nationalist community not only because it corresponded to its own sense of legitimacy, but also because it saw political advance and the possible redress of nationalist grievances in communal rather than individual terms.[76] In this sense the underlying premises of the act could be satisfactorily interpreted both through pre-existing frames of nationalist political culture and through emerging themes of identity politics, which drew on structural and contextual explanations of identity.

While the underlying justifications for the structures and practices established by the Fair Employment Act as well as the resulting policy and practice do share significant similarities with US legislation (causing some Unionists to detect the influence of the MacBride Principles and the US experience of positive and affirmative action), it is important to stress that elements of affirmative action were *not* adopted.[77]

These similarities made the act and its policy framework attractive to nationalists. In this sense, the Fair Employment Act represented a convergence between British policy-makers and nationalist and Republican politicians who increasingly drew on the discourse of group rights and positive discrimination as an antidote to historic injustice and communally-structured wrongs.

There were undoubtedly contradictions in the working of the act, especially the difficulty of acting upon the logic of communal rights while maintaining the principle of individual merit and avoiding charges of partiality. Perhaps because politicians and policy-makers were aware of the zero-sum game that characterized Northern Irish politics, they were reluctant to acknowledge the sectarian logic that flowed from the dominant discourse of a communal conflict between two traditions.[78]

---

76 Ruane and Todd, 1996, Chapter 6.
77 For example, see Needham quoted by Neumann, 2003, 143–144.
78 Neumann, 2003, 174

However, the general operation of the act, with its sectarian-orientated monitoring procedures and concomitant encouragement for social engineering by funding, ensured that the discourse of communal identity became encoded into the private and public spheres. This was further reinforced by British policy-makers' focus on the relative deprivation experienced by nationalists and unionists in the 1990s. There was an acceptance that this discrimination was 'the fundamental structural issue facing any government', and that the dominant theme of policy should be to eradicate inequality of opportunity and relative disadvantage.[79] This thinking was given added weight by the Good Friday Agreement and the resulting Northern Ireland Act (1998). Section 75 of the act required public authorities to actively promote equality of opportunity between and within categories of community defined by, amongst other things, religious belief, political opinion, race, gender and sexual orientation.[80] Public bodies responsible for allocating resources had to work within this framework and ensure that, through their policies and the use of equality impact assessments, there was equitable distribution and compliance with these aims. In establishing the funding regime and bureaucratic practice, this legislation increasingly defined the discursive framework and ideological context for nationalist community projects in the 1990s.[81]

The impact of this framework on Republican politics and community activism became clear in the 1990s. Although the Fair Employment Act was initially given no credibility by Republicans,

> it became some kind of marker beyond just winning individual cases because the act of revealing discrimination might create some imperceptible change. It was about doing some immediate good and revealing power structures. It was thought that the process of revealing resulted in politicization and activism.[82]

The Northern Ireland Act had a similar impact on the underlying discursive framework of Republican politics: arguments that the 'equality agenda' was not being adhered to during the allocation of resources became common-place in the everyday exchanges of politics in the 2000s. For example, Sinn Féin MLA Fra McCann argued that by exempting many high-level decisions

---

79 Sir Peter Brooke, Secretary of State for Northern Ireland speaking in the House of Commons, 5 March 1992, quoted in Neumann, 2003, 175.

80 See Northern Ireland Act 1998 (c.47), Part VII Human Rights and Equal Opportunities, http://www.opsi.gov.uk/acts/acts1998/ukpga_19980047_en_7.

81 Hadaway, 2004.

82 Claire Hackett, former Monitoring and Evaluations Officer, USDT and local history project worker, Falls Community Council, interview, 18 July 2005.

from screening under Section 75, 'civil servants ... frustrate change in the North and implement policies which fundamentally undermine the chances of attaining a level social and economic playing field'.[83]

The community policy initiatives that flowed from the Fair Employment Act and the Northern Ireland Act had a new framework of positive discrimination towards areas most affected by poverty. When combined with a distinctive focus on targeting social need, the result was that resources were directed towards the nationalist minority. The new focus on reducing differentials between the two communities was also reflected in the changing nature of political discourse in the 1990s, where positive achievement was measured against evidence of a reduction in the sectarian gap of advantage/disadvantage between the two communities.[84]

However, the emphasis on purely communal (as opposed to social class) deprivation, combined with identity politics, did not always produce positive results. It reinforced the existing sectarian dynamics and helped to ensure that this zero-sum attitude continued to be the dominant political framework into the twenty-first century. This was especially true in disputes over the allocation of resources by the state; it was frequently argued by both communities that government policies were 'favouring one section of the community over another'.[85]

Defining and representing the community?

Sir Richard Needham's fishing analogy stresses the superior force of the state and its ability to define the pattern of conflict between the British government and the Provisionals. In viewing the Provisionals as passive objects to be caught on the hooks of state policy, Sir Richard paradoxically reflects Republicans' own analyses of the thrust of British social policy. Leading Provisionals saw the normalization agenda as a 'blatant attempt by the British government to control, through blackmail, community groups and self-help schemes in the city [Derry]', which in turn was part of a conscious British strategy of controlling potential community resistance:

> Britain, having recognized the extent of the dependency it created, is now attempting to impose political and social control through the manipulation of these schemes. Britain has always feared the development of a community dynamic, believing it to be inherently subversive to establishment interests in the six counties.[86]

83 M. Hall, 'Equality undermined', *The Irish Democrat*, June/July 2006.

84 Neumann, 2003, 176.

85 Bairbre de Brún, Sinn Féin MEP, quoted in 'Nationalist anger over £3m mural paint plan', *Irish News*, 11 July 2006.

86 Mitchel McLaughlin, quoted in J. Plunkett, 'Community groups hit back', *An Phoblacht/Republican News*, 13 February 1986.

The state *was* sufficiently powerful to limit the strategic options open to the Republican movement, as well as possessing the resources to influence community development among the nationalist population. However, defining the relationship between the British state and subaltern groups as that of subject–object does not do justice to its complexity. The ideological state apparatus is not a lumbering threshing engine: the construction of consent is much more subtle than that.

The mechanisms for the construction of hegemony are located in the myriad connections between the formal structures of the state and nationalist civil society. Rather than imposition, the dominant consensus is the product of an unequal dialogue. To a certain degree, consent is a result of the internalization of these ideological influences within the structures of civil society. Thus the British state has a significant role in defining the discursive framework of the mutually-contending parties in the conflict in Northern Ireland. The Provisionals' attempts to develop a counter-hegemony in the form of the resistance community recognized the importance of this dialogic relationship between the state and nationalist civil society.

As large political questions and ideas receded in the late 1980s, the Republican project began to embrace, from below, peripheral, marginal and small-scale objectives as the only things that were achievable. The community and the activity of the micro-society fitted this scaling-down perfectly. The significance of the community and voluntary sector results from its growing importance in the political framework of the Provisionals. Simultaneously, from above, the language of partnership and conflict management, rooted in the discourse of consociationalism, provided models for the peace process and the structures of the Good Friday Agreement.

A brief history of community development in the Greater Ballymurphy/Upper Springfield area will illustrate the pattern. From the 1960s onwards and throughout the Troubles there had been community organizations operating in the area, such as the Ballymurphy Tenants' Association. Their functions had been seen in terms of collective representation, self-help and a concept of community development largely generated within the community itself.[87]

Other groups, such as the Springhill Community House and the Upper Springfield Resource Centre, had an approach that linked educational and social development to an explicitly political agenda, such as economic development. There was some dialogue and contact with the state, but distance and independence were highly prized and emphasized. In terms

---

87 The following sections are based on White, 2000.

of their operations and approach, with varying degrees of emphasis, groups like these could be fitted in to the resistance community frame.

The late 1980s represented something of a turning point, with the creation of mechanisms such as the Belfast action teams in 1987 and the Making Belfast Work initiative in 1988, whereby the voluntary and community sector could access government resources for innovative and worthwhile projects. As we have seen, the government was keen to use the voluntary sector in Northern Ireland (as it has been in Britain) as a means of delivering economic development, because it is cost-effective and it encourages the self-help ethos of the 'new right'. This very much followed British models of urban policy, which focussed on partnership and what would be defined in the 1990s as the 'communitarian stakeholder model'. These programmes, and similar programmes such as City Challenge, involved partnerships between statutory agencies, local councils, the private sector and the voluntary and community sector.

By 1993, this partnership approach culminated in the development of the Upper Springfield Development Trust (USDT), a local partnership drawing funds from Making Belfast Work and the EU to the tune of £6.9 million. The USDT drew in local community leaders, statutory agencies and business people to implement a 'programme of initiatives focussing on many of the underlying causes of deprivation as a means of positively transforming the entire social and economic life of the area'.[88]

Although initiatives like the Upper Springfield Resource Centre and Springhill House continued to operate autonomously, the main focus had shifted towards the USDT, which took on a significant social and economic role in the Greater Ballymurphy area. With a salaried staff of around 60 people, it was to become one of the largest employers in West Belfast.

The ethos of the USDT reflected the contemporary language of community empowerment, with its mission to tackle economic and social obstacles to individual development through the provision of education and training. For social and community activists, bodies like the USDT provided a platform for activism, while shaping the political and social agenda at the community level.

This discursive framework was very much in tune with the mood of the times, having been described as 'the language of communitarianism merged with the language of American management speak, very New Labour in style, with its references to stakeholders, partnerships, mission statements and social inclusion.'[89] Given the range of community programmes that a

88 'Upper Springfield Development Trust Annual Report 2004' (Belfast, 2004), 2.
89 Pauline Hadaway, former Arts Project Coordinator, USDT, 1997–1999, interview, 9 August 2004.

body like the USDT would undertake (covering employment, training, health, parenting, childcare, restorative justice, culture, public art and sport), its functions went beyond mere fundraising and project coordination. It became almost a form of embryonic local government. This role could be seen most clearly in its function as a mediator between the community and other centres of power. As Hadaway argues:

> The USDT is very mission-oriented and focussed, and is able to embed these approaches into the communities that it operates in, for example by translating the ideas of the Good Friday Agreement into projects on the ground. Drawing power and authority from the community base, it uses its advocacy function both to represent and define the community to external authority.[90]

For critics of this discourse, it can appear that government funding regimes and the needs of the 'pacification agenda' have imposed an ideology and a practice of community activism on formerly anti-establishment radicals. 'These structures make you dependent on the establishment you are trying to overthrow. All these strings come with it and they dull the sharp edge of your politics', was how one community worker described this process.[91] Yet the origins of individual project workers from within the sector and the growth of these hybrid structures within the community movement point towards a different process taking place.

The direct involvement of community groups on the boards of projects such as the USDT rules out any simple command model of social engineering by funding application, or of the imposition of an alien ideology by main force. It is a process of engagement with the hegemonic discourse of communitarianism. This internalization betokens an ideological shift beyond mere compliance to ensure the continued operation of the project.

This process produces some hybrid ideological and organizational forms. As with the explicitly political framework of the peace process, some activists were aware that the discourse and practice of community development are not neutral and could serve different agendas than those of community organizations. This engagement can be justified in instrumentalist terms. It can also be explained in terms of a dialogue and a challenge to the state's discourse, making the agenda of community development part of the 'battleground between the state and radical community groups'.[92]

90 Ibid.
91 Tommy Gorman, former Republican prisoner and community activist, interview, 7 August 2005.
92 Claire Hackett, interview, 18 July 2005.

In community activism as it developed in the 1980s, this struggle increasingly took place on the field of language. In contemporary politics, the cultural turn means that meanings are shifted, not transformed. In the community arena, politics were increasingly conducted as a dialogue within a common discursive framework rather than as a contest for power between radically-opposed meanings. Rather than overthrowing centres of power, they were to be held discursively to account by 'the community'. The wider political implications of this battle of definitions for the wider Republican project were clear. As one community activist argued:

> People have always seen the potential for reformism and surrender in this engagement. We are aware of its limited nature, but it's too simplistic and deterministic to talk in terms of surrender to a dominant agenda. It is active, testing the cracks in the other position. There is a battle of discourse, we regroup and respond to new ideas and challenges and see how we can take community activism forward.[93]

The turn to community: *un nationalisme de gestion?*[94]

The election of the Blair government in 1997 gave added impetus to the British strategy of securing 'peace through prosperity'. This 'turn to community' was reflected in the Blair government's domestic agenda of social inclusion, which aimed to end alienation by rebuilding the social capital of communities with a combination of partnership, empowerment and direct intervention. These policies of strengthening civil society and community participation enthusiastically embraced European urban policy discourses that aimed to renegotiate relationships between the state and local people, defined as 'communities'.[95] These policies had the ambitious aim of transforming the region's economy *and* its social structure, as the starting point for the creation of a new political dispensation.

The discursive framework of Northern Irish politics after 1998 was provided by these communitarian themes, conjoined with a consociational institutional structures. Drawing on the patterns of social policy established in the region since the late 1980s and international models of successful peace processes, the Blair government's emphasis on political inclusion and addressing economic, cultural and social inequality placed civil society and the reconstitution of community at the heart of the new

---

93 Ibid.
94 Literally, a nationalism of management as opposed to a nationalism of protest. See X. Crettiez, 'IRA, ETA, FLNC: l'agonie des illusions militaristes', *Le Monde*, 23 August 2005. I am grateful to Liam O' Rourke for drawing the article to my attention.
95 Murtagh, 2001, 443.

dispensation.[96] These patterns of intervention were especially directed towards the community and voluntary sector, which was given a key role in implementing this policy agenda in Northern Ireland. Significantly for the consolidation of the third sector's central position in policy delivery and partnership with the state, this deepened the 'engagement between a centrist government and suspicious community activists'.[97]

The international experience of peace processes emphasized the importance of social and economic intervention in the transition from conflict to peace. In particular, middle-range actors and non-governmental organizations (NGOs) were seen as critical components of this transformational approach. These intermediate bodies provided a way for states to maintain significant connections to both the activists and the broader constituencies involved in the conflict. They also embodied an infrastructure for sustaining peace, acting as agents of influence and providing conduits for the external economic aid which addressed the structural inequalities frequently cited as a factor in protracted ethno-political conflicts.[98]

The British government applied these models in Northern Ireland by using the community sector as a middle range actor in the peace process. These policies were designed to consolidate its intermediary position and strengthen links with political and social actors in nationalist civil society. There was, however another distinct strand to these policies. The Blair government supported community initiatives as mechanisms and structures to develop civil society at all levels: the idea of a peace process was promoted as a grassroots exercise in promoting community cohesion and cross-community reconciliation.[99] In a reading that was widely quoted by policy-makers, the community sector could transform the established communal blocs by offering a potentially neutral cross-community sphere of activity.[100] In this sense, civil society represented an alternative vision of community against the reality of communalism.

These rhetorical forms of community and civil society entered the political mainstream and were deployed by the region's political parties in their manoeuvring for position in the post-Good Friday polity. A similar discursive and rhetorical influence was also apparent in the community and voluntary sector. The Good Friday Agreement and the Northern Ireland Act 1998 stressed the importance of equality of opportunity and targeting social need as over-arching policy priorities, showing the significance of these themes for British policy. The Good Friday Agreement's optimistic

96   Elliott, 2002, Appendix 6, 227–230.
97   Murtagh, 2001, 440.
98   Byrne and Irvin, 2001, 415–417.
99   Guelke, 2003, 61–78.
100 See, for example, Pollak, 1993.

belief in the transformative potential of civil society was manifested in the establishment of the Civic Forum, and related initiatives from community arts through to housing policy.[101]

It was not through the policy and actions of the British state alone that these assumptions became dominant in the region in the 1990s. The use of economic and social policies as instruments of political strategies of normalization was given further impetus in the 1990s by the EU and the International Fund for Ireland.

The development of the International Fund for Ireland from 1985 onwards reflected a dominant view in the USA that economic and social development was an essential underpinning to conflict resolution in Northern Ireland. President Clinton's high-profile political role and the support of US business for the peace process (from 1992 up to the Good Friday Agreement and beyond) echoes the importance of US economic aid in other peace processes in the 1990s.[102] This economic intervention was supplemented by US political and cultural influence. Together, they reinforced the idea that new forms of community could transform the conflict in Northern Ireland.

Likewise, at both the discursive and the material levels the impact of the EU was considerable. By drawing on a long-established culture of civil and social dialogue involving NGOs and social partners, the European language of civil society and subsidiarity was to enter the common currency of Northern Irish politics through funding regimes for the community and voluntary sector.[103]

One of the main channels for this ideological and structural influence was a variety of EU-funded programmes from 1995 onwards. The aims of the Special Support Programme for Peace and Reconciliation (which eventually ran to three peace programmes) encapsulated not only the underlying strategic approach and policy range of the EU-funded programmes, but also revealed the defining ideological premises of other political and social actors.[104]

These initiatives for promoting economic development, inter-community links, reconciliation and social inclusion shared considerable common ground with the communitarian interventionism of Blair's New Labour administration.[105] Taken with other EU structural funding and community initiatives in operation since 1995, these strands represented an

101 Guelke, 2003, 61–78.
102 Byrne and Irvin, 2001, 416.
103 Wilson, 1997; Murtagh, 2001.
104 Lahusen, 2004, 55–71.
105 European Union, 1995, 2.

essential continuity for British policy-makers. There was, however, some repositioning within the strategy that reflected the changed priorities of the peace process. Even greater attention was paid to the targeted needs of the alienated communities that produced paramilitarism.[106] This increased engagement with the socially excluded and marginalized mirrored the new forms of political engagement with Republicans in this period. These policies were a local example of a wider international pattern in which states increasingly engaged with anti-state insurgencies through social and economic mechanisms. The political impact of such interventions has been significant beyond the level of resources expended. These EU initiatives have brought insurgent forces into the mainstream and helped to transform their politics from protest to participation and lobbying.[107] This is not a tactical reorientation on their part; it points instead to a deeper malaise and disillusion in the radical project of European left-wing and nationalist politics. However, these initiatives did not cause this transformation; they simply accelerated the process. The political impact of such EU strategies in Catalonia, Corsica, the Basque country and Northern Ireland has been defined in the following terms:

> A nationalism of responsible and recognized business management promoted by the construction of the EU, which offers appropriate institutional tools (regional committees since 1994 and structural funds), is taking the place of a nationalism of protest. In addition, since an armed struggle is first of all made up of individuals, it is disillusion which is going to corrupt activism.
>
> *(Au nationalisme de protestation se substitue en Europe un nationalisme de gestion, responsable et reconnu, encouragé par la construction de l'Union européenne, qui propose des outils institutionnels adaptés (comité des regions depuis 1994 et fonds structurels). Plus encore, parce qu'une lutte armée est d'abord le fait d'individus, c'est la désillusion qui va gangrener l'activisme).*[108]

The Catholic middle class: the new risen people?

In Northern Ireland, these strategies of normalization attempted to manage the economic patterns of de-industrialization and transform existing political conflict. The development of new sociopolitical relationships that aim to transcend division by the common culture of consumption marks a shift from mere containment to a fundamental realignment of life in the region. In this way, 'the primary aim of state intervention has been to

106 Ibid.
107 See, for example, 'MEP's Diary: Bairbre de Brún', *An Phoblacht*, 29 June 2006.
108 X. Crettiez, 'IRA, ETA, FLNC: l'agonie des illusions militaristes', *Le Monde*, 23 August 2005. I wish to thank Dr I. McKeane for the translation.

regulate and/or restrain political antagonisms as well as accommodate new socioeconomic mechanisms of political hegemony.'[109]

In particular, the recruitment of Catholics into the realms of social power was intended to create a middle class to act as a buffer between the state and those Republican communities regarded as irreducibly hostile to the status quo. For Shirlow, this is a key component of British state strategy, which:

> extended to building new class alliances, so whilst it saw limited scope in working class urban areas, it deliberately and consciously attempted to bind the middle class to dependence on government resources, political guarantees and most crucially of all, publicly-funded jobs.[110]

The growth of a new Catholic middle class employed in the public sector, the housing executive and the civil service was increasingly commented on from the mid-1980s onwards.[111] British government fair employment and community relations policies intimately connected this emerging class with the state in myriad ways. This rapprochement between the state and the new Catholic middle class reflects wider patterns of social mobility, which in turn are facilitated by education, fair employment and the growth of public sector employment. By the mid-1990s, nearly one-third of jobs created in Northern Ireland were in the professional, managerial or administrative categories. The Catholic share of new employment grew by 32.8 per cent between the mid-1970s and the mid-1990s.[112] Combined with the emergence of a new class of nationalist business and social entrepreneurs, this 'new Catholic money' began to have an increasingly decisive political and social impact in the 1990s. Writing in the early 1990s, Eamonn McCann could describe the steady advance of the Catholic middle class, 'the group who had won the civil rights struggle', in the following terms:

> The fruits of this victory are on open display, along the leafy avenues of the Malone Road in Belfast or amid the eruption of Southfork replicas which now ruin the scenery along the Foyle... In the courthouse in Bishop's Street, it's now usually a Catholic who'll represent the Crown – unheard of a generation ago... Derry's only 'gentlemen's' club ...which did not admit Catholics in the 1960s, now has a majority Catholic membership.[113]

The buoyancy and self-confidence of the Catholic community and the rise of a new Catholic middle class have become staples of political analysis.

109 Shirlow, 1997a, 142.
110 Shirlow, 1997b, 87–107.
111 Wichert, 1999, 183.
112 Shirlow, 1997b, 87–107.
113 McCann, 1993, 52.

As a Secretary of State noted in 2000: 'Today, Catholics are part of the establishment as never before.'[114] This new Catholic middle class is now a significant political factor; it is qualitatively and self-consciously distinct from the old Catholic middle class, which served its own community in education, health, legal services and the licensed trade and knew its place in the world at large. As O'Connor noted in the early 1990s:

> The speed with which Catholic lawyers, doctors, accountants, and entrepreneurs of various kinds have developed access to political decision-making and made their way into an economic mainstream, once closed to them, has left nerves jangling inside the Catholic community and beyond it.[115]

Social conservatives have always invested a great deal of faith in the stabilizing effects of a property-owning democracy; the wider political impact that these rising expectations have had on the social psychology and political outlook of many Catholics has led some Republican activists to detect a similar connection when they argue that 'since there have been changes in living standards and expectations, with so much of today's society judged in material terms ... it is a completely different political and social context.'[116] Others link these social and economic changes to a political de-mobilization and the creation of a new nationalist elite as a result of the conflict:

> A whole generation has grown up with different priorities and attitudes. After 30 years of conflict, some people saw a political niche for themselves. Others saw the benefits of peace in material and social terms. For them, life's getting better. Whilst there is continued social and economic deprivation in West Belfast, there have also been increases in standards of living since 1994. These are not based on industry, but on various funding agencies and government subsidies so people get distracted.[117]

One result of these changes has been the development of new forms of Republican politics and the re-emergence of intra-communal divisions alongside the dominant inter-communal antagonisms. Indeed, evidence suggests that the consolidation of these affluent groups and the resulting social differentiation is greater within the nationalist population than it is within Northern Ireland as a whole.[118] It has also been suggested that

114 Dr John Reid MP, Secretary of State for Northern Ireland, 'Becoming persuaders: British and Irish identities in Northern Ireland', speech at the Institute of Irish Studies, University of Liverpool, 21 November 1999.
115 O'Connor, 1993, 16.
116 Jim Gibney, member of Sinn Féin Ard Comhairle, interview, 25 July 2005.
117 Tomás Gorman, member of Irish Republican Socialist Party Ard Comhairle, interview, 19 July 2005.
118 Sheehan and Tomlinson, 1996; 1999.

the fracturing of the monolithic blocs might be along class lines, with 'an increasingly divided and discordant material set of experiences for middle- and low-income Catholics'.[119]

If this differentiation continues, it could have a wider impact on the politics of the nationalist population. The increased social mobility and wider economic change that contributed to the consolidation of the Catholic middle class over the last twenty-five years will continue to be significant. However, the exact pattern of development remains hard to discern. One possibility is that these social processes will produce new political forms; in particular, these tendencies contribute to the fracturing of a monolithic Catholic identity and the development of new forms of nationalism. These emphasize cultural identity over political reunification, and accept the benefits of the new dispensation, whether under direct rule or devolved power-sharing. Furthermore, this rapprochement with the status quo combined with the shared class values and lifestyles of the middle classes of both traditions could potentially act to undermine existing patterns of national identity. For some who view this as a positive development, these forces might form the basis of a new cross-community type of politics: 'that fracturing ... may be the necessary precondition for recognition of what unites rather than what divides the community.'[120]

Another possibility is that this embourgeoisement continues to increase the political self-confidence and social self-assurance of Catholics within the region's polity. Republicans, in particular, claimed that their thirty-year campaign had ultimately produced the material and political benefits of the peace process for the nationalist population. 'In the 1970s the IRA's campaign put backbone into the SDLP [Social Democratic and Labour Party] when it negotiated with the unionists: nationalist confidence today in political negotiation and bargaining is a product of the Republican struggle,' argues one former senior Republican.[121]

However, this apparent strength conceals an underlying defensiveness within the nationalist population as a result of deepening segregation and continuing political polarization between the communities. The pressures for communal solidarity seem stronger than the tendencies towards political differentiation. Gerry Adams has described 'group Catholic thinking' as a significant factor in nationalist culture: 'About 80 per cent of northern Catholics ... are only one generation away from the land or the ghetto and it doesn't take a lot to concretize their views... There's a tendency in this state for some aspects of life to remind you where you came from.'[122]

119 Graham and Shirlow, 1998, 245–254.
120 Elliott, 2002, 169–188.
121 Danny Morrison, interview, 5 January 2004.
122 O'Connor, 1993, 87.

This widely-held sense of victimhood and ghettoization remains a key theme in nationalist politics, and is frequently mobilized by the Provisionals to great political advantage. The communalized nature of post-Good Friday Agreement politics has reinforced these trends. Former SDLP councillor Brian Feeney believes that the threats of loyalist violence reinforce this sense of fear and strengthen the existing organic links between the nationalist middle and working classes. He argues:

> continuing loyalist violence promotes Catholic solidarity. Even middle-class Catholics see it could happen to them if they move to the 'wrong area'. Every middle-class person knows someone still living in the areas that they came from: this middle class keeps up these links and they haven't forgotten their origins.[123]

One of the most important political and social impacts of this 'new risen people' has been on Republican politics. Sinn Féin's electoral strength still lies in its urban working-class and rural heartlands, but it is gaining more middle-class support. As the party continues to seek an increased share of the middle-class vote, some believe that this consolidation will result in yet further moderation of its political position.[124] While some activists see dangers in courting this vote, leading Sinn Féin strategists see the Catholic middle class differently. To a former leading Sinn Féin strategist, they are:

> an instrument for change. In the past we had a very small Catholic middle class: it was very rich, but it had no political power. What we have today is a very strong middle class. It has grown, it's very rich and now it wants political power. Tensions are created when they see the glass ceilings in our society: the way they continue to be excluded feeds back into the equality agenda and strengthens our politics.[125]

The peace industry

By the late 1990s, a combination of British government policies, wider social and economic change and the concomitant strengthening of these community organizations had created a hybrid form of civil society in Northern Ireland. This was reflected in what has been defined as 'a huge dependency culture in the community and voluntary sector'.[126] These structures are said to be key part of 'the peace industry', a term that

123 Brian Feeney, former SDLP councillor, interview, 3 August 2005.
124 Private information: former member of Sinn Féin Ard Comhairle, interview, 14 April 1999.
125 Tom Hartley, former General Secretary of Sinn Féin, interview, 30 July 2005.
126 F. Meredith, 'Putting a price on peace?', *Irish Times*, 10 January 2006.

conjures up images of 'hatchet-faced paramilitaries appropriating for their own dark purposes peace funds designed to promote healing and reconciliation'.[127] Given that it has been claimed that this sector is the region's largest employer 'with 30,000 workers being paid by 4,500 community organizations which have benefited from £1 billion in handouts from the European Commission and the British and Irish governments' since 1994, it seems possible to quantify the social and economic power that this sector represents.[128]

The significance of these programmes can be seen in the politics of resource allocation and bargaining, where MEPs pitch for increased funding for their communities. Unionists, for example, contrast the success of nationalist groups in gaining funding with the perceived failure of the unionist community groups 'to start applying for funding ...[to] get their fair share'.[129] This is of more than symbolic value in the zero-sum politics of communal advancement, since it has been argued that 'the future sustainability of the community and voluntary sector ... [is] increasingly uncertain' because of a 50 per cent reduction in funding for the PEACE III programme for 2007–2013.[130]

It is the range of activities and employment that gives the sector its significance as a network of social power and influence in the nationalist community. The impact of these developments, which linked the growth of community organizations to state funding, had been understood almost from the beginning. The British government's Action for Community Employment (ACE) programme in the early 1980s posed the question for many activists of whether to participate in the scheme to obtain state funding, or to boycott it because it aimed to buy off the radicalized resistance communities. The response was a practical, pragmatic one: 'the only reason why people wanted any contact with the state was money, it wasn't about any interaction with agencies as such ... but there's also the [question]: what else can we do?'[131] Others explicitly linked emerging divisions within the community to the nature of the funding regime:

> When the Catholic Church controlled all the ACE schemes it didn't make the community cohere or bond together. It split the community, because when the funding came around you had a feeding frenzy... Everyone just looked on their wee corner and fought over this scarce funding.[132]

127 Ibid.
128 Incore and Cresco Trust report, quoted in Meredith, 'Putting a price on peace?'
129 DUP MEP Jim Allister, quoted in Meredith, 'Putting a price on peace?'
130 Meredith, 'Putting a price on peace?'
131 Claire Hackett, interview, 18 July 2005.
132 Tommy Gorman, interview, 7 August 2005.

These external funding agencies provided significant funding for particular projects in the most deprived areas, and have a greater impact than
the amounts of money would suggest. Thus the extent of this 'soft power'
is not simply a function of the size of the state and the political and
social resources available to it. The significance lies in the specific focus
and disproportionate influence that is brought to bear in shaping the
social and political life of particular communities, such as the nationalist
working class of west Belfast. Consequently, the frames of their activity,
taking place within boundaries established by the funders and the regula-
tors, also acted to increasingly legitimize the state, *de facto* if not as yet
de jure.

As the example of the USDT illustrates, this process operates with
nothing as crude as a transmission belt. It is a subtle process that takes
the form of active engagement and dialogue between partners within
the many spaces where the state and sections of civil society meet and
fuse. In a pattern that became familiar in Northern Ireland from the 1980s
onwards, these organizations function as conduits for social resources as
well as mediating between the state and the community.

Characteristically, this scaffolding around the core structures of the
state is drawn not only from the structures of the clearly-defined quangocracy itself, but increasingly involves nominally independent NGOs as
well as elements of the community and voluntary sector. In this way, these
organizations become increasingly autonomous in relation to the communities that created them. This remoteness and lack of real accountability
helps to further blur the distinction between state and civil society. Some
Republican activists see these developments as the continuation of a
British counter-insurgency strategy by other means, albeit one that now
incorporates Republicans rather than relegating them to the margins:

> We get some sense of autonomy here in west Belfast – the People's Republic
> of West Belfast – because Sinn Féin are running everything and every-
> thing's grand. But these developments didn't empower, they softened up
> the community and added another layer to the state. A lot of these organiza-
> tions are seen as self-interested, self-identifying and self-perpetuating. It's
> a smokescreen. The reality is different from the perception... Generally in
> terms of participatory democracy they do very little.[133]

The typical forms of politics for these third-sector groups become those of
the pressure group, petitioning for reform and the redress of grievances
rather than organizing movements for transformation and mobilizing
challenges to the state. For example, the Special European Union Programmes

---

133 Tomás Gorman, interview, 19 July 2005.

Body, which administers the PEACE II and III programmes, is criticized for distorting the community sector's agenda by emphasizing economic change at the expense of social development and reconciliation.[134]

Partnership arrangements and social entrepreneurship in the delivery of services and functions normally associated with the core state, such as education and training, further strengthen the relationship between community organizations and the state.[135] Given the political and social milieu from which these organizations arose, this process of formalization and incorporation represents a radical shift in direction and function. This takes on a self-perpetuating form with often-unanticipated outcomes:

> Once the structure exists with its jobs, services, activities and projects you need to get funding: you become concerned to follow the funding. Community development did change as a result and organizations revised their activities according to what the funding criteria were. Increasingly, we used the language of value-for-money, monitoring and evaluation and effectiveness. It would limit what could be done and was a definite constraint.[136]

Increasingly, this process in the UK as a whole has turned 'charities and voluntary organizations into multi-million-pound businesses by contracting-out services provided by the state,' far removed from the 'cuddly image of the third sector'.[137] In this manner, the state–community sector complex supplements the military–industrial one. The very nature of this soft power continues to embody the characteristic contradictions and limitations of the modern state. Indeed, the terrain of the state is itself contested and partially occupied to some extent by potential challengers as part of this process.[138] Compromises and concessions have to be made by the state which, while ultimately resulting in the incorporation of challengers, will also alter the composition of state power. Thus the reconfiguration of hard and soft power and the reconstitution of state–civil society relationships arise from a position of relative weakness rather than confident strength.

However, even if the state faces a crisis of authority, this accretion of hard and soft power combined with the social and financial resources at its disposal and the comparable ideological exhaustion of the Republican project still makes it the most significant centre of power in Northern Ireland. Despite the mutual exhaustion of the contending parties, the state

134 F. Meredith, 'Putting a price on peace?', *Irish Times*, 10 January 2006.
135 Pierson, 1991, 121–126.
136 Claire Hackett, interview, 18 July 2005.
137 D. Hencke, 'Government turns charities into multimillion-pound businesses', *Guardian*, 3 July 2006.
138 Jessop, 1990, 267–268.

would appear to still have the whip hand. Thus, paradoxically in the light of the general crisis of the state internationally, it appears that the power of the British state in Northern Ireland in the twenty-first century has become even more central to the region's politics, while at the same time being even more difficult to define.

Shaping the agenda?

This chapter has assessed the nature of Northern Ireland's economic and social terrain and suggested how these structural factors, mediated through the British state, contributed to shaping the political context for the development of Provisionalism since the 1980s. This is not to suggest a simple causal relationship between societal base and political superstructure, but it does help us to understand how the political development of Republicanism is anchored firmly in this broader context.

This three-way relationship between the British state, nationalist civil society and the Provisionals is not a simple command relationship between subject and object. All the actors interact with and shape each other, although the flows of power and influence are by no means equal. The British state's decisive power gives it the ability to determine the terrain on which political actors operate; its obvious significance has been long recognized by Republicans, if only because it has been the main target of Provisional military and political campaigns since the 1970s.

The nature of nationalist civil society is itself another significant determining factor. The state had a disproportionate importance in the nationalist community generally and among the most deprived groups in particular, given the levels of unemployment, state-sponsored employment and welfare benefits in the 1980s and 1990s.[139] The dependency culture of the most deprived was just the tip of an iceberg of connection that included most of the nationalist community and quite wide sections of the unionist population too.

As we shall see in Chapter 2, civil society had a contradictory character for the Provisionals: it was both a zone of contestation and a zone of engagement with the state. The emerging structures of a civil society in the 1980s, such as community groups, became increasingly geared to seeking and being sustained by UK and European Union funding and support. Their activities and agenda likewise became closely bound up with the social and economic policies of the state. Although many community activists argued that by 'sometimes going along with the government

---

139 See, for example, figures on levels of child poverty and benefit take-up in West Belfast, taken from British government figures cited in the Falls Community Council's 'West Belfast: some of the facts behind the issues' (Belfast, 1987).

agenda it was possible to subvert them from within by creating a structure of your own', others saw how a wider social and political context could be determined by external agencies:

> I don't want to say that power corrupts, but it shapes the agenda... Co-option develops and a language of partnership with the state develops, especially as the state divests itself of a whole number of functions. For example, the West Belfast Forum in the 1990s started to look at the idea of partnership whilst the reconciliation and peace terminology of PEACE II [an EU-funded programme] focussed on cross-community work. Funding becomes a process of jumping through hoops set by these external agencies.[140]

The paradox of this development was that this engagement rested on the strength of those very elements and structures which provided the political constituency for Sinn Féin. The social networks, which had initially provided the supporting frameworks of the Provisional revolutionary project in the 1970s and 1980s, had now become forces for stabilization and channels for normalization and integration.

The formalization of these networks into community organizations is mirrored by a process of institutionalization and political adaptation by the Provisionals themselves. Drawn from the same social and political milieu, similar processes within community organizations and the Republican movement were bound to influence each other. Civil society was also a medium for ideological influence: community organizations were increasingly shaped by the politics of normalization as well as by the strategies of resource allocation. In the long term, it was to be these forms of politics that were to have the greatest impact on the evolution of Provisionalism.

The powerful forces of state, economy and society provided the external context for the ideological exhaustion of the Provisional national liberation project: they were decisive factors in a world in which radical anti-state politics were declining in salience by the late 1980s. Republicans did not simply surrender to these external forces. Provisional politics from the mid-1980s onwards attempted to counter the successful British strategy of military and political containment.

However, the possible options open to Republicans were limited by the changing balance of forces. The resulting politics of the peace process, by their very nature, could not achieve Republican political goals. Their culmination in the Belfast Agreement and the new political dispensation that haltingly developed after 1998 represented a decisive defeat for Republicanism. The new forms of Provisionalism that emerged in the 1980s

140 Claire Hackett, interview, 18 July 2005.

and 1990s refracted these external forces through the existing organizational and ideological structures and culture of the Republican movement. They also reflected the complexities of the movement's changing relationship with the nationalist population. The manner in which this range of political, organizational and cultural factors contributed to the process of institutionalization and fundamental ideological shift within Provisionalism will be the subject of Chapters 2 and 3.

Chapter 2

From Resistance Community to Community Politics

Ardoyne is a small community in Belfast, which has borne more than its fair share of suffering in the past 20 years of conflict. This week its people came together to remember their dead and to rededicate them to the struggle for lasting peace in their community and their country... The staunchness of the ordinary working-class community of Ardoyne and of many another communities like it across the Six Counties is a shining example to all the oppressed sections of the Irish people. Neither [sic] occupation, criminalization, extradition, imprisonment nor even assassination can defeat them. They are the real stalwarts of freedom.[1]

Characterizing the Provisionals has been a central issue in Northern Irish politics since the 1970s. Throughout the Troubles, it has proven difficult to fit Provisionalism into the theoretical categories of conventional politics. Stressing the 'traditional' nature of Republicanism or situating it solely within a terrorist paradigm ignores the complexities of the contemporary movement.[2] 'Terrorology' is as useful as theology in explaining the emergence of New Sinn Féin over the last sixteen years.[3]

Events since the signing of the Belfast Agreement have confirmed the scale of this transformation. The Provisionals' participation in the institutions of the Good Friday Agreement 'was a departure no previous Republican has endorsed. Not even de Valera when he departed Sinn Féin in 1926 argued that Republicans should end abstentionism in the context of parliamentary representation in Northern Ireland.'[4] The vast ideological distance that the Provisionals have travelled during the peace process was highlighted even more dramatically by Sinn Féin's cooperating with the Democratic Unionist Party (DUP) to form a restored executive in 2007. To understand the dramatic shift in Republican politics, we

1 'Stalwarts of freedom', *An Phoblacht/Republican News*, 30 March 1989.
2 For example, 'Northern Ireland: Future Terrorist Trends, November 1978'(the 'Glover report'), produced by British military intelligence in 1978, defined Provisionalism as 'committed to the traditional aims of Irish nationalism': its politics were 'motivated by an inward-looking Celtic nationalism'. See Cronin, 1980, 339–357.
3 Alexander and O'Day, 1984; O'Day, 1995; Maillot, 2005.
4 Rafter, 2005, 138.

need to understand Provisionalism's contradictory character as a hybrid combination of bureaucratic political party, popular protest movement and military organization.[5] For most of its history, this was an inherently unstable ideological and organizational form: the peace process itself was a prolonged working through of some of these contradictions, resulting in a new form of Provisionalism. Sinn Féin, according to Taoiseach Bertie Ahern, has 'done its utmost to move away from its past', and so is now deemed an acceptable partner in government by even its most vehement former enemies in the DUP.[6]

While it may be accurate to argue that in the contemporary world, 'no other party has undergone such a radical overhaul of its basic principles', questions remain: have the Provisionals followed previous generations of Republicans into the corridors of power by becoming a *fully constitutional* political party?[7] This lingering uncertainty was not simply the historical legacy of the Armalite and the ballot paper; other movements, both historically in Ireland and internationally, have combined electoral politics and armed struggle en route to the cabinet table. Nor were these questions simply part of the necessary political manoeuvring in preparation for a historic compromise between the DUP and Sinn Féin in 2007.[8]

The unresolved questions about contemporary Provisionalism arise from its character as a structure of power within nationalist civil society. The trajectory of the Provisional movement over the last thirty years illustrates how the founding moments of social movement organizations and political parties continue to exert 'a weight on ... [their] organizational structure even decades after'.[9] In this way, what can be defined as the politics of community were central to Provisionalism's founding moment and continue to remain an essential part of its genetic composition. Community is a keyword whose shifting meanings encapsulate both the past and the future of Republican politics.[10]

The ideological and organizational contradictions that remain at the heart of Provisionalism are not solely a product of these internal dynamics: powerful external factors have also shaped the movement's development. In particular, the changing balance of forces between the Republican movement and the British state during the 1980s was decisive in the

---

5 Irvin, 1999.

6 Bertie Ahern speaking on RTE Radio News, 15 October 2006; F. Millar and G. Moriarty, 'DUP and Sinn Féin move closer to agreement', *Irish Times*, 14 October 2006.

7 Rafter, 2005, 15.

8 G. Moriarty, 'Contingent commitment may be key to NI deal', *Irish Times*, 5 October 2006.

9 Panebianco, 1988, 50.

10 Williams, 1976, 65–66.

transformation of Provisionalism. In conjunction with underlying social and economic change, the successful British military and political containment of Republicanism determined the patterns of institutionalization and concomitant ideological change within the Republican movement.

A by-product of this process was the strengthening of the movement's social and political influence within the nationalist community, giving it some of the attributes of a form of state power. Paradoxically, this consolidation drew Republicans more firmly into the orbit of their senior partner, the British state. This relationship was developed through increasingly formal and informal engagement with the 'real state' at all levels, from local government and the community sector through to secret diplomacy and direct political negotiation.

The result was a new Republican politics that replaced the militant form of resistance community with an essentially electoral community activism prepared to work within the new dispensation established by the Good Friday Agreement in 1998. Chapters 3 and 4 show how this new orientation towards the British state developed, and why it produced a deeper ideological and structural realignment within Provisionalism.

Defiance and dinnseanchas: the founding moment of the Provisionals[11]

Provisionalism's founding moment during the Northern Irish state's crisis in 1969–1973 casts a long shadow over its subsequent history. It was a period marked by heightened communal polarization, the collapse of state authority and an insurrectionary mass movement; 'a community in revolt, rather than a hermetically sealed secret society of gunmen and bombers'.[12] The social movement organization that emerged from this crisis was much wider than the narrow base of pre-1969 Republicanism.

As such, it released a 'pool of energy' that many contemporaries considered tantamount to a revolution.[13] For many young nationalists, this was a period in which the forces and symbols of authority were thrown off: 'we realized that they weren't all-powerful... We had no-go areas and we had an armed organization... All of this resulted in a discussion about what could replace it.'[14]

From the start, the Provisionals deployed the language of community to

11 *Dinnseanchas* can be defined literally as topography, but in the Irish language tradition the term endows place with a particular mythological meaning.
12 T. McKearney, 'Putting the Provos in context', *Sunday Business Post*, 7 August 2005.
13 de Baróid, 1990, 27–31.
14 Felim Ó hAdhmaill, former Republican prisoner and community activist, interview, 25 August 2005.

mobilize support for the 'armed struggle'.[15] To Republicans, 'community' was not simply a product of the collective imagination: *resistance communities* were battlefields between the state and an anti-state insurgency, between a dominant hegemony and an emerging counter-hegemony.[16] Republicans consciously attempted to create a new radical *Gemeinschaft* of the resistance community to establish their own political dominance over the alternative definitions of 'community' advanced by the Catholic Church, constitutional nationalism and the state. The appeal of this strategy lay in the nature of civil society within the nationalist community. A whole range of organizations and social networks, products of both the pre-1968 period and the Troubles, provided a fertile field by enabling activists to be 'well-integrated in their communities and belong to tight-knit political networks'.[17] Like other social movements, these existing social structures provided 'the mechanisms that transformed social settings into sites of emergent collective action... Recruits were drawn in through existing ties, [and] along established lines of interaction.'[18]

By drawing on these networks, Republicans were relatively successful in building a micro-society within sections of the nationalist community from the 1970s onwards. For example, it has been suggested that Ballymurphy's later political development as a Provisional stronghold was influenced by the deep-seated oppositional culture that had developed there before 1969.[19] Their success shows how the idea of community mobilizes subaltern groups when it can be 'located within their traditions, their culture and their consciousness ... [which are] informed by a variety of influences such as land, religion, myth and folklore... [As such] it is not necessarily a class-consciousness, or a working class culture.'[20]

The importance of these local determinants and characteristics has led some to define the Provisional movement in its early period as a loose federation of locally-defined Republicanisms in which class, community and locale jointly produce distinctly different forms and styles of politics. Republican activists created a coherent coalition from these elements by redefining the collective identity of the community to accord with the aims of the movement.[21]

---

15 Brendan Hughes, former OC, Belfast IRA, interview, 12 August 1998; Mickey McMullan, former Northern Editor, *An Phoblacht/Republican News*, interview, 16 April 1998.
16 Gramsci, 1971, 416–418.
17 Casquette, 2001, 240–241.
18 McAdam, 2003, 131–132.
19 de Baróid, 1990, 30–31.
20 Robson, 2000, 36–37.
21 McAdam et al, 2001, 43.

The description of Ardoyne in North Belfast at the beginning of this chapter is an example of the essentially idealized characteristics of this resistance community. The defining feature was contained in the language of the ghetto, a term of abuse positively appropriated as an identity. This was a conscious attempt to identify the nationalist population with the contemporary Black American experience. The ghettoes were defined by their segregation and sense of imposed exclusion from society. These areas combined a contradictory sense of powerlessness and vulnerability with a strong family-like kinship and social network.[22] These features produced communal defiance and a high level of political consciousness in reaction to conditions of exploitation and oppression.[23]

These resistance communities were also characterized by a strong sense of place. The local was an important way to situate the individual within the national narrative, especially given the initially localized patterns of mobilization that created the Provisionals. Events from 1968 onwards conferred a further mythological status on particular locales, and situated them within a wider pattern of local and national meanings for Republicans.[24] For the Provisionals, the potent intersection and mutual reinforcement of themes of place, class and community were essential in the process of defining a new, radically different sense of community, illustrating the political significance of place as 'the terrain where basic social practices ... are lived out. Place is where everyday life is situated.'[25] This was not unique to Republicanism: the relationship between place and patterns of political mobilization is an important dynamic in a range of nationalist and popular movements internationally.[26]

The power of common local experiences in shaping a political outlook is important, causing one critic to argue that 'in the 1980s the Provos stood for an independent 32-county Republic of West Belfast.'[27] Many Republicans were drawn into military activism in response to events around them, and only then developed strategies that best corresponded to the reality on the ground.[28]

---

22 Burton, 1978, Chapter 3 and Adams, 1997 discuss the political importance of these social networks.

23 See J. Sosa, 'Ardoyne under a microscope: review of F. Burton's *The Politics of Legitimacy*', *Republican News*, 13 January 1979.

24 For example, see Brownie, 'Ghosts', *An Phoblacht*, 27 June 1981; Morrison, 1989; and Harnden, 1999.

25 Merrifield, 1993, 552.

26 Agnew, 1987; Smith, 1999.

27 Malachy O'Doherty, political and cultural commentator, interview, 23 July 2005.

28 For the importance of individual experience in shaping political ideas, see White, 1993, and Bean and Hayes, 2001.

In this process, they were assisted by the limited nature of the Republican theoretical tradition, whose elasticity enabled activists to be creative in developing new political strategies. The organic intellectuals of the Provisional movement successfully reworked these experiences into a new story of community oppression and resistance, which appeared to grow naturally from the old. While Republicans naturally drew on existing elements of nationalist political culture and the favourable social structures of the Catholic communities to 'fuse the social consciousness of Catholicism into a political practice', other external ideological and structural influences were to be just as potent in creating new forms and representations of community.[29] As one contemporary sociological study of Ardoyne noted, these frequently contradictory elements produced 'a remarkable ideology that can express its revolutionary claims one week in a thinly veiled religious and mystical form and the next in a style and reasoning much closer to Lenin and Mao than Aquinas.'[30] In this way, Provisionalism was not a mere reproduction of tradition. Its military and political practice reflected the harsher urban tones and contemporary experiences of the 'war zone'. The ashes of Bombay Street were more important in shaping the outlook of the young volunteers who flocked into the ranks of the IRA than the faintly glowing embers of the GPO.[31]

1968 and all that: Cú Chulainn and Coronation Street

The ideological and organizational characteristics of the Provisionals reflected wider contradictions within northern nationalist culture. As the revolutionary wave receded by the late 1970s and the Provisional challenge was contained, the contradictory tensions inherited from this culture re-emerged and continued to influence Republican politics into the twenty-first century. The exact balance of ideological forces within Republicanism was always unstable, representing a constant tension between existing tradition and new political forms. That this combination of communal rootedness and intellectual eclecticism can be an ideological weakness as well as a social strength was to emerge during the movement's transition into a mainstream organization. The growing emphasis on the local and the communal within Provisionalism at the expense of the universalist categories of nation and class was a reflection of this tendency and represented a clear scaling-down of Republican aspirations during the late 1980s and 1990s.

29 Burton, 1978, 128.
30 Burton, 1978, 75.
31 For an interesting discussion of the early origins of the Provisionals, see McIntyre, 1999, Chapter 3.

The central arch of nationalist political culture framework since the 1920s had been the imperative for communal solidarity.[32] This was to be a powerful strand in the common culture that Republicans could appeal to at particular moments of crisis. Explicitly nationalist groupings attempted to portray themselves as the representatives of the whole nationalist community: communal solidarity and the transcendence of internal class divisions were deemed vital in the face of a structurally hostile Unionist state.[33] While reunification was ostensibly the long-term goal at the heart of this political culture, in practice nationalist politics were essentially representational or clientelistic, seeking accommodation within the framework of the Northern Irish state after partition. During the 1970s, the SDLP absorbed most of the elements of constitutionalist nationalism. Its position as the political voice of the nationalist community seemed unchallenged; even Republicans initially appeared to tolerate it as an electoral expression of nationalist opinion.[34] During the 1980s, Sinn Féin increasingly emphasized these older traditions of nationalist unity as they began to claim the communal mantle from the SDLP in the fight against the common enemy at election time.

The hegemonic power of the Church over religious, educational, socio-cultural and political activity within the nationalist community strengthened this sense of communal unity. While secularization and challenges to the political, social and sexual authority of the Church have certainly taken place since the 1960s, Catholicism remains an important cultural influence and an underpinning element of communal common sense, even for lapsed Catholics. Despite Republicanism's frequently bitter battles for hegemony with the Church, the parish and the community of the faithful were to leave a deep imprint on the community politics of the Provisionals.[35]

Other traditions also had an important mobilizing role. Republicans legitimized their actions by drawing on the popular historical narratives of northern nationalist culture. This reflected the ambiguous historical relationship between sections of the nationalist population and Republicanism, which combined semi-derision with sceptical admiration for the IRA as 'a bulwark against loyalist attack'.[36] The defence of St Matthew's Church in 1970, for example, was described as 'the classic example of the traditional role of the IRA in Belfast, defending Catholic areas against

---

32 For the historical context and the development of a determining idea of community, see Elliott, 2000, xxxiii–xxxviii and Chapters 5–8.

33 Todd, 1990, 34–35.

34 Danny Morrison, former senior Republican strategist, interview, 5 January 2004.

35 O'Hagan, 1996.

36 O'Connor, 1993, 109.

hostile Protestant attack... It sent a clear message ... that the new Provisional movement was of and for the people.'[37] While some have discerned continuity with eighteenth-century Defenderism in this relationship, it is perhaps better understood in terms of the immediate impact of 'the pogroms of 1969' than as the expression of a continuous tradition.[38]

The events of 1969 were reinvented and retold, creating an influential symbolism to illustrate the organic relationship between Republicans and their community.[39] The idea of the IRA as the historically-sanctioned defender of the nationalist population remained a central theme in Provisional conceptions of community. It was to be a potent framing device for contemporary debates on IRA decommissioning and policing issues in the 2000s.

If the above elements could be categorized as the products of specifically local influences, other external factors expressed distinctly different universalist aspirations. The civil rights movement and its challenge to the state in the late 1960s and early 1970s was an important vehicle for these influences. These external factors were mediated through a new generation of activists who would be crucial in defining the politics of Provisionalism in the 1970s and 1980s.

These new political forms combined youth culture and the style of international popular protest. As such, they were as much a challenge to established authority within the nationalist community as to the state outside it. Media images of the war in Vietnam, the Black civil rights movement in the USA, radical student movements in Europe and the *zeitgeist* of the 'swinging sixties' are frequently mentioned by Republicans as important formative political influences.[40]

During this period, a whole range of community groups, tenants' associations and welfare rights groups developed, broadly influenced by radical ideas of community empowerment and a deep-seated anti-authoritarian culture.[41] In particular, the styles and ideologies of new left politics were influential among young Republicans. For example, the no-go areas in 1969–1973 were represented by these activists as 'new forms of self-government and social regulation, as opposed to alien state control, that grew out of working class experience and conceptions of

37 Quinn, 1999, 165.
38 Cronin, 1980, 209.
39 M. Armstrong, 'It was the people that asked for the IRA', *An Phoblacht/Republican News*, 13 August 1987.
40 Tommy McKearney, former Republican prisoner, interview, 30 May 1998; Danny Morrison, interview, 5 January 2004.
41 Claire Hackett, former Monitoring and Evaluations Officer, USDT and local history project worker, Falls Community Council, interview, 18 July 2005.

solidarity'.[42] The impact of these styles on Republicans was later described in the following way:

> Housing action groups, direct action, tenants' associations – all new terms to me in 1968. People were coming together, discontent was in the air... Revolution was in the air. Street fighters were to be seen in Paris, Berlin, Cleveland and Newark, and they looked the part. Masked and hooded, long-haired and angry, filled with wrath and fury, longing to pull down the establishment. Barricades, burning ... students and workers, the old left and the new, ready again to show the world that the 'Internationale' still meant something and that imperialism was not having it all its own way.[43]

This illustrates how the events of 1968 became mythologized, and Northern Irish politics interpreted through international frames of reference. It is further evidence of the range of cultural influences that shaped the nationalist population. British popular culture and the mass media ensured that sections of nationalist population partially inhabited a common cultural space with their working and middle-class counterparts in Britain. Pop music and an international youth culture were also important influences.[44] The significant impact of structural determinants, such as the post-1945 British welfare state and concomitant social changes in the politics and outlook of nationalists, were likewise significant.[45]

Such experiences produced more than a narrow ghetto tradition. These shifting patterns resulted in a cultural amalgam that was equally at home with Cú Chulainn and Coronation Street. Indeed, young Republicans were probably more familiar with Top of the Pops than they were with The Táin. Like many young people, influenced by culture and events in the wider world, they placed themselves and their community in a much wider frame than that of a provincial Northern Ireland.[46]

On the long road?

The history of the Provisionals from the mid-1970s onwards can be written as a series of attempts, military and political, to break out of Britain's successful containment and regain the initiative they held for a short period in the early 1970s. Levels of IRA activity declined after reaching an historic peak in 1972.[47] The so-called 'long war' strategy in 1977 was one

42 Felim Ó hAdhmaill, interview, 25 August 2005.
43 K. Gallagher, 'Revolution was in the air', *An Phoblacht*, 4 August 1979.
44 Danny Morrison, interview, 5 January 2004.
45 Devlin, 1969; Ó Dochartaigh, 1997; McCann, 1993.
46 Bean, 2005, 8–19.
47 Security information on the level of shootings, casualties and incidents from Wichert, 1999, 256–258.

of the first public recognitions of the strategic impasse that Republicans faced. The reorganization of the IRA under the 'cell system', the centralization of operations through Northern Command and the declining levels of IRA activity by the late 1970s all pointed to the emergence of a different type of movement: the localized and informal character of Provisionalism was being replaced by more formal and hierarchical structures.

The fundamental problem for the Provisionals was the demobilization of the broad social movement that had given birth to the IRA after the fall of Stormont. Initially, the Provisionals defined the community as a collective subject whose revolutionary potential could be realized through the agency of Republicanism.[48] As one Republican later explained, support was frequently taken for granted:

> community activism in the early 1970s was natural. At that point the major vehicle in the war was the IRA. Community and tenants' groups were something different, not part of the Republican armoury. Bobby Sands for example, in Twinbrook, didn't believe that we had to go in and take over groups. There was a belief within Republicanism that people would be supportive anyway.[49]

An important element of the long war strategy was a renewed focus on 'the base' as a means of overcoming the increasing isolation of the Provisional campaign.[50] The resistance community linking national and social liberation on both sides of the border was a key means of mobilizing for the struggle ahead. As Jimmy Drumm argued in words written to reflect the dominant leadership orthodoxy in 1977:

> We find that a successful war of liberation cannot be fought exclusively on the backs of the oppressed in the six counties, nor around the physical presence of the British Army... The isolation of socialist Republicans around the armed struggle is dangerous and has produced ... the reformist notion that 'Ulster' is the issue, which can somehow be resolved without the mobilization of the working class in the 26 counties.[51]

The stalemate could be broken if the resistance community could be remobilized and the battlefield broadened. This was possible because the nationalist working class, it was argued, had already moved 'from a position of supporting peaceful reform ... to guerrilla warfare... [This was] a revolution in itself, especially against a fairly powerful and influential Catholic middle class.' It was essential to break the hold of this class

48 'Soldiers of the People', *Republican News*, 24 February 1979.
49 Felim Ó hAdhmaill, interview, 25 August 2005.
50 'Secret', *An Phoblacht*, 12 May 1979.
51 J. Drumm, 'Annual Wolfe Tone Commemoration Speech', *Republican News*, 25 June 1977.

and the clergy 'on nationalist thinking, as part of an ongoing ideological struggle'.[52] Using an explicitly left-wing analytical framework, the core of this strategy stressed the importance of linking 'the advanced forces of Irish national liberation' and 'its other half: the struggling mass of workers and small farmers'.[53] In a stylistic conjunction of Leninism and Fenianism, the community exemplified 'the people'. The IRA was the vanguard of this vanguard community, 'the most *politically* [my emphasis] progressive, with implicit faith and conviction in the capability and conviction of the Republican leadership to overthrow British imperialist occupation.'[54] Members of the IRA and Republican activists were the critical subjective element because:

> The Volunteer is in everyday contact with the ordinary people whom he is fighting to liberate... He is in fact an ambassador of Republicanism and must propagate Republican philosophy... Apart from the practical reasons involved for the necessity for support, it must be remembered that these people are our fellow countrymen and women and their cultivation and education is, like ours, a prerequisite for the success of the revolution... The purpose of the war is nor [sic] merely to destroy, but to build alternative structures [the People's Councils]... [B]y radicalising and changing society we are automatically cementing gained ground and ... widening our base.[55]

Community thus became a central theme for what was now defined as a specifically socialist Republican project of revolutionary mobilization. In this reading, the community was both a site of resistance and a structure for the creation of a dual power challenge to the state.[56]

The prison protests and hunger strike campaigns of 1980 to 1981 represented an intensification of the existing strategy, and a turning point in terms of electoral politics. Many of the strategic developments in this period were accidental or pragmatic responses to circumstances, rather than the products of a long-term plan. The essential continuity in this period was the stress on community mobilization; the decisive break was the political and electoral success of the campaign.

52 P. Arnlis, 'The war will go on', *An Phoblacht/Republican News*, 10 September 1982.
53 'The tasks ahead', *Republican News*, 25 June 1977.
54 'Organise', *Republican News*, 4 December 1976.
55 Solon, 'Revealing revolutionary relations', *Republican News*, 30 July 1977.
56 These themes were developed in a series of influential articles during this period by Brownie (identified as Gerry Adams), including: 'Active abstentionism', *Republican News*, 18 October 1975; 'The republic; a reality', *Republican News*, 29 October 1975; and 'Active republicanism', *Republican News*, 1 May 1976, as well as letters and editorials in the paper, such as: 'Organise', *Republican News*, 4 December 1976; 'Reader slams republican interview', *Republican News*, 28 February 1976; and P. Mac Dermott, 'Movement must mobilise workers in mass movement', *Republican News*, 10 April 1976.

However, these successes were on a different basis to that originally envisaged by the long war strategy. From 1978 onwards, the National H-Block/Armagh Committee and the relatives' action committees had operated as broad fronts, including among their supporters those who did not necessarily support the IRA's armed struggle. In many ways, the hunger strikes were communal mobilizations illustrating the power of this sense of community, and marking 'a uniquely close identification between the nationalist population ... and ... physical force Republicanism', bringing thousands on to the streets 'by their umbilical cords'.[57] The electoral successes in Fermanagh and South Tyrone in 1981, and the support witnessed at hunger strikers' funerals and demonstrations, were motivated by a range of humanitarian and emotional factors, not just support for the Republican struggle.

Playing to the gallery? The ballot paper and the Armalite

The 'accidental' political and electoral mobilization of the hunger strikes showed new strategic possibilities. Combined with renewed activism this strategy would, it was hoped, revive the flagging campaign. The recruitment of a new layer of Sinn Féin activists in the wake of the hunger strikes and the developing activism of ex-prisoners who had been politicized in jail also made this strategy viable.[58] For many in the Republican leadership, the hunger strikes represented a seminal moment that would eventually produce the politics of the peace process:

> We learnt simple but very important lessons. Jim Gibney argued that we needed a broader alliance of forces: out of that came the H-Block movement, the electoral interventions and then the developments up to today. I think there is a logic there, although I am not sure it was clear at the time. You can be smart-arsed about it and say 'You didn't know where you were going', but we were on a learning curve and we're still on a learning curve. With the politics of looking for opportunities there are risks, and you never quite know where it's going to take you.[59]

---

57 O'Connor, 1993, 101–103. See also O'Malley, 1990 and Kearney, 1984, 9–12.

58 Patricia Campbell, former Tyrone Sinn Féin activist and member of Sinn Féin Ard Comhairle, interview, 6 January 2004; Anthony McIntyre, former IRA prisoner and Sinn Féin advice centre worker, Lower Ormeau, 1993–1997, interview, 17 May 2000. For something of the character and abilities of these new activists, see H. MacThomas, 'Sheena Campbell: a croppy who would not lie down', *An Phoblacht/Republican News*, 22 October 1992.

59 Tom Hartley, former General Secretary Sinn Féin and Belfast councillor, interview, 4 August 2005.

The hunger strikes certainly opened up new political opportunities for the Provisionals.[60] Participation in elections had been an unarticulated desire among some leading Republicans in the late 1970s. They realized how difficult such a transition to electoral politics would be in the light of the movement's history, but believed that building up a political movement would be a form of insurance policy that could open up a new front for the Provisionals.[61] Although the rhetoric was still revolutionary in the early 1980s – 'the war was going on' and armed struggle remained the cutting edge – some saw that an electoral strategy might yield future, if still uncertain, dividends.[62]

> A number of things were holding back the struggle, and that could lead to stalemate and defeat. We had to have as many options open as possible for all scenarios. By building up a political movement, we might at some stage be able to challenge the SDLP. I certainly saw it as a political investment. I thought: if there is a vacuum, let's fill it. If we can develop, then develop.[63]

The strategy that emerged was encapsulated in Danny Morrison's famous slogan 'the ballot paper and the Armalite'. According to Morrison, using this symbolic phrase 'was playing to that gallery at the 1981 Ard Fheis'.

> I had to convince a lot of IRA people … [and] reassure them that by taking part in electoral politics there was not going to be any diminution in the armed struggle. If they thought that, then we weren't going to get across that bridge [standing in elections], and we had to get across that bridge. I wasn't being deceptive, because at that stage I still saw armed struggle as being the priority. When I left my seat I didn't know what I was going to say. When I finished, Martin McGuinness turned to someone on the platform and said 'Where the fuck did that come from?'[64]

Whether the strategy really developed in such a haphazard manner remains unclear. What does emerge from these accounts is the importance of internal political dynamics and organizational culture in shaping Provisional strategy. Morrison's decision to play to the gallery in 1981 would not be the last time this method of persuasion was employed by the Republican leadership. This combination of pragmatism and reliance on leadership prestige, supported by the 'internal management' of opposition,

---

60 For a serious challenge to the dominant Provisional consensus concerning the conduct of the hunger strike and the leadership's strategy during this period, see O'Rawe, 2005.
61 Danny Morrison, interview, 5 January 2004.
62 P. Arnlis, 'The war will go on', *An Phoblacht*, 10 September 1982.
63 Danny Morrison, interview, 5 January 2004.
64 Danny Morrison, interview, 5 January 2004.

would prove to be very effective in the future development of Provisionalism.[65] By linking the armed struggle and the electoral strategy through the rhetoric of the resistance community in the 1980s, the Provisional leadership could reassure activists that the armed campaign still had primacy as the cutting edge of the Republican struggle.

For most Republicans, the electoral strategy was a continuation of the war by other means. Republicans, it was argued:

> did not approach elections from a reformist basis ... [they] did not believe that the six counties can be democratized... [The strategy aimed] to create the conditions whereby the Irish people may seize political and economic control of their own destinies.[66]

The ballot paper and Armalite strategy was initially successful in terms of electoral gains. The revolutionary will and political consciousness of the Provisionals were believed to be sufficient grounds to prevent elections resulting in incorporation by the state. For example, one of the earliest advocates of this strategy, Belfast Sinn Féin councillor Sean Keenan, argued that the Republican 'revolutionary outlook' and use of 'everyday issues as an educative and mobilizing strategy' would prevent a sell-out. He continued, 'It's up to the people themselves to fight their own battle; we're only there to assist them if they need it. The Housing Executive has ... tried to use us as a buffer between itself and tenants, but we've refused to fall into that trap.'[67]

This revolutionary rhetoric of struggle and mobilization – 'a process of politicizing people and building up their confidence in themselves' – was easily adapted to the different requirements of fighting elections.[68] This rhetoric retained its potency because there was considerable truth in the argument that Sinn Féin represented a community in revolt. While not everyone concurred with *An Phoblacht/Republican News* assessment that the key battle was between the nationalist middle class and an increasingly radicalized Republican working class, most media commentators explained Sinn Fein's electoral support as the product of nationalist alien-

65 See Moloney, 2002, 287–297 for examples of the Provisional leadership's tactics to ensure a majority for the resolution to end abstentionism at the 1986 Sinn Féin Ard Fheis. During the 1998 Sinn Féin Ard Fheis, the author witnessed the IRA's Adjutant-General and a member of the IRA Army Council 'lobbying and persuading' IRA volunteers to vote for the leadership's position on the Good Friday Agreement.

66 Sinn Féin Education Department, 1983.

67 S. Delaney, 'Housing in Belfast: building community confidence – interview with Sean Keenan', *IRIS*, December 1984, 34.

68 Ibid., 32–34.

ation and the political culture of the nationalist ghettoes.[69] For example, in the early 1980s it was argued that 'Sinn Féin had been able to mobilize hundreds of young and working-class supporters' while 'the SDLP quite plainly had not'. The contest between Sinn Féin and the SDLP was a battle of 'youth versus middle age, working class versus middle class and enthusiasm versus weariness'.[70]

The overall pattern of Sinn Féin results in Westminster, European, Assembly and local government elections throughout the 1980s confirmed these trends. In 1983, Gerry Adams won West Belfast and Sinn Féin's share of the vote across Northern Ireland rose to 13.8 per cent. This strength was concentrated in traditional rural Republican seats along with what were fast becoming Sinn Féin strongholds in the urban working-class areas of West and North Belfast and Derry.[71] There was a clear correlation between Sinn Féin's electoral success and indices of social and economic deprivation, but its support was not simply a product of 'poverty, repression and resistance', as Republicans themselves increasingly stressed.[72] Paradoxically, the strength of the results emphasized the Republican failure to establish a wider hegemony over the nationalist electorate. Sinn Féin had a strong electoral base, but one narrowly confined to particular communities.

The resistance community has put down deep roots, which provide more than a core vote for Sinn Féin. As the electoral setbacks of the mid-1980s were to illustrate, a vote for Sinn Féin did not mean unconditional support for the IRA. The Provisionals recognized from an early stage that:

> The public and supporters don't just accept everything that the IRA does, and at times they will probably register some form of disapproval, either withdrawing support or by not voting for Sinn Féin.[73]

However, there was considerable local support for and involvement in militant Republicanism in these base areas. The initial electoral base for Sinn Féin in the 1980s indicated this level of support, as did survey evidence

69 'Clearly defined', *An Phoblacht/Republican News*, 5 May 1983; W. Graham, 'Sinn Féin vote puts pressure on Britain', *Irish News*, 22 October 1982; 'A clear message' (editorial), *Irish News*, 22 October 1982; 'Lost opportunity' (editorial), *Irish News*, 11 June 1983.

70 E. Moloney, 'Success of Sinn Féin big threat to SDLP', *Irish Times*, 22 October 1982; 'Test for Sinn Féin electoral strategy', *Irish Times*, 22 March 1983.

71 Sinn Féin, 2005, 186–187 and 250–251.

72 Paxo, 'A question about Enniskillen', *Iris Bheag*, 5, 1987.

73 G. Kerrigan, 'The IRA has to do what the IRA has to do…; interview with Danny Morrison', *Magill*, September 1984.

in the 1990s, which continued to show that 'significant numbers of people within [Northern Ireland] ... have empathy with the methods and goals of terrorist organizations.'[74] A European values study in 2000 found that just over a quarter of respondents expressed some level of sympathy for Republican paramilitaries.[75]

The 'Republican community' has a tangible reality connecting the individual experience of tragedy and heroism(as they would see it) to that of a wider 'family' shaped by the violence over the 30 years of the Troubles. This is further sustained by family and intergenerational connections, social and geographical ties, the homogenizing experience of prisoners and prisoners families, and the power of bonding and sense of victimhood within IRA culture. A further imagined Republican community created by political activity, protests, jail and IRA experience across districts and areas supplements this 'immediate' family.

The language of family and community is significant, suggesting a sense of a unique shared experience and indissoluble ties. Given the numbers of people who have passed through the IRA and their wider family and communal links, it would be an unusual family in the nationalist areas that had no links, no matter how tenuous, with the Republican movement. This is reflected in the self-image many Republicans have of their movement: 'Republicans are part of a community, not separate from the rest of society or divorced from their ordinary working-class community. They are respected as having sacrificed and given a lot.'[76]

Likewise, a popular Republican culture and folklore constantly reinforces and reinvents the tradition and emphasizes the identification between Republicans and the community.[77] The commemorative culture of murals, memorials and rallies also reinforces this sense of place and locale. In that sense, all politics are local in Provisionalism. This was to be especially important for the young as the Troubles extended over several generations, and the early heroic periods of the 1970s and 1980s started to fade into legend by the end of the twentieth century.

74 B. Hayes and I. McAllister, 'Who backs the bombers?' *Fortnight*, May 2004.

75 Cited in B. Hayes and I. McAllister, 'Who backs the bombers?'

76 Felim Ó hAdhmaill, interview, 25 August 2005.

77 This collective memory is represented in de Baróid, 1990, 27, and Ardoyne Commemorative Project, 2002. It is also reflected in the features sections of local nationalist newspapers, such as *Andersonstown News*. For up-to-date examples of murals, see belfastexposed.org and cain.ulst.ac.uk.

Mandates and mediation

Sinn Féin's electoral support waxed and waned in the 1980s and 1990s before representing a majority of the nationalist electorate by 2001. Although the armalite and ballot paper strategy used the language of revolutionary mobilization, in practice electoral politics was now a key indicator for the Republican leadership. The last great waves of activism and mobilization within the nationalist population were the hunger strikes. Despite attempts to recreate the momentum of this period, revolutionary politics for Sinn Féin increasingly meant electoral contests.

These electoral successes had significant effects on the politics and the organizational structures of the Provisional movement. The movement shifted resources from armed struggle to community politics, resulting in the development of Sinn Féin's network of advice centres, the growth of a party apparatus and an increased profile for local Sinn Féin councillors.[78] There was also a higher level of campaigning activity, not just on traditional Republican issues but also around community and non-political issues.[79] Sinn Féin activists combined revolutionary gesture politics with a focus on the traditional concerns of nationalist local politics, such as municipal corruption and discrimination.

Provisional rhetoric stressed the importance of 'principled leadership' and 'a proven record of real representation'. Republicans believed they had been successful in 'introducing politics into the [council] chamber', as well as exposing the SDLP's 'alleged nationalism and perceived class politics [and] their *pipe dream of partnership* [my emphasis]'.[80] Sinn Féin councillors were presented as pragmatic and responsible representatives of 'their community'. As one councillor put it:

---

78 Former Chief of Staff and close colleague of Gerry Adams, Ivor Bell, believed that this strategy would result in the eventual scaling-down of the armed campaign. In 1984 he was court-martialled for 'treason' along with a number of Belfast IRA Volunteers because of their opposition to the political direction that the Provisionals were taking. Among the other volunteers was Danny McCann, who was one of the three IRA members who were killed at Gibraltar in 1988. Public criticisms of the IRA, or suggestions that the armed campaign be scaled-down (much less ended), were not acceptable, whatever the private thoughts of some leading Provisionals. Leading Sinn Féin activist Sean Keenan fell from favour for his criticism of some IRA operations in the mid-1980s. The time was not yet ripe for such comments. Note of conversation with former member of Belfast Brigade, IRA staff.

79 Collins, 1997, Chapter 17; Patricia Campbell, interview, 4 January 2004; and M. Armstrong, 'All in a day's work', *An Phoblacht/Republican News*, 31 March 1983.

80 P. T. O'Hare, 'Advancing under attack: Sinn Féin in the council chamber', *An Phoblacht/ Republican News*, 2 March 1989.

the loyalists [Unionists] and the council officials were genuinely apprehensive of Sinn Féin in the council chamber, but within a short period of time they saw that we were *genuine* and *reasonable*... [Sinn Féin councillors] rightly received admiration ... from many quarters ... and a *grudging respect* ... from a hostile media and the government agencies, all of whom are in daily contact with Sinn Féin at every level.' [Emphasis added][81]

The active subjectivity of the political project was replaced by the idea of the activist as mandated delegate. The role of the Sinn Féin's elected representatives was defined as being '*representative of the local people who have elected them*... [O]ur policies must be geared to avoid a conflict of interest, Party versus People' [emphasis added].[82] The language of representative democracy became increasingly central, replacing the revolutionary conception of the 'risen people' with the passive phraseology of 'the electorate'. Restrictions placed on Sinn Féin councillors in the 1980s, for example, were attacked as attempts to nullify their election through the popular vote, and illustrated the need to 'defend their right and mandate to represent the nationalist/Republican electorate':

> Politically and judicially ... every law and procedure has been employed by the British administration ... and by the loyalist councillors *to marginalize, exclude and disenfranchise the councillors and their electorate*. [Emphasis added][83]

While attempting to overthrow the state through armed struggle, Sinn Féin's elected councillors and community activists were simultaneously attempting to democratize it. The use of 'British imperialist' courts to support these claims on occasions only served to highlight the wider contradictions that were emerging.[84] Sinn Féin's local government and community activism raised questions of political legitimacy and the nature of the mandate for armed struggle that had been immanent within Provisionalism from its founding moment. The armalite's legitimacy was revolutionary, while the mandate of the ballot paper was liberal-democratic. The ballot paper and armalite slogan avoided this ideological contradiction in 1981 by pragmatically arguing that the armed campaign's existence was its own justification.

The issue of mandates, whether historically derived from the Second Dáil or conferred by the contemporary support of the nationalist population,

81 Ibid.
82 Education Department, background reading document on involvement in the local community, October 1987; *Iris Bheag*, 3, 1987.
83 O'Hare, 'Advancing under attack: Sinn Féin in the council chamber'.
84 For example, see, E. Tracy, 'Council Commissioner moves in', *An Phoblacht/Republican News*, 17 April 1986.

remained a central ideological issue for Republicans. The idea that the Republican movement represents a form of state, a 'Republic virtually established', has been deeply rooted in its history since the nineteenth century.[85] At the foundation of the Provisionals, the political argument that Republicans should work 'towards the reassembly of the 32-County Dáil ... which will ... rule all Ireland' was strengthened by the quasi-legal argument that the IRA leadership were the direct representatives of the 1918 Dáil and, as such, the lawful government of the Irish Republic.[86] For some Provisionals, however, these legitimations were mere sophistry: the struggle had more immediate justifications.

> No one who joined the Republican movement post-'69 had heard of the theology that the Army Council was the legitimate government of Ireland... As far as I was concerned this was a bit farcical... You could only argue the justification for armed struggle in the North came from the conditions under which we live. *The mandate would come from the support you had in the community.* [Emphasis added][87]

This view coexisted with another strand that justified the IRA's armed struggle by reference to the right of resistance to secure national self-determination. As Gerry Adams argued:

> *The IRA does not need an electoral mandate for armed struggle* – it derives its mandate from the presence of the British in the six counties... The use of force is justified [because] they don't give people much choice. At the end of the day they won't be argued or talked out. [Emphasis added][88]

Electoral politics transformed the revolutionary justification of '*the support you had in the community*' into the liberal-democratic conception of electoral mandates and consent. This local government and community experience was to have a significant influence on both the ideology and the

85 MacDonagh, 1983, 83; and de Paor, 1997, 39–42.

86 For those who see Republicanism as a historically-defined tradition, the initial statements of the Provisional leadership provide strong evidence. Thomas Maguire, 'as sole surviving member of the executive of Dáil Éireann', declared that the Official Army Council was illegal and that 'the government authority delegated in the Proclamation of 1938 [by the 'surviving faithful members of the latest 32-County Parliament of the Irish Republic'] now resides in the Provisional Army Council and its lawful successors.' 'Comdt.-General Thomas Maguire's statement', *An Phoblacht*, February 1970. See also 'Attempt to take over the Republican movement', *An Phoblacht*, February 1970. These were powerful arguments that seemed to accord the Provisionals not only historical legitimacy in continuing the struggle against Britain, but also a high degree of legal authority. See English, 2003, 213–214.

87 Danny Morrison, interview, 5 January 2004.

88 G. Adams quoted in M. Farrell, 'The armalite and the ballot box', *Magill*, July 1983, 13–17.

wider political strategy of the Provisional movement. Increasingly, Republican political practice was framed in a new discourse of mandates and consent which betrayed a much deeper revision in underlying aims and legitimating discourse. As this style of community activism and electoral politics developed in the 1980s and 1990s, Republicans were increasingly operating within a political context defined by the structures and policy framework of the British state. This ideological and practical engagement over many years at local level between Sinn Féin councillors and the state was to provide a working model for the later politics of the peace process.

Despite electoral success and evidence of increasing support in the nationalist community, the strategy was not without its critics. Many Provisionals saw dangers implicit in community activism and electoral politics.[89] While elections had long been used by Republicans as platforms for revolutionary mobilization, electoral politics were believed to be a stepping stone towards compromise and incorporation by British imperialism. A sense that the party was becoming conventional in its style was often taken to represent deeper political and cultural changes representing a growing respectability or demilitarization of the movement.[90]

Critics argued that the movement's methods were 'indistinguishable from Fianna Fáil's', and that mere representational politics would make clientalism inevitable in the absence of a clear *political* differentiation between Sinn Fein and other parties.[91] Likewise, the advice centres had 'achieved nothing more than can be had from Citizens' Advice Bureaus [sic]. From the outset we tried to ensure that we were not ... a buffer between the state and the people. Can we honestly say we are not?'[92] Similar criticisms focussed on weaknesses in the roles of local councillors, the low levels of political activism, the emerging bureaucratic structure of the organization, and the failure to develop local initiative and leadership because of the 'non-democratic authoritarian ethos of the party'.[93]

Throughout the 1980s and 1990s, leading Republicans saw a positive connection between electoral politics, these types of campaigning and the formalization of the party structure. Much of the internal discussion in

89 Collins, 1997, Chapter 17.
90 Tommy McKearney, interview, 30 May 1998; Patricia Campbell, interview, 6 January 2004; Ruairí Ó Brádaigh, former President of Sinn Féin, interview, 15 February 1999; discussion paper for Sinn Fein internal conference on community politics, Belfast, undated: June 1991?.
91 Tuck, 'More than an election party?' *Iris Bheag*, 2, 1987; Nanoon, 'Community work plan', *Iris Bheag*, 4, 1987.
92 J. McQuillen, 'The politics of work in advice centres', *Iris Bheag*, 12, 1988.
93 McQuillen, 'The politics of work in advice centres', *Iris Bheag*, 12, 1988; Co. Meath supporter, 'A strategy to re-launch Sinn Féin', *Iris Bheag*, 27, 1990.

the Republican movement, authorized by the leadership, linked electoral and community politics to wider questions of broadening the base and the development of a 'broad front' strategy. This was now becoming a code among leading Provisionals for wider strategic and ideological shifts in the late 1980s.[94] Gerry Adams, for example, argued that:

> It seems that in fighting the elections, Sinn Féin has consolidated our base, *built middle leadership* and proved our vote was not personation. The councillors have *speeded up the politicization of Sinn Féin* and laid a solid foundation stone for those who inherit their roles. [Emphasis added][95]

In contrast to the open democratic project portrayed by Provisional politicians at Ard Fheiseanna in the 1990s, critics linked electoral politics to a wider process of institutionalization within Provisionalism. The most fundamental criticism was that electoral politics, focussing on the role of the elected representative at the expense of the collective subjectivity of the community, simply reinforced the powerlessness of communities. In this sense, the electoral mandate was defined as passive and potentially disabling for the base, imprisoning them in conventional politics rather than empowering and mobilizing people for real change.[96]

Different types of battles?

By 1985, there were signs that the armalite and the ballot paper strategy was beginning to stall. The central political problem for the Provisionals was the success of the Anglo-Irish Agreement within the nationalist community. This was reflected in Sinn Féin's failure to overtake the SDLP: after the dramatic successes of the pre-1985 period, its vote remained at around 10–11 per cent in local government and Westminster elections until the beginnings of the peace process in the early 1990s.[97] The 'Southern' strategy of mass mobilization, even when scaled down from the revolutionary scenario of the late 1970s to the mundane aspirations of Dáil representation after 1986, had also patently failed.[98] Increasingly, Republican

94 M. Mac Diarmada, 'Broadening the struggle', *An Phoblacht/Republican News*, 29 May 1986; 'Education through commemoration', *An Phoblacht/Republican News*, 11 February 1988; 'Broadening the base', *An Phoblacht/Republican News*, 30 June 1988; and 'Ard Fheis report: towards a mass base', *An Phoblacht/Republican News*, 3 February 1989.

95 O'Hare, 'Advancing under attack: Sinn Féin in the council chamber'.

96 D. McDermott, 'Is our electoral strategy consistent with revolutionary politics?', *Iris Bheag*, 12, 1988.

97 Figures taken from 'Political party support in Northern Ireland, 1969 to the present', cain.ulst.ac.uk.

98 Sinn Féin failed to poll above 2 per cent in Dáil elections until 1997. Coakley and Gallagher, 1999, 367.

strategic options were limited by the successful British containment of their campaigns, reflected in the declining levels of IRA violence after the defeat of its offensive in 1987–1988.[99] These failures increasingly resulted in the questioning of the effectiveness of armed struggle as a political instrument. As one senior Republican commented later:

> There was talk of a kind of Tet offensive... I was totally opposed to it because ... the IRA wasn't strong enough... We weren't ready. And this is where some suspicion comes in. Why opt for that strategy? Given the way things worked out a lot of people died needlessly.[100]

The context of military and political activity had changed dramatically for the Provisionals by the late 1980s because 'the state had taken control of the areas: it was now a different type of war with different types of battles.'[101] This resulted in a major reassessment of British strategy and the implications of the Anglo–Irish agreement for Republican politics.[102] The result was that abstentionism was dropped (1986); a broad-front strategy directed towards constitutional nationalism resulted in talks with the SDLP (1988) and contacts with the Dublin government; and secret contacts with the British government were revived. In practice, a fundamental realignment of Provisionalism was underway; in essence, all the elements of the Provisional strategy during the peace process were in place by 1989.

One aspect of this strategy attempted to increase the Provisionals' electoral bargaining power with London, Dublin and the SDLP with a renewed focus on electoral politics and community activism. Initially, this seemed to be an intensification of established patterns rather than a completely new departure for Republicans; however, the new political and military context decisively altered the impact of this strategy, as one Republican community activist recalled:

> In the late 1980s, some Republicans argued that getting directly involved with community groups was one way of circumventing censorship and *going directly to the people in the local areas*... Also, that was the only way that we were going to have *some sort of contact with state agencies*: they wouldn't talk

99 Wichert, 1999, 256–258.
100 Brendan Hughes, interview, 12 August 1998;
101 Felim Ó hAdhmaill, interview, 25 August 2005.
102 Morrison, 1985. Dr Garret FitzGerald believed that the Anglo–Irish Agreement had a significant impact on Republican understanding of British aims in Northern Ireland during this period, and that this resulted in a reassessment of the Provisionals' strategy. Dr Garret Fitzgerald interview, RTE Radio, 14 August 2005. Former leading Provisional strategist Tom Hartley confirms that the agreement did have an influence on Republican thinking: Tom Hartley, interview, 4 August 2005. See also Art Rooney, 'Analysis of the SDLP position re: Hillsborough', *Iris Bheag*, 9, 1988.

to us directly, but would indirectly through community groups. Sinn Féin activity was also limited in that the state was refusing to have any contact with Republicans, but *legitimate authority* such as councillors could be in contact with the state. [Emphasis added][103]

In this way, a strategy that was ostensibly designed to remobilize the Republican struggle and rebuild links with local communities actually strengthened the tendencies towards adaptation to the British state. Republicans were well aware by the early 1990s of how this might occur because of Britain's successful undermining of Provisional influence in the nationalist community. This 'penetration of local communities' had resulted in 'self-censorship' and the marginalization of Sinn Féin, because the 'British government are portraying themselves in a positive light', a conference of activists was told in 1991.[104] In this reading, Republicans had failed to establish a wider hegemony beyond their base areas, and even there they were under threat. One participant questioned whether the British strategy could be resisted:

> How many people outside our own base recognize the same things? And within our base, is recognizing the same as being able to resist?... We have allowed the Brits to plant the doubt that we may be more of a liability than anything in all but restricted 'policing' roles within our areas... We have left our people isolated and in fear of being associated with us or supported by us.[105]

British success was ascribed to political and organizational failures by Republicans, including the lack of a long-term strategy, the insularity and elitism of the Provisionals and a failure to develop empowering partnerships with community activists.[106] These criticisms were taken to heart organizationally in a reorientation towards the community; Republican activists developed internal and community networks in an attempt to broaden the base in the 1990s. Although it appeared to be successful in terms of building electoral and wider community support, this came at a price.

Republican politics were drawn even further into the ideological framework and terrain defined by the state. The paradox was that a strategy designed to counter the British drew the Provisionals and the wider nationalist community into even deeper contact with the state, and further facilitated the Provisionals' institutionalization. The question posed to activists in 1991 – 'Can our communities and our movement withstand another five

103 Felim Ó hAdhmaill, interview, 25 August 2005.
104 'Report of internal conference on community politics', Belfast, undated: June 1991?
105 'Altering the sea we swim in: British government attempts to change and control the community', discussion paper, Belfast, undated: June 1991?
106 'Report of internal conference on community politics', Belfast, undated: June 1991?

years [of British strategy]?' – was to be answered in the negative by the practice of Republican community politics throughout the 1990s.[107]

This focus on organizational matters ignored what was perhaps the major issue facing not only the Provisionals but also other forms of radical and transformative politics in this period. Leading Republican strategist Jim Gibney argued in 1989 that:

> I don't believe that the political philosophy that has emerged from the struggle ... has the capacity any more to motivate people. The anti-imperialist community in this country, before it's too late, have got to produce a liberating ... ideology which is capable of motivating people again, which is capable of bringing people out of the apathy which they are sunk under, under the type of society that we're living in today.[108]

Gibney's arguments reflected a wider crisis for radical and left politics internationally pre-dating the fall of the Berlin Wall and the collapse of the Soviet bloc between 1989 and 1992. This general retreat of the left affected Republicanism in a period when the Provisionals were becoming increasingly isolated anyway, causing what had been formerly peripheral to move to the centre of Republican politics. This was an ideological and existential crisis rooted in the failure to inspire support for the political project, rather than a product of the limitations of Republican activism.

Green Ken and Red Gerry

Situating the Provisionals within the wider context of radical politics internationally is a useful way of understanding their development. While leading Provisionals denied that their organization was Marxist, Republican rhetoric in the late 1970s and early 1980s was an eclectic mixture of leftist and national liberation themes defined as Republican socialism.[109] The Provisionals were not Marxist in either the orthodox Soviet or Trotskyist sense; their Republican socialism had more in common with the anti-imperialism and radical nationalism of guerrilla groups (see

107 'Altering the sea we swim in: British government attempts to change and control the community', discussion paper, Belfast, undated: June 1991?.

108 J. Gibney, 'A liberating philosophy', *Socialist Republic*, August/September 1989.

109 Gerry Adams defined himself as a Republican socialist and specifically denied any Marxist influence in the Provisional movement in the late 1970s. See English, 2003, 216. However, leftist currents continued to be a factor within the Provisionals, especially within the jails. The internal magazine *Iris Bheag* and Sinn Féin's Education Department were centres of leftist influence in the 1980s. By this point, the leadership had moved to the right and leftism lacked real influence within the movement as a whole. Private information from former member of Sinn Féin Education Department.

Chapter 5).This eclecticism reflected the porous nature of the Republican theoretical tradition and its susceptibility to the ideological pull of external forces.[110]

Other influences closer to home were to become more important in providing an ideological model for the development of Provisional community and electoral politics. The relationship that Republicans enjoyed with sections of the British left continued to be a feature of their politics into the 1990s. Not only did the Provisionals see a radical solidarity movement among activists of the far left as a possible harbinger of a broader mass movement, but there was also bilateral traffic in ideas, with many of the emerging Provisional leaders in the late 1970s influenced by some elements of leftist ideology and practice. [111]

The Provisionals' own electoral successes in the Assembly elections in 1982 and in the 1983 Westminster election in West Belfast may also have had some impact on the development of a new diplomatic orientation in their British strategy. The armed struggle still had the predominant place in the English campaign, but there was an increasing awareness among the Republican leadership of the need to broaden the battlefield in Britain as well as Ireland. This broadening would involve a very different dialogue and a new set of relationships with the elected representatives of the Labour left.

In an interview given in 1984, Danny Morrison argued that Republican electoral successes had made a 'big impact' by 'demoralizing the Brits and making the news ... internationally'. He went on to argue that 'Ken Livingstone's visit here ... Gerry Adams going to London ... all of these things have been very important in terms of the struggle,' because:

> the Republican movement, through having *elected representatives*, has increased credibility. It does make it easier [for British Labour Party politicians] ... to engage in discussion and to realize that we haven't got horns and to realize that what we're saying, that there is a validity to it. [Emphasis added][112]

110 Tommy McKearney, interview, 30 May 1998. There were also frequent articles in *An Phoblacht* on revolutionary guerrilla war in this period, e.g. a series of articles on Cuba, China, Vietnam and Nicaragua, *An Phoblacht*, February–March 1980. The introduction to each argued that 'Irish Republicans can learn and draw inspiration for our own struggle' from these successful cases, which showed that 'every struggle for national liberation and socialism has involved armed struggle'.

111 Note of a conversation with Dr Bob Purdie, former member of the International Marxist Group, 18 April 2004. For another example of these supposed links, see Secretary of State Merlyn Rees's comments on alleged Trotskyist influences on Belfast Provisionals in 1974, quoted in R. Bourke, 'Britain's secret talks with paramilitaries', *Irish Times*, 4 January 2005.

112 Kerrigan, 'The IRA has to do what the IRA has to do...'

The contacts between Sinn Féin and the Labour left were to have a greater long-term ideological significance than immediate political gains for the Republican movement. In the course of these contacts, Republicans stressed the comparable nature of the mandate held by elected representatives from Belfast and London. It also meant that Republicans became closely involved with attempts to influence the policy agenda. For example, Gerry Adams in 1988 directly intervened, at the request of Irish-American campaigners, with a left-wing pressure group, the Labour Committee on Ireland (LCI), to influence British Labour Party conference decisions on the MacBride Principles. As one account of these contacts between the Sinn Féin leader and British activist Martin Collins puts it: 'presumably ... [the Irish-Americans] felt that the pro-MacBride constituency Labour parties would take more notice of a request coming from the President of Sinn Féin via Collins than just Collins.'[113]

During visits to the Greater London Council (GLC), Labour conference fringe meetings and press conferences at the House of Commons, Sinn Féin councillors and Assembly members referred positively to the radical aspects of British Labour traditions and drew on the then-fashionable discourse of community empowerment and militant local government socialism. While at this stage the armed struggle was still defended in unapologetic terms as a legitimate form of resistance, in these contacts it was the legitimacy of their electoral mandate that was the focus of Republican politics. Parallel to this political engagement is an ideological conjunction in which Sinn Féin's community politics and emerging electoral strategy begin to resonate with the style and politics of Ken Livingstone's GLC.[114]

Until the late 1980s, the dominant strands of radical politics were very much a product of the post-1968 currents of the 'new left'. New-left politics were an extremely inchoate mixture that emphasised the revolutionary role of new social forces, such as students and women, while privileging spontaneity, participatory democracy and decentralization over the bureaucratic hierarchies of traditional left politics, trade unionism and, of course, the state, which had been a focus of social democratic politics in Western Europe.[115] These new ideas of democracy and self-organization

---

113 MacNamara, 2006, 175. Adams allegedly argued that, for tactical reasons, it was better to focus on the MacBride Principles at the conference rather than the LCI's more usual calls for reunification.

114 See, for example, 'From Invitation to exclusion', *An Phoblacht/Republican News*, 9 December 1982; 'Belfast welcome for GLC leader' and 'Interview with Ken Livingstone', *An Phoblacht/Republican News*, 3 March 1983; 'Sinn Féin in London', *An Phoblacht/Republican News*, 28 July 1983; 'Sinn Féin at Brighton Conference', *An Phoblacht/Republican News*, 6 October 1983.

115 Ali and Watkins, 1998; and Heartfield, 2002, Chapter 7.

entered the political bloodstream, resulting in a politics that 'envisaged radically different state institutions, involving new, more vigorous forms of democracy and more responsive forms of social administration'.[116]

The GLC was an influential example of these forms of politics on the British left during the 1980s. This style of leftism replaced the class-based concepts of traditional Labourism and social democratic redistribution with an emphasis on community empowerment and identity politics that privileged diversity.[117] These new approaches raised questions of political agency and mobilization similar to those initially encountered by Sinn Féin at the outset of its 'politicization' project in the early 1980s, and perhaps even more strikingly at its emergence as a significant force in local government. This fusion of community and identity politics certainly had a direct influence on Republican politics; the ideological framework and underlying approach of Sinn Féin's community politics can be sited within the same political and cultural framework as that of Livingstone's GLC and the Bennite Labour left in the 1980s. However, it was the strength of Livingstone's personal interest and public statements on Irish politics that reinforced this ideological connection. Livingstone himself made the comparison in the following terms:

> I was struck by the similarity in the position of what you might call the new radical left in the Labour party and the radical left in Sinn Féin. I had no doubt that in different circumstances, if I had been born in West Belfast, I would have ended up in Sinn Féin. Equally, if Gerry Adams and Danny Morrison had been born in London, I'm sure they would have ended up supporting some Left current in the Labour party.[118]

Livingstone situated his politics and those of Sinn Féin within the radical decentralized left that had rejected vanguardist positions and was attempting to win popular support for radical policies. He cited Gerry Adams's personal style of politics as evidence of Sinn Féin's collective leadership and its rejection of the charismatic macho style: 'clearly a lot of thinking has gone on in Sinn Féin over the last few years: there has been as much a change in style as in policies of the leadership.'[119]

Identity politics informed the practice of the GLC by fusing concepts of community, localism and identity. As one supporter of this radical localism argued, this involved a new form of decentralized power that 'delegated council resources to *democratic community and voluntary groups*' [emphasis added], involving them in decision-making rather than

116 Wainwright, 2003, 5.
117 Livingstone, 1988.
118 K. Livingstone quoted in Collins, 1989, 17.
119 Ibid.

merely consulting them. In this way, 'the GLC did not seek simply to take hold of the reins of state and steer it in a benevolent direction, as traditional reformers had done.' Instead, it was conceived as an emancipatory agency for releasing the hitherto repressed potential of a population defined in terms of identities and communities.[120] The Irish, as a defined ethnic and cultural group, figured strongly in this political project and provided models for a developing pattern of identity politics in the multicultural city.

These strands of cultural politics, community empowerment and local government practice increasingly found their way into Republican thinking during the 1980s.[121] This was not simply as a consequence of direct political interaction between Sinn Féin and the British Left; this new cultural political agenda was congenial to elements of an established Republican discourse which already stressed community and identity and reflected the tension at the heart of the Republican project between universal and particularistic elements. The practice was increasingly a mixture akin to the community politics of traditional clientalist nationalism and the activism of the GLC. It was a close political relationship that was to be strengthened by the peace process in the 1990s. Ken Livingstone himself illustrated the distance the Provisionals and he had travelled when he remembered the initial links between them and compared the political journeys they had made:

> I ... have continued to say that these were people trying to address the same issues as us in the far more difficult and tragic circumstances of Belfast... I don't think either [Alex Maskey or I] imagined that we would be mayors of our respective cities twenty years on. Nor did we imagine that either of us would be following the inclusive politics that we now are.[122]

From City Hall to Stormont

The combination of external forces and internal dynamics that produced the new Republican politics of community is perhaps best exemplified by Sinn Féin's performance in local government since the 1980s. The containment of the Provisionals' universalist project based on nation and class

---

120 Wainwright, 2003, 8.
121 See 'Sinn Féin in London', *An Phoblacht/Republican News*, 28 July 1983, where Sinn Féin's community politics are described as 'leading people away from dependency and patronage'; and M. Armstrong, 'Belfast welcomes GLC leader', *An Phoblacht/Republican News*, 3 March 1983. Gerry Adams's review, 'Citizen Ken', *An Phoblacht/Republican News*, 20 May 1984 is positive about GLC local government politics and Livingstone's role in particular.
122 McCaffrey, 2003, 7 and 210.

encouraged the re-emergence of particularist communal politics. Forms of accommodation replaced the politics of transformation. This new organizational and ideological configuration was an unstable amalgam that shifted uncertainly between the old and the new, the universal and the particularist, and the subjective and the representational forms of politics.

These tensions and contradictions were most apparent during the 1990s in the Provisionals' broad-front diplomatic strategy and the politics of the peace process. However, it is in the more limited sphere of municipal and community politics that these forms first emerged and proved to be a significant model – a preview, in US Democratic politician Tom Hayden's words – for what was to follow on the wider political stage after 1998.[123] Much of this change was expressed rhetorically or through highly-charged symbolism, simply because of local government's political impotence under direct rule. Despite this, or perhaps because of these limited functions, this symbolism did accurately signpost the political future for Sinn Féin.

As the key political battleground during the Troubles, Belfast serves as a good case study for these new forms of representational and communal politics. In Provisional discourse, the city is now represented as a site of transformation and potential emerging from a constricting and oppressive space. These contradictions reflect the duality of the resistance community and its changing relationship with the city over the last 30 years. The institutions of the city, its local government and zones of public life appeared exclusive and excluding. The Provisional bombing campaign in the city centre during the 1970s reflected this sense of alienation from the centres of power and the commercial life of the city.

The resistance community was a place and a people apart; the distance between Ardoyne and the Edwardian imperialist splendours of the City Hall was more than a few miles. The Sinn Féin councillors who took their seats from 1983 onwards were entering into enemy territory; the hostility they encountered and the battles they fought – sometimes literally – were evidence of that.[124] The resistance community was external and hostile to the city and its government; as late as 1990, Republicans continued to echo this outcast status by calling for either a separate west Belfast council or a cantonal system that would 'end forever discrimination against the Catholic ratepayers'.[125]

123 Hayden, 1999, xi.
124 For examples of the intensely confrontational atmosphere within the council chamber, see Ó Muilleoir, 1999, 1–3 and Chapter 8.
125 'Boundary review prompts call for restructured council', *An Phoblacht/Republican News*, 30 August 1990.

By 1993 the emphasis had shifted, both rhetorically and in practice. Sinn Féin's local government strategy now situated the nationalist community firmly within the city and focused on the need for nationalist engagement in its government.[126] Sinn Féin councillor Mairtin Ó Muilleoir appealed to Unionists and other political opponents in these early attempts at detente by arguing that 'it is necessary for us all to work together and make common cause on the issues which unite the working people of this city of Belfast.'[127]

Today, Republicans self-confidently portray the present and the future in markedly different terms. The changing definition of community *within* the city meant that Republicans began to identify the city and the state as being potentially capable of serving all communities. Just as the politics of identity see the nation as an assemblage of traditions, so Republicans echo the 1980s GLC in portraying the city as a collection of communities whose diversity can contribute towards the transformation of the whole city. In Republican rhetoric, the city and the resistance community are now joined together and united by the common name of 'Belfast, man and woman'.

For thousands of individuals, the changing patterns of social and economic life make this process appear natural and unremarkable. Young men in Celtic shirts may now regard the city centre differently as it becomes their neutral leisure space, leaving politically symbolic issues of territory to the communally-defined flashpoints on the interfaces. For Republicans it marks a significant change, symbolized by the claiming of space and the assertion of territorial rights at the symbolic and political heart of the city. During the first Republican demonstration to be allowed into the Belfast city centre in 1995, Sinn Féin banners in front of Belfast City Hall proclaimed that it was 'Our city also'. Its significance for Republicans was explained thus:

> Look at [Belfast] City Hall, which we've never seen as ours. But it's just as much ours. Just because there's a Union Jack flying over it doesn't mean it isn't ours, and we've started to express and deal with what is ours, where before we were totally distanced from it.[128]

Sinn Féin's electoral strategy is frequently seen as the crucial element in the transformation of Provisionalism into a form of conventional political movement. Beyond the rhetoric, the experience of local government and community politics proved to be very different from the expectations of

126 'Sinn Féin drive to democratise City Hall', *An Phoblacht/Republican News*, 14 January 1993.
127 M. Ó Muilleoir quoted in *Fortnight*, January 1993.
128 Brendan Hughes quoted in Stevenson, 1996, 182.

revolutionary struggle. As one contributor to an early internal Republican debate on the strategy remarked:

> Experience on the six-county council [and surely the 26-county councils] has shown us how quickly the contradictions arise while participating in any part of the system, and how small our potential for making real change is. It also shows us starkly where rhetoric and being 'anti-' falls flat on its face in double time when it is not, and perhaps cannot, be matched by suitable action.[129]

Others hoped that the pressures of electoral politics and participation in local government would inject a sense of constitutional responsibility and realism into Republican politics. Some feared that this would produce 'persistent pressures to divide its ranks, co-opt its leadership and smother its Republican heart in the coils of compromising tokenism'.[130] The Republican experience in Belfast bears out these hopes and fears. The results might be ascribed to experience of individual Republicans working with the state, which wears down the abrasive edges of the revolutionary project. It certainly reflects the wider experience of layers of Republican activists and public representatives 'who had become part of the City Hall furniture'. In making the inevitable compromises of office, relationships between British government ministers, senior civil servants and Sinn Féin became 'embarrassingly warm' in the 1990s.[131]

These relationships between Republicans and the structures of the state have moved beyond the pragmatic necessities of seeking funding for a community project or activists using local government as a revolutionary platform. In Provisional theory, the state and its institutions remained agencies of British imperialism. Provisional practice, however, was qualitatively different. The view of the state had shifted as a result of community politics; rather than being an agency of repression, it had become a potentially neutral instrument that could at least be pressured if not used positively to further the Republican project. In advancing the new nationalist agenda that highlighted civic pride in identity, culture and the rights of citizenship, the state might seem a logical facilitator, at first locally, but later on a larger stage.

If, as Tom Hayden suggests, Máirtín Ó Muilleoir's model for Belfast really was Barcelona, with its separate language, autonomous regional government and vibrant city culture, then partnership with the state was perfectly natural and inevitable, even if 'the Europeans are more used to proud, assertive nationalists and cultural diversity ... [whereas] The

129 Fixit, 'Mainstream politics', *Iris Bheag*, 3, 1986.
130 Hayden in Ó Muilleoir, 1999, x.
131 Ó Muilleoir, 1999, 177 and 203.

Brits don't have any of that.'[132] The fashionable Barcelona model, with its ideological origins in the European politics of regionalism, devolution and new nationalism, was the perfect exemplar for the new Sinn Féin. It also was cognate with the devolved models of regional governance and the rhetoric of the 'new localism' of the Blairite project in the rest of the United Kingdom.

These ideological strands, conjoined with older traditions of nationalist politics and Sinn Féin's contemporary experience of local government, directly affected Provisional politics. In contrast to the acrimony and confrontational bear-pit politics of the 1980s and early 1990s, Belfast has become a possible model for new forms of politics that aim to manage or even transcend rather than reinforce communal division. These forms are portrayed as a 'different type of struggle ... in which dialogue can create the possibility of change and new political environments'.[133] In this way, the Provisionals now define the day-to-day business of local government with its compromises and negotiations as a new site of struggle, replacing the armalite as the motor of political change. That this seems credible is because increasingly it is symbolic issues of identity rather than substantial constitutional questions that provides the stuff of politics in Northern Ireland. The cultural politics of commemoration, funding allocation and community identity fought on a largely rhetorical battlefield have replaced the previous bitter clashes of irreconcilable ideologies in the council chamber.[134]

This experience was important in the late 1990s; by drawing on the experience of local government, the leap in the dark of the Good Friday Agreement could be made less frightening for Republicans. Following the introduction of 'proportionality' in 1999, Belfast City Council was cited as an example of how devolved government could work for Republicans given that '90 per cent of decisions are taken on a cross-party and cross-community basis and power-sharing is a reality.'[135] To the Provisionals, this experience seemed to offer potential for a more fundamental transformation of politics throughout the region. As one former north Belfast Sinn Féin councillor explained:

> We already know what happens when the institutions are up and running because we have been doing that on Belfast City Council and other district councils for twenty years. We have engaged at community level and with the state for a longer period of time, so we know in a broad sense what happens

132 Ó Muilleoir, 1999, ix.
133 Eoin Ó Broin, former Belfast Sinn Féin councillor, interview, 17 July 2005.
134 'Belfast City Council to pay for St Patrick's Day', *An Phoblacht*, 12 January 2006.
135 Eoin Ó Broin, interview, 17 July 2005.

when Unionist and nationalist engagement reaches a certain level. When it becomes a reality it opens up all sorts of other political engagements that were not possible before.[136]

However, other less positive readings of this evolution are possible. The constant battles within Belfast City Council produced a surreal atmosphere in the 1980s and 1990s.[137] Sinn Féin behaved 'impeccably and constructively' as Unionists disrupted council meetings; the Unionist reaction to the presence of Republican councillors undermined local government and weakened the reputation of Unionism as force in Belfast politics.[138] In a reversal of roles, Republicans used the High Court to establish the legitimacy of their position as elected representatives, while Unionists were surcharged and injuncted for their conduct in excluding and obstructing Sinn Féin councillors.[139] According to former SDLP councillor Brian Feeney, this experience fed into later Republican strategy in other ways:

> it was a forerunner of what Sinn Féin aimed to do during the peace process and the operation of the power-sharing elements of the Belfast Agreement – that is, to divide Unionism and to destabilize the politics of Northern Ireland.[140]

By 2001, Sinn Féin was the largest single party on Belfast City Council, capturing 28.4 per cent of the overall vote and fourteen councillors. This was a significant stage in the party's development, which would culminate in the election of a Sinn Féin Lord Mayor, Alex Maskey, in 2002, marking the full participation by Republicans in the official civic life of the city. If Maskey's election was symbolic for Republicans, then his conduct while in office dramatically illustrated the ideological shifts that had taken place within Provisionalism.[141]

In laying a wreath before the main Somme commemoration in 2003, Maskey saw his role as one of 'uniting and including rather than dividing and excluding' all the citizens and communities in the city.[142] He criticized the failure of civic leadership and the history of sectarian divisions: 'the council should be an example to the city as to how different traditions can dialogue and work together for the benefit of everyone who lives in

---

136 Eoin Ó Broin, interview, 17 July 2005.
137 Ó Muilleoir, 1999, 177 and 203; McCaffrey, 2003.
138 Brian Feeney, former SDLP councillor and political commentator, interview, 23 August 2005.
139 McCaffrey, 2003, 55–78, 104–117, 128–130.
140 Brian Feeney, interview, 23 August 2005.
141 McCaffrey, 2003, 151–170.
142 A. Maskey, 'The memory of the dead; seeking common ground' (speech), 26 June 2002 (copy held in Northern Ireland Political Collection, Linen Hall Library, Belfast).

Belfast.'[143] It was one of a number of significant gestures that were recognized by some as an example of 'Maskey's fantastic job in reaching out to Unionism'.[144] Above all, it was a gesture that, in combining the themes of identity politics and communal reconciliation, showed (to paraphrase Ken Livingstone) how far the Provisionals had travelled since 1983.[145]

Pressure-group politics

Several Republican campaigns against aspects of British government policy in the late 1980s and 1990s illustrate the Provisionals' turn away from the politics of revolutionary mobilization towards forms of pressure-group politics and lobbying. While the Republicans still drew heavily on the *rhetoric* of the resistance community, the *form* of politics was increasingly representational, radically changing the original conception of community as a site of resistance. Lobbying and representations to centres of power now involved a much wider cross-section of the community. Attendance at a conference in West Belfast on British government employment strategy, for example, now included 'businesspeople, lawyers, community workers, trades unionist, elected representatives, managers and workers within government training and education programmes and people on the receiving end of those programmes'. Significantly, contacts were also increasingly extended to senior civil servants and the statutory agencies of the British state.[146]

The genesis of this strategy was a result of the British government's proposals in 1985 to stop funding a number of voluntary and community projects that were either deemed to be 'Provo fronts' or closely associated with Republicanism.[147] The political battle over vetting enabled the Provisionals to consolidate their image as defenders of the community and to mobilize groups of activists around this issue. As one activist recalled: 'Because it was *so* overt it was possible to mobilize against political vetting.'[148] The withdrawal of funding was seen by many community activists as an attempt to undermine the emerging community base of the Provisionals, so that 'for a brief period community action became synonymous with Republicanism.'[149]

143 McCaffrey, 2003, 226.
144 David Adams, former loyalist prisoner and political commentator, interview, 23 July 2005.
145 McCaffrey, 2003, 7and 210.
146 'Making Belfast appear to work', *An Phoblacht/Republican News*, 7 June 1988.
147 Parliamentary report, *The Times*, 28 June 1985; J. Plunkett, 'SDLP back Brit vetting of community groups', *An Phoblacht/Republican News*, 6 February 1986.
148 Claire Hackett, interview, 18 July 2005.
149 Robson, 1999, 44.

The campaign combined the usual street protests at City Hall with a new politics of lobbying, which involved meetings with European Commission representatives and mainstream umbrella organizations such as the Northern Ireland Council for Voluntary Action.[150] As well as new forms of politics, there were also new forms of argument against government policy. For example, Sinn Féin's argument that 'everyone should have access to public funds, providing such money is accounted for ... nobody should be sacked without having the opportunity to be heard' indicated an implicit acceptance of the British state's role in social policy.[151]

Other issues also drew the broad currents of Republican support into direct engagement with the state. These campaigns around local and immediate issues involved lobbying for resources or presenting challenges to government plans in ways similar to community politicians in other parts of the United Kingdom.[152] In taking part in a conversation with agencies of the state, such as the Housing Executive or the Department of the Environment, lodging formal planning objections or calling for independent inquiries into transport proposals, Sinn Féin's practice could be situated within mainstream community and representational politics.[153] Within the broad currents of Republicanism, groups like the West Belfast Economic Forum functioned and developed new relationships with the state that were the epitome of modern pressure-group politics. The forum defined its role as 'monitoring the impact of government economic and social policies ... informing and encouraging debate within local communities on current policies and future developments' and 'continuing to attend meetings with interested parties and government bodies to express concerns and to influence policy.'[154]

The most significant campaign in this period was Sinn Féin's support for the MacBride Principles and its related opposition to the British government's proposed fair employment legislation in 1987. The Fair Employment Act 1989 and its related policy initiatives went on to establish an important

150 'Grants withdrawal conference', *An Phoblacht/Republican News*, 8 May 1986; D. Wilson, 'Playing the ACE card', *An Phoblacht/Republican News*, 3 July 1986.

151 T. Ryan, 'Political vetting of community groups', *An Phoblacht/Republican News*, 3 July 1986.

152 K. McCool, 'Derry's debate', *An Phoblacht/Republican News*, 23 July 1987.

153 'Black taxis under threat' and 'Divis residents plan future', *An Phoblacht/Republican News*, 26 March 1987. As a symbol of the quite literal integration of the once oppositional into the mainstream of the city, the new bus interchange in the Castle Street area of Belfast has provided facilities for the 'black taxis', thus integrating public transport and a former 'alternative service' into the same framework. Where 'black taxis' go, Republican politicians follow.

154 'Still not working: West Belfast Economic Forum', *An Phoblacht/Republican News*, 23 May 1991.

ideological framework for society and politics in Northern Ireland. This framework was further consolidated by the Belfast Agreement and thus continues to be influential into the twenty-first century. Both in the manner of presentation and in the actual arguments themselves, there is clear evidence of an underlying shift in Sinn Féin's political strategy. Republican arguments against the British fair employment proposals were put forward in what has been described as 'an impressive document, carefully researched and well-drafted'. [155] Although support for the MacBride Principles among the Irish-American supporters of the Provisionals in Noraid may have been designed initially to embarrass the British government, the campaign in Northern Ireland itself had a different orientation. [156]

Sinn Féin's response began with the traditional Republican analysis that discrimination was an historical product of 'economic apartheid on which the state is maintained [and on which it was founded]', before going on to oppose ostensibly reformist solutions 'within the confines of the six-county state or under the auspices of a British government'. [157] However, the detailed policy proposals to remove the structures of discrimination were somewhat at variance with this approach. The established Republican position that it was impossible to reform an unreformable state was carefully sidestepped. After this perfunctory genuflection towards Republican pieties about the impossibility of worthwhile reforms within a partitionist context, the Republican proposals drew on a left-wing discourse that regarded affirmative action as the solution to the problems of structural discrimination. Political pressure was to be directed towards Britain as 'as the creators and apologists for the six-county state' and the 'de facto government' of the region:

> until evidence of positive qualitative and quantitative effect is produced, until discrimination practices are eradicated and until equality of opportunity is realised ... the ultimate criterion of any proposals is the actual effect of their implementation – they must lead to an end to sectarian discrimination in employment within tangible timescales. [158]

This neutrally bureaucratic tone is reinforced by a policy framework rooted in the discourse of positive discrimination. Sinn Féin called for contract compliance, monitoring and comprehensive legal sanctions by

155 MacNamara, 2006, 260.
156 Martin Galvin, a leading Noraid member, supported the MacBride Principles from an early stage for this reason. His motives and approach were in stark contrast to the position adopted by Sinn Féin. For Galvin's role, see MacNamara, 2006, 260.
157 'Setting the criteria: tackling discrimination – Sinn Féin proposals', *An Phoblacht/ Republican News*, 22 October 1987.
158 Ibid.

statutory (that is, British government) agencies to eradicate discrimination. Its proposals were influenced by the broad framework of the MacBride Principles, which, according to Gerry Adams, were 'the only realistic challenge to the institutionalized inequality of the six-county state'.[159] This approach also reflected the majority of nationalist opinion and, as such, helped to draw Sinn Féin closer to the political mainstream.

Most significantly, Sinn Féin made demands on British policy-makers that were at odds with the Republican analysis of the colonial nature of the British presence in the north. The proposals were framed as part of an implicit debate with the British government. Gerry Adams, for example, argued that 'If they [the British] were serious they would accept the MacBride Principles, which do represent an effective first step towards equality of opportunity.'[160] By demanding that Britain 'dismantle the system of economic apartheid' and recognize its 'historical responsibility … to tackle this historic/structural problem', it suggests that Britain could act against its own imperialist interests. Significantly, this analysis mirrors aspects of the British presentation of the problem by suggesting implicitly that Britain was a potentially neutral party to the conflict and could act as a positive force for change.[161] Although at this stage these arguments were not explicitly stated, these underlying assumptions about Britain's potential role as a persuader were to form a central part of Sinn Féin's peace strategy in the early 1990s. In particular, this approach to the British state prefigures the more developed political arguments that appeared in one of the founding Provisional documents of the peace process, *Towards a Lasting Peace in Ireland.*[162]

Learning to lobby

This chapter has attempted to understand the origins of the new politics of Sinn Féin as the product of the institutionalization of the Provisional movement in the 1980s and 1990s. The nature of this process is encapsulated by the experience of former IRA volunteer and community activist Tommy Gorman:

> We had a meeting in 1996 about economic development in west Belfast and someone said, 'We're going to have to learn how to lobby', and we talked about paying lobbyists to meet our elected representatives! If I want to see

159 Gerry Adams reported in *Irish News*, 12 February 1987, quoted in MacNamara, 2006, 260.
160 Ibid.
161 'Setting the criteria: tackling discrimination – Sinn Féin proposals', *An Phoblacht/ Republican News*, 22 October 1987.
162 Sinn Fein, 1992.

Gerry Adams, I have to see a lobbyist! This is a sign of the times. These people are just beyond reach now. We used to think we were very lucky because we had this direct continuity from the ground right through to Stormont and the corridors of power, but now this big gap has opened up between the people and this middle strata in the political movement.[163]

Much attention has been paid to the way in which electoral politics increasingly drew Republicans into the embrace of the state and facilitated the movement's development into a 'slightly conventional' political party during the 1990s. While electoral success was a visible indicator of change, the transformation of the Provisionals was the product of much wider processes of institutionalization. This changing relationship between the movement's base and an emerging party apparatus was reflected in new definitions of community, which in turn were evidence of a shift away from subjective agency towards more particularist forms of politics. Going beyond mere electoralism, these community politics embraced new organizational and ideological forms across the nationalist population and pointed towards new types of relationship with the state and revised narratives of political progress.

From the 1970s onwards, the Republican movement attempted to dominate its immediate environment and redefine the wider political and social context by achieving British withdrawal. The mobilization and redefinition of the community as 'the resistance community' was a key instrumental theme in this process. To do this, the Provisionals had to create a framework for the imagined resistance community that reflected significant elements of the existing communal culture and organisational forms. Building on an established cultural pattern, these invented traditions set down deep roots and continued to shape the dynamics of Republican politics into the 1990s. These networks of social integration, which sustained collective mobilization in the 1970s and 1980s, were later to form the basis for successful electoral politics in the form of an 'electorate of belonging'.

However, the concept was ambiguous since it contained contradictory ideas of a particularist communal identity alongside universal concepts of class and nation. Initially, these purely sectional or recognitional elements were subsumed within a wider project of national and social emancipation. However, by the late 1980s, while the phraseology apparently remained constant, a discursive shift was being undertaken, hollowing out the concept from within and bringing a narrower representational focus to the fore.

---

163 Tommy Gorman, former Republican prisoner and community activist, interview, 7 August 2005.

This shift can be linked to the beginnings of the formalization of Republican organization and a strengthening process of organizational mediation between the activist and the community. In this way, the resistance community enabled the Provisionals to partially shape their constituency and define the political culture of the base. However, Republicans were unable to widen their hegemony beyond the narrow base of these communities. The containment of the Republican project was more than the result of a successful British state strategy. Electoral politics and the compromises it entailed, coupled with the politics of pan-nationalism, allowed the Provisionals to expand their electoral base but at the expense of their hegemony. In practice, the Provisionals had always seen the community as an inanimate object; it was to be Republicanized, and, by being thus acted upon, transformed and mobilized in revolutionary struggle. This static view of politics remained essentially unchanged. However, by the mid-1990s the only transformation that had occurred was a discursive one within Provisionalism. The resistance community had become an electorate to be mobilized at the ballot box in the limited form of electoral politics; appeals to community now were attempts to re-engage with an increasingly demobilized and disengaged population, rather than calls to arms.

This raises deeper questions of political agency and subjectivity and the degree to which political actors facilitate the activity or passivity of their constituency (or, in Provisional terminology, their base). Traditional social democratic understandings of the state seem apposite to the development of the Provisionals' community strategy, and more generally to the sense of disillusionment felt in most contemporary political projects. As one critic of the traditional left has put it:

> the predominant conception was of the state as an agency for change operating *on* [her emphasis] society, effectively from above, like an engineer fixes a machine. The role of the labour movement, the mass supporters, was to get the social engineers into place so that they could deploy the instruments of state. Implementation of policy was seen as a technical matter, best left to the experts.[164]

These questions also resonate with the historical debates within radical politics between revolutionaries and revisionists about whether the bourgeois state can be utilized as an instrument for the emancipation of the working class. Echoes of these radical positions also fuse with strands in the Republican tradition that refuse to recognize the 'partitionist states' and seek their overthrow rather than their reform. This is reflected in Provisional terminology, which was influenced by these themes. 'Reformism' was applied to the SDLP's policy of participating in an 'internal settlement'. The debates within the Provisional movement in the 1980s and 1990s about community politics, the broad front and revolutionary strategy show that for many Republicans these were questions of more than merely historical interest.

Furthermore, what was left unresolved theoretically was determined by pragmatic practice as Republicans increasingly engaged with the state.[165] A growing focus on localism and the communal reflected a scaling-down of ambitions as the Provisionals' national project of transformation shifted towards a more limited representational role of petitioning within the political and social framework of the status quo. Thus, a process that had begun at this limited level would ultimately end in Republican participation in government after 1998.

This shift also reflected the growing ideological influence of communitarianism, transmitted into Northern Irish life by the powerful external forces and resources of the British state and the European Union. This new language of community, popularized by Tony Blair's 'Third Way', resonated with existing Republican ideas of community politics and representation. The buzzwords of localism, community empowerment, transforming neighbourhoods and political re-engagement have increasingly entered the lexicon and intellectual framework of Provisionalism since the mid-1990s.[166] As such, this process of intellectual and practical engagement was simply the latest phase in a process of adaptation that had been underway since the mid-1980s.

164 Wainwright, 2003, 11.
165 Ó Muilleoir, 1999, 172–175.
166 A. Perkins, 'Off the main stage', *Guardian*, 12 October 2005.

Chapter 3

'They Haven't Gone Away, You Know': The Withering Away of the 'Provisional State'?[1]

[Michael Corleone:] Kay, my father's way of doing things is over – it's finished. Even he knows that. I mean in five years the Corleone family is going to be completely legitimate. Trust me. That's all I can tell you about my business.[2]

'Let's not kid ourselves that we are better than… the Sticks were or Fianna Fáil'[3]

By 2007, the Provisionals' long journey into Northern Ireland's political mainstream seemed complete. From sitting in a 'partitionist assembly at Stormont' through to the decommissioning of IRA weapons, and now jointly heading a devolved government with the DUP, the previously unthinkable had become the commonplace for the Provisionals.[4] Taking responsibility for policing and taking the pledge of office upholding the rule of law were more than just symbolic acts to restore devolution.[5] Recognizing the state's legitimate monopoly of violence and its ultimate right to enforce its will marked 'the irrevocable final step away from trying to overthrow the state'.[6] Given what these symbols represented for longstanding Republican aims, the belief that this acceptance of 'Britain's illegal claim to sovereignty in Ireland' and 'their total immersion into the English system in Ireland' constituted defeats seemed accurate.[7]

1 Gerry Adams talking about the IRA in 'They haven't gone away you know', *An Phoblacht/Republican News*, 17 August 1995.

2 Puzo and Coppola, 1972.

3 Ruairí Ó Brádaigh quoted in 'Ard Fheis report '86', *An Phoblacht/Republican News*, 7 November 1986. 'Stickyism' is a reference to the Official Republicans, who transformed themselves into a conventional left-wing party during the 1970s and 1980s.

4 P. Ferguson, 'Anyone for tennis?', *Weekly Worker*, 4 August 2005; F. O'Connor, 'The most formidable of pairings', *Irish Times*, 20 October 2006.

5 G. Moriarty, 'Formula for nomination of NI ministers sought', *Irish Times*, 17 November 2006.

6 F. O'Connor, 'The most formidable of pairings', *Irish Times*, 20 October 2006.

7 V. Browne, 'Adams was IRA chief of staff', *The Village*, 5 August 2005; 'For what died the sons of Róisín?', *Sovereign Nation*, April–May 2006; 'Adams accepts British police', *Saoirse*, November 2006.

There were other signs of significant political change within the Provisional movement. Twelve years after the first IRA ceasefire it seemed that the balance of power within the movement had finally shifted away from the armalite towards the ballot box. The IRA statement of July 2005, instructing volunteers to dump arms and 'assist the development of purely political and democratic programmes through exclusively peaceful means … to advance our Republican and democratic objectives, including our goal of a united Ireland' appeared to end the central ambiguity in Provisionalism between electoral politics and the military instrument.[8] Other evidence in 2006 seemed to confirm that the IRA was indeed going away: according to the Gardai, the Provisionals had 'abandoned organized crime' in the Irish Republic, while the Independent Monitoring Commission's eleventh report in September 2006 declared that:

> [The IRA] is not engaged in terrorist activity, by which we mean undertaking attacks, planning … them, or developing a terrorist capability by … procuring weapons or training members. The leadership is opposed to the use of violence in community control, has taken a stance against criminality and disorder amongst the membership and has been engaged in successful dialogue to prevent violence during the 2006 parades season.[9]

Despite these positive statements, many Unionists remained unconvinced: to them Sinn Féin remained a revolutionary organization, making it impossible to go into government with 'people who were at the beck and call of terrorists'.[10] From the opposite viewpoint, Republican critics also questioned the Provisionals' democratic credentials when they continued to combine 'normal bourgeois democratic politics at one level backed by a militia at another'.[11] Underlying these differing assessments was a common theme that Sinn Féin was not yet a conventional political party and that its power rested on more than an electoral mandate. What remained unclear was the nature of that power and the future influence it would have in Northern Irish society. It also raised much wider questions about the nature of normalization in Northern Ireland, and in particular whether the political and social structures created during the Troubles would continue to exert power under the new dispensation.

The official rhetoric of transition used during the peace process implied positive movement towards a qualitatively different future in

---

8 D. McKittrick, 'The IRA's farewell to arms', *Independent*, 29 July 2005.

9 S. McKinney, '"Organized crime abandoned by IRA" in Republic', *Irish News*, 10 October 2006; D. Sharrock, 'Provos "have key role in peace"', *The Times*, 7 September 2006.

10 J. Allister, 'Why I have doubts over the proposals', *News Letter*, 17 October 2006.

11 Anthony McIntyre, former IRA prisoner, interview, 29 July 2005.

Northern Ireland.[12] However, instead of distinct boundaries between past and future, this transitional process has produced an indefinite and hybrid form of polity that looks increasingly permanent. The ideological and organizational forms of the Provisional movement exemplify the characteristics of this new dispensation. While some British and Irish politicians regard the fundamental ambiguities within Provisionalism as grey areas that will be eventually resolved by devolved government, it is not just Unionists who disagree with this interpretation of the movement's future role. Former Provisionals have criticized the movement as a totalitarian structure of power that is intent on controlling the nationalist community. Other commentators have accused London and Dublin of effectively turning a blind eye to these activities in order to preserve the status of the Provisionals as interlocutors during the peace process. [14]

While there was understandably much focus on the IRA during the peace process, Provisionalism has always rested on a much more complex nexus of social power than armed bodies of men and women. The extent of this power weakens the reassuring parallels between the development of the Provisionals and Fianna Fáil's journey from the Legion of the Rearguard to the natural party of government. Unlike Fianna Fáil, the Provisionals constituted a form of state power even before they entered government. After 30 years of conflict, the Provisional movement has consolidated its power and sunk deep roots in society; it is not a defeated and outcast band of ex-guerrillas.

The ambiguous nature of this power revived the idea, first popularized by the British government and journalists in the 1970s, that the Provisionals are a form of mafia.[15] Some critics from within the Republican tradition have drawn on similar rhetoric to describe the Provisionals as a new social form, 'the Rafia', combining political and criminal power to raise itself above its community.[16] The analogies between Provisionalism and the mafia as forms of pseudo-state are not simply journalistic conceits or anti-Republican propaganda. Both of these armed bodies are historically residues, albeit very powerful, left behind by the receding tide of

---

12 Tony Blair quoted in O. Bowcott, 'Uproar at Stormont as loyalist killer with bomb tries to storm assembly', *Guardian*, 25 November 2006.

13 Bertie Ahern interview, RTE Radio, 31 July 2005; Peter Hain, Secretary of State for Northern Ireland, quoted in W. Graham, 'IRA committed to peace: McDowell', *Irish News*, 26 July 2006.

14 John Kelly, former senior Republican activist and Sinn Féin MLA, interview, 23 August 2005; E. Moloney, 2006, 80–81.

15 'Double blind', *Atlantic Monthly*, April 2006; McDonald, 2004, 197–199.

16 Anthony McIntyre, interview, 29 July 2005. The term 'Rafia' is a neologism combining the IRA's nickname, 'the Ra', with 'mafia'.

collective demobilization.[17]

In this way, the Provisional movement alienates itself from nationalist civil society by taking on some of the characteristics of the state. It maintains its power by turning the political capital and communal solidarity gained from 'the struggle' back against the resistance community from whence the movement emerged. The result is a form of Provisional state-within-a-state, a hybrid type of institutionalization: that is, a process by which movements that formerly aimed to transform social or political structures are themselves transformed into permanent natural systems integrated into the established order. In the case of the Provisionals, the pattern of institutionalization was decisively shaped by a combination of British state strategy and wider social and economic change. While it is easy to see this process of institutionalization as the Provisional movement being dragged gradually into the British net, a more nuanced approach is to define it as the result of a dialectic between the state and the Provisionals.[18] Consequently, any understanding of the transformation of the Republican movement must begin with the partnership between the British state and the Provisionals that created this state-within-a-state.

As we have seen in Chapters 1 and 2, this interaction was not just with the traditional 'hard' state power of armies and bureaucracies: most significantly, the institutionalization of the Provisionals was determined by the 'soft' power that surrounds the 'postmodern state'.[19] What emerged from this process was a successful transition into the political mainstream alongside an ambiguous structure of power within nationalist civil society.

A state-within-a-state?

An extensive literature, both academic and activist, has developed over the last 100 years to explain the transformation of revolutionary movements into conventional parties.[20] This literature of social movements and political sociology helps us to understand the institutionalization of the Provisionals as a dynamic shaped more by interactions with other actors than by purely internal processes or the operation of an iron law of oligarchy.[21] Key factors in this process are the changing structure of the state and

17 This pattern is also relevant to the decline of the UDA from a mass movement in the early 1970s to little more than cliques of gangsters in the early 2000s. See, for example, Taylor, 2000; McGovern and Shirlow, 1997; Crawford, 2003.

18 Ruairí Ó Brádaigh quoted in 'Adams accepts British police', *Saoirse*, November 2006.

19 Cooper, 2003, 50–54.

20 The classic account is by Michels, 1959. For some useful surveys of the literature, see Barker, 2001; della Porta and Diani, 1999; Kriesi and Rucht, 1999; Rucht, 1999; and Oliver and Myers, 2003.

21 Oliver and Myers, 2003.

the new forms of relationship that have developed between the state, the economy and civil society in the late twentieth century.

The classic models were developed to theorize the institutionalization of the modernist party organization and highly structured ideological forms of the twentieth century, such as the pre-1914 German SPD or the post-1945 Italian Communists.[22] However, these approaches remain useful in interpreting the assimilation of contemporary social movements into the different party structures and less coherent political ideas of the twenty-first century.[23] With some modification, they are directly applicable to the organizational evolution of the Provisional movement.[24]

Radical parties like the Italian Communists acted as organizations of social integration, creating parallel social and political structures that almost constituted a state-within-a-state. Initially, these party-movements were designed formally to overthrow or at least transform the state. Institutionalization replaced transformation with accommodation. The needs of the organization and its leadership predominated; organizational stability and survival become the movement's *raison d'être*.[25]

The growing formalization of power within the organization reflected the growth of a bureaucratic hierarchical structure. This took the form of a growing distinction between the leadership and the membership, the professionalization of the movement's apparatus and the leadership's control of decision-making. This created a passive, demobilized and deradicalized membership and the 'renouncement of each powerful idea and each strong action' by the movement.[26] Alongside this process of bureaucratization, the autonomous movement associations and supportive networks that initially aided collective mobilization were transformed into agencies for accommodation and integration.[27]

In this process, the movement's original aims remained rhetorically significant to maintain collective identity and legitimate the leadership. In practice, the goals become more vague and aspirational, resulting in a gap between the official ideology and the pragmatic behaviour of the leadership. Despite ostensible revolutionary goals, the politics of these parties became essentially reformist and representational.

22 Craig, 1981, 266–270; Panebianco, 1988; Koff, 2000, 24–25, 35–37 and 85–90.
23 For a discussion of the relevance of these models, see della Porta and Diani, 1999, 32–40.
24 Some have rejected these comparisons because 'The old PCI did not back up their polity with arms'; McDonald, 2004, 203. My argument is that they do have significant value because the contemporary Provisional movement's power does not spring solely or largely from force of arms.
25 Panebianco, 1988, 50–72.
26 Michels, 1959, 68; Rucht, 1999, 151–153.
27 Tarrow, 1998, 210.

Institutionalization is frequently linked to particular economic and social patterns, such as the development of a labour aristocracy or conscious state strategies of political integration.[28] Above all, the institutionalized movement is of necessity intimately integrated into the state, acting as both mediator and channel between the formal structures of state power and subaltern groups. As the fount of power and resources, the state becomes increasingly the focus of politics, with lobbying replacing collective mobilization. As the process of institutionalization deepens, the power of the movement becomes measured more by its ability to obtain resources and political benefits from the state on behalf of its constituency than by its commitment to radical change.

Coercion and consent

The power of the Provisionals does not simply grow out of the barrel of a gun or even from a barrel of red diesel. Its influence derives from a complex network of political, economic and social power mirroring some of the characteristics of the contemporary state. This analogy is not an echo of the legalistic Republican argument that the IRA 'is the direct representative of the 1918 Dáil Éireann parliament and that as such it is the legal and lawful government of the Irish Republic', but it does accurately describe Provisionalism's organizational configuration.[29] Like a modern representative state, the movement rests on a shifting combination of coercion *and* consent. In normal periods, power is largely exercised through forms of consent.[30] For both the British state and the Provisionals, consent is preferred to coercion, which is usually the last resort.[31] This distinction between consent and coercion is frequently blurred in practice; political consensus, conferring a degree of legitimacy and authority, can be a manufactured hegemony normally resting on other facets of social power backed by a monopoly of 'legitimate force'.[32]

These networks were the product of the dialectic between the British state and the nationalist population, acting in conjunction with rapid social and economic change within nationalist civil society. Alongside thirty years of collective mobilization, this has resulted in a social integration movement not only capable of manufacturing consent within the micro-

28 Graham, 1993, 28. The classic Leninist thesis on imperialism stressed the political importance of the integration of the 'labour aristocracy' for the stabilization of capitalism. See Lenin, 1973, 127–129.

29 Extracts from the 'Green Book' (IRA training manual) in O'Brien, 1993, 289.

30 Przeworski and Wallerstein, 1982, 215.

31 Taylor, 2005, 71–77.

32 Gramsci, 1971, 245–263.

societies of its base areas, but able also to exert direct and indirect influence over much wider sections of the nationalist community. These community organizations and movement networks have produced an intertwined apparatus of party and community functionaries, with many of the characteristics of a bureaucratic nomenklatura within civil society.

The overlapping membership of committees and management boards drawn from the familiar faces of the Republican great and good, for example, illustrates the existence of a Provisional quangocracy mirroring, and intimately connected through funding and function with that of the British state.[33] 'It is a tactic of control by Sinn Féin. West Belfast is full of these groups. A lot of them are seen as self-interested, self-identifying and self-perpetuating,' says one Republican socialist critic.[34]

These networks are no longer solely concerned with political or even electoral mobilization, but now exist largely to maintain a movement counter-culture or meet specific social and economic needs. They cover a wide range from community and self-help groups through to economic development and cultural organizations. In some instances, these social movement elements have evolved from community activities into free-standing businesses, completing a transformation from organizations of social and political mobilization to commercial enterprises. The evolution of the *Andersonstown News* from a news-sheet of the Andersonstown Central Civil Resistance Committee in 1972 to a privately-owned media group of locally influential newspapers is an illustration of this process. Others were effectively privatized by their practical autonomy from the communities that they claim to represent. The means of mobilization have become ends in themselves.

These structures can act as centres of social power and gatekeepers within nationalist civil society. This *collective* power within society is distinct from the rapid social mobility of *individual* members of a new Republican bourgeoisie, whose lifestyle is frequently contrasted with that of ordinary Republicans.[35] For many in the nationalist population, association with the Provisional movement will provide a variety of identity, status and

33 Umbrella organizations like the West Belfast Partnership Board and the Falls Community Council have important community and economic development roles as well as education, training and health-promotion functions that are closely linked to the state. See *Falls Community Council Annual Report 2005*, Belfast 2005.

34 Tomás Gorman, member of the Irish Republican Socialist Party (IRSP), Ard Comhairle interview, 12 August 2005.

35 For the alleged links between the black economy and the Provisionals, see McDonald, 2004, 198–201. For comments on the 'exploitation' of former comrades by the new post-ceasefire elite, see S. Breen, 'Decommissioned Provos on scrapheap of history', *Sunday Tribune*, 16 April 2006.

limited material benefits. The interests that have evolved may take the form of selective incentives, such as funding for community projects, employ-ment and other material benefits, or status incentives, including access to local political and social influence. These limited forms of clientalism and patronage often underpin Provisionalism's power in these areas.

One key aspect of this social power is the ability to define the circum-stances of everyday life and work: it is in the mundane and the quotidian that real power lies. For Republican ex-prisoners, as an example, sources of employment connected to the movement remain important; those closest to the leadership secure paid work in the community sector, while others are employed in businesses owned by or supporting Republicans, such as security companies, bars and taxi firms.[36] These employment patterns can be used as a blunt form of social control, acting as rewards for past activity and guarantees of future loyalty. Provisional activists vigorously reject these allegations of *de facto* political vetting against community and ex-prisoners' groups, and paint instead a picture of an inclusive, pluralist community open to all.[37] However, the evidence points to a Provisional movement whose wider social and economic power affects individual life chances in ways that, despite being concealed, are none the less effective. As ex-IRA member Anthony McIntyre puts it:

> People would testify to their inability to gain employment in west Belfast unless they toe the Shinner line. It would be impossible to get a job in the black economy or even to take part in social life: they can make your life uncomfortable. People with a public profile can find it easier, but there's a lot of people who don't have the publicity… That's the worst thing you can be because these people will make it very difficult.[38]

Rising with your class

The classic accounts of the institutionalization of radical parties focus on the emergence of embourgoised worker-militants as a key factor in the formation of a party bureaucracy. Since the mid-1980s, the Provisionals have developed such a leadership of MPs, TDs, MLAs and senior politicians alongside a mid-level leadership of councillors and functionaries drawn from the ranks of the movement's activists, many of them ex-prisoners. Since many conventional careers were not open to these people, polit-ical and community activism provided alternative forms of meaningful activity and status along with some limited material benefits.

36 Brendan Hughes, former OC Belfast IRA, interview, 12 August 1998.
37 A. Morris, 'Ex-IRA prisoner's criticism unjustified says Tar Isteach', *Irish News*, 17 October 2006.
38 Anthony McIntyre, interview, 29 July 2005.

The development of this activism also relied on the strength of a culture of community among Republicans. Significantly, for many activists these benefits did not result in a social mobility that took them *outside* their community; it essentially confirmed their place *within* it. For the generation whose lives were shaped by military and political activism during the Troubles it was a case of 'rising with your class, not out of your class'.[39] As one community activist explained it:

> British government initiatives saw education and training as a way to encourage movement away from the community; they assumed a selfish individualism would result in social mobility. I don't think they anticipated that there was a strong ethos of people wanting to stay and work in the community.[40]

During the 1990s, Sinn Féin expanded beyond its original working-class heartlands to become the largest nationalist party in Northern Ireland. The system of interests that sustained Sinn Féin was extended to include the nationalist middle class. Increasingly, many activists came from other backgrounds less steeped in the traditions of the struggle and had different experiences and attitudes. As one former Republican prisoner and Sinn Féin official put it: 'Many of these people would be better working for a charity like OXFAM. They've never handled anything more deadly than a pen.'[41] MLAs such as Catriona Ruane and the MEP Mary Lou MacDonald are frequently cited as prominent examples of this new type of Sinn Féin politician.[42]

For some established Sinn Féin activists, these new high-flyers are essentially well-meaning liberals whose 'politics of reconciliation' mean that they had nothing to with Republicanism during the 'struggle', and only joined Sinn Féin when it was safe to do so. Inevitably, the political attitudes of these new and younger activists were largely shaped by the politics of the peace process and developments after 1994.

Far from challenging the old guard, this influx of new activists and natural generational shift had the political effect of consolidating the policies and personnel of the existing leadership. 'The kind of people who were being promoted from the early 1990s were totally dependent on the leadership for their newly-elevated positions, and there was no way they were going to challenge anything', was how one former senior activist described these new Sinn Féiners.[43]

---

39 D. Morrison, 'Rise with your class, not out of your class', *Daily Ireland*, 26 July 2006.
40 Claire Hackett, former Monitoring and Evaluations Officer, USDT and local history project worker, Falls Community Council, interview, 18 July 2005.
41 Private information.
42 Rafter, 2005, 167–168.
43 Private information.

These patterns of recruitment mirrored those of the 1980s, following Sinn Féin's first electoral successes when the integration of new layers of activists provided effective support for the Adams leadership during the debates on abstentionism in 1985 to 1986. Furthermore, the organizational tactics of 'managing the base' developed by the Adams leadership in this period were to prove extremely successful during the next twenty years. As Danny Morrison explained in 1984: 'The leadership can't get ahead of the grassroots. It has to bring the grassroots along with it.'[44]

This process would have been aided by a long-established culture of loyalty that, in conferring Weberian charisma on leadership and valuing unity as the cardinal virtue, proved to be a very significant factor in the political evolution of the Provisionals. Most of the senior Provisional leadership are long-established Republican activists: 'these were not Blairite yuppies, but leaders forged in life-and-death struggle.'[45] The common experience shared by leaders and activists, the political successes that their strategy had brought, and the changing climate of politics after 1989 strengthened the position of the leadership within the movement. Thus, it would be wrong to ascribe the institutionalization of Provisionalism to an influx of yuppies and careerists after the ceasefire. Comparisons of this type between New Sinn Féin and New Labour are inaccurate. The movement's style of leadership is more Old Labour: to paraphrase Herbert Morrison, Republicanism is defined as what the leadership says that it is.

Voices of banana Republicanism?

To complement these organizational forms of power, the Provisional state had other means to manufacture consent. A similar pattern of influence developed through a range of interlocking media and cultural organizations that amount to an ideological state apparatus that defines the social and political agenda for sections of the nationalist community.[46]

The history of the *Andersonstown News* exemplifies this power. Originally published as little more than an extended handbill in the early 1970s, it has grown into a flourishing bi-weekly publication with a large readership and great influence. According to its editor Robin Livingstone,

44 G. Kerrigan, 'The IRA has to do what the IRA has to do: interview with Danny Morrison', *Magill*, September 1984.
45 P. Ferguson, 'Anyone for tennis?', *Weekly Worker*, 4 August 2005.
46 E. Lynch, '*Andersonstown News*: Voice of banana Republicanism?', *Irish Echo*, 11 June 2003.
47 Quoted in O' Rourke, undated – 2004?
48 O'Rourke, undated – 2004?

the paper has been described as an 'ultra-reliable barometer of nationalist opinion'; 'If west Belfast really is the cockpit of the North, the *"Andytown News"* has become its instrument panel.'[47]

The origins of the paper lay within the resistance community, reflecting what was seen as a disenfranchised, disaffected and unofficial subculture. Today, as a commercial venture, it reflects the new nationalist community and growing Catholic business interests; the paper's ability to court mainstream advertisers illustrates the economic power and growth in nationalist areas. The paper's strong community orientation often appears to have a 'certain dose of vanity and self-satisfaction' in its celebration of the economic, educational and cultural achievements of nationalist west Belfast.[48]

Editorially it has 'absorbed the dominant values, attitudes and styles of the corporate mainstream' media in its coverage of 'moral panics around anti-social behaviour and the demonization of the youth', bringing it closer to the *Daily Mail* than its radical roots.[49] Politically, it has been criticized because it:

> serves much the same function for Sinn Féin as *Pravda* once did for the Soviet politburo and that Fox News now does for the Bush administration. It is a dependable organ of banana Republicanism, promoting Dear Leadership and attacking dissenters with zeal.[50]

The Féile an Phobail/West Belfast Festival is another example of this ideological power that combines identity politics and politicized forms of culture to define the nationalist community. With its community focus, its relationship with the state, its voluntary and community sector funding regime, and its stress on empowerment and recognition, the Féile has become the embodiment in cultural form of the master-narratives of contemporary Provisionalism. It is also a significant factor in the economic and social life of west Belfast, with a turnover of £500,000, over 50,000 visitors annually and a team of development workers and volunteers.[51]

With its wider agenda of building self-confident communities and empowerment through economic and social regeneration in west Belfast, the Féile is located at the intersection of self-help and community development, government social and economic policies and objective-led funding regimes. The Féile locates itself within a new west Belfast as an expression of a new identity and an agency for change. In an area that was:

---

49 Tomás Gorman, interview, 12 August 2005.

50 E. Lynch, *'Andersonstown News*: Voice of banana Republicanism?', *Irish Echo,* 11 June 2003

51 Féile an Phobail 2004 website at http://www.feilebelfast.com/aboutus/

once a battlefield between the IRA and the British army and its people prey
to loyalist assassins, *West Belfast is transforming itself* and Féile an Phobail
is proud to play a leading role in the transformation. It has embraced change
and cheerily meets every challenge, with *its people exuding confidence* in the
future and pride in their achievements. [Emphasis added][52]

The range of partner organizations and funding sources for the Festival
as well as its declared aims shows how the community now accommo-
dates itself to and works with the state and its agencies.[53] The perennial
disputes over funding reflect this orientation towards the British state
and the impact of its policy agenda. In 2006, for example, Féile organizers
attacked 'the complacency from statutory organizations ... [and] particularly government departments about what we and others have achieved –
in terms of replacing communal strife – and what we could achieve if given
proper and adequate core funding.' [Emphasis added][54]

The Féile's main ideological role is the projection of this new discourse
of Provisionalism, with its aims of celebrating diversity, developing
community participation and overcoming social exclusion.[55] As one
development worker explained, the Festival's ethos of partnership and
outreach has a wider agenda:

> The organizers would still see the Féile as being political ... you could argue
> that the Féile has been a small part in moving the political situation to where
> it is today... We're keen to facilitate Unionists or ethnic minority community
> leaders coming into West Belfast to talk about the situation in their commu-
> nities ... and to let local people hear at first hand. We also want local people
> to put their views across to these people and to discuss things amongst
> themselves.[56]

The Festival's success is cited as evidence that a powerful sense of community is still strong in nationalist west Belfast.[57] The degree of political
engagement is said to be high: 'although people here get very down because
the levels of political activism are less than ten or twenty years ago, you
still find more activity than in a similar working-class area in England.'[58]
The range of political debates at the Féile and the involvement of younger
activists are cited as proof of that vibrancy.[59]

52 Ibid.
53 Féile An Phobail, 1994, 13–14, 27–33.
54 O'Hare, 2006, 4.
55 'What are Féile an Phobail's aims for the next three years?', www.feilebelfast.com.
56 Glen Phillips, Féile Community Development worker, interview, 3 July 2005.
57 Felim Ó hAdhmaill, former Republican prisoner and community activist, interview,
    25 August 2005.
58 Glen Phillips, interview, 3 July 2005.
59 Claire Hackett, interview, 18 July 2005.

For the Provisionals, the Féile is a model of political engagement. As leading Republican Jim Gibney argues:

> We are very keen for people to shape their own political lives ... we like the community to express itself, not as a mirror image of what Sinn Féin wants, but as mirror image of itself. The Féile is a model for the type of politics we favour ... *we haven't moved away from the idea that community politics is the cornerstone of political life.* [Emphasis added][60]

Others are less convinced and see the Féile as part of an underlying shift in the patterns of Republican politics that have 'become more and more establishment, and more and more managed. There's no real argument or spontaneity. The Féile now is all pre-planned and controlled.'[61] Whatever the degree of control, the Féile is a powerful medium both for projecting an image of the nationalist community to the wider world and for representing the community back to itself. This gives the Féile a key role in the increasingly important battle for memory, by which means the Provisionals attempt to define political life in contemporary west Belfast.

The New Old IRA: stalwarts of the peace process

If the Provisional state could successfully manufacture consent, what was the future role of its coercive arm, the IRA? The history of Republicanism in the twentieth century offered a number of possibilities. Fianna Fáil's early ambiguous relationship and separation from the IRA during its transition into a 'slightly constitutional party' was one model. Another was the Official IRA, the shadowy existence of which as a party militia in the 1970s and 1980s combined individual criminality and organizational fundraising within the Workers' Party.[62] The disintegration of the Irish National Liberation Army (INLA) into organized crime and drug dealing offered a further, if unlikely, possibility.[63]

Continued allegations of Republican criminality, whether 'privatized' or 'sanctioned', only seemed to confirm that the IRA could not go away; it was an inherent and essential part of the Provisional movement.[64] While it

60 Jim Gibney, member of Sinn Féin Ard Comhairle, interview, 25 July 2005.
61 Tommy Gorman, former Republican prisoner and community activist, interview, 12 August 2005.
62 Dunphy, 1997, 117–138.
63 Holland and MacDonald, 1994.
64 See A. Chrisafis, 'IRA offered to shoot McCartney killers', *Guardian*, 9 March 2005; D. Fowler, 'One family taking on the IRA', *Marie Claire*, July 2005; M. Brennock, 'Opposition calls again for end to IRA criminality', *Irish Times*, 11 February 2005; J. Allister, 'Why I have doubts over the proposals: response to the St Andrews Agreement', *News Letter*, 17 October 2006; and B. Hutton, 'IRA "killed man during ceasefire"', *News Letter*, 19 October 2006.

was clear that the IRA's war against the British state was over, some argued that the IRA could not simply become a benign veterans' group, because it had evolved into either a localized mafia or an agency of repression that maintained Provisional control over the nationalist community.[65]

The preferred option of London and Dublin was the Fianna Fáil/Old IRA model. The assumption that the IRA would fade away as volunteers pursued 'purely political and democratic programmes through exclusively peaceful means' was publicly accepted by the British and Irish governments in order to restore devolved government.[66] The clear implication was that the IRA had 'constitutionalized its aims and methods' and that the Provisionals were on the road to becoming a conventional political party.[67]

The St Andrews Agreement of 2006 illustrated Tony Blair's pragmatic view of 'the reality that there is no way of getting a government in Northern Ireland that does not have Sinn Féin as part of it', while Bertie Ahern confidently distinguished between Sinn Féin and the IRA because 'Sinn Féin are doing their utmost to move away from their past.'[68] Drawing on Fianna Fáil's history, he suggested that the future of the IRA might lie not in disbandment, but in a 'new mode' in which the Provisionals might go the way of the Old IRA and become an old comrades' association.[69] This attempted transformation of the IRA's image, 'internally painless and externally acclaimed', was publicly unveiled at the Provisionals' annual Bodenstown commemoration in 2005.

> Gone were the paramilitary trappings, and in their place a colour party wore green blazers. It could have been a parade led by tennis umpires at Wimbledon… The image they gave the commemoration was similar to … members of the Royal British Legion marching down Whitehall on Remembrance Sunday.[70]

Thus the IRA's evolution from 'Western Europe's most feared terrorist group' to 'pillars of the Ulster community and stalwarts of the peace process' left little room for its continued existence in any other than a ceremonial form as the New Old IRA.[71]

If the Royal British Legion was one model, then the Officials' Group

---

65 C. Chrisafis, 'Men in green blazers: the future of the IRA?', *Guardian*, 29 July 2005; Comerford, 2003, 21; and McIntyre, 2001 and 2003.

66 D. McKittrick, 'The IRA's farewell to arms', *Independent*, 29 July 2005.

67 Bertie Ahern interviewed on RTE, 15 October 2006.

68 P. Wintour, 'Prime Minister's answers', *Guardian*, 5 July 2006; G. Moriarty, 'Governments take comfort from response', *Irish Times*, 14 October 2006.

69 Bertie Ahern interview, RTE Radio, 31 July 2005.

70 P. Murphy, 'IRA rebranding makes transformation painless', *Irish News*, 28 June 2005.

71 Sharrock, 'Provos "have key role in peace"', *The Times*, 7 September 2006.

B was another. The possibility that the Provisional IRA's future was as a party militia similar in function to the Official IRA in the 1970s and 1980s was given weight by the McCartney murder (2005) and the Northern Bank robbery (2004). In the same way that the Official IRA's fundraising exposed contradictions within the politics of the Workers' Party, so the McCartney murder and other alleged cases of criminality revealed contradictions within the Provisional movement.

To some, the McCartney murder symbolized the hidden power of the Provisionals in Northern Irish society; it was a 'shocking reflection of life in a typical, nationalist area of Belfast, where the IRA are the "protectors" of the community.'[72] One Short Strand resident argued in the wake of the murder that 'there's a very low element associated with the Provisional IRA in this area nowadays. I don't think it's Republicanism. It's all about money and thuggery and power.'[73] Some traditional nationalists argued that these activities showed that Republicans had 'the smell of fascism' about them, while the peace process was a 'deep dark menacing shadow … [in which] destruction by peace is a new and deadly tactic' used by the Provisionals.[74]

Republicans have always been insistent that theirs is a justified political struggle and have distanced themselves from any taint of criminality.[75] The reaction of leading Provisionals during the McCartney case mirrored that of police chiefs when confronted with wrongdoing by individual constables. They argued that the problem was not systemic or institutional; it was a case of individual bad apples within the movement.[76] Likewise, the Provisionals denied any 'responsibility for the number of former Republicans who have embraced criminal activity. They do so for self-gain. We repudiate this activity and denounce those involved.'[77]

The Provisional response to the accusations of criminality drew on this historical experience by attempting to deflect the charges with a display of righteous anger. The IRA's Easter 2005 message, for example, argued that the political outcry surrounding the McCartney case was an attempt by British and Unionist politicians to 'criminalize the Republican struggle' comparable to Margaret Thatcher's. It continued:

72 A. Chrisafis, 'Wall of silence', *Guardian*, 31 October 2005.
73 Kate Meighan quoted in S. Breen, 'The cost of being a friend of Robert McCartney: beatings and banishment', *Sunday Tribune*, 28 May 2006.
74 A true nationalist, but the Church's man above all', obituary for Monsignor Denis Fall, *Irish Times*, 24 June 2006.
75 See, for example, Ruairí Ó Brádaigh's views on gangsterism quoted in White, 2006, 404.
76 A. Chrisafis, 'IRA offered to shoot McCartney killers', *Guardian*, 9 March 2005.
77 'Óglaigh na hÉireann Easter Message 2006', *Fuascailt*, Spring/Summer 2006.

Our patriot dead are not criminals. We are not criminals… Ten of our comrades endured the agony of hunger strike and died defeating the criminalization strategy. We will not betray their courage by tolerating criminality within our own ranks.[78]

If these events show the coercive power of the IRA over the community, other strategies were designed to maintain a degree of consent. The need to retain the support of the base meant that Provisional leaders had to respond to evident communal unease and the effective grassroots campaign by the McCartney family. Sinn Féin leaders publicly backed the search for the truth by inviting members of the McCartney family to Sinn Féin's 2005 Ard Fheis; IRA courts martial disciplined volunteers involved in the cover-up and 'offered to shoot the offenders'.[79]

The IRA's call, 'in the strongest possible terms', for those involved to 'come forward and to take responsibility for their actions', along with a decision by Sinn Féin to give the names of party members involved in the case to the Police Ombudsman, highlighted both the pressures the Provisionals faced within the community and their ambiguous relationship with the state.[80] An even further departure from Republican practice was the Sinn Féin leadership's call for four Republicans suspected of kidnapping of a dissident Republican, Bobby Tohill, in 2004 to surrender to the authorities. The choreography of the Tohill case was probably less a result of community outrage than part of the Provisionals' *modus vivendi* with the British state.[81] These tentative and ambiguous connections with the legal system through the halfway house of the Police Ombudsman pointed towards Sinn Féin's future participation in the policing and justice system, which acceptance of the St Andrews Agreement entailed.[82]

Criminalizing the Republican struggle: Sicily and the Short Strand

The tendency to lump together a range of incidents, from smuggling through to murder, under the heading 'Republican criminality' hid as much as it

---

78 IRA statement, 23 March 2005, on BBC website, http://news.bbc.co.uk/go/pr/fr/-/hi/ northern_ireland/4076520.stm

79 A. Chrisafis, 'IRA offered to shoot McCartney killers', *Guardian*, 9 March 2005; IRA statement, 23 March 2005, on BBC website, http://news.bbc.co.uk/go/pr/fr/-/hi/ northern_ireland/4076520.stm; and M. Devenport, 'Sinn Féin on horns of policing dilemma', 4 March 2005 on BBC website, http://news.bbc.co.uk/go/pr/fr/-/hi/ northern_ireland/4076520.stm

80 Devenport, 'Sinn Féin on horns of policing dilemma'.

81 'PSNI urged to release pictures of kidnappers', *Irish News*, 3 November 2006.

82 M. Hennessey, 'Qualified welcome for St Andrews proposals from SF', *Irish Times*, 7 November 2006.

revealed.[83] The significance of these activities lay in the differing functions of this criminality, either as an inevitable by-product of transition or as a strategically directed instrument of control.[84] Thus, the origins of the McCartney case in an *individual* dispute make it different in character from sanctioned murders, such as those carried out by Direct Action Against Drugs or the shooting of Joe-Joe O' Connor (which was designed to eliminate a military and political rival).[85]

Nevertheless, despite the Provisionals' attempt to distance the organization from it, the McCartney murder did illustrate the movement's power within sections of the nationalist community. The individuals involved drew on its authority to obstruct investigations into the murder. In this sense, the movement created the conditions and the structures that enabled such events to take place; they were the by-products of the power structures that the Provisionals have developed over 30 years of conflict.[86]

For Unionists, these 'institutionalized criminal structures' were an integral part of the Republican movement and, as such, continued to pose a fundamental threat to the state. Unionists frequently referred to the Republican 'multi-million-pound criminal empire' as an obstacle to devolution. The DUP's Peter Robinson, for example, argued that:

> democracy cannot tolerate a situation where criminality is institutionalized at the heart of the state, and that is exactly what would be done if we permit an organization like Sinn Féin, which is still seamlessly linked to paramilitary and criminal activity, into government.[87]

Given that its fundraising operations were alleged in the early 2000s to be worth £20 million per annum in West Belfast alone, the IRA's involvement in the black economy and smuggling throughout the country amounts to a substantial criminal enterprise.[88] Other activities allegedly linked the Provisionals to robberies and a criminal empire of money-laundering

---

83 For example, J. Allister, 'Why I have doubts over the proposals', *News Letter*, 17 October 2006; and 'Horror attack "litmus test for Republicans"', *News Letter*, 9 November 2006.

84 Bertie Ahern referred to these 'grey areas during the transitional process' in an interview on RTE Radio, 31 July 2005.

85 A. McIntyre, 'Is Gerry a McCarthy?', *Fourthwrite*, Autumn 2000. Direct Action Against Drugs was a cover name for the Belfast IRA in the mid-1990s. Moloney, 2002, 437–440.

86 D. Fowler, 'One family taking on the IRA', *Marie Claire*, July 2005; and A. Chrisafis, 'IRA offered to shoot McCartney killers', *Guardian*, 9 March 2005.

87 G. Moriarty, 'Warning criminality must not be "institutionalized"', *Irish Times*, 6 February 2006.

88 See McDonald, 2004, 200 and Rafter, 2005, 188–218 for estimates of income raised by the Provisionals in this way.

through pubs, hotels, businesses and property.[89] It was also alleged that individuals have 'built considerable property-based personal wealth' as a result of these activities, which blur the distinction between revolutionary fundraising and the personal spoils of war.[90]

When combined with other investments and the laundering of this income in legitimate businesses at home and abroad, this makes the Provisionals, individually and collectively, a significant economic and social power far beyond the ghettoes and villages that are usually regarded as their power base. By the 1990s, the phrase 'Sicily without the sun' was used to describe a *whole* society in which, after 30 years of conflict, paramilitary criminality is endemic rather than limited to deviant places in 'bandit country'.[91] In questioning the motives of the Northern Bank robbers, some former Provisionals have raised wider issues about the nature of the contemporary movement. As former IRA member Dolores Price argued after the robbery:

> Call me old-fashioned if you like, but there used to be standards, codes of conduct, that sort of thing when I was a volunteer... The 'liberated' funds [from bank robberies] would buy weapons, feed volunteers on the run, help look after the families of those in jail and keep the war machine ticking over... The war is over, we are told. Guns paid for from those bank robberies are to be melted down, some already have been. So this 'big one' [the Northern Bank robbery] is not about buying guns... What is all this money needed for?[92]

The uncertain boundaries that exist between private gain and fundraising for the movement indicate that some of these structures have taken on a life of their own and will be difficult to control, let alone dismantle. Individual Republicans will not willingly surrender the status and power that membership of the IRA gives them in some nationalist communities. A combination of historical inertia and the extent of its penetration of society means that the IRA's structures of power cannot be removed as easily as military posts in south Armagh.

These patterns lend some support to the comparisons between the IRA and the historical forms of mafia. As the products of social disruption and communal resistance to authority by 'those who make themselves

---

89 For an example of the nature of these allegations, see V. Browne, 'The "framing" of Phil Flynn', *The Village*, 16–22 March 2006.

90 C. Lally, 'IRA bank money was for investment in Bulgaria', *Irish Times*, 26 July 2006.

91 McDonald, 2004, Chapter 7; and Harnden, 1999.

92 D. Price, 'Money... Money... Money...', *The Blanket*, 17 January 2005, http://lark. phoblacht.net.phprint.php.

respected', both groups share some elements of social banditry.[93] However, it is as the products of collective demobilization that their organizational trajectories have the greatest similarities.

The Sicilian Mafia's development is typical of these forms of social rebellion. The movement emerged in the nineteenth century following an unsuccessful revolutionary challenge, and went on to become a strong-arm rural bourgeoisie operating within a 'double underworld' of official structures of power and unofficial social networks.[94] Like other historic groups of social rebels, it did not challenge the existence of the state or existing social relations; indeed, its position relied upon the continued existence of these social and political structures to provide an arena within which it could operate. Force and fear were used as forms of bargaining and social power in a type of moral economy limited by convention and the power of the state.

Thus, the evolution of social banditry through the medium of organized crime into 'legitimate' commercial activity and political brokerage was a quantitative rather than a qualitative change. However, the ambiguities and contradictions inherent in operating in a double underworld continued to be a feature of its power in legitimate society. It became essentially a parasitic mediator between the community and external authority; being entirely part of neither one nor the other, its power rested on this intermediary status. In the Italian case, it went on to develop close links with established political parties; in South America, it developed into a form of populism.[95]

These models are applicable to Northern Irish politics. The Provisionals' movement into conventional politics and their ambiguous relationships with official society replicate some of these historic patterns of collective demobilization. Northern Ireland's own double underworld is formed by the modus vivendi that has developed between the structures of the British state and the social power of the Provisionals. These contradictory forms exist because the British government was prepared to allow 'a criminal phase in … [Provisionalism's] democratic evolution' as a necessary, if distasteful, form of compromise.[96] This phase, British ministers argued, was bound to be uneven and indefinite, since 'it was unrealistic to expect the Provisionals to deliver a state of absolute perfection' during this transitional period.[97]

93 Hobsbawm, 1985, 36.
94 Hobsbawm, 1985, 40.
95 These historical patterns are discussed in Hobsbawm, 1985, Chapters 1 and 2.
96 H. McDonald, 'Sinn Féin on the edge of the abyss,' *Observer*, 6 March 2005.
97 Peter Hain, Secretary of State for Northern Ireland, quoted in W. Graham, 'IRA committed to peace: McDowell', *Irish News*, 26 July 2006.

However, the evidence seems to show that, far from withering away with the ending of the armed struggle, these working relationships between the British state and the Provisionals have actually increased the movement's power within the nationalist community since 1994. This double underworld seems set to remain a permanent feature of political and social life in Northern Ireland, and given that, is it feasible that the IRA *as an organization* can be as easily decommissioned as its arsenal was in 2005?

'A quiet word with the man from the IRA'

The contradictions in this double underworld were revealed by issues of policing and community control that arose after 1994. These grey areas were examples of the constructive ambiguity at the heart of the normalization process, and posed questions about what constituted normality in Northern Ireland.[98]

Throughout their history, the Provisionals had several related motives in dealing with crime and anti-social activity. This concern formed a key part of the resistance community strategy by enabling the Provisionals to undermine the legitimacy of the state and demonstrate their role as communal defenders.[99] However, their real concerns were not crime and social order, but control of the community and consolidating their own state forms.

Paradoxically, taking on the mantle of a community police force placed the Provisionals under a degree of pressure from the community. Rising crime rates and an exaggerated fear of crime have become features of life in urban working-class neighbourhoods throughout the United Kingdom since the 1980s. Consequently, many claimed to see the growth of a 'hood [hooligan] culture' and concerns about crime in Northern Ireland as signifiers of normalization.[100] There was also an increasing focus on young people and criminality in what was to become a familiar form of moral panic.[101] Republicans became increasingly aware that the disaffection of sections of nationalist youth threatened to undermine the community solidarity necessary to maintain the struggle.[102]

These concerns brought an attendant politics of fear in the nationalist community around anti-social behaviour and 'ordinary decent crime'.[103]

98   Bertie Ahern interviewed on RTE Radio, 31 July 2005.
99   Brendan Hughes, interview, 12 August 1998.
100 'No-go areas for hoods', *An Phoblacht/Republican News*, 19 January 1989.
101 Walton, 2002.
102 P. Harrison, 'The hoods: a candid and controversial assessment', *An Phoblacht*, 12 November 1981.
103 A. West, 'Notes from a war zone', *An Phoblacht/Republican News*, 25 February 1988. This review (of Conroy, 1988) realistically discusses the problems of anti-social

When faced with problems like this, many members of the nationalist community turned to the IRA squads and found themselves involved in an ambivalent complicity that strengthened the movement's social power.[104] The neighbours who reported a suspected child abuser or the woman who had a 'quiet word with the man from the IRA' about the teenagers who 'tortured' (harassed) her were typical of this acquiescence in IRA punishments.[105]

The Provisionals were responsive to communal anxieties; these collective moods could be contradictory, with support for rough justice for offenders quickly switching to sympathy for the victims of kneecappings.[106] It means that, as one critic argues, many people who publicly dissociate themselves from these punishments 'were denying to themselves that they really did ask for the IRA to take action. They are locked in their own denial... A lot of that kind of energy works in areas like Poleglass, Twinbrook and the Falls.'[107]

The Provisional strategy for combating the criminal results of this alienation was a contradictory mixture of revolutionary rhetoric, traditional communal punishment and direct action.[108] These elements were mutually reinforcing; harsh punishments and vigilantism could be justified as the expression of the anger of the resistance community. In this way the rhetorically revolutionary, which emphasized immediate action, took precedence over the reformist solutions of social policy.[109] The result was that:

> their social power is all around. It's not just the McCartney killing ... or Mark Robinson, McGinley, Barney Mac Donald, etc. You live in these areas and you know who the power is. People when they talk, talk about the power of the Provos. The kids in the street talk about the Provos and talk about being afraid of the Provos. 'The IRA will sort them out', they say. The first line of contact with authority in these areas is not with the state, it's with the Provos.[110]

---

behaviour and the complex power relationships within nationalist working class communities.

104 For example, the IRA in one Belfast area in the early 2000s dealt with a range of issues, from domestic violence and sexual abuse through to drug-dealing and teenage 'misbehaviour'. Private information.

105 Private information, and McCann, 1993, 20–24.

106 Private information, former members of Belfast Brigade, IRA.

107 Malachy O'Doherty, political and cultural commentator, interview, 23 July 2005.

108 'Plan To combat vandalism', An Phoblacht, 5 January 1984.

109 'Action against sex attacks', An Phoblacht, 23 February 1984.

110 Anthony McIntyre, interview, 29 July 2005.

This conception of community is implicitly authoritarian, presupposing a general will that can be mobilized through 'marches against rape' or putting pressure on the pushers.[111] It can also take the less liberating forms of vigilantism and communal intimidation. For example, Republican involvement in the Concerned Parents Against Drugs Campaign in Dublin in the 1980s and other actions against crime and anti-social activity was frequently cited as evidence of the ambiguities within this form of communal mobilization.[112]

The McCartney case showed how these politics of fear could manufacture consent, or, failing that, silence and acquiescence. These forms of power are complex and shadowy, resting on implied threat and the creation of a communal consensus against perceived opponents and deviants. By linking anti-social behaviour and political deviance, the Provisionals:

> use the term 'community' in a bullying way within these neighbourhoods; if you're not part of the community then you can be frozen out. The joyrider, the young offender and the dissident can be regarded as offenders and deviants against the community and alienated or even exiled from the community on that account.[113]

The intimidatory behaviour and social ostracism directed towards the McCartney family and their friends following his murder illustrated just one facet of this power.[114] These intimidatory forms of political mobilization carry echoes of the premodern forms of 'rough music' or *charivari* used 'against individuals who had offended against certain community norms'.[115] Other examples include intimidatory visits to potential Republican dissidents, Sinn Féin-organized 'spontaneous demonstrations' and pickets at the homes of two former IRA members (Anthony McIntyre and Tommy Gorman), and the alleged murder of Real IRA volunteer Joe-Joe O'Connor in 2000 by the Provisionals.[116] Harassment of this type brought forth accusations that the Provisional collaboration with the state in the policing of 'dissidents' ensured that 'British colonial rule continues in Ireland with the support of lackeys and quislings.'[117]

---

111 J. Plunkett, 'March against rape' and 'Anti-drug action demanded', *An Phoblacht*, 1 March 1984.
112 Rafter, 2005, 164–165.
113 Malachy O'Doherty, interview, 23 July 2005.
114 S. Breen, 'The cost of being a friend of Robert McCartney: beatings and banishment', *Sunday Tribune*, 28 May 2006.
115 Thompson, 1991, 467.
116 See, for example, *Fourthwrite* Special Supplement, November 2000, dealing with events surrounding the murder of Joe-Joe O'Connor. Anthony McIntyre, interview, 27 November 2000.
117 'No surrender to British rule: Continuity IRA statement', *Saoirse*, October 2005.

Policing the community

The central role of the IRA since the early 1990s has been to act as an instrument of power *within* the Provisional movement and the wider nationalist community. This change of function occurred as a result of the winding down of the IRA's campaign against the British state.[118] By the late 1980s, the Adams–McGuinness leadership had recognized that the armed struggle had decreasing strategic effectiveness, and that ultimately the IRA as an offensive instrument would have to be surrendered as a bargaining counter in return for political gains.[119] The political and strategic logic of the leadership's position meant the end of the Provisionals' war and the acceptance of a settlement that fell far short of the movement's original aims.

The IRA remained central to the management of this retreat for several reasons. The continuing military potential of the IRA made it a valuable negotiating tool that could not be surrendered lightly; the peace process became essentially a long-drawn-out auction of the IRA as a going concern. The process had necessarily to be prolonged because of the difficulties in managing the base and dismantling the IRA's offensive capability in an orderly fashion. There was significant opposition within the IRA to the leadership's strategy, reflected in the breakdown of the ceasefire in 1996 and pressure to continue the armed struggle.[120]

For these reasons, the IRA could not be disarmed and disbanded overnight; the process had to be managed carefully, since the complete decommissioning of weapons and the disbandment of the organization would be the ultimate concession, revealing the end of the Republican challenge and the Provisionals' acceptance of the *status quo*. This would have significant psychological and political effects, leaving a vacant space for a new group to emerge, laying claim to the historical and political legitimacy of the IRA. If for no other reason, this meant that the Provisional IRA could not go away while any possible potential challengers remained in the field. As one former senior Sinn Féin strategist explained:

118 Tommy Gorman, former Republican prisoner and community activist, interview, 7 October 1997, on his feelings that 'the war was running down in the late 1980s'. Tommy McKearney similarly believed that the leadership felt the war was effectively over by this period (interview, 10 May 1999). However, senior Republican Brendan Hughes was unaware of any 'peace strategy' in the late 1980s or attempts to end the armed campaign during that period (interview, 11 August 1998). See Moloney, 2002, 261–279 for some of the first indications of a strategic shift in the leadership's thinking.

119 For some of the straws in the wind, see Danny Morrison's letter to Gerry Adams in October 1991. Morrison, 1999, 240–242.

120 For details of these complex manoeuvres and manipulation see Moloney, 2002, 428–480.

The leadership realized that you don't ensure the primacy of politics by dismantling the military machine and creating a political machine. If you don't bring the thought processes and the ideology of the military machine with you then you will not succeed, because you will leave behind a rump that may eclipse you.[121]

The British and Irish governments understood the necessity for this realpolitik. Taoiseach Bertie Ahern argued as late as 2005 that the continued existence of the Provisional IRA was still essential to provide structures of control over its own followers and potential dissidents. Although there would continue to be grey areas, he believed that these functions were vital to ensure that the Provisionals as a whole made an effective transition from paramilitarism to constitutional politics.[122]

From the relative political security of the post-Good Friday Agreement world, Gerry Adams was to argue that:

one of the objectives of this [peace] process is to see the IRA out of existence. When I say that we want to bring an end to physical-force Republicanism, that clearly means bringing an end to the organization or the vehicle of physical-force Republicanism.[123]

However, rather than disbandment, 'ending physical-force Republicanism' meant that the organization's focus would shift towards a new 'internal front'. How this was to be achieved reveals much about the political culture and organizational forms of the Provisional movement. Increasing attention was paid to consolidating the power of the Provisionals within the nationalist community and to preventing 'dissidents' mounting a political and military challenge to the peace process.

Some Republicans went as far as arguing that there was a tacit agreement between the Provisionals and the British, Irish and US governments to 'police' the peace process within the nationalist population. In return, the Provisionals were 'given latitude in terms of criminality and quasi-authority, to police their own communities and their own areas'.[124] For a founding member of the Provisionals, John Kelly:

it was a political strategy to keep the nationalist population under their [the Provisionals'] subjugation… This was strengthened by the Good Friday Agreement and all the talk that you had from Mo Mowlam about 'housekeeping' matters. The British would not get involved with 'housekeeping'…

121 Private information.
122 Ahern interview, RTE Radio, 31 July 2005.
123 G. Adams, 'Trimble knows the old days are over', *Sunday Business Post*, 28 September 2003.
124 John Kelly, former senior Republican activist and Sinn Féin MLA, interview, 23 August 2005.

If you can shoot Joe-Joe O'Connor, you can shoot somebody else; if it will be considered as mere housekeeping by the British authorities then you have a free hand... It's as if they said: 'You can do that lads, but don't shoot soldiers or plant bombs.'[125]

Mirroring the common practice of the 'real' state, the dissident threat could also be wheeled out for political advantage by the Provisional leadership during periods of crisis.[126] Some take this argument further and argue that the exceptional needs of a transitional period may become permanent. Like the temporary emergency legislation of a conventional state, this war-footing, used against internal opposition, and its accompanying politics of fear could continue indefinitely as a feature of the Provisional state. Consequently, some Republicans argue that control of the community, in whatever form it is exercised, has become the *raison d'être* of the Provisional project. The future of the IRA will be to act 'as a policeman over its own communities ... because there was a developing pattern within Provisionalism ... that has become totalitarian and almost fascist in its attitude towards its own people. They are afraid of losing control.'[127]

The paradox was that the greater the rhetorical emphasis by Republicans on consent in the region's politics, the greater the real reliance on coercion as an instrument of political control *within* the nationalist community.[128] However, the communal image presented by the Provisionals is one of diversity and pluralism. Supporters of the leadership argue that Republicans are probably more tolerant now than they were during the armed campaign. Republicans, it is suggested, are less able to enforce their will on the community because in peacetime such domination lacks legitimacy. Thus, according to this argument, forms of community hostility towards dissent result from spontaneous peer pressure rather than organized campaigns by Republicans.

This argument assumes a natural and close affinity between the movement and the community that results in:

---

125 Ibid.
126 See, for example, the argument that the Provisionals exaggerated the strength of 'the dissidents' for political advantage during the discussions following the St Andrews Agreement: G. Moriarty, 'Word of threat easy to believe as stakes are underlined', *Irish Times*, 14 November 2006.
127 John Kelly, interview, 23 August 2005.
128 For some examples cited by 'dissidents', see 'Vicious attack on Republican family', *Saoirse*, July 1998; 'Provo action: denial of freedom of speech and political expression', *Saoirse*, October 1998. *The Blanket* website and archive also carries a number of articles on this topic. See http://lark.phoblacht.net

an intolerance based on community support for the leadership and opposition to people who are criticizing the leadership. They [the community] see ex-members of the IRA, in particular, as traitors who are not maintaining unity. It's probably more insidious than leadership threats.[129]

It also minimizes the degree to which the Provisionals have used their social networks to create this 'righteous anger' and mobilize against those who transgress against what is defined as the communal consensus.

Managing the legion of the rearguard

The subjective factor of leadership was of critical importance in these political and organizational manoeuvres. The success of this management strategy in preventing a major split in the Provisionals and minimizing the effectiveness of dissident groups can be claimed as one of the historic achievements of the Adams–McGuinness leadership.[130] However, when the general lines of the peace strategy started to emerge in the late 1980s, it is probable that not even Gerry Adams and his closest supporters were aware of exactly where the strategy would lead. As one Sinn Féin insider explained in the late 1990s:

> The leadership of Adams and company is epitomized by its pragmatism not by its politics… In some ways the strategy is being made up as they go along. There were clear objectives to get from A to B but with little notion of how to deal with eventualities in-between. It was very dependent on personalities, and a lot was left to chance. The objective was to end the isolation of Sinn Féin, develop a mandate for Sinn Féin … and a degree of support via the democratic process. *The specifics were worked out as events unfolded.* [Emphasis added][131]

Gerry Adams's style of leadership is bonapartist. He is portrayed as embodying the movement's essential characteristics while at the same time balancing between tendencies and standing above them as the final arbiter of events.[132] His strategy relied on a secure organizational control; along with Martin McGuinness, he also drew on his reputation to cultivate the belief among activists that his political strategy would succeed in obtaining Republican goals. During high-level internal meetings, Adams would play upon 'his status and charisma rather than the force of argument. Basically

129 Felim Ó hAdhmaill, interview, 25 August 2005.
130 Currie, 2004, 433–434.
131 Private information.
132 This 'Eighteenth Brumaire' was reflected in Gerry Adams's personal tactics. As one former Sinn Fein activist argues: 'Adams himself largely stayed out of or above the debate, as befitted his emerging presidential role in the overall movement. However, it was clear where he stood.' P. Ferguson, 'Anyone for tennis?', *Weekly Worker*, 4 August 2005.

he was saying that if he wasn't given the necessary latitude to do as he saw fit, then he would resign and they could get someone else.'[133]

If the details of strategy were developed ad hoc, the tactics of its implementation were not. The internal management process was designed to maintain unity at all costs and to minimize the numbers and operational strength of those who would inevitably leave. Adams's and McGuinness's tactics drew on the experience of the leadership that they had replaced in the late 1970s:

> We were very, very conscious not to make any of the mistakes that were made during 1975... The lesson that Republicans learned in the 1990s was that *the most important constituency that you negotiate with is your own*. [Emphasis added][134]

How this success was achieved indicated the future political role of the IRA. The IRA's coercive functions were combined with those of an inner party cadre within the movement. The distinction between the IRA and Sinn Fein at senior levels was a transparent fiction; although 'Sinn Féin and the IRA were the two sides of the same coin', the exact balance of power between the military and political wings of the movement was one of creative tension.[135] Senior IRA figures were assigned to work in the party and an IRA representative would attend Sinn Féin Ard Comhairle meetings to 'explain the Army's position'.[136] All major decisions and changes adopted by Sinn Féin had in effect to be first approved by an IRA Army Convention or the Army Council, making clear the relative distribution of power between the two wings of the movement.[137]

This relationship had historical precedents going back to the 1916–1923 period: however, in the 1970s the 'long war' strategy gave it a new emphasis.[138] Then the aim had been to radicalize Sinn Féin using politically-educated IRA volunteers. The party would become a transmission belt for the mobilization of the Republican base to support the cutting edge of the armed struggle.[139] In the 1980s, as Sinn Fein's membership

---

133 Private information.
134 M. McGuinness, 'The lessons of history', *An Phoblacht*, 12 January 2006.
135 Irish Minister of Justice, Michael McDowell quoted in M. Brennock, 'Ball now firmly in court of Provisional movement', *Irish Times*, 11 February 2005.
136 Private information.
137 For example, Sinn Féin's decision to end abstentionism in 1986 was preceded by an IRA convention that allowed volunteers to consider the question and hence vote for the leadership's position on taking seats in Leinster House at the Sinn Féin Ard Fheis.
138 Rafter, 2005, Chapter 4.
139 These ideas were developed in the 'Brownie' articles and the 'Staff Report'. The 'Brownie' articles were attributed to Gerry Adams, and discussed aspects of Republican strategy in *Republican News* and *An Phoblacht/Republican News* in the late 1970s and early

grew, IRA volunteers at all levels, from local Cumainn to Ard Comhairle and Revolutionary Council, formed a vanguard who directed the politics and activity of the broader Republican movement.[140] IRA volunteers operating under military discipline acted as a caucus to ensure that the 'Army line', as defined by the leadership, would prevail throughout the movement.[141] Thus, as one former IRA member has noted, 'the party is ruled by the ethos of the army.'[142]

Within the IRA itself this political culture and the bureaucratic centralization of decision-making was strengthened by the IRA's cellular reorganization in the 1970s and the subsequent development of Northern Command.[143] When combined with the IRA's conspiratorial tradition and militarist ethos, this form of democratic centralism, originally designed for revolutionary mobilization, became instead an instrument for the command and control of the wider movement.

The leadership managed the process internally by balancing between the different centres of power within the Provisional movement and by manoeuvring externally between the British government, the Unionists and Republican activists. Gerry Adams's apparently throwaway line in 1995 – 'they haven't gone away you know' – was a small example of this choreographed process, in that it reassured activists that the leadership would not sell them out while at the same time appearing to put pressure on the British government as well as angering Unionist leaders.[144] By this stage, the British government at least understood the calculations behind the remark and the leadership's real intentions, even if it would take others until July 2005 to discern their true import.

Manipulating the symbols

Republican leaders proved adept at manipulating the symbols and transitional language of contemporary politics to obscure their ultimate

---

1980s. The 'Staff Report' was a captured IRA document of the 1976–1978 period, which discussed the reorganization of the IRA and Sinn Fein. See Clarke, 1987, 251–253.

140 See Collins, 1997, 219–232 for an example of how this relationship worked on the ground.

141 For example, see Moloney's account of the Sinn Féin decision to end abstentionism: Moloney, 2002, 287–297. During the 1998 Sinn Féin Ard Fheis, the author witnessed the IRA's Adjutant-General and a senior Army Council member strenuously 'lobbying and persuading' IRA volunteers to vote for the leadership's position on the Good Friday Agreement.

142 Anthony McIntyre, interview, 30 May 1999.

143 Tommy McKearney quoted in McIntyre, 2003, 193.

144 Gerry Adams, quoted in 'They haven't gone away you know', *An Phoblacht/Republican News*, 17 August 1995.

objectives from many of their own supporters. There were sound reasons, rooted in the need to preserve the unity of the Republican movement, for the Adams leadership to use a language that bridged the old positions of armed struggle and revolutionary mobilization with the newer discourse of diplomacy and pragmatic accommodation.[145]

The TUAS document is an example of these tactics. Written for IRA internal briefings before the first ceasefire, it used the language of struggle to mask an entirely different purpose. This strategy was variously defined as 'tactical use of armed struggle' or 'totally unarmed strategy'; the very ambiguity of its title indicated how the Provisional leadership managed activists and supporters.[146] This political sleight of hand had a clear purpose, as one former senior Sinn Féiner explains it:

> TUAS was a sop... They wanted to convince IRA volunteers, who had come from a very militaristic tradition, that their usefulness and their role in the struggle for Irish freedom was as relevant in 1994 as it was in 1916, whereas the reality was that in the 1990s things were completely different and there was a need to be more pragmatic.[147]

Its success relied on a culture of *ex post facto* IRA briefings and the management of opposition rather than democracy and debate. This culture precluded any serious political debate within the Provisional movement. One former Sinn Féin activist describes a pattern of stage management and manoeuvres within the party:

> The full politics of the pan-nationalist position were never ... debated openly. Every step of the way, the leadership cynically denied the direction in which they were headed and used their considerable standing ... to pursue policies which were never laid out openly for the membership to debate, let alone vote on.[148]

Likewise, before the 1994 IRA ceasefire, for example, it was likely:

---

145 McIntyre convincingly argues that Provisionalism has always been in many ways a departure from pre-1969 Republicanism, illustrated in the way that new discourses have 'unceremoniously usurped' the 'vestiges of tradition' in, for example, the abstentionism debate. McIntyre, 2001, 193.

146 The political significance of the different titles is obvious, and was much commented upon at the time. A paper with the acronymic title 'TUAS' was circulated among members of the IRA in the period leading up to the first IRA ceasefire in 1994. Copy of paper in author's possession.

147 Private information, former Sinn Féin Ard Comhairle member.

148 P. Ferguson, 'Anyone for tennis?', *Weekly Worker*, 4 August 2005. A former IRA volunteer in Collins, 1997, 219–232 presents a similarly negative view of the political culture within the Provisional movement in the 1980s.

that there would have been some discussion and debate [within the IRA] around ... the strategy. But the idea of genuine consultation is slightly different in the IRA. It is more someone coming from the strata above to explain the leadership's position.[149]

This culture remains strong within the movement. Paradoxically, the supposedly more open and democratic politics of the peace process have actually strengthened it. Like the skilful generals they are, the Provisional leaders never undertake a political manoeuvre without securing their base. Despite the public statements on 'the important task of consulting with party members and the wider Republican community' about the St Andrews Agreement, the Sinn Féin leadership followed a similar pattern of management, which produced a similar majority for the leadership's position.[150]

Other aspects of managing the IRA in the 1990s entailed a diversionary 'Grand Old Duke of York' strategy of responding to internal pressures by keeping activists occupied by mobilizing around contentious parades or maintaining the movement's civil administration structures in the areas.[151] It also involved a great deal of micro-management by the leadership as it attempted to win support for the 'new departure'. While it was clear by the mid-1990s that ending the war was a major element in the leadership's strategy, volunteers on the ground were constantly being told in briefings that 'we're going back to war' if the peace process failed, or that there would be no decommissioning under any circumstances. It meant that for IRA members in this period, life must have been a constant and confusing process of doublethink, when the events in the world around them flatly contradicted what their leaders were telling them.[152]

Another important factor that helped the Provisional leadership was the length of the process. Playing the long game during the interminable discussions and meetings over sixteen years of the peace process was a tactic directed not only at the British government and the Unionists. This war of position was also a war of attrition directed against activists and potential opponents within the wider Republican movement.

Disillusion and apathy with the Republican project in general and

---

149   Tommy McKearney, former Republican prisoner, interview, 30 May 1998.
150   'Proposals deserve careful consideration', *An Phoblacht*, 19 October 2006; 'Sinn Féin leadership to decide on St Andrews', *Irish News*, 6 November 2006; S. O'Driscoll, 'Adams tells US supporters of possible splits over policy', *Irish Times*, 11 November 2006.
151   Punishment beatings by Republicans showed a marked increase in the period leading up to the first ceasefire and during its operation (1993–1996). See analysis of RUC/PSNI figures in Monaghan and McLaughlin, 2006, 171–186.
152   Private information, former member Dublin Brigade IRA.

its Provisional incarnation in particular became widespread among IRA members and political activists 'caught with the Provisional disease'.[153] Worn down in this way, many became inactive or left altogether, leaving behind a Provisional movement reduced to a pliable corps of loyal followers. This favourable position for the leaders was not simply a result of organizational manoeuvres or a lack of real debate within the movement. Many of their opponents appeared to have little to say.

The failure of both the internal challenges to the Adams leadership in the 1990s and of small groups outside the Provisionals to build viable political or military alternatives only served to strengthen the leadership's position. This process was helped by the changing climate of opinion after the Omagh bombing in 1998. There really seemed not to be an alternative to the peace process when:

> the dissidents cannot sustain a propaganda newspaper or magazine. They have not produced a programme. They have not offered a compelling analysis or even a woeful one. Their spokespersons have been spectacularly unimpressive and inarticulate.[154]

Even Republican critics recognized the political and tactical abilities of the Adams leadership: 'like everyone else, Adams and others were searching for ways of achieving overriding objectives. Gerry had an answer when the rest of us hadn't really articulated an alternative,'[155] A former Sinn Féin strategist speaking in the aftermath of the Belfast Agreement was clearly aware how successfully the leadership had manipulated the activists and navigated its way through a dangerous political situation to bring about a remarkable ideological transformation:

> The transformation of the thinking in the Republican base and the IRA over the last ten years has been phenomenal. *There is no doubt that ten years ago, if you had said 'let's return to Stormont' or 'implement a ceasefire' you would have got kicked to death, whereas now they seem the most logical and practical steps and the most realistic way forward.* [Emphasis added][156]

153 L. Ó Comain, 'If you cannot organize a meeting, how can you expect to organize a revolution?', *The Blanket*, 3 September 2006, http://lark.phoblacht.net/phprint.php
154 D. Morrison, 'When one doesn't mind being called a Provo', *Daily Ireland*, 6 September 2006.
155 Tommy McKearney, interview, 30 May 1998.
156 Private information, former Sinn Féin Ard Comhairle member.

'Fuck Constable Adams and the PSNI'[157]

The other side of the double underworld was illustrated by Sinn Féin's developing relationship with British state and its willingness to contemplate acceptance of policing and judicial structures within Northern Ireland. The Provisionals' endorsement of the PSNI would be 'its most neuralgic decision of the peace process' and would 'mark the end of the ideological road for Republicans and render the IRA "defunct"'.[158] Policing had a fundamental political and symbolic significance for Republicans. Acceptance of the judicial system meant the complete *de jure* recognition of the British state, enshrined in the legal system and the legitimate monopoly of force within society.[159] In terms of the historic Republican aim of overthrowing the state, this acceptance was a public acknowledgement of defeat.

The contradictions within these arrangements were widely recognized by both supporters and opponents of the Provisionals. The graffito quoted in the heading at the beginning of this section was one clear response to these ambiguities. Other reactions reflected unease within the wider Republican base, which questioned whether 'any Irish Republican [can] accept a six-county partitionist police force ... controlled by Britain... There is a difference [between] supporting law and order and supporting a British-sponsored police force.'[160] The Provisionals attempted to elide this criticism by arguing that the devolution of justice and policing to a reconvened Assembly would replace 'British political policing' with 'proper civic democratic and accountable policing' under local control.[161]

This position seemed to indicate that a fundamental shift was occurring. In the run-up to the St Andrews Agreement, the British and Irish governments accepted the assurance of the Provisionals that their views on community policing had changed. The Independent Monitoring Commission reported in autumn 2006 that 'the [IRA] leadership is opposed to the use of violence in community control, [and] has taken a stance against

---

157 Graffito from Lower Falls area of Belfast, 5 November 2006.
158 F. Millar, 'Will a pragmatic Paisley finish his career by "doing the deal"?', *Irish Times*, 11 November 2006.
159 The Provisionals' acceptance of the framework documents in 1995 and the Belfast Agreement was clearly *de jure* recognition of the British state in Northern Ireland. Acceptance of policing and law and order through the St Andrews Agreement was simply the final confirmation of this recognition.
160 'Concerned Republican, law and order and "state police" are not the same', letter, *Irish News*, 8 November 2006.
161 M. McGuinness, 'Republicans must plot the way forward together', *An Phoblacht*, 19 October 2006.

criminality and disorder amongst the membership.'[162] Statistics pointed to a sharp reduction in Republican punishments and other indicators of IRA activity since 2001.[163] With something of a vacuum emerging, others stepped into the gap to claim the role and the legitimation of community police. Some went as far as suggesting that the PSNI could become more acceptable within nationalist areas 'who are moving away from traditional hostility to the police'.[164] Another claimant to the role was the Continuity IRA, which justified a series of paramilitary-style attacks in the autumn of 2006 in language reminiscent of the Provisionals in the 1980s.[165]

The Provisionals' strategy to deal with criminality and 'anti-community behaviour' was now said to depend on statutory agencies, social services, local authorities and local residents working in a partnership to 'ensure that the quality of life in our communities is protected'.[166] This multi-agency approach was in stark contrast to the IRA's direct action against gangsters in the 1980s and 1990s.[167] Sinn Féin's discursive framework now appears close to that of mainstream Blairite communitarianism, with its calls 'to direct young people's energies to enhance communities and make them feel they have a stake in the future', and appeals to schools and parents to instil 'respect for ... neighbours and for the community in which they live'.[168]

As a further indicator of change, it was now Sinn Féin that found itself condemning the suffering inflicted by punishment attacks and criticizing such dissident activities as threats to the peace process.[169] In this vein, Sinn Féin spokespeople argued that now they would not 'simply respond to the community clamour for direct action', and that following the IRA statement of July 2005 'it is evident that the days of IRA intervention are gone.'[170] If the language echoed the British government's 'respect agenda', the partnerships that were emerging reflected the very different realities

162 Sharrock, 'Provos "have key role in peace"', *The Times*, 7 September 2006.
163 For trends in punishment shootings and beatings, see analysis of RUC/PSNI figures in Monaghan and McLaughlin, 2006. The majority of 'Republican' punishment attacks since 2005 have been attributed to 'dissidents'. See K. Bourke, 'Paramilitary assaults are down by half', *Irish News*, 20 October 2006.
164 SDLP councillor Alex Attwood quoted in A. Morris, 'Shot man believed to be on dissident Republican hit list', *Irish News*, 20 October 2006.
165 A. Morris, 'CIRA claims paramilitary-style attacks', *Irish News*, 17 October 2006.
166 R. McCartney, 'Teaching citizenship to our children', *Daily Ireland*, 31 July 2006.
167 'Belfast IRA take action against gangsters', *An Phoblacht*, June 14 1984 and 'IRA statement on crime', *An Phoblacht* September 27 1984.
168 R. McCartney, 'Teaching citizenship to our children', *Daily Ireland*, 31 July 2006.
169 A. Morris, 'Shot man believed to be on dissident Republican hit list', *Irish News*, 20 October 2006.
170 R. McCartney, 'Teaching citizenship to our children', *Daily Ireland*, 31 July 2006.

of Northern Irish society. While the acknowledgment of the British state's authority was a defeat for the historic Republican project, it was not an unconditional surrender that required the dismantling of the Provisional state.[171]

What emerged instead from the peace process was a new form of relationship between the Provisionals and the British state. This *quid pro quo* meant that while the Provisionals acknowledged that ultimate power resided with the British state, some of the state's functions were, in effect, sub-contracted to the Provisionals. By swearing fealty in this way, the Provisionals maintained their power within the nationalist community at the expense of nullifying Republicanism's historic aims. Thus, the forms of Provisional power might change, but its substance, now resting on a *de facto* partnership with the state, remained intact.

One example of this relationship was the 'very close contact' Sinn Féin activists developed with the PSNI to defuse localized 'interface' conflict, such as in north Belfast.[172] 'Our intent was to de-escalate the situation, de-militarize it', was how leading Republican Gerry Kelly described the role of Provisional activists during a contentious Orange Order parade in Ardoyne in 2006.[173]

The best examples of these new forms of partnership were community restorative justice (CRJ) and community watch schemes. The schemes were given a degree of official recognition by the British government, and opened up the possibility of some indirect involvement by Republicans in policing through community-based initiatives and multi-agency partnerships involving public, private and voluntary sectors.[174] In nationalist areas these schemes were widely perceived to be linked to the Republican movement, resulting in criticism that British government protocols on the operation of the schemes made too many concessions to paramilitarism.[175] The SDLP believed that the protocols were designed to allow Republicans to participate in the schemes without dismantling paramilitary structures. According to SDLP leader Mark Durkan, they showed that 'the culture of paramilitary control persists in some communities, leaving people too scared to speak out' and allowing the Provisional movement 'to have its own state-funded quasi-police'.[176]

---

171 For examples of some Republican criticisms of this 'endorsement and acceptance of the British occupation of Ireland', see 'Mala Poist', *An Phoblacht*, 2 November 2006.
172 Private information.
173 G. Moriarty, 'SF leaders tell of contacts with PSNI', *Irish Times*, 14 July 2006.
174 G. Moriarty, 'Plans for local justice schemes outlined', *Irish Times*, 26 July 2006.
175 A. Maginness, 'Communal justice or vigilantism?', *Fortnight*, March 2006.
176 G. Moriarty, 'SDLP voices profound concern at CRJ schemes', *Irish Times*, 26 July 2006.

The development of CRJ schemes consolidated the power of the Provisionals by producing 'what is effectively a Sinn Féin policing structure in nationalist areas of the North'.[177] This power drew on the historically-sanctioned forms of communal mobilization that have been developed by Republicans during the last thirty years and which, as we have seen, continue to be deployed to maintain their political and social control over sections of the nationalist population.[178] While the British government stressed that the schemes 'must be locked into policing and comply fully with the rule of law... [because] society would not tolerate officially-approved schemes becoming a tool for local paramilitary control', a sufficient number of grey areas remained, resulting in accusations that these schemes are 'too closely identified with Sinn Féin and the IRA and that [they] shield Republicans from criminal justice'.[179]

The blurred boundaries between formal judicial authority on one hand and community justice on the other are very much in keeping with the ambiguous forms of the new Northern Irish politics. Dr FitzGerald's criticisms of 'Sinn Féin policing' accurately characterize these contradictions, but overstate the challenge community justice presents to the authority of the state.[180] These schemes are an accommodation with the state, not an attempt to undermine it. In one sense, British policy is a realistic appreciation of the structure of power within the nationalist community, in that it pragmatically recognizes the Provisional state as a way to manage political conflict. This power is, in turn, further consolidated and formalized by this recognition by the British.

British policy also strengthens the tendencies towards communal particularism within Northern Ireland. For example, the consociational framework of the Belfast Agreement, British community development policy and the proposed local government reform continue to create the political context for increased Balkanization.[181] Should policing powers be eventually fully devolved, the new district policing boards and other politically accountable aspects of policing might reflect this structurally-determined pattern too.

There is, of course, outright official hostility to the idea of communalized

177 G. FitzGerald, 'Revised CRJ protocol is still unacceptable', *Irish Times*, 29 July 2006.
178 For a defence of the operation of the CRJ schemes, see K. McEvoy, 'Restorative justice, politics and local communities', *Fortnight*, March 2006.
179 D. Keenan, 'Seeking justice from within', *Irish Times*, 29 July 2006. These charges were vigorously denied by West Belfast CRJ activist Jim Auld.
180 G. FitzGerald, 'Revised CRJ protocol is still unacceptable', *Irish Times*, 29 July 2006.
181 I. Graham, '"Super council" plans unveiled amid warnings on sectarianism', *Irish News*, 8 November 2006; and P. Shirlow and B. Murtagh, 'Entrenching sectarian goals', *Fortnight*, September 2006.

policing (in which nationalists police nationalist areas and Unionists police Unionist areas), and the structures of a reformed PSNI will formally ensure that the state's writ runs throughout the region. However, the underlying patterns of segregation and the growth of parallel structures within society will undermine this in practice. These forms of particularism will also continue to strengthen the political and social power of the Provisional movement, ensuring that it remains an indispensable partner for the British state in the governance of Northern Ireland.

Soldiers of the past, heroes of the future[182]

In the summer of 2006, Republican areas were festooned with facsimile posters and black flags commemorating the 25th anniversary of the 1981 hunger strike. In a series of rallies and commemorative events, speakers highlighted the importance of historical legitimation in the contemporary politics of Provisionalism by making the connection between the turning point of 1981 and the contemporary 'golden opportunity to advance a new era in our long struggle'.[183] Gerry Adams expressed this continuity even more directly:

> When we went to meet Tony Blair and his cabinet at Downing Street, I remember thinking that our side of the table was terribly crowded. There was Bobby [Sands], Máiread [Farrell] and many many others, keeping us right, helping to steer us in the correct way.[184]

The importance of the commemorative culture as a means of rallying the faithful and presenting an image to the world was an established part of the Republican tradition.[185] As well as these directly political purposes, commemorative activities have a number of social functions and multiple meanings for participants and observers.[186] As Dolan has pointed out, Republican commemorations:

> are a chance to see who are remembered, how they are commemorated and the numbers of men and women who attend. There is a chance also to catch a glimpse of what Republicanism might mean to the people these honoured martyrs were supposed to have died for.[187]

Few speeches to Republican audiences were complete without 'a special appreciation... [to the IRA,] not just dead comrades and their families, but

---

182 Poster on sale in Sinn Féin bookshop, Belfast, July 2005.
183 G. Kelly, 'Standing on the threshold of historic change', *An Phoblacht*, 22 June 2006.
184 J. Nawaz, '"Think big" for Irish unity', *Daily Ireland*, 14 August 2006.
185 Bell, 1989, 436.
186 Bryan, 2000.
187 Dolan, 2003, 142.

the IRA today, sitting near you, proud to bring peace and justice too our society' [emphasis added].[188] The current political needs of the Provisional leadership are reflected in their tributes to the IRA's 'most pivotal role in this phase of the struggle' and the commitments to 'take up the mantle and do the best we can in the era that we live in. We must lead, strategize and use tactics suitable and workable for the twenty-first century. *That is the onerous task our fallen comrades leave us'* [emphasis added].[189]

This flattery was part of the leadership's management of the IRA to reassure volunteers about the importance of their role in past struggles. It was an important part of a contemporary battle of memory in which alternative versions of the past and of the future were in bitter dispute. Increasingly, the battle for memory was at the heart of conflicts about the future.[190] This role was especially significant when Republican opponents attacked the Provisionals as:

> Stormont parliamentarians [who] tell us that the hunger strikers were the beginning of their moves to accept the Good Friday surrender... No matter how often Mr Adams and his hangers-on perform the Pontius Pilate manoeuvre ... they will convince nobody that Bobby Sands ... died on hunger strike rather than wear a prison uniform no more than he died ... in order that young men and women could join the RUC/PSNI and wear a peeler's uniform.[191]

The IRA was not just an armed body of men and women; it also embodied a range of symbolic meanings that could be read by both supporters and opponents of the Provisionals. That the IRA was a name and a legitimating memory worth fighting over was evident from the Provisionals' earliest period, when they laid claim to the inheritance of the 'good old IRA' of the Tan war era.[192] However, these new forms of commemorative politics had a wider function than the traditional purpose of keeping the faith alive. The IRA could not go away just yet because it was too valuable an instrument to be abandoned. Like the Old IRA and Fianna Fáil, its presence was essential to prove that the Provisionals were still Republicans. Thus, the IRA's ideological role was probably more important than its overt paramilitary

188 Gerry Adams, quoted in J. Nawaz, '"Think big" for Irish unity', *Daily Ireland*, 14 August 2006.
189 G. Kelly, 'Standing on the threshold of historic change', *An Phoblacht*, 22 June 2006.
190 For example, see the reaction to Richard O'Rawe's claims about the 1981 hunger strike and the controversy surrounding a biography of Bobby Sands in A. Peddle, 'O'Rawe's nonsense', *An Phoblacht*, 1 June 2006; J. Hanley, 'Sands book controversy', *Forum*, February–March 2006; and D. O'Hearn, 2006.
191 S. Maguire, 'Bobby Sands and his comrades died on hunger strike rather than wear a prison uniform,' *Saoirse*, July 2006.
192 Sinn Féin, 1984; Danny Morrison, interview, 5 January 2005.

functions during a period when the Provisionals were preparing to enter devolved government.

In the new politics of Sinn Féin, the IRA was a significant resource in determining the authorized meaning of the past and thus shaping political understanding of the present as well. The hunger strike commemorations, posters and historical accounts published in 2006 showed that the legitimation of the present by the appropriation and commodification of the past has become central to the Provisional project, proving that there really is 'no better way to forget something than to commemorate it'.[193] This is especially true as the key turning points of Provisionalism's journey into the mainstream recede into history and become the distant past for people under 40.[194] The heroic names of the past become icons and sanitized relics; real history becomes packaged as 'Republican heritage', digestible for an era of Troubles tourism and hen parties transported in converted Saracen armoured cars. It is less 'lest we forget' and more 'lest we remember'.

The Provisional leadership did more than use the considerable historical prestige and contemporary political capital of the IRA to legitimate and further its political project. It translated the organizational charisma of the armed group into a form that portrayed Republican politics as the continuation of war by other means.[195] This militarization of politics gave the IRA vital symbolic and practical functions that were essential to the success of the transition from armed struggle to constitutional politics.

In this sense, the IRA had already gone into 'a new mode' after 1994 by transmuting into a 'political' form; at a time when politics is about the manipulation of meanings rather than real change, the Weberian charisma of the IRA, with just a whiff of cordite, is a potent and suitably ambiguous symbol. In a polity frozen by stasis and the mutual exhaustion of its contending ideologies, the leadership hopes that the historical memory of the IRA will offer some sense of political meaning in response to the predominant mood of disillusion.

For many, this search for meaning is an escape into the heroism and purpose of the past, not the rebirth of a new subjective form of political action. In this way, the IRA encapsulates a form of politics 'where the dramatization of past wrongs deflects the focus of concern away from the problems in the here and now ... [and] where the act of bearing witness

193 A. Bennett, *The History Boys* (screenplay), 2006. The Provisionals also demonstrate another of Bennett's aphorisms: 'There is no period so remote as the recent past.'

194 For examples of the rebranding of the IRA during this transitional period as it is reflected in the murals and popular culture of Republican areas, see Rolston, 2003, 3–16.

195 See Panebianco, 1988, 44–48 on the impact of charismatic power on the organizational form of a political party.

becomes an act of closure, an end in itself.'[196] In this way, a strategy that appears to offer a way forward is in fact a step backwards.

Even though these sub-cultures retain emotional power and resonance, their usefulness for direct political mobilization is increasingly limited. The general pattern was for forms of street politics and communal activism to meet with decreasing success by the late 1990s. Paradoxically, the rallies and events to commemorate the 25th anniversary of the hunger strike in 2006 were well attended, and this encouraged some to believe that the historical links had not been broken. However, what distinguished these events from the political activism of the 1970s and 1980s was that they were essentially commemorative, remembering a past that had clearly gone.[197] They were nostalgic gatherings of old soldiers, not the mobilization of new waves of activists. Despite the differences in scale and attendance, they shared a similar tone to those much smaller gatherings of dissidents in country churchyards remembering comrades of long ago.[198]

The withering away of the state?

The conventional wisdom is that the Provisional movement is finally coming to the end of a long transitional period that will see it emerge as more than a 'slightly constitutional party'. The analogy with Fianna Fáil is deliberate, but not complete. Despite taking on many of the styles and forms of conventional politics, there are still fundamental contradictions within Provisionalism. Fianna Fáil emerged from a political and military struggle that lasted ten years. Provisionalism has had 36 years to consolidate, not simply as a political movement, but as a structure of power with deep roots in Northern Irish society.

The consolidation of the Provisionals in the 1980s and 1990s broadly followed the patterns established when 'social movement organizations become players in the conventional political process, thereby losing their initial character as challengers to the *status quo* and the forces in power.'[199]Given that the British state played the decisive role in creating a new political and social terrain in this period, any understanding of the transformation of the Republican movement must begin with the relationship between the British state and the Provisionals.

Thus, while it is possible to disagree that this relationship has transformed the Provisional IRA into 'the armed militia of the British state', the paradox remains that the *character* of contemporary Provisionalism

196 P. Hadaway, 'Review of *Ardoyne: The Untold Truth*,' *Fourthwrite*, Spring 2003.
197 'Freedom in our time', *Daily Ireland*, 14 August 2006.
198 'Séan Mac Diarmada commemorated', *Saoirse*, July 2006.
199 Rucht, 1999, 153.

is significantly determined by the state.[200] The boundaries that frame its continued existence are defined by that power; even the strategic functions of the IRA, formally the part of the movement most structurally antithetical to British rule, are shaped in this way. The British state has been successful in achieving the main aim of all strategy: to force your will on an opponent with the minimum expenditure of resources.

However, the state's victory was not total or unqualified. The Provisionals were defeated, not destroyed. Any new political dispensation that sought permanence would have to accommodate them and their constituency in some form. The resulting synthesis was an uncertain one of constructive ambiguity, rather than the clear result that characterized 'victory' and 'defeat' in the politics of modernity. Timothy Garton Ash has argued in a similar vein, comparing Hizbullah, Hamas and the Provisionals in the context of 'building democracy' in the Middle East:

> Up to a point, you can fight the terrorist side while encouraging the political side. In fact, the name of the game is precisely to shift their calculus of self-interest towards peaceful politics, by increasing both the costs of violence and the benefits of participation... [A]long the way you have to negotiate with nasty people and regimes... [I]n this dirty, complicated world, advocates of armed struggle – terrorists if you will – can become democratic leaders. Like Menachem Begin. Like Gerry Adams. Like Nelson Mandela.[201]

Furthermore, although the British state had contained and largely integrated the Provisionals by 1998, it was through a process of co-evolution, which profoundly influenced the forms of state power in Northern Ireland.[202] This contradictory relationship was the product of a more complex dialectic than simply that 'the most powerful governments in the world... [wanted] Sinn Féin as a junior partner in pacifying a partitioned Ireland.'[203] Indeed, this co-evolution between the British state and the Provisionals had the effect of both institutionalizing and *strengthening* the movement as a political and social force in Northern Ireland.

The British and Irish governments have been tolerant of this hybrid form during the transitional period, and will continue to be for as long as the Provisionals are necessary interlocutors for the future political stability

---

200   Marian Price, a member of the Thirty-Two County Sovereignty Committee, quoted in White, 2006, 340. She was referring to Joe-Joe O'Connor, a member of the Real IRA, who, it was alleged, was murdered by the Provisional IRA.

201   T. Garton Ash, 'A little democracy is a dangerous thing – so let's have more of it', *Guardian*, 3 August 2006.

202   Oliver and Myers, 2003.

203   Hayden, 1999, x.

of Northern Ireland.[204] This transitional period has acquired an increasingly permanent character in which seemingly irreconcilable contradictions between constitutional politics and criminality – Bertie Ahern's grey areas – are ignored in the interests of moving the process forward.[205]

The journalistic comparisons between Republican criminality and the mafia probably owe more to the films of Francis Ford Coppola than to the sociology of insurgency. However, the Provisionals are presented with similar problems to those facing the fictional Corleone family in their transition from crime to legitimate activity. In both cases, the distinction between illegitimate and legitimate activity is ambiguous, because ultimately their legitimate business rests on the power and resources gained through illegitimate activity. Despite their respectability and status, neither can entirely break away from their past. In this way, contradictions are built into the institutionalized power of the movement, which ensures that the Provisional state is unlikely to wither away. Whatever the balance between the Armalite and the ballot paper, the Provisional movement's will to power remains undiminished. Its organizational forms may change, but in essence, it cannot go away.

204 For an example of this tolerance, see Peter Hain, Secretary of State for Northern Ireland, quoted in W. Graham, 'IRA committed to peace: McDowell', *Irish News*, 26 July 2006.
205 Moloney, 2006.

Part II

The Historic Compromise?

Introduction to Part II

For many, the pictures of Gerry Adams and Ian Paisley around the table in Stormont signalling their intentions of going into government together were a 'telling and forceful image' marking the end of the Troubles and the start of a new era in which 'real politics can begin' in Northern Ireland.[1] This was just the latest in a line of what one Secretary of State for Northern Ireland called 'it'll-never-happen moments', which reinforced the sense of normalization that had been a central strand in the narratives of the peace process since the early 1990s.[2]

If there was widespread agreement that these events were historic, there were contrasting views among the participants about their true meaning. For Gerry Adams they represented 'a new start ... with the potential to build a new, harmonious relationship between nationalists and Republicans and Unionists.'[3] Ian Paisley was characteristically more direct, claiming them as 'a great victory for the Unionist people' because 'Gerry Adams will sit in our Assembly – a British institution of the British state ... [and] will take an oath to ... support the rule of law,' which meant 'the end of Republicanism'.[4]

While the Provisionals claimed that they remained 'unrepentant Republicans', some within their political tradition agreed with the Democratic Unionists that it was they who were 'writing the agenda ... and forcing Republicans to adhere to their demands.'[5] To these other 'unrepentant Republicans', the historic compromise was a fundamental defeat for the Republican project, and marked a decisive shift in Northern Irish politics.[6] Other commentators pointed to the contradictions within this 'curious kind of peace', which they defined as simply the continuation

1   D. McKittrick, 'Two worlds come together to broker a new era of hope', *Independent*, 27 March 2007.
2   P. Hain, 'This time, it's we who will say "No surrender"', *Observer*, 11 March 2007.
3   O. Bowcott, 'Northern Ireland's arch-enemies declare peace', *Guardian*, 27 March 2007.
4   G. Adams, speech to Sinn Féin Ard Fheis, *Irish Times*, 29 January 2007; I. Paisley, 'We can lay the foundations for a better future', *News Letter*, 31 March 2007.
5   Paisley, 'We can lay the foundations'.
6   A. McIntyre, 'The cul de sac called "futility"', *The Blanket*, 27 March 2007, http://lark.phoblacht.net/AM1270307.html.

of war by other means.[7] In these assessments, a political Rubicon had not been crossed in 2007; the essential political conflict 'driven by invariant understandings of nationhood and political identity' remained intact.[8] So while the Provisional IRA had changed from being a revolutionary movement committed to overthrowing the state to a constitutional party prepared to govern it, many questions still remained unanswered about what exactly was ending and what was beginning as a result of this new departure.

One response is to explore how changes in Northern Irish society gave rise to new ideological forms, so that the new politics of Sinn Féin can be understood as a product of the new political economy within the region. Chapters 1 to 3 outlined how the hybrid organizational form of contemporary Provisionalism resulted from a dialectic between external forces of social and economic transformation refracted through the British state, and localized structures of power within the nationalist community. This interaction was as much ideological as organizational, and has continued to be a feature of Provisional politics throughout the peace process.

However, if this describes the *process* of institutionalization, it does not entirely explain the particular political *form* that Republicanism has taken in the 1990s and 2000s. To do this, many have drawn an analogy between Blair's modernization of the British Labour Party and Adams's transformation of the Provisional IRA into a party of government in the 1990s.[9] However, while it is easy to chart the Provisionals' apparent political evolution through a number of decisive events such as the Good Friday Agreement in 1998, the IRA's commitment to exclusively peaceful politics in 2005 and the recognition of the PSNI in 2007, simply labelling them as New Sinn Féin is not completely adequate as a definition of their politics. Indeed, it begs a number of further questions about the contradictions within the ideological structure of contemporary Provisionalism, and about how far these tensions are inherent within Republicanism as an historical force.

Provisionalism is perhaps best described as an ideological configuration rather than a unified body of ideas; it has remained a work-in-progress throughout its history because it is a site of contestation between elements of the universal and the particular, revealed especially in the tensions between civic and ethnic conceptions of identity and the nation. The pattern of Provisional ideological development is one of the emergence of the 'new ' from the 'old', rather than a narrative of radical breaks and

7 R. Dudley Edwards, 'Northern Ireland: a curious kind of peace', *First Post*, 28 March 2007, http://www.thefirstpost.co.uk.

8 P. Shirlow, 'Crossing the Rubicon?', *New Statesman*, 27 March 2007.

9 Maillot, 2005, chapter 2.

discontinuities. Thus, 'really existing Provisionalism' provided much of the raw material for the later discursive shift, showing how its changing characterization of loyalism, for example, reflected changes in the underlying structures of Republican politics.

Trying to determine the balance between these diverse strands of continuity and change within Republican politics is further complicated by the radical transformation of the wider ideological landscape that has taken place during the past quarter of a century. The weakening of traditional categories of left and right and the emergence of new forms of nationalism, for example, have produced contradictory patterns of politics that rendered the established ideological taxonomies unserviceable. These ideological changes have taken place alongside other major shifts in the nature of politics and structures of power, both domestically and internationally since the end of the Cold War. Taken together, these developments have made it increasingly difficult to characterize parties and ideologies in an age of political uncertainty.

The remaining chapters will discuss the impact of these new forms of politics on Provisionalism and, paraphrasing Tony Blair, consider whether Republicans have indeed become 'less Republican'. The politics of the peace process, and thus the new politics of Sinn Féin, have been decisively shaped by the decline of universalist ideologies and the acculturation of politics in the form of new types of identity politics. The impact of these changes at a discursive level was illustrated by Gerry Adams's frequent references to 'the process of peace-making and national reconciliation' as a way of overcoming 'the sad history of orange and green'.[10] Likewise, when Tony Blair echoed Adams's desire to 'build a new harmonious relationship' he drew on language that what would have been considered impossible before the peace process, but now forms the everyday platitudes of Northern Irish politics:

> [Paisley/Adams] won't stop Republicans or nationalists being any less Republican or nationalist, or making Unionists any less fiercely Unionist. But what it can mean is that people can come together, respecting each other's point of view, and share power.[11]

This argument would have previously been a *non sequitur* because, as *political ideologies*, there could be no compromise between Republicanism and Unionism. As in all forms of modernist politics, the victory of one meant the defeat of the other. The historic aim of an independent republic

---

10 Gerry Adams, quoted in D. McKittrick, 'Two worlds come together to broker a new era of hope', *Independent*, 27 March 2007.

11 D. Sharrock, 'No time for handshakes, but this was history in the making', *Times*, 27 March 2007.

was in contradiction to the maintenance of the Union. Throughout the nineteenth and twentieth centuries, Republicans had not sought an 'historic compromise'; rather, they wanted an historic victory that would transform Unionists into citizens of an all-Ireland state. However, the new politics constructed a radically different theoretical plane, illustrated by the moral framework and therapeutic language of the peace process. It was in this parallel realm of discourse rather than in the real world of politics, as traditionally understood, that these opposing ideologies were to be redefined and thus reconciled as *cultural identities*. Instead of a universalist narrative that transcends the divisions of particularism, identity politics become a form of conflict regulation that both manages and maintains the patterns of communal division in society.

Viewed in this light, the new politics of Sinn Féin take on a different appearance. For example, the central tensions within Provisionalism over the last twenty-five years have usually been defined as a struggle between the politics of the past and the politics of the future, frequently represented respectively by the armed struggle and electoralism. This is a false distinction, because these 'new ' forms are ultimately rooted in the particularist forms of identity politics and, as such, are cognate with long-established particularistic elements within Republicanism. Thus through an 'adroit nurturing of sectarian nationalism' in the communalized politics essential to the new dispensation, the Provisionals have secured 'a following that Republicanism at its most popular failed to attain'.[12]

In this way, the new politics of Sinn Féin are not a complete ideological break with their past. Reinforced by the structures of the post-Good Friday Agreement polity, Provisionalism retains significant elements from its own founding moment and from earlier forms of the northern nationalist political tradition. However, this legacy is not simply passed on unaltered; as we have seen, Republicanism's ideological trajectory is also determined by its interaction with external structures. Understanding how this dialectic between external forces and the Republican tradition determines the changing forms of the politics of identity and the politics of transition is the key to understanding the shifting balance between aims and means that underpins the new politics of Sinn Féin as a whole.

12 A. McIntyre, 'The cul de sac called "futility"', *The Blanket*, 27 March 2007, http://lark.phoblacht.net/AM1270307.html.

Chapter 4

The Ideological Origins of New Sinn Féin

The crisis consists precisely in the fact that the old is dying and the new cannot be born; in this interregnum a great deal of morbid symptoms appear.[1]

It is too early to say. [Chinese leader Zhou Enlai in 1989, when asked about the effects of the French Revolution.][2]

The party of moderate progress within the bounds of the law?[3]

Sinn Féin's decision in January 2007 to accept the legitimacy of the PSNI completed a process that fundamentally changed the nature of Provisional ideology, and radically transformed the contours of politics throughout Ireland.[4] The hand of history was felt on a great many shoulders in this period, but, for once, the description 'historic' was no mere political soundbite.[5] The logic of Provisional politics from the late 1980s seemed to lead inexorably towards this point, a process described by one Provisional as 'moving from an historical position, strategy and culture of resistance to one of engagement, negotiation and governance'.[6] It reflected a widely-held view that the vote signalled not merely the end of one form of Provisionalism, but, more generally, the passing of militant Irish Republicanism as a historic force.[7]

Beginning with the abandonment of abstentionism in 1986 and ending with the vote on policing in 2007, the Provisionals had revised so

---

1 Gramsci, 1971, 276.
2 Zhou Enlai, *Guardian*, 2 May 1989, quoted in Cohen and Cohen, 1995, 420
3 Hasek, 1973.
4 V. Browne, 'This is a good time for Ireland', *Irish Times*, 31 January 2007.
5 Tony Blair, speaking during the talks preceding the Good Friday Agreement, said: 'I feel the hand of history on our shoulder in respect to this'. Quoted on 'Blair tries to allay unionist concern', http://news.bbc.co.uk/1/hi/events/northern-ireland/latest-news/75664.stm.
6 L. McKeown, 'Out from behind the doors', *An Phoblacht*, 25 January 2007. For example, see the early Hume–Adams statements (quoted in V. Browne, 'This is a good time for Ireland', *Irish Times*, 31 January 2007), and the Provisionals' public reaction to the Framework Document 1995, outlined in McIntyre, 1995b, 25–26; and McLaughlin, 1995, 89–91.
7 Editorial, 'Not so alone', *The Times*, 29 January 2007.

many positions previously regarded as fundamental and crossed so many Rubicons that this sense of a qualitative historical shift within Republicanism seemed fully justified. Just as cultural critics had defined Ireland as a 'post-nationalist' society, it now seemed possible to use similar terminology to define the Provisionals as 'post-Republican'.[8]

It became commonplace to compare the Provisionals' trajectory with other revisionist projects. For example, the Provisionals' effective public relations and ideological modernization drew comparisons with New Labour's vacuous politics of presentational slickness and abandonment of core values.[9] Other comparisons were prompted by historicist parallels between the Provisionals' evolution into 'constitutional revolutionaries' in the 1990s and Fianna Fáil's embrace of 'slight constitutionality' in the late 1920s.[10] The Big Lad was following The Chief: the latest 'legion of the rearguard' had been transformed into yet another 'party of moderate progress within the bounds of the law'.

Similar assessments placed these developments within the historical context of northern nationalism and the narrowing of the political options open to Republicans from the mid-1980s. The Provisionals were contained within the common political space they shared and contested with constitutional nationalism, making it inevitable that in time New Sinn Féin would became the old SDLP writ large.[11]

However, if the process of ideological change was easy to describe, explaining its dynamics has proved less straightforward. No single narrative, whether told by commentators outside the movement or by the Provisionals themselves, seemed able to encompass entirely the dramatic ideological changes that have taken place.

Some explanations went beyond the cynical calculations of everyday politics and used the moral narrative of reconciliation to explain the Provisionals' movement into the political mainstream.[12] A related therapeutic discourse that has underpinned many accounts of the peace process interpreted these political developments within Republicanism as a form

---

8 Bean, 2002, 129–142.

9 A frequent criticism made by Republican 'dissidents' and contributors to *The Blanket*, http://lark.phoblacht.net.

10 The reference to 'constitutional revolutionaries' was made by a delegate, Paul O'Connor, at the Sinn Féin Extraordinary Ard Fheis of January 2007. See G. Moriarty, 'SF leadership get their way over support for PSNI', *Irish Times*, 29 January 2007. For these historical parallels, see C. Brady, 'No change on the IRA front', *The Village*, 26 February–4 March 2005.

11 Todd, 1990; Murray and Tonge, 2004, xvi.

12 Power, 2005, 55–68.

of closure and a new beginning.[13]

If this therapeutic language was not always convincing when applied to, or used by, the Provisionals, it did, however, point to the possible depth of the change in the movement's political psychology.[14] This process of psychological change was described by one leading Provisional as 'a long road moving from wishful thinking to accepting material conditions and then working to change those conditions'.[15] In this account, the shift from ideological absolutism to a more pragmatic relativism is not simply a story of political maturation. Rather, it renounces the previous emotional attraction of the images of a revolutionary struggle that almost 'seemed more appealing than reaching the objective itself. In hindsight it was never going to happen that way because Ireland is not Cuba or Vietnam.' In Sinn Féin's new politics of the 'real world', 'the struggle' is not synonymous with 'one particular tactic' alone and now requires new methods to achieve the movement's goals.[16] Benefiting from hindsight, it is a narrative that challenges the underlying assumptions of the Provisional project and indicates a lack of confidence in the possibilities for transformative politics in general.

In this reading, the ending of the IRA's armed struggle and its commitment to electoral politics represents a form of liberation, ending the fusion of self and ideal image that is held to be central to the animating *imaginaire* of 'utopian ideologies' such as nationalism and Marxism.[17] In similar vein, a sympathetic commentator argued that it was the strategy of armed struggle that cemented the movement's identity, rather than a specific ideology: the peace process enabled 'a new Sinn Féin to emerge, one that has gradually emancipated itself from its old partner [the IRA]' and its old politics.[18]

However, most Provisionals would rather not define their movement's political development in terms of such a liberation from the past, preferring to stress essential continuity rather than radical change. Consequently, the New Sinn Féin label was strongly rejected by the Provisionals themselves

---

13 D. McKittrick, 'Their aim? Reconciliation. Their means? Talking', *Independent*, 29 November 2006; Furedi, 2004, 172–174.

14 For a discussion of these wider issues of conflict, memory and reconciliation, see Arthur, 2002.

15 L. McKeown, 'Out from behind the doors', *An Phoblacht*, 25 January 2007. Significantly, McKeown drew on the experience and historical prestige of the prison struggles to justify his pragmatic strategy, echoing a familiar theme in Provisional politics.

16 McKeown, 'Out from behind the doors'.

17 See O'Brien, 2003.

18 Maillot, 2005, 4–5.

because of its overtones of Blairite revisionism and slickness.[19] Instead, they described these changes in position as essentially tactical accommodations, in which the Provisional head pragmatically overruled the Republican heart in order to achieve cherished long-term goals.[20]

These new forms of politics were presented as new forms of *struggle* that required 'an imagination that can see the "new" beginning to take form whilst the old still exists': it also required 'a rejection of absolutist positions' and a 'capacity to duck and dive, twist and turn in true guerrilla fashion to counter opponents' tactics'.[21] This 'imagination' helped the Provisional leaders to argue that their long-term strategy still remained that of 'ending Partition and removing the British state from Ireland', whilst they pursued immediate objectives 'to critically engage with the structures of society that affect the lives of the people we represent'.[22]

The distinction between immediate engagement and long-term objectives was one defining characteristic of New Sinn Féin's ideological structure; the softer language of transition and gradualism has replaced the maximalist imperatives of a revolutionary party. New Sinn Féin's rhetoric of transition elided the distinction between the maximum and the minimum programme to produce an image of 'a party which is, on one hand, pragmatic, prepared to make compromises and to listen, and on the other, [is] unswerving about its fundamental commitments'.[23]

For Republican critics of the contemporary Provisional project, this flexibility meant the abandonment of principle and the triumph of 'yes men and ceasefire soldiers ... who only got involved when it became trendy to be a Republican'.[24] New Sinn Féin typified the fashionable expediencies of contemporary political life, which these critics starkly contrasted with Republicanism's fixed sense of tradition and historical continuity.[25]

Merely comparing presentational techniques and political style does not interrogate ideological change. Republicanism cannot be theorized successfully within its own self-referential tradition; simply counterposing New Sinn Féin to an authentic, historically-defined Republican tradition

19 Eoin Ó Broin, Sinn Féin Director of European Affairs, interview, 17 July 2005.

20 Martin McGuinness referred to his own individual ideological battle in these terms. See G. Moriarty, 'SF leadership get their way over support for PSNI', *Irish Times*, 29 January 2007; P. Taylor, 'Paisley the peacemaker?', *Guardian*, 31 January 2007.

21 McKeown, 'Out from behind the doors'.

22 Sinn Féin Chairperson Mary Lou MacDonald quoted in A. Foley, '"We can create a new beginning to policing"', *An Phoblacht*, 1 February 2007.

23 Maillot, 2005, 4–5 and 23.

24 Letter to the editor, 'Did we fight for more than 30 years to achieve nothing?', *Irish News*, 16 December 2006.

25 A. Morris, 'We and SF are like oil and water: Ó Brádaigh', *Irish News*, 14 February 2007.

in reality tells us little about Irish Republicanism in general or Provisionalism in particular. Despite the makeover, Sinn Féin is not just another constitutional nationalist party. Both its history and its contemporary form as an institutionalized structure of power ensure that the contradictions between a revolutionary past and reformist present will continue to define its ideological trajectory. While some of these ambiguities can be explained as parts of a deliberate leadership strategy to reassure activists, the dynamics for this ideological and strategic shift cannot be solely found in the secret diplomatic history of Gerry Adams.[26] We need to examine a much wider range of forces and ideological currents, both within and without Provisionalism.

'The most powerful forces in the modern world history'[27]

There were several analytical problems in defining the politics of New Sinn Féin as they emerged in the last quarter of the twentieth century. The ideology of Provisionalism that emerged in the 1970s and 1980s contained many disparate and often contradictory elements. Whilst some of these could be considered traditional, many more were responses to events as they unfolded or were strongly influenced by other external ideological forms. By the strict yardstick of Republican tradition, Provisionalism, especially when expressed in the harsh urban tones of the 'war zone', was never traditional.

Radical critics saw these contradictions as fundamental political flaws: Republicanism was too broad and insufficiently critical an ideology, which 'obstructs the elaboration of a coherent revolutionary theory ... and is often only a short step away from opportunism'.[28] Others pointed to the theoretical limitations of Republicanism that 'confused ideology, principle, strategy and tactics'.[29] Defining Provisionalism as an essentially ambiguous and unstable ideological form accords perfectly with its history, although not with how that history and tradition have often been presented.

These issues were to emerge continually during the peace process. For example, one Republican in the late 1980s drew attention to these intellectual weaknesses during a discussion of the crisis of ideology within Provisionalism by arguing that:

---

26 See Moloney, 2002 for an influential account that stresses this conspiratorial narrative.
27 English, 2003, xxiv.
28 Tommy McKearney, former Republican prisoner, interview, 30 May 1998.
29 Eoin Ó Broin, interview, 17 July 2005.

> We need to be clear what our ideology is: what sort of beliefs does an Irish
> Republican have? If you think that this is only stating the obvious, then ask
> each member of your cumann to write down the four most important beliefs
> in Republicanism and compare answers.[30]

The other analytical problems are more general and rooted in the difficulties of defining ideologies in an era when the established political categories and classifications appeared increasingly inadequate. New ideological structures and forms have displaced the established terminology of left and right, and the 'old politics' of class and the nation that characterized the politics of modernity. Thus to understand exactly what was beginning and what was ending in Irish Republicanism engages much broader questions about the nature of politics in a period that supposedly saw the 'end of ideology'.[31]

Many Republicans saw their ideological history as a continuous unbroken tradition, but others saw instead 'a heterogeneous, hugely contested project which has been influenced by different political contexts and historical moments'.[32] This was reflected in the way that activists identified the major elements of Republicanism. These were frequently exemplified by the contributions of individuals such as Pearse and Connolly, who respectively embodied the cultural separatist and republican socialist strands.[33] Others stressed the historical tensions between the Republican goals of national and social liberation, and the influence of other ideological currents outside the Republican tradition.[34]

Republicanism was a broad church, which historically drew from a range of discontents and oppositional projects that embodied:

> the most powerful forces in the modern world history: the intersection of
> nationalism and violence, the tension between nationalism and the state, the
> interaction of nationalism and socialism and the force of aggressive ethno-
> religious identity as a vehicle for historical change.[35]

Whilst its central political demand for self-determination and the political independence of the nation are part of the ideological legacy of the Enlightenment, there are also strong particularist and essentialist strands within historical Irish Republicanism and contemporary Provisionalism,

30 Editorial, 'Crisis of ideas and ideology', *Iris Bheag*, 11, 1988.
31 For a discussion of the problem of defining the morphology of ideologies in the
    contemporary world, see Eccleshall et al, 2003, 9–11 and 217–236.
32 Eoin Ó Broin, interview, 17 July 2005.
33 Jim Gibney, interview, 2 August 2005.
34 Eoin Ó Broin, interview, 17 July 2005.
35 English, 2003, xxiv.

such as Catholic Defenderism and forms of ethno-nationalism.[36] Repub-licans themselves claim that their beliefs derive from the Enlightenment tradition (embodied in the French revolutionary goals of liberty, equality and fraternity) rather than in the explicitly Romantic forms of cultural nationalism.[37] They defined their political inheritance from the United Irishmen as 'the Republican tradition of separatism, secularism, anti-sectarianism and progressive nationalism'.[38] As one former leading Sinn Féin strategist put it:

> We are still fighting over the ideas of the French Revolution. Although we are in a different political space than ten or twenty years ago, these ideas are still important. While governments, political institutions and political landscapes change, these ideas continue to haunt us and dominate our political thinking.[39]

Republican claims to this common intellectual patrimony enable us to define its ideology in terms of another political legacy of the Enlight-enment: the distinction between the universal and the particular. These tensions between the politics of universalism and the politics of difference constitute a central contradiction within Provisionalism and, as such, provide a way of defining its ideology by relating it to the wider currents of historical and contemporary thought.[40]

These categories can be further refined by equating the politics of universalism with assertive ideologies that are culturally blind, stress a neutral civic equality and are theoretically based on the individual subject. The politics of difference, on the other hand, focus on identity by seeking recognition through parity of esteem, positive discrimination and collective rights. Taylor describes the central distinction as follows:

> With the politics of equal dignity, what is established is meant to be univer-sally the same, an identical basket of rights and immunities; with the politics of difference, what we are asked to recognize is the unique identity of this individual or group, their distinctness from everyone else.[41]

Exploring this unfolding dialectic between the universal and the particular

36 For an example of what is very much a minority current of ethno-nationalism within contemporary Republicanism, see G. McGeough, 'Inside view', *Hibernian*, October 2006, which argues that 'for the Irish nation, culture and language to survive and thrive our society must be permeated with Catholicism ... Ireland must be Catholic and free from the centre to the sea.'
37 Tom Hartley, former Sinn Féin General Secretary, interview, 19 August 2005.
38 Sinn Féin Education Department, no date.
39 Tom Hartley, interview, 19 August 2005.
40 Bourke, 2003, 1–20.
41 Taylor, 1994b, 38.

within Republicanism reveals an ideology and political form that is 'richer, more complex, layered and protean than is frequently recognized'.[42] It also reveals that the new politics of Sinn Féin are rooted in the older forms of Provisionalism. The particularist forms of identity and communal politics that were always implicit within its political configuration have moved centre-stage as a dominant form, reflecting the radically different external political environment and the changing patterns of social and economic life in Northern Ireland. Thus Sinn Féin was immanent within 'really existing Provisionalism', making it at the same time both a departure from and a product of the contradictions within Republican ideology.

If these political contradictions and ideological weaknesses within Provisionalism shaped the new *forms* of Republican politics, external forces significantly contributed to their substance. These factors ensured that the Provisionals could not simply become another Fianna Fáil or SDLP: all three parties have very different organizational trajectories and structural contexts, both during their founding moments and throughout their later development.[43] Above all, New Sinn Féin was born during a very different historical moment and in very different social and political terrain than either of its constitutional predecessors.

Some of these forces can be located in the new geopolitical framework and new forms of politics that emerged in the post-Cold War world. In particular, the emergence of particularist forms of cultural identity increasingly displaced the universalist categories of nation and class as a basis for political activity and public policy. Other influences were closer to home and reflected cultural and ideological change within Irish nationalism, as well as the organizational and ideological interaction between the Provisionals and the British state.

This resulted in new forms of Provisional identity and communal politics combining older particularist ideologies of community with the dominant British framing discourse of consociationalism and communitarianism. In this new international and local context, the fundamental questions about the politics of universalism and the politics of difference that had been posed since 1789 and 1798 were to be raised again in a new form and with different, yet familiar, results.

The deluge of the world

Just as Provisional ideology in the 1970s was influenced by wider currents and events outside Ireland, so the politics of New Sinn Féin were the product of the very different world order that came into existence in the

42 English, 2003, xxiv.
43 Murray and Tonge, 2004, xvi.

last quarter of the twentieth century. The period 1985–2005 saw dramatic changes that had as fundamental an impact on global politics and ideology as the First World War, or the decolonization of the European empires after 1945. The collapse of the Soviet Union and the apparent triumph of liberal capitalism, the ending of a bi-polar system of international relations and the emergence of apparently new forms of threat, such as 'fundamentalist' Islam, contrived to give Western democracies in the late twentieth century a contradictory character of both triumphalism and exhaustion.

The triumph was seen in the changing international context of what was referred to as the 'New World Order' in the early 1990s, and the defeat of a wide range of oppositional projects such as socialism and nationalism. For some, this process internationally went beyond a merely temporary setback for radical politics to become, as one former Provisional activist described the new politics of Sinn Féin, 'a sorry end to a once-inspiring revolutionary struggle'.[44]

This new 'deluge of the world' in the 1980s and 1990s ushered in a period of instability and challenge after the certainties that had underpinned the 'modes of thought of men, the whole outlook on affairs' for most of the twentieth century.[45] In this way, the ending of Hobsbawm's 'short twentieth century' could be defined as a qualitatively new historical period, which represented a failure of all transformative ideologies and political projects.[46] In particular, it posed an existential challenge to national liberation movements internationally, which were not only contained from without by the *force majeure* of the new international dispensation, but were also defeated from within by a sense of futility and disillusion. In the early 1990s it was clear, as McCann pointed out, that these movements – such as the Palestinian Liberation Organisation (PLO), the Sandinistas and the African National Congress (ANC) – were 'now in political and organizational disarray, diminished in the eyes of their own people ... as they seek a deal with imperialism to bring them in from the cold'.[47]

Increasingly, the changing shape of the post-Cold War world and its echoes in the world of ideas had a direct impact on Northern Irish politics, in particular producing 'the climate of cynicism and low expectations [that] has taken its toll on popular engagement in the nationalist cause'.[48]

44 P. Ferguson, 'Anyone for tennis?', *Weekly Worker*, 4 August 2005.
45 Winston Churchill speaking in the House of Commons, 16 February 1922, quoted in Stewart, 1977, 179. He was describing the cataclysmic changes that followed the First World War and their limited impact on Irish politics.
46 Hobsbawm, 1995.
47 McCann, 1993, 39.
48 Ryan, 1994, 9. See also Cox, 2006, 427–442.

This major shift in the social psychology of political radicalism and the decline in popular mobilization was a key factor in a number of peace processes that originated in this period.[49]

Republicans were aware of the impact of these developments on the political space within which they operated. Whilst most political decisions were directly influenced by local Irish conditions, many believed that events in the wider world influenced ideological development, even if only in an indirect way.[50] As one Provisional strategist describes it:

> the general retreat of the left had an impact on Republicanism when Republicanism was becoming increasingly isolated anyway... A while array of ideological positions no longer seemed applicable... [I]t was a period of flux and change when there was a sense of crisis and a lack of ideological certainty.[51]

During the Provisionals' Republican socialist phase in the late 1970s and early 1980s, they positioned themselves as national liberationists and closely identified with like-minded movements in the postcolonial states. However, unlike the Workers' Party, the Provisionals had not had sustained ideological or material links with the former Soviet Union or its allies.[52] The failure of these radical nationalist projects and the changing patterns of geopolitical power following the collapse of the Soviet Union as 'a counter-balance to western Imperialism' added to the Provisionals' own sense of containment and stalemate, which was growing in the early 1990s.[53] Ideologically, this saw a scaling back of socialist and populist rhetoric that 'moved the agenda of debate and thought within Republicanism away from changing society'.[54] Strategies of diplomatic *realpolitik* orientated towards the sole superpower and architect of the New World Order replaced revolutionary mobilization and international solidarity.

The strategic justification for this turn also had a wider conservative impact on Provisional politics and ideology. One leading Sinn Féin activist described the political implications of this new position:

> The politics of nationalist consensus were at the greener end of the Republican spectrum as opposed to the redder end of it. They were successful in ending Republican political isolation by building new relationships with Fianna Fáil, the SDLP and Irish America. These things happened coincidentally, yet simultaneously coalesced with the retreat of the left and the shift away from radical rhetoric by leading Sinn Féiners.[55]

49 Ryan, 1994; Ryan, 1997, 72–83.
50 Tom Hartley, interview, 19 August 2005.
51 Eoin Ó Broin, interview, 17 July 2005.
52 Danny Morrison, former senior Republican strategist, interview, 4 January 2004.
53 Eoin Ó Broin, interview, 17 July 2005.
54 Felim Ó hAdhmaill, former Republican prisoner, interview, 17 March 2006.
55 Eoin Ó Broin, interview, 17 July 2005.

The broad nationalist alliance involving the Dublin government, the SDLP and Irish America was directed at securing US diplomatic support and pressure on Britain.[56] The impact of US diplomatic intervention throughout the peace process is well established as a moderating influence on the Provisional leadership. This orientation towards the USA was one of the most consistent elements in the Provisionals' peace strategy and also one of the most problematic, causing tensions between the remnants of its leftist populist image and the reality of an alliance with conservative foreign interests identified with neoliberal exploitation.[57]

Some of the most important external influences on the ideological development of the Provisionals came in the form of the discourse and practice of peace processes, especially the South African experience. This occurred at a variety of levels. Seeing Republican leaders pictured with world leaders and playing the part of statesmen added to the credibility and prestige of the strategy in the context of a new political situation:

> This high profile made the strategy easy to sell. People were saying: when did this ever happen before? When had we world leaders wining and dining representatives of the Republican movement?... Pictures of Gerry Adams with Mandela and Arafat showed that we're not just an isolated group: we're on the move here.[58]

The very different experience of South Africa provided a blueprint and ideological master-narrative for the Provisionals. Not only was the moral authority of the struggle against apartheid appropriated by the Provisionals' explicit comparison between the ANC's campaign and that of the IRA, but there were also rhetorical and strategic borrowings from the South African experience of the 'politics of transition'.

The South African connection also served to influence and legitimate Provisional ideology and strategy more directly. Prominent members of the ANC spoke publicly in support of the leadership's strategy at Sinn Féin Ard Fheisanna, as well as at internal briefings and visits to Republican prisoners.[59] For some Republican critics of the Provisionals' strategy, the South African connection was both a template for the leadership's politics and a warning of its future conservative direction.[60]

56 As justified in the TUAS document, summer 1994. Reprinted as an appendix 2 in Moloney, 2002, 498–501.
57 D. O'Hearn, 'A radical political force for Ireland?', *Left Republican Review*, May 2003, 15.
58 Felim Ó hAdhmaill, interview, 17 March 2006.
59 See, for example, ANC support for the Republican leadership in the form of a visiting South African government minister during the policing debate in 2006–2007, cited in J. Gibney, 'See the opportunities – seize the moment', *An Phoblacht*, 11 January 2007.
60 Felim Ó hAdhmaill, interview, 17 March 2006.

It was not just radical critics who compared the Provisionals' trajectory to that of movements like the PLO and the ANC.[61] In its contacts with Sinn Féin, the Major government referred to the Rabin–PLO deal as a precedent for negotiations, and the peace process model that was established internationally during the 1990s became a point of reference for both the British government and Republicans, especially after the election of Tony Blair in 1997.[62] In this way, the transformation of the Provisional movement and its growing partnership with the British government was a local variant of a wider pattern in which 'the outsiders had become insiders ... [meaning that] the world looked a very different place from the new perspective'.[63]

Ennui and the end of history

This 'incredible journey' from the margins to the centre took the Provisionals into a very different and uncertain political mainstream from that of the 1980s.[64] The sense of crisis was not confined to the unstable polities and revolutionary movements of the developing world. Far-reaching changes in the forms of domestic politics in the west, such as the collapse of class-based politics, growing disillusionment with the political process and challenges to the legitimacy of the liberal democratic state, prompted widespread discussion about the nature of politics and even the future of ideological projects.[65]

One widely-acknowledged symptom of this trend has been an apparent de-politicization, linked to a crisis of meaning with regard to the concept of 'the political'. The increased privatization of life seemed to render the political process irrelevant. Declining electoral turnouts and falling membership rolls contributed to this sense of the collapse of organized mass parties, whether class-based or ideologically defined, which had been the main means of political engagement since the advent of universal suffrage.[66]

Even where grassroots politics seemed to survive, they became fragmented and particularist in form, disconnected from national and

---

61 McCann, 1993, 38.
62 For the Provisionals' account of these contacts, see Sinn Féin, 1994, 41. For one comparison among many between the Northern Irish peace process and international developments, see K. Cullen, 'Wise lessons from South Africa nurture peace in North', *Irish Times*, 13 May 2000. For a comparative analysis of these peace process models, see Darby and McGinty, 2003.
63 McGinty, 2006, 129.
64 'Northern Ireland: the incredible journey continues', *Guardian*, 29 January 2007.
65 For example, see Gray, 2003; 1995; and 1997.
66 Hobsbawm, 1995, 581.

global issues of a universalist character. In what is seen as an increasingly corporate-dominated consumerist culture that stresses individual interests, politics have lost their inspiring and empowering character, throwing the public sphere into a deep crisis.

In such a climate, citizens become consumers and political parties take on the character of pressure groups. These anxieties about the lack of faith in politics continued into the twenty-first century, which remained 'a paradoxical age ... a democratic society where there has been an unparalleled opportunity to address government and form networks, and never before has there been such a ubiquitous frustration about democratic politics. Politics has become disconnected from everyday life.'[67]

These strengthening symptoms of disillusion and disengagement from political life were the reflections of a fundamental ideological shift in developed societies in the last quarter of the twentieth century. This pervasive pessimism and a 'sense of terminus' suggested that the essential bases of politics that had been dominant since the Enlightenment were exhausted and devoid of further potential or even relevance to real life.[68] Ideas such as the 'end of politics' or the 'end of history' reflected a sense not only of closure, but also a crisis going beyond mere institutions and political structures.[69] This crisis was widely perceived to be universal and fundamental with an impact that was not just political and economic, but social and moral in character.[70] Moreover, it was an ideological exhaustion that seemed to affect both rulers and ruled, as confidence and certainty drained away from the political classes and former challengers alike.

It might reasonably be argued that such an apparently politicized and polarized society as Northern Ireland runs counter to these trends, suggesting that as in the aftermath of an earlier 'deluge of the world ... the integrity of their quarrel is one of the few institutions that has been unaltered in the cataclysm which has swept the world'.[71] However, commentators increasingly stress that the 'normalization' of northern Irish society is undermining these exceptionalist arguments. They point to those features that Northern Ireland is starting to share with other Western societies, such as declining political engagement and activist demobilization, differential electoral participation and a widespread boredom with conventional politics. One experienced observer accurately

---

67 S. Coleman quoted in P. Wintour, 'Defying political gravity from inside Whitehall', *Guardian*, 10 February 2007.
68 Furedi, 1992, 214.
69 For example, see Boggs, 2000; Mulgan, 1994; and Fukuyama, 1992.
70 Hobsbawm, 1995, 10–11.
71 Winston Churchill speaking in the House of Commons, 16 February 1922, quoted in Stewart, 1977, 179.

summed up the prevailing political mood that had been established by the early 2000s:

> Everyone up here is disillusioned. Even the staunchest supporters of the Belfast Agreement have grown weary of the endless cycle of crises and crux negotiations… In pubs, taxi depots and cafes, in-depth analysis focuses on the race for the English Premiership, not that for the peace deal. The strategies of Sir Alex Ferguson and Arsène Wenger arouse much more interest that those of Gerry Adams and David Trimble.[72]

If these patterns were true for Northern Irish politics in general, they were especially valuable in providing insights into the ideological and organizational shifts in Republican politics during the 1990s. Throughout the 1980s, many media commentators described high levels of popular engagement in politics in Republican areas, evidenced in electoral participation, public support for meetings and demonstrations, and political and cultural activism such as the West Belfast Festival.[73] The picture of political demobilization that emerged in the 1990s and 2000s was in marked contrast to this vibrant activism. As one Republican strategist explained it, this shift showed that 'there is an alienation at work in terms of the formal expression of politics, but it's contradictory because there are still other forms of informal community activism'.[74] Sinn Féin's perceived failure to mobilize significant support on the streets during contentious marches during the 1990s was typically described as a symptom of this deeper malaise:

> The Sinn Féin leadership didn't realize the significance of what was happening down here. They took their eyes off the ball by concentrating on the talks at Stormont. They're becoming men in suits and losing touch with what is happening on the ground.[75]

In this period, the Provisionals moved from the politics of the streets into the anterooms of power: the days of revolutionary mobilization in any thing other than a commemorative or rhetorical sense were long over. However, many activists had believed in 1994 that the new forms of post-ceasefire politics would see a return to 'the mass mobilizations of the civil rights period, producing a type of republican intifada'.[76] They were to be disappointed, both in the unwillingness of the nationalist population to

72 S. Breen, *Irish Times*, 25 April 2003.

73 For an example of the mobilization of new voters and a new base in the 1980s, see E. Moloney, 'Success of Sinn Fein big threat to SDLP', *Irish Times*, 22 October 1982; and 'Test for Sinn Fein electoral strategy', *Irish Times*, 22 March 1983.

74 Jim Gibney, interview, 2 August 2005.

75 Gerard Rice, member of Lower Ormeau Residents Group, interview, 7 April 2003.

76 Felim Ó hAdhmaill, interview, 17 March 2006

be drawn back into these politics and because Provisional strategy itself was now essentially one of managed retreat and negotiation.

Criticisms of the growing remoteness of Sinn Féin politicians, their attempts to restrict debate and the alienation of 'the base' made during the Republican debate on policing before the Sinn Féin Ard Fheis in 2007 echoed similar complaints made about establishment politics throughout Western society.[77] Taken together with other indicators of the level of political and community activism, this evidence shows an increasing trend towards a political disengagement in Northern Ireland, similar in character to other European polities.

The 2007 assembly elections confirmed these trends. Electoral contests across Northern Ireland are shaped both by the communal dynamic *between* Unionism and nationalism, and competition *within* the communal bloc between parties competing for votes. This produces a series of contradictory and differential patterns that can be attributed to class and geographical factors, alongside increasing political apathy towards traditional communalized politics.[78] Examples of the current tendencies towards apathy rather than activism include a decline in those registering to vote (especially in working-class nationalist wards such as the Upper Springfield area of West Belfast), limited interest in Sinn Féin-organized protests, and electoral turnout figures in line with those in rest of the UK and the Irish Republic.[79]

77   For criticisms and examples of this political disengagement within Provisionalism, see 'Republicanism – a failed ideology?', *New Republican Forum*, February 2003, G. Moriarty, 'Sinn Féin battles for Republican hearts and minds over policing', *Irish Times*, 29 November 2006; T. Catney, 'Always tell the truth', letter to the editor, *Irish News*, 2 December 2006; and C. Simpson, 'Sinn Féin "threatens" objectors to policing', *Irish News*, 3 January 2007.

78   See, for example, the differential turnout between rural nationalist areas west of the Bann (averaging at 72.1 per cent) and urban areas in Greater Belfast (62.3 per cent). Data from http://news.bbc.co.uk/1/shared/vote2007/nielection/html/main.stm.

79   In the 2005 Westminster election, turnout in Northern Ireland was 62.9 per cent, compared with 61.3 per cent for the UK as a whole. The equivalent figure for the Irish Republic was 62.7 per cent. Data from http://cain.ulst.ac.uk (accessed 14 February 2007), and Kennedy, 2002. The average turnout in local government and Northern Ireland Assembly elections from the early 1980s is 63.2 per cent. W. Graham, 'Dramatic changes lie ahead on the political landscape', *Irish News*, 28 November 2003. Voter registration also reflects these contradictory patterns. The latest electoral register showed a fall of 7 per cent from 2005 to 2006, resulting in 82,000 fewer people on the register. West Belfast showed the largest fall, 15 per cent, followed by North Belfast with 10 per cent, which resulted in a vigorous voter-registration campaign by Sinn Féin to re-engage with these key constituencies. D. McCarney, 'One in four voters not on the register', *Andersonstown News*, 7 December 2006; 'Register now', *Nuacht an Iarthar/West Belfast News*, December 2006.

The election campaign itself was described as 'one of the most low-key in recent memory', because 'no single new issue has emerged ... to capture the imagination of the wider public'.[80] Despite the 'historic' nature of the election, there were widespread comments on political apathy within the nationalist population.[81] Whilst the communal Orange and Green voting blocs remained intact (and were indeed strengthened to some extent), it was widely argued that these elections were also increasingly about bread-and-butter issues, and how these would be dealt with by a devolved government.[82] As one British journalist observed, 'the border issue – for so long the only issue that mattered – has for the first time disappeared from the electoral agenda'.[83] The overall turnout, at 63 per cent, continued to fall compared to 1998 and 2003. The nationalist electorate had already taken the possibility of a Sinn Féin–DUP executive into account in making its electoral calculations. Sinn Féin proved to be an effective electoral force, consolidating its position as the largest nationalist party and remaining the dominant representative of nationalist opinion in Northern Ireland by increasing its share of the vote and gaining seats at the expense of the SDLP.[84]

The real battles were within the nationalist bloc to decide who would best represent the communal interest in the post-election bargaining with Unionism and the British government, as well as in the battles in the executive that would inevitably follow. In 2007, despite some remaining uncertainties about the DUP's attitude to working with the Provisionals in a devolved executive, 'Sinn Féin's enthusiasm for government was now taken for granted'.[85] The Provisionals declared themselves 'eager to get down to the business of tackling the very many social and economic issues which came up on the doorsteps, be it water charges, rates increases or health and education cuts'.[86]

This electoral success was built on that synthesis of new and existing ideological forms which had proved eminently serviceable to meet the immediate political needs of the Provisionals during their transitional

---

80 'Fire has gone out of election', editorial, *Irish News*, 26 February 2007.

81 'No excuse for election apathy', editorial, *Irish News*, 6 March 2007.

82 M. Devenport, 'A bread and butter election?', BBC News, 25 February 2007, http// www.bbc.co.uk/blogs/election07/northern-ireland/2007/02 a_ bread_and_butter... ; S. McKinney, 'Challenge to SF on police may upset the status quo', *Irish News*, 1 March 2007.

83 D. Sharrock, 'From murder rates to water rates', *The Times*, 5 March 2007.

84 Data from http://news.bbc.co.uk/1/shared/vote2007/nielection/html/main.stm.

85 D. McKittrick, 'Hain resumes peace push after Northern Ireland elections', *Independent*, 19 March 2007.

86 Sinn Féin's chief negotiator, Martin McGuinness, quoted in McKittrick, 'Hain resumes peace push'.

phase. However, its long-term success remains uncertain; attempts to address Provisionalism's deeper ideological exhaustion since the late 1980s by producing 'a liberating ... ideology which is capable of motivating people' and overcoming the apathy of the 'anti-imperialist community' have failed in their own terms.[87] In the new Northern Ireland, where 'politics seem to be about how much additional expenditure party leaders can jointly secure from the Treasury', Republicans are unlikely to prove to be ultimately more successful than other politicians elsewhere who draw on the particularistic language of identity and tradition in their attempts to rally the faithful and breathe new life into tired politics.[88]

The politics of identity and community

One ideological response to this ideological crisis in western societies was derived from the currents of postmodernism. This contemporary movement in thought has been characterized by its rejection of the possibility of objective knowledge, scepticism towards the possibilities of truth, unity and progress, and hostility to those meta-narratives that claimed rationality and universality, such as Marxism and liberalism.[89] These patterns of thought became increasingly influential as the traditional categories of left and right were deemed no longer relevant to contemporary politics.[90]

In comparison with political projects that made fundamental critiques of the status quo or aimed at radical transformations, the dominant discourse at the end of the twentieth century reflected a scaling-down of ambition that ultimately adapted and accommodated itself to the world as it is. As one critic accurately argued, 'the ideology of the end of modernity and progress corresponds to a sense of retreat from radical ambition'.[91] In these forms, postmodernity was both a rejection and a product of modernity; as such, it was both a radical break with the Enlightenment project and a direct result of the defeat of the left.[92]

Forms of identity politics, official multiculturalism and changing conceptions of the nation epitomized this retreat from radical political ambition. Originating in the anti-establishment politics of the post-1968

---

87 J. Gibney, 'A liberating philosophy', *Socialist Republic*, August–September 1989.
88 'Butter or guns', editorial, *The Times*, 5 March 2007.
89 Eagleton, 2003, 13.
90 For an interesting discussion of some of these themes, see Anderson, 2005.
91 Heartfield, 2002, 103.
92 Davidson, 2006. For examples of the implications of this break with modernity, see, Bauman, 1992; Baudrillard, 1988; Eagleton, 1996; Callinicos, 1989; and Furedi, 1992, viii.

'new left', these political and cultural ideologies increasingly focussed on identity and its parent framework, tradition, as the central organizing principle of contemporary politics. With the failure of the class-based politics of the 'old left', which looked to the working class as the agency for change, the 'new left' found alternatives in other new social movements, such as developing world national liberation struggles, feminism and gay rights.[93]

These politics of difference were identified with radical anti-establishment politics because they adopted as their starting points the construction of identities oppositional to dominant norms. In calling into question the claims of hegemonic cultures, the formation of counter-cultural identities becomes the main site of resistance and action. Conditions of oppression and exclusion were frequently inverted to become a source of strength and pride, as in the case of Black Power in the USA and in some forms of Irish cultural nationalism. Identity was thus presented as a product of exclusion and oppression that could also become a source of inner strength and nobility. By placing the definition, negotiation and constant reinterpretation of identity at the heart of politics and culture, the result is the acculturation of contemporary politics.[94] If the personal is political, then the political is now cultural.

Despite an iconoclastic reputation, these ideas can be considered as deeply conservative, implicitly rejecting forms of politics based upon the transcendence of existing categories of identity. The historical origins of these forms of politics can be located in the Romantic reaction against the Enlightenment. Identity politics are cognate with essentialist forms of nationalism rooted in the concept of the *ethnos*.

With its stress on the uniqueness of the *Volk*, this tradition emphasized the irrational and given nature of the nation as a community of fate. The *Volksgeist*, defined as the eternal soul of a people, is reflected in primordial elements such as language and race, which set a people apart and produce cultures that are authentic and to be valued in their own *particularist* terms, rather than by the *universal* criteria of the Enlightenment.

Within this framework, 'identity is the passive by-product of history… As it were, one is simply born into it, history supplies the rest.'[95] As such, identity politics represent the victory of tradition over consciousness and, for the left, abandon 'secular universalism for ethnic particularism'.[96] Political projects of change are thus replaced by projects

---

93   Chaliand, 1976; della Porta and Diani, 1999, 1–20.
94   Barry, 2000, 72–73.
95   Furedi, 1992, 258.
96   Malik, 2005, 54.

of cultural formation, stabilization and management. For its critics, new postmodernist is but old conservative writ large.

Identity politics have been criticized as the product of ideological disintegration and a way of rationalizing the left's impotence in the 1990s, becoming, in the process, 'the ideology of an era without ideology'.[97] As the US critic Russell Jacoby has suggested, 'stripped of a radical idiom, robbed of a utopian hope, liberals and leftists retreat in the name of progress to celebrate diversity. With few ideas on how a future should be shaped, they celebrate all ideas.'[98]

As we shall see, these essentialist elements were already present within Provisionalism in the form of cultural nationalism and particularist forms of communal identity. These internal tendencies were strengthened by this wider climate of ideas, and the influence of other ideological projects and external forces with which Republicans came into contact. For example, the US experience of affirmative action and positive discrimination, as encapsulated in the MacBride Principles and rooted in particularist categorization, was a significant ideological influence in the late 1980s as the Provisionals developed policies to eliminate discrimination and disadvantage.[99]

However, it was the British state and the British left that most directly influenced the ideology and practice of Provisional communal and identity politics. The discourse of the British state, which reflected forms of multiculturalism in its language of communal reconciliation between the 'two traditions', was a powerful influence throughout Northern Irish society. The forms of identity politics developed by Ken Livingstone and others on the British Labour left, and implemented through the diversity policies of the GLC in the 1980s, presented a radical counter-narrative that was adapted by Republicans to their ideological needs. Identity politics certainly resonated with established nationalist discourse. In defending these forms of identity politics, some Republicans argued that their ideology has:

> always recognized the plurality of different kinds of struggle in comparison with the rigidities of class-based meta-narratives such as Marxism: the development of 'identity politics' meant that the political left has simply discovered political and cultural realities that have been around for hundreds of years.[100]

---

97 Ibid.
98 Quoted in Malik, 2005, 55–56.
99 See MacNamara, 2006.
100 Eoin Ó Broin, interview, 17 July 2005.

However, identity politics in the contemporary world are ultimately contradictory. They are frequently framed as subversive counter-narratives to a dominant discourse, whilst at the same time seeking forms of legitimation and recognition rooted in the hegemonic discourse they claim to challenge. This was particularly true when identity politics were translated in the 1990s into public policy as a form of communitarianism that Amartya Sen defined as 'plural monoculturalism'.[101] This attempted to redefine the relationship between alienated individuals and society by recreating the idea of community as an organic *gesellschaft* in which individualism and particularist interests are subordinated to the common good.[102]

Frequently expressed in nostalgic terms and moral panics, it can appear to be a lament for a world we have lost by counterposing organic definitions of community to the contemporary destruction of communities by social and economic change, and an unbalanced emphasis on individual rights.[103] Hobsbawm describes these attempts at reinvention in terms evocative of contemporary Northern Ireland:

> It was not a crisis of one form of organizing societies, but of all forms. The strange calls for an otherwise unidentified 'civil society', for 'community' were the voice of lost and drifting generations. They were heard in an age when such words, having lost their traditional meanings, became vapid phrases. There is no other way to define group identity, except by defining the outsiders who were not in it.[104]

The central aim of these politics is to strengthen solidarity and political legitimacy by reworking themes of identity, community and nation in a convincing collective narrative.[105] Communitarianism was a way of rebuilding not only social solidarity, but also the broader authority of states, institutions and parties increasingly challenged by apathy and quiet hostility from their citizens. Although communitarian theorists and political advocates have frequently been drawn from what can be defined as the left, the appeal of this approach is its success in drawing on discursive elements from across and beyond what is increasingly seen as the irrelevant polarities of right and left.[106] However, the very terminology of

101 Malik, 2006, 64–66.
102 Etzioni, 1995.
103 For specifically Irish examples of communitarian discourse, see U. Mallaly and K. Rafter, 'Is Bertie really following the advice of his guru?', *Sunday Tribune*, 11 September 2005.
104 Hobsbawm, 1995, 11.
105 For some examples of a wide-ranging debate in the Anglophone world, see Wolfe and Klausen, 2000; and Goodhart, 2006.
106 Giddens, 1994.

reinvention is itself suggestive of crisis and collapse, drawing as it does on 'such conservative words as family, kin, neighbourhood and community [which] have long held appeal for the political clerisy in the West'.[107]

The ideological strands of identity politics and communitarianism became central in defining the framework for political and social life in Northern Ireland. These discourses were central to the Third Way project and domestic politics of Tony Blair and Bill Clinton in the 1990s.[108] Communitarianism was also at the heart of EU social and economic policy as applied to Northern Ireland.[109] One of the attractions of communitarianism is that its origins can be located in the discourse of Catholic social teaching, making these apparently new approaches congruent with established nationalist culture and politics in Ireland.[110] By drawing on these older traditions and communal structures, the discourse of cultural identity was strengthened both in nationalist civil society and amongst a range of political actors. In conjunction, these forms defined the ideological climate in which the Provisionals formulated their aims, made their demands to the state and mobilized their supporters on behalf of 'their' community.[111]

The politics of recognition in Northern Ireland

The conflict between the politics of difference and the politics of universalism is fully reflected in the public and political sphere in Northern Ireland. Conflicting identities are widely perceived to be the central dynamics of political and cultural conflict in the region, subsuming and marginalizing other explanations rooted in universal categories such as class.[112] As the dominant power in the region, the British state's framing discourse stresses the fundamental duality of the conflict, and emphasizes that political structures should ensure equality between the two traditions.[113] It is this understanding that shapes the public sphere in Northern Ireland, rather than the aim of constructing an alternative political space to the particularized structures of Republicanism and Unionism.

Attempts at political settlement since the 1970s have been rooted in

107 Nisbet, 1986, 107.
108 For one example (among many) of the political influence of this discourse, see P. Wintour, 'Blair plans new social contract', *Guardian*, 24 November 2006.
109 Murtagh, 2001.
110 Robson, 2000, 114–135.
111 For a discussion of the British state's social and ideological impact on aspects of community development in the nationalist community, see McVeigh, 2002. For evidence of Republican awareness of this impact, see Sinn Fein, undated 1991?.
112 Ruane and Todd, 1996.
113 McGarry and O'Leary, 2004, 270–272.

these politics of difference and have been designed to manage rather than resolve conflict.[114] For example, the framework document agreed by the British and Irish governments in 1995 reiterated what had been a central theme since 1972: the starting point for a political settlement in Northern Ireland must rest on 'the balance of legitimacy' between the two traditions and communities.[115] Politics within Northern Ireland, it was argued, should 'respect the full and equal legitimacy and worth of the identity, sense of allegiance, aspiration and ethos of both unionist and nationalist communities'. Furthermore, the British government guaranteed that the administration of the region should be based on 'full respect for and equality of, civil, political, social and cultural rights, and freedom from discrimination for all citizens, on parity of esteem, and on just and equal treatment for the identity, ethos and aspirations of both communities.'[116]

The Good Friday Agreement itself continued these themes. The *Irish Times* described the forces that shaped the agreement as arising from patterns of cultural change, in which 'nineteenth-century concepts of political exclusivity built around the nation-state are yielding to more complex notions of identity and allegiance... The way forward is in compromise, in trust and in a true willingness to respect diversity.'[117] The agreement's three strands and institutional structures bestowed equal legitimacy on two fundamentally conflicting Republican and Unionist aspirations, reflecting not simply a skilful piece of political legerdemain but also the absorption of political discourse into a cultural framework.[118]

Specific British government policy initiatives across the public sphere supported the development and consolidation of this new discursive framework. The structures of 'civil society' in particular were defined as a decisive arena for shaping political attitudes. This was reflected in a developing policy consensus within the political class and key opinion formers in civil society such as the churches, the media and the voluntary sector. Through these social channels, the politics of difference began to be reflected at all levels of cultural production, political discourse and social activity.

The framing discourse of the British state, expressed in these multicultural terms, also determined the form of social and economic strategies for community development. Given that the imperatives of identity politics structured funding regimes and resource allocation, this discourse had an obvious influence on community organizations and activists within the

114 Cunningham, 2001; Dixon, 2001; Neumann, 2003.
115 Nic Craith, 2003, 55.
116 'The Framework Document 1995' in Elliott, 2002, 215.
117 'Easter 1998', *Irish Times*, April 1998.
118 Elliott, 2002, 223–225.

nationalist population. Ranging from background financial support for the activities of the voluntary and community sectors through to direct intervention to encourage diversity and cross-community partnerships, this process might be defined as social engineering by mission statement and funding application.[119] Alongside the voluntary sector, the work of statutory bodies and supporting initiatives such as the Cultural Traditions Group, the Central Community Relations Unit, the Northern Ireland Community Relations Council and Education for Mutual Understanding aided the development of new political models. The transmission of new ideas into existing structures was reflected in the facility with which community relations and cultural traditions funding supported the growth of the community sector in nationalist areas throughout the 1990s.[120]

The strength of this discourse in civil society, and indeed the increasingly politicized use of the idea of 'civil society' as an alternative framework, was indicated by the evidence, findings and report of the Opsahl Commission in 1993.[121] The methodology of the citizens' inquiry, it was argued, provided 'a shared space where dialogue and debate can begin to take place ... away from the barriers of a divided society'.[122] Opsahl focused on managing the central problematic at the heart of the paradigm of self-determination and majority rule in a divided society by arguing for political institutions based on the concept of parity of esteem and the politics of cultural identity.[123]

Politics in the region are thus conducted through such discourses of identity and recognition, which one observer sees as a process where 'the recognition of cultural diversity is essentially an acknowledgement of cultural otherness ... an acknowledgement of difference legitimizes the existence of separate groups with distinct identities'.[124] This has also strengthened the idea of politics in Northern Ireland as simply a form of communal bargaining and supplication for resources from the state.[125]

In this respect at least, Northern Ireland can no longer be considered an exceptional case. These patterns of multiculturalism and identity politics have become dominant in public life and discourse in Western societies generally, ostensibly shifting power from the centre to the periphery. In these 'new economies', where access to state resources remains vital for the marginalized and socially excluded, the functions of mediation and

---

119 As discussed in Chapters 2 and 3.
120 Cultural Traditions Group quoted in Nic Craith, 2003, 52.
121 Pollak, 1993.
122 Ibid., 393.
123 Ibid. See also Gallagher, 1994.
124 Nic Craith, 2003, 16.
125 For a fuller discussion of these issues, see Chapters 1 and 2.

cultural politics may provide focus points of activity for those political actors seeking to appeal to such disempowered groups.[126] In this way, the power of the state to define the categories of these differences and thus ultimately the patterns of politics in the region is increased through these processes of recognition.[127] The result, as one critic has argued in another context, is that the 'politics of difference' becomes a:

> formula for manufacturing conflict, because it rewards groups that can most effectively mobilize to make claims on the polity, or at any rate it rewards ethno-cultural political entrepreneurs who can exploit its potential for their own ends by mobilizing a constituency around a sectional set of demands.[128]

Much of the public sphere and cultural practice in Northern Ireland functions in this way. As O'Doherty has convincingly argued, it is a conscious strategy used by the state and political entrepreneurs alike to define and delineate separate communities for the purposes of mobilization or resource allocation. The result is that:

> The politician reads 'culture' as allegiance and 'community' as support. Public bodies have been trained by a political process into thinking and operating within these frames... The ossification of culture is a political project in Northern Ireland. It suits the basic model for describing our politics and our conflicts to include everything in the categories that political movements have established. That way, political movements feel entitled to take responsibility for wider areas of our thinking and to demand conformity.[129]

Identity politics and the 'imagined Ireland'

Another set of important influences on the Provisionals' ideological development were the changing patterns of Irish nationalist culture and politics on both sides of the border. This was part of a much wider intellectual shift produced by a combination of the wider 'deluge of the world' and the

126 It has been argued that this notion of group empowerment within postmodern political arrangements is illusory. Barry, for example, argues that any society from which the notion of the objectivity of truth has disappeared can only function as a dictatorship: 'There is no way in which decisions taken by a majority can be accepted by the minority unless both sides occupy a common universe ... (and) only by the exertion of absolute power could a set of common (if constantly changing) beliefs be established'. Barry, 2000, 21.

127 For example, Democratic Unionist politicians argued that they had gained a series of benefits from the British government on behalf of 'their community' during the negotiation of the St Andrews Agreement. S. Dempster, 'Leaders of DUP and UUP meet over St Andrews', *News Letter*, 8 November 2006.

128 Barry, 2001, 21.

129 O'Doherty, 2003, 74–75.

specific local characteristics of Irish culture and society in the 1980s and 1990s.[130] Social and economic change from the 1960s onwards prompted a wider debate about the nature of Irish society and identity that challenged the dominant political and social orthodoxies of the southern state.[131] The Troubles had also reopened some old questions about the national project and the methods necessary to realize it.

By the 1980s, Catholic and nationalist certainties were perceived to be in retreat before the forces of modernization and secularization, meaning that 'the real force behind the changes in Irish politics has proved to be not so much the force of the new as the decay of the old'.[132] The accelerated economic and social changes ushered in by the 'Celtic tiger' in the 1990s and 2000s also had a significant impact on how the nationalist project was to be defined, by friends and foes alike.[133] The developing social and economic position of sections of the nationalist population within Northern Ireland also contributed to a greater sense of self-confidence and helped to shape a new understanding of their specific cultural identity.[134]

The confluence of these factors resulted in a wide-ranging political, cultural and historiographical debate about the historical origins and contemporary nature of Irish identities.[135] Although largely dealing with matters of ostensibly cultural and academic interest, these controversies had an impact far beyond the seminar room and editorial office. The vigour of the debate was a product of this wider ideological significance and political impact. As Howe describes it:

> The intensity of these culture wars, the unusually high profile of literary politics in Ireland and its intrinsic intertwinement with arguments over historical interpretation, national identity and politics … in the … conventional sense help explain the sharpness of the contestation.[136]

In one sense, these questions continued the concerns of earlier 'decades of debate', but the answers given showed the emergence of new voices in Irish public life clearly influenced by the new forms of identity politics

130 Brown, 2004; Ferriter, 2004, 1–27.
131 Fennell, 1986.
132 Ryan, 1994, 95. McDonald 2004 also considers the impact of socioeconomic change on Irish cultural values and identity.
133 The impact of the 'Celtic tiger' phenomenon on the psychology and politics of Northern Ireland has yet to be fully assessed, but it does appear to have contributed to the mood of nationalist self-confidence and sense of Unionist retreat. For example, see C. Heatley, 'Unionists look south as job cuts bite deep,' *Sunday Business Post*, 29 October 2006.
134 O'Doherty, 2003, 79.
135 Brady, 1994.
136 Howe, 2000, 142.

and cultural criticism that emerged in western societies during the 1970s and 1980s.[137] One influential strand of this cultural criticism argued that political conflict could be transcended and resolved by the unifying force of culture.[138] Writers for Field Day, for example, discussed the idea of the 'Fifth Province' as a cultural space for the development of new ideas and identities annexed to the other four provinces.[139]

Another influential counter-narrative reflected the considerable impact postcolonial theory had on Irish political and cultural discourse from the 1970s onwards.[140] These critics drew from a range of anti-colonial thinkers and activists such as Frantz Fanon and Edward Said, and stressed the significance of the residual psychological and cultural impact of colonial rule on former colonial societies.[141] By defining Ireland as postcolonial in this way, the cultural left stressed the country's unique historical position and contradictory contemporary culture.[142]

This resulted in some criticism that these new approaches were simply traditional nationalism 'expressed in the accents of fashionable theory'.[143] Moreover, some responses from the cultural left to the challenge of revisionist public intellectuals seemed to confirm this alignment. The intellectual climate was indicated by one influential theorist who argued that 'the rhetoric of revisionism obviously derives from the rhetoric of colonialism and imperialism'.[144]

In one sense, the insights of the cultural left were cognate with the established narratives of Republicanism, in that they valorized the subaltern and celebrated an historically-informed victimhood.[145] In identifying with the politics of the cultural left, it might appear that Republicans were simply maintaining their traditional position and defending the conventional pieties of nationalist culture.[146] However, by arguing for an historical and contemporary voice for the excluded and the marginalized, the cultural left posited its own form of pluralism, which challenged

---

137 The description of the 1960s and 1970s as 'the decades of debate' is made in Brown, 2004, 254–296.
138 For some examples of this debate, see Pine, 1985; Witoszek and Sheeran, 1985; and Kearney, 1991.
139 See, for example, Kearney, 1997; and Deane, 1991.
140 For one contemporary response to this debate, see Fennell, 1983.
141 For example, see Kiberd, 1995, 184–186 and 557–558; and Deane, 1991, 608.
142 See Coulter, 1990.
143 Brown, 2004, 406.
144 Seamus Deane quoted in Brown, 2004, 406.
145 Howe, 2000.
146 For examples of these intellectual and political currents, see the contributions to Cullen, 1998.

traditional Republicanism and helped to reshape Provisional politics in ways that would become obvious only during the peace process.[147]

Despite the clear battle-lines between postcolonialism and revisionism, both intellectual currents, in their several ways, popularized concepts of Irish identity as plastic, malleable and capable of a variety of readings. Both revisionism and the cultural left developed alternative narratives of Irish history and culture that challenged established positions and contributed to the formation of a new climate of opinion. In these forms of cultural criticism, Ireland was a blank canvas to be painted on by the artist and brought into life by an act of creation, a true representation of the 'imagined' or 'invented' Ireland. The concept of the 'imagined' Ireland also opened up the possibility of choosing and mixing from a range of equally legitimate and authentic identities and becoming whatever type of Irish person one wanted to be.

The ethnos or the demos?

These debates on Irish identity echoed a wider discussion within western societies on the nature of nationalism and the nation. This critical debate assumed greater salience in the 1980s and 1990s as a result of the crisis of legitimacy within states, the decline of the class politics of the left and the emergence of new forms of nationalism.[148] Whatever form the discussion took, the key question remained: was nationalism to be located within the politics of universalism or the politics of difference? This distinction has been explored theoretically by considering the contrasting ideas of civic and ethnic nationalism. Civic nationalism is rooted in the democratic and secular traditions of the Enlightenment, which stressed the citizens' identification with the state and the nation as a voluntary and conscious choice. This western tradition is based on the identification and affinity of the citizen with a political community, while the eastern, ethnic tradition is rooted in the concept of the *ethnos*, a community of fate that defines the nation in terms of primordial elements such as language, culture, tradi-

147 For example, see 'An exercise in revisionism', *An Phoblacht/Republican News*, 6 April 1989; 'Challenging revisionism', *An Phoblacht/Republican News*, 7 December 1989; P. Beresford-Ellis, 'Revisionism and the new anti-nationalist school of historians', *IRIS*, August 1990; and M. O'Riain, 'The final run from the 1798 presses', *An Phoblacht/Republican News*, 17 December 1998. F. Lane, 'Bad history – Mala Poist', *An Phoblacht/Republican News*, 12 October 1989 attacked T. Hoppen's definition of the causes of conflict in Northern Ireland for using the categories of 'tradition' and 'identity', which would themselves by commonplace terms amongst Provisionals within a few years.
148 For an introduction to the very extensive literature on this debate, see Bhabha, 1990; Gellner, 1983; Hobsbawm, 1990; McCrone, 1998; Ozkirimli, 2000; and Smith, 1995.

tion and race. With its stress on the *Volk*, this tradition emphasizes the irrational and given nature of national identity. As Gellner has argued, these civic and ethnic elements remained in creative tension in the development of nineteenth- and twentieth-century nationalisms that defined the nation-state as a sovereign entity representing and acting on behalf of a culturally homogeneous people.[149] This analytical distinction between civic and ethnic nationalism has been useful for our understanding of Irish nationalism and Republicanism as historical forces and contemporary political currents. Many historians and cultural theorists have emphasized the strength of ethnic and essentialist elements in Irish nationalism and Republicanism, whilst others have seen the modernist conception of the nation as the key element in its ideological framework.[150] Issues such as the relationship between nationalism and socialism, the nature of democracy and self-determination, and the definition of the nation in Ireland – which are central to the politics of modernity – continue to define the contradictions between the Republican politics of universalism and nationalist politics of difference.[151]

One attempt to resolve these contradictions more generally in the west resulted in the development of what has been defined as 'new nationalism'.[152] This response to the collapse of established ideologies and parties was a type of *nationalisme de gestion*, a wave of regionalist, autonomist and separatist movements that represent, in varying degrees, a revolt of the marginalized and the peripheral against the centre and the metropolis.[153] As exemplified by the movements for autonomy and/or sovereignty in Quebec and Catalunya, and devolution in Wales and Scotland, these new nationalisms reject ethnically-based, nation-state-building projects and reconnect with the civic elements that were previously submerged.[154]

---

149 E. Gellner, 1983, 1.

150 Among the most powerful advocates of the 'ethnic' interpretation of Irish nationalism has been Conor Cruise O'Brien: see O'Brien, 1970; 1972; 1994; and Garvin, 1981; 1987. Eagleton, 1999, 50 argues the contrary case. Some of the controversy surrounding Peter Hart's work on the IRA continued the debate on the 'ethnic' and sectarian nature of twentieth-century Republicanism. For a flavour of these exchanges, and other similar controversies about the nature of Republicanism, see Hart, 1998; and Lane, 2006.

151 The relationship between univeralism and particularism was an important issue for socialist Republicans. See English, 1994 for an historical account of the difficulties in distinguishing between these categories.

152 McCrone, 1998, 128–129.

153 Translated as a nationalism of management as opposed to a nationalism of protest. See X. Crettiez, 'IRA, ETA, FLNC: l'agonie des illusions militaristes', *Le Monde*, 23 August 2005.

154 The following defining elements of new nationalism are drawn from McCrone, 1998, 128–129.

These movements define themselves in pluralist terms and emphatically claim that their roots lie in the *demos* rather than the *ethnos*.[155]

Other characteristics mark them out as different from classical nationalist movements. Breuilly suggests that new nationalism has a specifically political orientation and is frequently driven by the social and economic concerns of key social groups, such as the upwardly-mobile managerial and business classes.[156] These nationalisms are also of a liberal and social-democratic character, in which self-consciously progressive political and socioeconomic themes outweigh the conservative and backward-looking elements of traditional nationalism. Most significantly, these movements are based in regions charaterized by coherent, developed civil society and a certain level of wealth. These are nationalisms of rising expectations rather than the despairing cry of the alienated poor.

Another marked contrast with earlier forms is the complex relationship between political and cultural nationalism. With its stress on a civic rather than an ethnic discourse of identity, this appears to mark a step away from the simple particularism of descent and ethnicity towards the flexibilities of identity politics. Nairn, for example, argues that this type of nationalism is qualitatively different from the anti-modernist and Romantic-based movements of the nineteenth and early twentieth century, and instead represents an engagement with the contemporary world.[157] Rather than the clear cultural framework of the state-building nationalisms, this new form reflects a deep uncertainty about who 'we' are, even in those nations with an apparently clearly-defined sense of identity supported by the political structures of the nation-state. In the contemporary world, identity is portrayed as a culture of hybridity and a work in constant progress, rather than a pure, fixed form embodied in a coherent set of propositions or simple set of political arrangements.[158] Thus new nationalism, like cultural identity:

> belongs to the future as much as the past. It is not something which already exists, transcending time, place, history and culture ... like everything which is historical they undergo constant transformation. Far from being eternally fixed in some essentialist past, they are subject to the continuous 'play' of history, culture and power.[159]

A similar hybridity is evident in new nationalism's understanding of political power. In this respect, new nationalism is very much a product of its time, reflecting the dominant post-ideological and pragmatic politics

155 See, for example, Conversi, 1997, 187–221 and McCrone, 1998, 147.
156 Breuilly, 1993, 333–338.
157 Nairn, 1977, 127.
158 Bhabha, 1990.
159 Hall, 1990, 224.

of the late twentieth century.[160] Its discourse is studiedly ambiguous, drawing on concepts of process, transition and movement rather than fixed points, defined destinations and clear aims.

By these means, the simple triad of people–state–nation is replaced by an expanding and developing continuum that relates to both supranational bodies and to the distribution of power and organizing structures within the state itself. New nationalist demands for 'independence within Europe' and devolved power-sharing at all levels show the application of these ideas and the almost limitless variety of interpretations that can be placed on them in theory. This is a reflection of both postmodern politics and a more diverse social base of support than those that sustained nineteenth- and early twentieth-century nationalisms. The ultimate aim of these movements remains constantly ambiguous and irresolvable, combining as they do elements of independence and forms of autonomy within an existing but culturally reconfigured state.

Thus, the essence of these new ideological forms is their Janus-like ability to incorporate contradictory elements and to shift the ideological pattern and direction of their message. As an adaptable ideological framework, nationalism has always had this ability, but new nationalism takes this a stage further by combining vertical patterns of historical memory and invented tradition with horizontal issues of contemporary political, economic and cultural power. This 'gives neonationalism its power and significance in the territorial politics of western states'.[161] Consequently, it enables these niche nationalists to 'present themselves as on the left as well as on the right, as in favour of neoliberalism as social democracy, as civic as well as ethnic depending on the circumstances'.[162]

The godfathers of New Sinn Féin

Many of these ideological characteristics of new nationalism can be applied to New Sinn Féin. This process of the acculturation of politics can be seen in the way that political discourse, which previously turned around traditional concepts of power, authority and legitimation, increasingly drew its inspiration from the language of culture and identity.[163] The language of identity politics and the discourse of transition have been significant parts of Provisional politics since the early 1990s. Likewise, as a nationalism of rising expectations this ideological form accurately reflects the changing social and economic position of the northern nationalist population in

160 For examples of this pattern, see McCrone's discussion of case studies from Scotland, Catalunya and Quebec in McCrone, 1998, 129–147.
161 Ibid., 148.
162 Ibid., 145.
163 FitzGerald, 2003, 176–184.

the 1980s and 1990s. The scaling-down of Republican aspirations and the studied ambiguity of its project all mark it out as sharing the features of these new types of nationalist politics. Perhaps most importantly, not only is it possible to compare the Provisionals to other movements within Europe, but the existing political currents within Ireland itself gave Republicans models and a corpus of ideological influences to draw upon.

The most coherent and consistent political exponents of these forms of new nationalism throughout the Troubles were Garret Fitzgerald and John Hume. However, by the early 1990s this discourse was widely influential across the nationalist political spectrum and had become one of the master-narratives of the peace process.[164] Hume deserves to be considered as not only one of the architects of the peace process, but also as an attentive godfather who assisted at the birth of New Sinn Féin. Along with Fianna Fáil, the SDLP's engagement with the Provisionals from the late 1980s was to have a significant impact on their political development.[165] This contribution had begun with Hume's fundamental redefinition of constitutional nationalism within Northern Ireland, which replaced territorial nationalism with more pluralist concepts of identity. Instead of reunification in a unitary state, he argued for political institutions that would reflect the complexity and diversity of the conflicting identities, and which could secure the allegiance of Unionists and Republicans.[166]

This analysis and the SDLP's policies of power-sharing were ultimately rooted in a culturalist variant of internal explanations of the Northern Irish conflict.[167] It revised traditional nationalism by downplaying the 'imperialist' role of the British government and proposing a model of nationalism where nation and state are nor congruent. Hume's focus was instead on the 'multiple locations where political interaction could and should take place'.[168] This emphasis on diversity and the plural nature of Irishness was reflected ideologically and politically in the acceptance that these multiple identities and cultures were equally legitimate. Although this political terminology was influenced by soft concepts of power, in many ways the discursive focus on the particularism of culture and identity with its attendant focus on justice and communal rights can be accommodated within what Todd has defined as the essential and pre-existing triad of northern nationalism: community, nation and justice.[169]

164 See, for example, Cunningham, 1997 and Hume, 1996.
165 Moloney, 2007, 277–83.
166 Todd, 1990; Murray and Tonge, 2004.
167 Brian Feeney, former SDLP councillor and political commentator, interview, 9 August 2005.
168 Nic Craith, 2003, 30.
169 Todd, 1990, 32.

This analysis of the conflict, which emphasized the recognition of identity and the need to accommodate it politically, was reflected in the New Ireland Forum report of 1984 and the Irish government's contribution to the Anglo–Irish Agreement. It also figured greatly in much of the later language and style of the peace process.[170] These pluralistic themes positively celebrated diversity and particularism, as opposed to what were seen as the political and cultural straitjackets of the traditional nationalist discourse of a united Ireland.

As defined by John Hume, this analysis of the conflict drew heavily on themes of cultural and identity politics, starting from the position that the nature of Northern Ireland is multifaceted. As a frontier zone of Britishness and Irishness, the region has Irish and European regional characteristics, as well as a broader international dimension through its links to the USA.[171] It also neatly dovetailed with the themes of British government policy that had been established in the early 1970s, and their understanding of the key elements that would be required in any future political settlement.[172] The Forum for Peace and Reconciliation, established as part of the peace process by the Irish government in 1994, exemplified this narrative in its attempts to promote a 'durable settlement respecting fully each tradition's rights and interests', and in its recognition that 'conventional labels no longer do justice in describing … actual positions', because 'the parties themselves seem to recognize the complexities engendered by clashing identities in Ireland'.[173]

The extent of this cultural transformation was clear in the nationalist contribution to the discursive framework and institutional structures of the Good Friday Agreement. The pluralistic discourse of the agreement was a significant departure, which, according to Coakley, was not 'a diluted version of traditional Irish nationalism', but represented instead 'a new form of nationalism' that is 'neither anti-nationalist nor non-nationalist'.[174]

New nationalism in Ireland

The result has been positively defined as an end to insularity and the opening up of a more fluid and uncertain sense of cultural and national identity that might pave the way for the 're-emergence of a significant, but temporarily disrupted, tradition of egalitarian and pluralist republicanism

170 Hume, 1996, 79–106; FitzGerald, 1991.
171 Hume, 1996, 58–59.
172 Goodall, 2002; Cunningham, 2001; Neumann, 2003.
173 C. McGuinness, 'Open door to dialogue', *Fortnight*, January 1995.
174 Coakley, 2002, 152.

in Ireland'.[175] One influential Fianna Fáil intellectual, for example, illustrated this when he defended the Good Friday Agreement as the product of the will of the 'living people of Ireland'. He distinguished this contemporary population from the abstract 'historic Irish nation', whose subsisting rights to self-determination, traditional nationalists had argued, trumped those of an existing electorate. In this way, the Agreement allowed Irish people to choose their identity:

> without being encumbered by ideological straitjackets that require that some of the people on this island have proper rights that override theirs or that definitely assign them to a non-Irish category. Under the terms of the agreement, people in Northern Ireland can be Irish or British or both. There is no necessary incompatibility between being Unionist and Irish.[176]

The idea that New Sinn Féin has adopted just another version of constitutional nationalism is commonplace amongst Republican critics and political commentators alike. Before we can conclude that, we need to consider the contradictory ideological influences that have shaped New Sinn Féin. It is not a product of new nationalism alone, but also reflects the powerful pull of old nationalism and the other communalized forms that are inherent in the structures of politics in Northern Ireland.

In historical and contemporary terms, there is a strong case that the Northern Irish nationalist population has been shaped by a 'profound sense of community', both in the sense of being part of an all-Ireland national community and as a distinctive community within the Northern Irish state.[177] Northern Irish nationalist politics have been defined in terms of a powerful and historically adaptable ideology, with 'a rich and flexible conceptual structure which allows it to express divergent interests and accommodate very different political tendencies'.[178] The framework of this ideology has been located in the themes of nation, community and justice, which, it has been convincingly argued, formed a common heritage and a discursive framework for both Sinn Féin and the SDLP.[179]

Given the greater sense of the collective in this communal culture and these underlying patterns of nationalist politics, it could be argued that the new politics of difference would be more easily assimilated by nationalists.[180]

175 Frost, 2006, 281.
176 M. Mansergh, letter to *The Village*, quoted in Lane, 2006, 58.
177 Coulter, 1999, 81.
178 Todd, 1990, 34.
179 Todd, 1990; Murray and Tonge, 2004.
180 For a discussion of the formative period of Northern nationalist political and communal culture see Elliott, 2000; O'Connor, 1993; Todd, 1990; Hepburn, 1996; Staunton, 2001; Phoenix, 1994.

However, there are tensions within this framework between civic forms of nationalism and a more particularist approach based on the communal traditions of Northern nationalism.[181] These conflicts exhibited themselves throughout the history of the SDLP as a split between the green and the red, but this ideological distinction between the universal and the particular has, as we have seen, a much older pedigree, both within Ireland and internationally.[182]

The strength of this hybrid form of *nationalisme de gestion* is illustrated by the convergence between the two parties' positions on the EU and its role in conflict resolution in Ireland. The SDLP had always stressed the European dimension of the conflict in Northern Ireland. John Hume's view that the EU's institutional structures could provide a model for 'addressing common concerns but protecting ... essential diversity' in the region was an early example of his new nationalist discourse.[183]

The Provisionals' changing attitude towards the EU increasingly brought them within a similar ideological framework. Sinn Féin's critical engagement with the EU since 2001 has modified its previous total opposition and is an indicator of the deeper shifts in its politics towards these new forms of nationalism.[184]

The call for a 'Europe of equals' and Sinn Féin's membership of the European United Left/Nordic Green Left group of MEPs are further evidence of this new ideological development.[185] This engagement mirrors its earlier attitude towards the British state, in that it combines lobbying for resources and 'support for Europe-wide measures that promote and enhance human rights, equality and the all-Ireland agenda' with 'principled opposition' to a European superstate.[186]

'Vote-catching seoiníns in the political mainstream'?[187]

This chapter has attempted to understand the underlying ideological forms of New Sinn Féin by situating the party within a broader political taxonomy than that of traditional Republicanism. Drawing on these wider

181 Bourke, 2003, x–xvi.
182 Murray and Tonge, 2004.
183 Hume, 1996, 47.
184 E. Ó Murchú, 'A delicate balance between maturity and compromise', *The Village*, 16 February 2006.
185 'Traditional nationalists' attacked this group of MEPs as 'an alliance of Italian Stalinists, militant feminists and Communist parties'. P. Ó Floinn, 'Themselves alone', *The Hibernian*, December 2006, p29.
186 See 'North-west delegation in Brussels', *An Phoblacht*, 14 December 2006; and the introduction to the website of Sinn Féin's MEPs, www.sfguengl.com.
187 P. Ó Floinn, 'Themselves alone', *The Hibernian*, December 2006, 28.

frameworks is not only analytically secure, but it accurately reflects the political and ideological reality of contemporary Provisionalism. Assessing ideological shifts within a party wholly or even largely by reference to its own traditions is never satisfactory. It has always been the case that in general ideological terms no man, woman or movement is an island unto itself, but is always part of the main.

In the case of Republicanism, it is even more so given that its own theoretical and analytical tradition is weak and that it was never an hermetically-sealed tradition. The Provisional movement, in particular, interacted with external structures and forces, both as subject and object, from the moment of its birth. It was ideologically promiscuous in its borrowings and naturally susceptible to the ideological and organizational gravitational pull of other, more powerful forces. Closer engagement with the British state, the SDLP and Fianna Fáil from the late 1980s onwards simply enlarged the scope and opportunities for such influences.

This process follows most of the established historical patterns for the containment and integration of radical Republican challengers by the state and the established parties. It enables Republican critics to make parallels with Collins and De Valéra, and predict that in time the Provisionals will turn on their old comrades if that is necessary to maintain the status quo.[188] It also sustains a myth that explains the success of New Sinn Féin in terms of the betrayal of principle and takes comfort in the familiar circularity and certainty of the pattern of defeat, or in a chronicle of a betrayal foretold. For those who are not part of the New Sinn Féin project, the purity of these explanations allows them to continue the struggle, certain that 'a proud history gives confidence of [eventual?] victory'.[189]

The Provisionals themselves have rejected the New Sinn Féin label, with its overtones of Blairite revisionism.[190] Instead, they argued that they remained committed to their ultimate goals whilst engaging with the realities of the new dispensation to serve both immediate and long-term aims. It is commonplace to argue that this rhetorical attempt to disguise the extent of the Provisionals' revisionism using the language of essential continuity echoed previous generations of Republicans who successfully moved from the extremist margins to the constitutional mainstream. However, what distinguishes the Provisional project from its earlier predecessors in Fianna Fáil and the Workers' Party is not just the mood of defeat, but the sense of collapse and terminus. Republicanism appears intellectually

188 John Kelly, former Sinn Féin MLA and founding member of the Provisional IRA, interview, 23 July 2005.
189 Dalton and Hayden, 2006.
190 Eoin Ó Broin, interview, 17 July 2005.

exhausted, giving the appearance of an ideological project that has run its historical course. In this sense, the New Labour comparison has more than illustrative value, since the Blairite project arose from the defeat and the ideological collapse of welfare Labourism and the consolidation of Thatcherism. As we have seen, New Sinn Féin arose in a similar way from a sustained period of containment and long defeat that replaced the 'long war'.

This characterization of the ideological context that has shaped the politics of New Sinn Féin is grounded in more than the transient moods and episodes of political and social life. By looking at the fundamental ideological bases of politics and public policy in Western societies, it is clear that the great ideologies grounded in universal principles are in disarray, whilst the essentialist and particularist politics of difference have become predominant in the public arena. Given the historic tension between these forms within Republicanism, it is not surprising that in era when the structures of politics, the power of the state and the dynamics of economic life support these particularist ideologies, these elements should come to the fore in the ideological framework of New Sinn Féin.

Chapter 5

On the Long Road: The Provisional Politics of Transition[1]

The only objective I ever heard in the early days was to get the Brits out of Ireland ... through armed resistance, engage them in armed conflict and send them back across the water with their tanks and guns. That was the Republican objective.[2]

We have seen the tentative beginnings of a real process of national reconciliation between Orange and Green. The prospect of a peaceful transition to Irish unity has never been closer.[3]

Denying the existence of the country in which they hold office

In the early days of the devolved executive, one of the new Sinn Féin ministers, Conor Murphy, reportedly issued guidance to his civil service staff to 'use language he was comfortable with' in speeches and statements issued in his name. In particular, staff were asked to refer to Northern Ireland as 'here' or 'the North', and the Irish Republic as 'all-Ireland'.[4] The resulting political row was predictable, and echoed the familiar controversies surrounding place-names and titles that had long been a feature of public life in the region.

While some found amusement in the minister's attempts to redefine the region's constitutional status through place-names, one Unionist response to the memo unwittingly made a telling assessment of the New Sinn Féin project.[5] In suggesting that 'Mr Murphy appeared to be trying to deny the

---

1 The title of the chapter echoes the words of a Republican ballad whose words include the phrases:

We're on the one road,
It may be the wrong road
But we're together now, who cares?

See Smyth, 2005.

2 Brendan Hughes, former OC, Belfast Brigade IRA, interview, 10 August 1998.

3 'Sinn Féin: the only real alternative', editorial, *An Phoblacht*, 17 May 2007.

4 'Minister defending language memo', http://news.bbc.co.uk/go/pr/fr/-/1/hi/northern _ireland/6676659.stm.

5 G. Moriarty, 'DUP not lost for words when it comes to here and there', *Irish Times*, 22 May 2007.

existence of the country in which he holds office', the DUP MP Gregory Campbell pointed to a central contradiction within Provisional strategy.[6] Conor Murphy's attempt to re-order reality was just one small example of a Republican politics of denial that sought to claim in the realm of discourse victories that had not been won on the fields of power.

In the early days of devolution, Unionists were fond of highlighting similar contrasts between Republican rhetoric and political reality. Jeffrey Donaldson, for example, described Martin McGuinness's claims that Republicans 'have now entered the end phase of our struggle ... [and] begun the countdown to a united Ireland' as 'feeble rhetoric'.[7] For Unionists, such rhetoric masked:

> the reality that Mr McGuinness is Deputy First Minister of Northern Ireland, part of the United Kingdom. He will be a minister of the crown and will have to make an oath of allegiance and give support to a British police force and a British judicial system... The situation is a world removed from his comments... It is a fantasy that there will be a united Ireland.[8]

Democratic Unionists and dissident Republicans seemed to share a common analysis. Republican critics did not see the new Stormont Assembly as a stepping-stone to reunification; to them, it remained an instrument of British rule and 'an obstacle to Irish freedom and unity'.[9] Both were agreed that neither Conor Murphy's linguistic turn nor Martin McGuinness's 'feeble rhetoric' fundamentally altered the substance of the new dispensation in Northern Ireland; simply denying the state or even giving it a new name did not transform it.

Yet the Provisionals continued to claim that theirs was a transformative project. Sinn Féin leaders argued that they still 'believe absolutely in a united Ireland' that would be achieved not by armed struggle but by Republicans seeking to 'develop ... build, and seek support for our vision of an ... Ireland of Equals.' They also spoke of opening up 'the potential for new beginnings' and working for a 'real process of national reconciliation ... building a new relationship between the people on this island' that will 'change the political landscape from here on out.'[10] Some Republicans believed that the interim results of this strategy had been so

6 Quoted in 'Minister defending language memo'.
7 Martin McGuinness, quoted in '1916–2007 Easter commemorations', *An Phoblacht*, 12 April 2007; Jeffrey Donaldson MP quoted in L. McKay, 'McGuinness's "fantasy" – Donaldson', *News Letter*, 9 April 2007.
8 McKay, 'McGuinness's "fantasy" – Donaldson'.
9 'Stormont: an obstacle to Irish freedom and unity', *Saoirse*, June 2007.
10 Gerry Adams quoted in 'A good day for Ireland', *An Phoblacht*, 10 May 2007.

successful that they could claim they were 'closer to a united Ireland now than we were ten years ago.'[11]

If this contemporary language of a 'transitional vision towards reunification and the All-Ireland Agenda' was much softer than the previous discourse of revolutionary overthrow and a thirty-two-county socialist republic, it was also much more ambiguous.[12] This strategy for transition rested on a number of diametrically-opposed assumptions that were so rarely questioned within the movement that they had achieved almost axiomatic status among Republicans. This framework combined an element of strategic realism with a large amount of wishful thinking. The central theme in the strategy was the belief in 'a law of historical development moving inexorably towards the achievement of nationalist destiny.'[13] Republicans argued that there was an almost predestined process of 'steady demographic, political, social and economic change, undeniably pointing in one direction towards support for a united Ireland.'[14] These 'underlying dynamics' would ensure that what the Provisionals regarded as the 'interim structures' of the Good Friday Agreement would help to 'hollow out the Union' and facilitate the 'all-Ireland agenda'.[15]

Missing from this schema were the structural mechanisms and the real political dynamics to achieve reunification. As Unionists had come to understand, a close examination of the strategy to 'facilitate the all-Ireland agenda' revealed fundamental flaws. Unionists accurately argued that Republicans were now committed to working within the institutions of a Belfast Agreement that structurally precluded any form of transition towards a united Ireland.[16] The DUP, for example, believed that no such dynamics existed; the process of reunification envisaged by Gerry Adams was impossible, and they delighted in mischievously and continually reminding Republicans that, irrespective of their rhetoric, Sinn Féin was now part of a British administration.[17] It was for precisely these reasons that they felt confident enough to agree to go into government with the Provisionals in 2007. Thus, behind the Provisional rhetoric of dynamic process and historical momentum was a strategic void combined with a

---

11 Declan Kearney, Sinn Féin spokesperson, speaking in a debate on policing at Conway Mill in West Belfast, 29 November 2006. Note taken by author.

12 M. Anderson, 'The Great Experiment', *An Phoblacht*, 16 October 2003.

13 Aughey, 2003, 7.

14 Mitchel McLaughlin quoted in R. Cowan, 'Census hits Republican hopes', *Guardian*, 20 December 2002.

15 Aughey, 2003, 7.

16 D. Kennedy, 'Dressing up "Brits out" in a language of legal correctness', *Irish Times*, 9 September 2003.

17 P. Robinson, 'The big man was right', *Belfast Telegraph*, 20 April 2007.

seemingly naive optimistic faith in the power of 'relentless negotiation' to achieve Republican goals.[18]

In one way, it was easy to explain these contradictions as doublethink that New Sinn Féin had inherited from Provisionalism. The language of radical transition was a necessary nonsense enabling the Provisional leadership to persuade 'the base' not only that had the movement's core aims remained unchanged, but also that a new sophisticated form of politics was going to achieve them.[19] Moreover, this calculated ambiguity only served to confirm the cuteness of Republican strategy by appearing to wrongfoot Unionists and increase divisions within their ranks. Every howl of outrage from a 'rejectionist Unionist' at the 'latest concessions to Sinn Féin' only acted to strengthen the impression that the Provisionals had remained true to their roots. Thus, Unionist critics of the ilk of DUP MEP Jim Allister stood surety throughout the peace process for the continuing revolutionary credibility of the Provisional project.

On the other hand, this structural duplicity was not simply an example of the tactical and ideological flexibility that had long characterized the movement,[20] nor was it merely the product of careerism or a 'carefully-orchestrated cult of the individual which surrounded Gerry Adams and his closest conspirators.'[21] The Provisionals' linguistic turn was a new form of politics that did represent a decisive break with the movement's ideological and strategic traditions. Historically, Irish Republicanism had relied on the decisive agency of the IRA supported by the political mobilization of the 'risen people' to achieve its aims. This strategy did not rely on historical inevitability or gradualist conceptions of transition; the essential dynamics for political change in this schema were the revolutionary subjectivity of the Irish nation and its Republican vanguard.

Republicans increasingly doubted their ability to achieve their aims as traditionally understood. This was not simply a reflection of tactical weakness or limited political resources, nor was it a form of new realism that believed that 'the struggle' was not synonymous with 'one particular tactic' and that new methods were required to achieve Republican objectives.[22] This declining belief in the movement's ability to shape events was a product of an underlying loss of historical confidence and a sense of ideological exhaustion within Republicanism. The new strategy was thus a fundamental psychological and ideological defeat that replaced long-established certainties with an ambiguous and uncertain politics of

18 G. Adams, 'Time to show courage and take risks', *An Phoblacht*, 4 January 2007.
19 'SF resurrects old Easter message', editorial, *News Letter*, 9 April 2007.
20 Maillot, 2005, 3.
21 'Mac Cool', 'Is the party over? Father of all debacles?', *Saoirse*, June 2007.
22 L. McKeown, 'Out from behind the doors', *An Phoblacht*, 25 January 2007.

transition. At its heart lay a radically different understanding of the world and of the power of political actors to change it.

These ideological and strategic characteristics were not unique, either to Provisionalism or to the politics of Northern Ireland. The diminishing sense of agency, which produced the strategic flaws and political confusion at the centre of Republican politics, exemplified a much wider loss of confidence that came to dominate the political sphere globally in the closing years of the twentieth century.

This chapter will trace this changing balance between what might be termed the politics of transformation and the politics of transition within Republican strategy over the last 25 years. Within this broad characterization, it is possible to see three phases: namely, the politics of the 'broad front' in the late 1980s, diplomatic manoeuvring in the early 1990s, and the politics of accommodation from 1994 onwards that culminated in Provisional participation in the government of Northern Ireland after the Good Friday Agreement. While ideologically and strategically distinct, these phases overlapped and shared a common intellectual framework. This evolutionary pattern was determined by a combination of factors, such as the internal dynamics of the Republican movement, wider social and economic change, and the external pressures of other dominant political actors. The result was that an uneven process of natural selection had radically transformed Provisional ideology by the late 1990s and produced the politically contradictory and strategically ambiguous form of New Sinn Féin.

Dílseacht and the politics of revolution[23]

In common with other political ideologies that claim descent from the French Revolution, Irish Republicanism historically believed in human agency and subjectivity as the means of political and social change. This belief in the decisive subjectivity of a universal category such as the nation or the working class was a central tenet of ideologies such as nationalism and socialism, and formed the basis of all forms of political activity in the nineteenth and twentieth centuries, from protests and strikes through to armed insurrections. Significantly, many of these models of historical change emphasized the crucial role of the revolutionary vanguard in mobilizing the nation or the class. The agency of the activist minority could ignite the subjectivity of the masses and propel them into epoch-changing action.[24]

23 See note 34.
24 For an analysis that places the Republican tradition within this framework, see de Paor, 1997.

The Republican tradition, especially embodied in its Fenian incarnation and the experience of 1916 and the Anglo–Irish war, stressed that the subjectivity of an organized group of activists could make history and determine the future of the nation.[25] It also drew on a contemporary discourse of national self-determination, rooted in the democratic subjectivity of 'the people' as a form of legitimating mandate for armed resistance.[26] The development of the Provisionals in the 1970s and 1980s seemed to confirm this perspective, as did the history of other national liberation movements since 1945, such as those in Algeria and Vietnam. The 'long war' strategy, in particular, was underpinned by the military-political rationale that history could be made by the revolutionary agency of the 'risen people'. Republicans believed that it was possible to weld together the oppressed nationalist population in the 'occupied zone' and the workers and small farmers in the 'free state' in a revolutionary movement capable of sweeping away British imperialism and both collaborationist states.[27]

If the underlying assumption of these politics was that the nation or the class had the potential to make its own history, then their frequent failure to do so had also to be explained. The conscious revolutionary subjectivity of the vanguard was considered essential in countering the defeats and the political demobilization that had characterized the history of Republicanism. This emphasis on the movement and 'the party' not only fully accorded with Republicanism's own Fenian organizational tradition, but also echoed the fashionable leftist rhetoric of the 1960s and 1970s.[28]

However, the resulting Republican critiques of these frequent setbacks usually combined a denunciation of the movement's organizational inadequacies with a moralistic narrative of individual betrayal by the leadership. Thus the defeats of the past and present were ascribed variously to leaders such as Collins and De Valéra, who were 'not true revolutionaries', or to the Irish people, who had been 'deliberately distracted from the supreme issue ... the unity and freedom of Ireland.'[29] Other explanations

25 Even in its most mystical form developed by Pearse, Irish Republicanism stressed subjectivity as the means whereby the nation achieved its destiny. See Dudley Edwards, 1977.

26 Augusteijn, 2003.

27 J. Drumm, 'Annual Wolfe Tone Commemoration speech', *Republican News*, 25 June 1977.

28 These trends are best exemplified in the late 1970s and early 1980s by the 'Brownie' articles on revolutionary strategy and organization. See, for example, 'Brownie', 'Scenario for establishing a socialist Republic', *An Phoblacht*, 17 February 1980.

29 E. Walsh, *An Phoblacht*, 21 November 1985: IRA statement ending the 1956–1962 campaign quoted by G. Adams, 'Time to take risks and show courage', *An Phoblacht*, 4 January 2007.

focussed on informers and 'the dark forces that destroyed the Republican struggle' from within.[30] These forms of analysis have remained popular with some Republican critics of the Adams/McGuinness leadership who have continued to explain the Provisionals' own political trajectory in such terms.[31]

This emphasis on revolutionary agency and the transformative potential of 'the struggle' situated Provisionalism within a common ideological framework of national liberation and radical movements internationally. The becalming of these projects by the late 1980s resulted in the emergence of forms of particularist politics that implicitly rejected collective political subjectivity and instead encouraged a passive strategy of 'realistic' accommodation with the status quo. In the case of the Provisionals, the ambitious subjectivity of the historical Republican project was replaced by a much narrower set of aims that redefined revolutionary transformation in the gradualist language of transition. During the peace process, this was further reflected in the emerging forms of identity politics that drew on existing cultural elements within the Republican and northern nationalist traditions to produce a 'new' conservative ideology of representation and recognition.

The first outlines of this change have been discerned in a number of strategic debates within the Provisional movement following the 1981 hunger strike and the initial successes of the electoral strategy.[32] The debate on abstentionism in 1985 to 1986 is frequently taken as a starting point for the revisionist process within Provisionalism, marking, according to political taste, either a realistic pragmatism or the beginnings of the fatal embrace with constitutional politics.[33] The supporters of abstentionism appear to make a simple, theological defence of tradition, summed up in the word dílseacht, which is variously translated as 'right', 'loyalty', 'fidelity', 'genuineness' and 'allegiance'.[34] Thus, 'traditionalists' such as Ruairí Ó Brádaigh saw abstentionism as:

---

30 See, for example, '"A man with whom we can do business": an analysis of the Denis Donaldson affair', *Sovereign Nation*, February–March 2006.

31 For an example of this position, see Brendan McLaughlin's oration quoted in '1916 Easter Commemorations 2007', *Saoirse*, May 2007.

32 Kearney, for example, identified tensions between what he saw as mythic discourse and anti-mythic pragmatic frameworks of thought within Provisionalism as early as the hunger strike period. See Kearney, 1984, p13.

33 Lynn, 2003, 74–94.

34 *Dílseacht* was the title of a biography of Tom Maguire and a general statement of the 'traditional' Republican case. See Ó Brádaigh, 1997. Sinn Fein, 1986 summarized the arguments in favour of ending abstentionism.

the very principle on which the Republican movement has been built ... to enter Leinster House would be a complete betrayal of the all-Ireland Republic, a betrayal of all those who gave their lives... Ernie O'Malley would turn in his grave if he thought that this motion was before this Ard Fheis.[35]

This implied a frozen form of politics whose essence was loyalty to a fixed body of doctrine. This sanctified inheritance was to be preserved and passed on in turn for future generations.[36] This version of Republicanism seems almost Burkean in its conservatism and its reverence for the legitimation of tradition. As a politics of faith, it seems far removed from revolutionary subjectivity.

Certainly, this was how the proponents of change portrayed 'traditional' Republicanism during these debates. Their arguments attacked this form of Republicanism as political sectarianism isolated from the Irish people. The Republic was a political option that the people could be persuaded to take, rather than a tradition sanctified by esoteric constitutional scholasticism. It was, above all, an aspiration of living people that rested on universal rights rather than the petrified mandate of the past.[37] As one supporter of ending abstentionism put it, the opponents of change were 'content to sell Easter Lilies and attend commemorations. History should have taught us that somewhere along the road we have been doing something wrong.'[38] The conclusion that the Provisional leadership drew from this reading of history was that Republican strategy should consequently develop through:

a process of continual interpretation and refinement in response to constantly changing social and political reality ... if we have no concept of winning we can remain as we are – a party apart from the people, proud of our past, but with little involvement in the present and only dreams of the future.[39]

This 'responsiveness to reality' recognized the limitations of the revolutionary project. It also marked the beginnings of a fundamental shift in Provisional politics that paralleled previous revisionist projects 'created by the strategic response of a section of the movement to prevailing circumstances.'[40] The result was that the Provisionals became 'less dogmatic ... more pragmatic ... and more politically aware in much the same way as [their] predecessors' in Fianna Fáil and Clann na Poblachta had.[41] Like

35 'Ard Fheis report '85', *An Phoblacht*, 7 November 1985.
36 See, for example, Mansergh, 2003, 304–309.
37 Danny Morrison, former senior Republican strategist, interview, 5 January 2004.
38 Seán Crowe quoted in 'Ard Fheis report '85', *An Phoblacht*, 7 November 1985.
39 G. Adams, 'The politics of revolution', *An Phoblacht*, 6 November 1986.
40 Augusteijn, 2003, 8.
41 Lynn, 2003, 92.

them, they were also ultimately to become much less revolutionary and more than slightly constitutional.

To many activists in 1986, such an outcome would have been inconceivable. Not only were they reassured by Gerry Adams and Martin McGuinness that the Provisionals remained committed to a revolutionary strategy, but history had shown that it was possible to combine an electoral strategy with forms of insurrectionary politics.[42] However, the leadership's electoral strategy implicitly replaced revolutionary transformation with a more passive form of evolutionary politics. These radically different assumptions were ultimately rooted in a very different understanding of the processes of historical and political change.

These new strategies did not regard the radical transformation in the consciousness of the Irish people as a necessary precondition for political change. Instead, Republicans sought to work within the grain of existing opinion; given that the majority of people recognized the legitimacy of the southern state, Republicans must do so too and utilize its institutions to further their project.[43] While still at an embryonic stage in 1986, this ideological and strategic framework prefigures *in form* the underlying rationale for the Provisionals' peace process strategy and their later participation in the institutions of the Good Friday Agreement. The arguments that were used to justify taking ministerial portfolios at Stormont in 1999 were, in essence, the same as those applied to taking seats in Leinster House in 1986.

'This is not 1921'

The ending of abstentionism began a period of reassessment that was to set the pattern of Provisional politics for the next 25 years. By the late 1980s, some Provisional leaders privately believed that the failure of the ballot paper and Armalite strategy could result at best in an unfavourable compromise, or at worst an open defeat. As a leading Republican explained in 1992: 'We know and accept that this is not 1921... We're not standing in the airport lounge waiting to be flown to Chequers or Lancaster House; we have no illusions of grandeur.'[44] This was a telling distinction, and in marked contrast to their attitude in talks with the

---

42 See, for example, 'Electoral interventions', *IRIS*, November 1981; and '50 years ago – four TDs elected in 26 counties', *Saoirse*, March 2007.

43 For an early example of these emerging ideas of legitimacy and the nature of the Republican mandate, see G. Adams, 'Bodenstown commemoration', *An Phoblacht/Republican News*, 23 June 1983.

44 J. Gibney, 'It is our job to develop the struggle for freedom: Bodenstown Address', *An Phoblacht/Republican News*, 25 June 1992.

British government during the 1970s.[45]

By this time, Republicans hoped to use the position that they had gained through 'the struggle' to obtain a result that could be presented positively as an honourable compromise. The means to achieve this was through 'finding vulnerabilities in the armour of our enemies, seizing the high moral ground and using the ingenuity for which we are renowned.'[46] This assessment of the strategic bind facing the Provisionals was accurate, while the description of the strategy to overcome this problem proved to be a remarkably prescient outline of what would actually emerge during the 1990s and 2000s.

However, the actual development of the strategy was much more ad hoc. Both at the time and in retrospect, there appeared to be no clear line of march or strategic direction.[47] What was frequently conducted as a pragmatic debate was in fact a now-open, now-concealed struggle for the future of Provisional Republicanism. This was especially illustrated by the radically different understandings of political agency that emerged during the discussion of the broad front strategy.

Given the political culture and organizational structure of the Provisional movement, this political reassessment was a largely internal process, controlled and directed by the leadership, but its echoes can be traced in printed form, providing a valuable insight into its political development. Although the discussion developed its own ideological dynamics, it was decisively shaped by significant changes in the external ideological climate and political context.

Probably the most significant factor was the relative success of Britain's political and military strategies to contain the Provisionals. The terrain on which Republicans operated was also decisively determined by the state's social and economic strategy.[48] Politically, Sinn Féin's advance had been halted after the dramatic successes of the pre-1985 period, and remained becalmed at around 10–11 per cent in local government and Westminster

45 Ruairí Ó Brádaigh, former President of Sinn Féin, interview, 15 February 2002. He discussed the 'negotiations' between an IRA delegation (which included Gerry Adams) and the British government in 1972 at Cheyne Walk, Chelsea in terms that stressed the parallels with 1921.

46 Morrison, 1999, 288–292. These comments were part of a longer article for *An Phoblacht/Republican News* that was not printed because the editor argued that it would be seized upon by opponents as a sign of division within the Provisional movement. See Morrison, 1999, 293.

47 Tony Catney, former member Sinn Féin Ard Comhairle, interview, 14 April 1997.

48 For further details of this important aspect of British strategy and its influence on the development of Provisional politics, see Chapter 1.

elections until the beginnings of the peace process.[49] This stagnation was even more apparent in Sinn Féin's poor showing in elections for the Dáil, where the expected breakthrough after the ending of abstentionism in 1986 failed to materialize.[50] Given the significance of the southern strategy within Republican politics, this was disastrous, and suggestive of a need for some form of political reorientation within the movement.

A similar pattern of military containment was reflected in the decline in the measurable levels of violence after the defeat of the IRA offensive in 1987–1988.[51] These failures were increasingly seen as not just technical or practical operational problems or a reflection of the imbalance of strength between a guerrilla army and a powerful state opponent. Some activists, for example, believed that, in the aftermath of the failure of a major IRA offensive in 1987, elements within the leadership were not fully committed to the continuation of the military campaign and were seeking a new type of strategy.[52]

Likewise, the rising levels of loyalist attacks during the late 1980s and early 1990s fatally undermined the IRA's claim to 'defend' the nationalist community and dealt a serious blow to the Provisionals' own sense of legitimacy. Indeed, some aspects of the IRA's campaign had actually increased sectarian and communal polarization rather than diminished it. These factors were evidence to many that the Provisionals' military-political strategy as a whole had not worked, and that the premises on which it was based were seriously flawed. Not only had the military-political campaign failed to obtain a British declaration to withdraw, but by the late 1980s this seemed even further away than it had in the early 1970s.

The broad front strategy was an attempt to break out of this political containment. Its main strategic premise was that 'only the combined forces of Irish nationalism can defeat imperialism in all its forms ... [and] end ... partition.' This involved the building of a mass movement, which was declared to be the main vehicle for national liberation, placing more emphasis on 'revolutionary mobilization' than 'armed struggle' to achieve Republican aims.[53]

The politics of the broad front were strongly influenced by a particular reading of the experience of the prisons and hunger strike campaigns in the

49 Electoral data taken from 'Political party support in Northern Ireland, 1969 to the present', cain.ulst.ac.uk.

50 Sinn Féin failed to poll above 2 per cent in Dáil elections until 1997. Coakley and Gallagher, 1999, 367.

51 'Security' information on shootings, casualties and incidents from Wichert, 1999, 256–258.

52 Private information.

53 All quotations from a resolution passed at the Sinn Féin Ard Fheis 1992 quoted by O' Brien, 1993, 225.

late 1970s and early 1980s.[54] This was a decisive period for many Republicans, and the electoral and campaigning politics of that time were a touchstone for later debates.[55] The mobilization of the same level of popular support and the reconstruction of a similar coalition among the nationalist population became central strategic goals for the Provisionals. This policy was underpinned by a number of assumptions that would later provide the essential framework for the politics of New Sinn Féin in the 1990s.

The leading edge of Irish nationalism?

Pivotal to this new strategic framework was a growing sense that the revolutionary tide had receded and that Republicans were going to have to adjust to the politics of a new world.[56] In situating Republicanism in 'a different world to the one that existed in the mid-60s' and stressing the impact of the 'more recent changes sweeping across the globe', the Provisional leadership appeared to be preparing 'the base' for a dramatic shift in position.[57]

The essence of the strategy was a declining belief in Provisionalism's ability to shape events as a subjective agent. This was combined with a correspondingly 'realistic' evaluation of the power of other political actors. Explicitly, the Republican movement no longer considered itself strong enough to achieve even limited aims on its own, and so required allies drawn from a bloc of progressive social forces.

These potentially demoralizing assessments were, however, given a positive gloss. The broad front was presented as a new site of struggle rather than an admission of strategic weakness. The Republican leadership argued that a number of factors aided this new direction. Most importantly, there was said to be considerable latent support for Republican objectives throughout nationalist Ireland.[58]

Consequently, the Provisional leadership argued that there were potentially progressive anti-imperialist elements among SDLP and Fianna

---

54 Clarke, 1987, 84–109.

55 Tom Hartley, former Sinn Féin General Secretary, interview, 12 August 2005.

56 Tony Catney, interview, 27 April 1998.

57 J. Gibney, 'It is our job to develop the struggle for freedom: Bodenstown Address', *An Phoblacht/Republican News*, 25 June 1992. The speech at Wolfe Tone's grave at Bodenstown is a public statement of the Republican leadership's position, and Gerry Adams often used the occasion to fly ideological kites through a third party to test reaction among the activists. As one former Sinn Féin strategist has argued: 'Don't listen to what Adams says, because Adams never uses himself to break new ground. He always uses someone else': Tony Catney, former member of Sinn Féin Ard Comhairle, interview, 27 April 1998.

58 Adams, 1986, 46.

Fáil supporters that could be won to the cause of national liberation. The medium for achieving this was a coalition brought together for limited common objectives, such as campaigns on extradition or the Single European Act. These broad fronts had the potential to eventually evolve 'through struggle' into a coherent and stable grouping capable of revolutionary mobilization under Republican leadership.[59] The orientation towards the 'green' wing of the SDLP and 'traditionalist' Republicans in Fianna Fáil was in marked contrast to the early 1980s, when these parties had been variously denounced as 'servants of the queen' and 'imperialist lickspittles'.[60]

These general assumptions about the 'revolutionary potential' of nationalist Ireland took a particular form when applied to Northern Ireland. Here, this discourse assumed the existence of a 'nationalist community' whose communal identity and interests transcended the divisions of class, and which was capable of mobilization through a common political project. In this case, theory followed practice.[61]

The strategy had been partially shaped by the Provisionals' experience of local government, and their increasing involvement in community politics. As a result, the language of communal unity began to replace the rhetoric of class struggle in the late 1980s. Criticisms of the SDLP were softened; constitutional nationalists were no longer 'cowardly collaborators'.[62] Now they were defined as potential allies, and rebuked because the 'continuous and ongoing confrontation between the two main nationalist parties ... divides and weakens the political negotiating power of the *broad nationalist community*' [emphasis added].[63] Building 'a northern nationalist consensus on the basis of constitutional change' and extending it to include constitutional parties throughout Ireland would become a key dynamic in Provisional strategy in the 1990s.[64]

As part of this revisionist project, existing forms of 'revolutionary' politics were criticized as objectively passive and ineffective. Previously unthinkable positions first considered during this period emerged publicly in the politics of New Sinn Féin. For example, the tactical use of armed struggle and a ceasefire to secure political advantage were aired

---

59 Tonto, 'The internal conference: some reflections', *Iris Bheag*, 1, 1987: notes taken at the 1988 Sinn Féin Internal Conference by a senior activist (copy in possession of author).
60 M. de Barra, 'Seirbhisigh na Banriona', *An Phoblacht*, 29 August 1981; 'Statement at end of second hunger strike' in Campbell et al., 1994, 259–264.
61 For further examples of the impact of this community strategy on Provisional politics, see Chapter 2.
62 Campbell et al., 1994, 259–264.
63 A. Rooney, 'Analysis of the SDLP position re. Hillsborough', *Iris Bheag*, 9, 1988.
64 TUAS document, summer 1994, printed as Appendix 2 in Moloney, 2002, 499.

during internal discussions in 1988.[65] Even defining Leinster House and Stormont as, at best, 'platforms of propaganda and at worst institutions of national and class betrayal' indicated a willingness to move into radically different political territory as part of 'the new phase of struggle'.[66]

The new direction was portrayed as a means of reinvigorating the Republican struggle by reaching out to new layers of support. It could also re-engage with the movement's existing base, as one activist explained:

> We have a 'vision', we put it before the people, we expect them to support it and believe in it because it is a 'noble' ideal... When we see that armed struggle is not enough we, with inevitable reluctance, involve ourselves in some political/social/cultural activity to attract others to 'give support' to our cause – a sort of mutual exchange – even if it is a nuisance!...What then is the role of the Republican movement? Is it to 'gather support' for its policies or to make a revolution in Ireland?[67]

Such limited challenge as there was to the new strategic direction came from those who argued that Republican socialism was incompatible with nationalism and alliances with mainstream parties. Despite the declining salience of socialism as an ideological force internationally, for some sections of the Provisional movement it still acted as an important ideological framework.[68] To these Republicans, constitutional nationalism would always remain an essentially middle-class Catholic Hibernianism whose 'interests inevitably made them neutral to partition and open to collaborate with British rule.'[69]

One early contributor to the debate expressed something that was becoming a very marginal viewpoint when he argued that pan-nationalism would be a repudiation of the 'anti-imperialist struggle for the sake of ineffectual posturing' and that 'there cannot be any pan-nationalist alliance between FF, SDLP and SF unless the latter was to abandon it's [sic] support for revolutionary armed struggle.'[70] To these critics, the general direction and political implications of the leadership's strategy were clear:

> The discussion raises the question of whether we in Sinn Fein see ourselves as the leading edge of Irish nationalism – Republicanism being the more politically advanced form of nationalism – or whether we see ourselves as a

65 H-Blocks Education Committee, 'The need for a broad front now', *Iris Bheag*, 11, 1988.

66 L. Gorman, 'Pan-nationalism or an anti-imperialist front', *Iris Bheag*, 13, 1988.

67 L. McKeown, 'Gathering support for ideals or building revolution?', *Iris Bheag*, 7, 1988.

68 Penfold, 'The capitalist class and the Irish national question', *Iris Bheag*, 7, 1988.

69 Silver, 'National self-determination', *Iris Bheag*, 6, 1987.

70 Ibid.

socialist party... Is the Republican movement a broad movement of all classes who see unity and independence as their goal, a movement broad enough to mobilize the majority of the Irish nation? Can our socialism allow us to see nationalist parties such as Finna [sic] Fail or the SDLP as in some sense our allies?[71]

TUAS or Tús nua?

As the strategy unfolded in the 1990s, it became clear that the Provisionals' 'socialism' would indeed allow them to ally with constitutional nationalism. Gerry Adams and Martin McGuinness's version of the broad front was far from revolutionary; instead of a militant coalition of progressive Republican and nationalist forces, it quickly narrowed into a diplomatic marriage of convenience between the Republican leadership and constitutional nationalist politicians on both sides of the border. The mass movement of the hunger strike period was not reborn; this essential revolutionary dynamic failed to materialize. It was doubtful that the Provisional leadership ever really thought that it would, or even wanted it to. By following the underlying political assumptions of the broad front through to their logical conclusion in this way, the Provisionals' strategy effectively became one of managed retreat rather than revolutionary advance.

The key period for the development of this strategy was 1992–1994. Two documents – one public, one internal – crystallized a number of strategic themes that had either appeared previously in incomplete form, or been discussed privately at a senior level within the Provisionals.[72] These strategic refinements established the framework for Provisional politics throughout the peace process, and thus decisively shaped what would become New Sinn Féin. The master political narrative was outlined in a Sinn Féin position paper 'Towards A Lasting Peace In Ireland', published in 1992; the strategic rationale was provided in an internal briefing paper known by the acronym TUAS, issued to IRA volunteers in 1994.[73] Ideological change and strategic shift were intimately interlinked, revealing the considerable degree of political weakness and uncertainty that was to be the hallmark of the Provisionals during this period.

The most dramatic changes in their public position occurred in the analysis of the nature and means of resolving the conflict in Northern

---

71 TippEx, 'Should SF bring down Charlie Haughey?', *Iris Bheag*, 1, 1987.

72 See, for example, the discussion on the tactical use of a ceasefire in H-Blocks Education Committee, 'The need for a broad front now', *Iris Bheag*, 11, 1988; Danny Morrison's views on the future of the movement in Morrison, 1999, 288–293; and emerging ideas on the nature of the conflict in Sinn Féin, 1988.

73 Sinn Féin, 1992; TUAS document in Moloney, 2002, 498–501.

Ireland.[74] While Republicans apparently rejected the 'current fashionable propaganda' that the conflict resulted from 'divisions between the Irish people', a new focus on Britain's potential role as a facilitator became increasingly conjoined in Republican analyses with an 'acknowledgement that peace in Ireland requires a settlement of the long-standing conflict between Irish nationalism and Irish Unionism.'[75] Thus, 'Towards A Lasting Peace In Ireland' argued that:

> Britain created the problem in Ireland. Britain has the major responsibility and role in initiating a strategy which will bring a democratic resolution and a lasting peace. This must involve, within the context of accepting the national right of the majority of the Irish people, *a British government joining the ranks of the persuaders* in seeking to obtain the *consent of a majority of people in the north* to the constitutional, political and financial arrangements needed for a united Ireland. [Emphasis added][76]

This implicit definition of the conflict as one *internal* to Northern Ireland shows the increasing salience of particularistic elements of identity politics within Provisional discourse. Republicans would have dismissed the underlying premises of this argument as 'reformist' just a few years earlier.[77] The depth of the ideological shift is also indicated by the idea that negotiation and the momentum of 'the peace process' can resolve the conflict. Combined with the language of persuasion and the emerging vocabulary of consent, this schema implied a new form of transitional period preceding British disengagement. Republicans now accepted that:

> the British government's departure must be *preceded by a sustained period of peace* and will arise out of negotiations ... such negotiations will involve the different shades of Irish nationalism and Irish unionism, engaging the British government either together or separately to secure *an all-embracing and durable peace process*. [Emphasis added][78]

Reunification was increasingly defined as an evolutionary process of transition rather than a decisive moment of revolutionary transformation. Decolonization was evidently to be a longer and rather more involved process than was suggested by simple acts of ratifying political change, such as hauling down a flag at midnight and seeing soldiers depart from Belfast Lough.

74 For further discussion of this ideological development, see Chapter 6.
75 'Sinn Féin maps road to peace', *An Phoblacht/Republican News*, 20 February 1992.
76 Sinn Féin, 1992, 12.
77 See, for example, K. Currie, 'Strengthening partition: the development of constitutional nationalism', *An Phoblacht/Republican News*, 17 June 1986.
78 J. Gibney, 'It is our job to develop the struggle for freedom: Bodenstown Address', *An Phoblacht/Republican News*, 25 June 1992.

The strategic implications of this analysis were far-reaching. This new start did share many of the 'realistic' assessments made during the debate on the broad front strategy. However, if the rhetoric of the broad front had looked back to the early 1980s for a model of successful political mobilization, the strategic reality in the 1990s was very different. The Provisional leadership explicitly acknowledged the political weakness and isolation of the movement: 'Republicans at this time and on their own do not have the strength to achieve the end goal'.[79] They relied instead on a combination of favourable external factors to achieve their aims.

All political actors assess how the strengths and weaknesses of their opponents will influence their projects. What distinguished this new Republican strategy was the extent to which it relied on other political actors and objective factors to achieve its aims. It was this reduction in ambition and agency that was to mark such a significant political and psychological shift in Republican politics in the 1990s and 2000s.

For the Provisionals, the dynamics of political change were now to be found in a specific unique conjuncture and an underlying sense of historical momentum. This sense of momentum was comparable to wider international patterns of political change; the experience of other peace processes was frequently cited as evidence by the Provisionals of how Northern Ireland could also be transformed. For example, Mitchel McLaughlin talked about a new international 'atmosphere of support for the democratic rights of nationalities' reshaping the politics of Europe, the Middle East and South Africa in the 1990s.[80] Others saw lessons for Republicans in the experience of other liberation movements that were coming to terms with the new realities of the post-Cold War world.[81]

The specific circumstances that were 'unlikely to gel again in the foreseeable future' included key leaders such as John Hume, Albert Reynolds and Bill Clinton, the increasing influence of the Irish-American lobby, and the fact that 'for the first time in 25 years ... all major Irish nationalist parties are rowing in roughly the same direction.'[82] This model confirmed that the Provisionals saw the central dynamic for change as the alliance between Sinn Féin, the SDLP, the Dublin government and the Irish-American lobby.

For Republicans, this strategic shift from the subjective politics of the revolutionary vanguard to diplomatic forms of manoeuvre could, at best, only secure concessions far short of Republican goals. The real balance of

79 TUAS document in Moloney, 2002, 498.
80 'Ard Fheis report', *An Phoblacht/Republican News*, 8 February 1990.
81 See, for example, Danny Morrison's comments on Sandinista strategy in Nicaragua in Morrison, 1999, 291.
82 TUAS document in Moloney, 2002, 501.

power within this diplomatic coalition meant the abandonment of Provisional ambitions to be the leading force in the national revolution; the acknowledged leader of nationalist Ireland throughout the peace process was not Sinn Féin, but the Dublin government, which successfully drew the Republicans into the orbit of conventional politics.

The public face of this strategy was the Hume–Adams initiative and the strengthening of links with Fianna Fáil, resulting in what the Provisionals referred to as the 'Irish peace initiative'. This took shape through a series of private contacts and public dialogues between Republicans and constitutional politicians from the late 1980s onwards.[83] To contemporaries, the discussions between Sinn Féin and the SDLP were the most important channel, but the private conversations between Republicans and Fianna Fáil (both in and out of office) were ultimately to prove the most ideologically and strategically significant.[84] By 1993, the strategy was publicly revealed in the form of the Hume–Adams contacts, and the role of Fianna Fáil Taoiseach Albert Reynolds in drawing the Provisional movement into negotiations with the British government was acknowledged.[85] The success of this new diplomatic focus was best exemplified by the pictures of John Hume, Gerry Adams and Albert Reynolds smiling together outside government buildings shortly after the first IRA ceasefire in September 1994.

This picture also emphasized the junior status of the Provisionals in the partnership. Although Sinn Féin would go on to achieve electoral dominance beyond its wildest expectations and become the political expression of the northern nationalist community, it would do so only as part of a constitutional settlement ultimately determined by the British government. The Provisionals' new diplomatic orientation was an acknowledgement of their permanently inferior status and further evidence of a declining belief in the movement's ability to secure its historic goals.

Sites of struggle

In June 2007, three Sinn Féin members 'stepped across a threshold that Republicans have never crossed before into a new theatre of struggle' when they took up their seats on the Northern Ireland Policing Board.[86] One of the three, Alex Maskey, explained how participating in these struc-

---

83   Sinn Féin, 2005, 203.
84   O'Donnell, 2003.
85   Moloney, 2002, 261–286.
86   Alex Maskey quoted in P. McDaid, 'Just the beginning', *An Phoblacht*, 7 June 2007.

tures meant that 'the last power base of the Unionist state' had crumbled. He argued that this 'new site of struggle' would have an all-Ireland dimension, and would be a way of 'ensuring that local communities play a full role in creating a representative, civic, police service.' Maskey encapsulated more than the party's approach to the Policing Board when he concluded that:

> we will only be limited in what we can achieve in this struggle by ourselves… [W]e are about challenging the status quo at every opportunity. And we are confident that we now have the tools to make the necessary progressive and radical changes.[87]

Maskey's analysis encapsulates some of the key elements of New Sinn Féin politics as they developed after 1994. A central trope is the idea of struggle: each new development or revision of a long-established position, from entering Stormont through to decommissioning IRA weapons, was defined either as a 'new site of struggle' or as a means to advance the struggle by other means. In 1994, IRA volunteers were told that 'TUAS has been part of every other struggle in the world this century. It is vital that activists realize that the struggle is *not* over' [emphasis in the original].[88] In a similar vein, Gerry Adams could argue in 1998 that:

> the Good Friday Agreement is not an end in itself, but a transition towards a full national democracy. For Irish Republicans the struggle for full independence and sovereignty is not over. The struggle continues.[89]

Although the Provisional leadership had effectively abandoned the armed struggle as a political tool by the late 1980s, there necessarily remained a great deal of ambiguity during the 1990s about what constituted 'the struggle' as far as Republicans were concerned. Republican discourse in this period continued to combine revolutionary themes with the realities of electoral politics; the legitimating language of 'mandates' was used in a number of different ways. In 1998, Adams overlaid fundamentally liberal-democratic conceptions of the mandate with the language of struggle:

> We go into this next phase of struggle armed only with whatever mandate we receive, armed only with our political ideas and our vision of the future

---

87 McDaid, 'Just the beginning'.

88 Given the context, the acronym TUAS here can be taken to mean '*tactical* use of armed struggle' as opposed to '*totally* unarmed struggle'. See TUAS document in Moloney, 2002, 501.

89 G. Adams, 'Presidential Address to Ard Fheis 1998', http://www.sinnfein.ie/peace/ speech/6.

... moving into uncharted territory. It is our responsibility to liberate that territory.[90]

The use of military metaphors was not confined to Republican activists, as the Lord Chief Justice of Northern Ireland had commented during Gerry Adams's trial for IRA membership in the 1970s.[91] However, given the uncertain relationship between the ballot paper and the armalite, this language has a significant role as an indicator of deeper strategic change within Provisionalism. The long-drawn-out process of decommissioning and the statement formally ending the IRA's role as a military organization clarified that the armalite had been put away, but Provisional rhetoric still harked back to this earlier language of militant politics. A 'strategy wedded to mobilizations, campaigning, street activism and the international dimension' not only straddled conventional protest and revolutionary activism, but also drew on the historical and contemporary experience of the Northern Ireland civil rights movement, the Palestinian *intifada* and the ANC in South Africa.[92]

With their implied civil disobedience and refusal to recognize the legitimacy of the state, these struggles were deemed to represent as fundamental a challenge to the status quo as the armed campaign. However, apart from the sporadic and localized 'mobilizations' during periods of tension around contentious marches such as Drumcree, protest activity was largely confined to conventional demonstrations or white-line pickets in support of essentially electoral politics.[93] The objectives of these forms of struggle were contained within quite clearly defined and restricted limits. The main thrust of 'the struggle' after 1998 was to gain 'sufficient political strength to realize our primary and ultimate aims ... [through] popularizing Republican ideas and mobilizing, organizing and strategizing how we achieve a free, united Ireland.'[94]

One of the key sites of struggle is the state itself. Maskey's characterization of events since the Good Friday Agreement focuses on the transformation of the state and destruction of centres of Unionist power such as the RUC. This model of change places the Provisionals at the centre of

90 Ibid.

91 Moloney, 2002, 173.

92 G. Adams, 'Presidential Address to Ard Fheis 1998', http://www.sinnfein.ie/peace/speech/6.

93 For example, a demonstration in Belfast city centre calling for Sinn Féin's inclusion in all-party talks in August 1995 was reported as an assault on a bastion of Unionism, but this was a rather hyperbolic description for what was essentially a conventional protest march. See 'They haven't gone away you know', *An Phoblacht/Republican News*, 17 August 1995.

94 G. Adams, 'Time to show courage and take risks', *An Phoblacht*, 4 January 2007.

politics and argues that the decisive factor is the pressure that Republicans can exert to secure further advances. In 1998, Republicans argued that 'our peace strategy has transformed the Irish political landscape over the past five years. It contains the dynamic which led to the Irish peace initiative and to the cessation of military operations by the IRA ... in 1994.'[95] Likewise, according to one leading Republican, Provisional strategy within the new dispensation after 1998 maintained this dynamic for change. Actions such as the final IRA decommissioning in 2005 were designed 'to create the maximum amount of goodwill for our cause', and as such 'this point in our struggle ... is ... a moment of decisive revolutionary opportunity.'[96] The initiative gained would 'turn that goodwill into real political muscle and support' that could be used 'to advance more quickly toward the Republic'.[97]

Underlying these perspectives was a confidence that there were no structural limitations on what Republicans could achieve; history was moving in their favour and the dynamics were in place to ensure that 'progressive and radical changes' were made possible by the Good Friday Agreement.[98] The language of transition and opportunity constantly reinforced the leadership's message that the agreement was not the end but the beginning, 'a staging post on the road to a peace settlement.'[99] This sense of relentless advance and historical momentum had been initially useful in countering arguments that the agreement 'wasn't much of a treaty to come out of a long hard war', and that the Union and the sectarian divisions that underpinned it remained intact, if not strengthened.[100] However, by 2004 the widespread, if frequently grudging, acceptance among Republicans that the Good Friday Agreement might function as a vehicle to further Republican aims had been replaced with scepticism. The suspension of the executive and the Assembly in 2002 and the failure of the transitional process to materialize in the form promised by the leadership had created a mood of disillusion and criticism. Even supporters of the leadership's strategy commented that it was 'an unusual feature of the times' that while the nationalist population generally had been 'energized' by the Provisionals' peace strategy, 'many activists, particularly in the Six

---

95 G. Adams, 'Presidential Address to Ard Fheis 1998', http://www.sinnfein.ie/peace/speech/6.

96 J. McVeigh, 'A moment of revolutionary opportunity', *An Phoblacht*, 29 September 2005.

97 Ibid.

98 McDaid, 'Just the beginning'.

99 G. Adams, 'Presidential Address to Ard Fheis 1998', http://www.sinnfein.ie/peace/speech/6.

100 M. Anderson, 'The great experiment', *An Phoblacht/Republican News*, 16 October 2003.

Counties, remained paralyzed by self-doubt and confusion.'[101] Arguments that saw the Belfast Agreement as a 'temporary renunciation of revolutionary demands' that could be justified because it was 'a bridge to the future ... [with] considerable potential', enabling Republicans 'to move beyond its limitations', seemed contradictory and lacking in strategic clarity.[102] It was not only the usual 'dissident' suspects who failed to see any possibilities of a transformation, beyond the transformation of Sinn Féin into the slightly constitutional form of Fianna Fáil.

The great experiment

The need for an imaginative and convincing analysis became all the more important following the 'strategic watershed' of the 2003 assembly elections, which strengthened Sinn Féin's position as the leading party among the nationalist electorate and also saw the emergence of the DUP as the largest Unionist party.[103] Given the DUP's public opposition to the Good Friday Agreement and its explicit hostility to any form of power-sharing with 'Sinn Féin/IRA', the Provisional leadership needed to explain how the Good Friday Agreement could facilitate the 'transition to a united Ireland' in a way that was not simply dependent on the goodwill or political agreement of the DUP.

The operation of the agreement since 1999 had shown the potential for Unionists to prevent any political development they were uncomfortable with, and the suspensions of the executive and the other institutions illustrated that constitutional power still ultimately lay with the British government. Privately, senior Republicans believed that the 'logic of events' would produce a restoration of devolution and that the logic of the DUP's own position was that they too would ultimately take part in government with the representatives of the nationalist electorate.[104] This possibility had been floated since at least 1998 in speeches and articles that stressed the essentially 'pragmatic' nature of the DUP and the 'realistic' possibilities of an 'historic compromise' between Unionists and nationalists.[105]

101 S. McCann, 'Beyond the Good Friday Agreement', *An Phoblacht/Republican News*, 29 January 2004.

102 Ibid.

103 D. Kearney, 'Assembly elections 2003: strategic watershed', *An Phoblacht/Republican News*, 11 December 2003.

104 Jim Gibney, Sinn Féin Ard Comhairle member, interview, 2 August 2005.

105 G. Adams, 'Presidential Address to Ard Fheis 1998', http://www.sinnfein.ie/peace/speech/6.

Republicans argued that the peace process had its own dynamics and that there was 'no stopping the wheels of change ... the DUP may be afraid of change, but they cannot stop it.'[106] The political dynamics for this change were said to lie in the existence of a pro-agreement majority within the electorate as a whole, providing the basis to 'build a pro-agreement project that will either compel the DUP into the institutions or, if they refuse, will leave them behind.'[107] However, this 'explanation' only went so far. Even if 'the wheels of change' and ' political dynamics' might ultimately lead to cooperation in government between the DUP and Sinn Féin, it remained unclear how the reunification process might proceed further given the DUP's implacable hostility to the nationalist project in even its mildest form.

One set of explanations advanced by the Provisional leadership argued that it was the structures and institutions of the agreement itself, in combination with other external factors and the political activism of Republicans, which could provide the dynamics and mechanisms for the success of the long-term transitional project. Although described as an 'ongoing revolution ... an amazing, extraordinary, path-breaking project on the world stage of the struggle for justice', this model of political change seemed to owe more to a belief in a Fabian-like inevitability of gradualness than to a revolutionary transformation.[108] The central argument turned around the 'strand two' elements of the agreement, such as the north–south Ministerial Council and the supporting cross-border implementation bodies, the Consultative Civic Forum and the legislative frameworks for human rights and equality of opportunity in Northern Ireland.[109] These structures provided 'an architecture for an all-Ireland government', forming 'part of the seed that could grow into all-Ireland governance' through:

> the possibility of all-Ireland justice and policing, accountable to the people; an all-Ireland economic strategy, or growth path, for a human rights-based economy; all-Ireland governance of environmental, health, rural development, education – not just a united Ireland, but a new Ireland of equals, of human rights.[110]

The cross-border implementation bodies were 'a vehicle for driving this agenda forward' because *'the potential of all-Ireland structures, as set out*

106 'No stopping the wheels of change', editorial, *An Phoblacht/Republican News*, 4 December 2003.

107 'Gerry Adams: We are determined to see the agreement implemented', *An Phoblacht/ Republican News*, 4 December 2003.

108 M. Anderson, 'The great experiment', *An Phoblacht/Republican News*, 16 October 2003.

109 The Good Friday (Belfast) Agreement (April 1998), printed as Appendix 6 in Elliott, 2000b, 226–229.

110 M. Anderson, 'The great experiment', *An Phoblacht/Republican News*, 16 October 2003.

in the Good Friday Agreement is unlimited and should be promoted as a means of demonstrating ... the benefits of an all-Ireland approach to social and economic development' [emphasis added].[111] The limited experience of the full operation of the institutions of the agreement before 2007 was regarded as a 'start and had great importance in themselves in their own restricted way, towards *eroding the border* through creating all-Ireland institutions *for self determination'* [emphasis added].[112]

This model of political change combined some imaginatively utopian rhetoric with a belief that the existing state structures on both sides of the Irish border could be easily utilized for such a radical project of reunification by stealth. Other strands in the evolving policy were much more in tune with the pragmatic tenor of the times and drew heavily on the gradualist practice that had characterized Provisional engagement with the structures of the Northern Irish state since the 1980s. The cross-border bodies were regarded as the most 'practical strand of the plan for a united Ireland' by 'providing us with institutional channels to further all-Ireland development.'[113] The way that this could occur in practice was outlined by one Sinn Féin official who believed that the areas covered by the cross-border bodies could be expanded, given:

> [Sinn Féin's] previous experience in the Executive and with *the addition of a stronger Sinn Féin presence in Leinster House, we can turn these bodies into genuine instruments of government,* particularly in the areas where the party will have control over ministries. Certain policy areas, such as agriculture and rural development are particularly suited towards this type of all-Ireland approach. [Emphasis added][114]

Alongside this focus on the structures of government were more radical strands that stressed that legislative and institutional change simply created 'a skeleton that needs flesh on its bones ... it is the space for further struggle.'[115] As we have seen, this rhetoric of struggle was a common theme in Provisional politics, but when applied to the 'framework for transition'

111 M. McLaughlin, 'Free-statism needs to be tackled', *An Phoblacht*, 3 August 2006.
112 M. Anderson, 'The great experiment', *An Phoblacht/Republican News*, 16 October 2003.
113 M. L. McDonald quoted in J. Corcoran, 'The most practical strand of the plan for a united Ireland', *An Phoblacht/Republican News*, 23 January 2003.
114 M. Treacy, 'Creating an all-Ireland government', Mála Poist, *An Phoblacht/Republican News*, 23 October 2003. Significantly, Sinn Féin took the ministries of Regional Development, Education and Agricultural Development in the restored executive in 2007, which appeared to confirm this perspective. See W. Graham, 'Shape of Stormont taking form as parties select their ministries', *Irish News*, 3 April 2007.
115 A M. Anderson, 'The great experiment', *An Phoblacht/Republican News*, 16 October 2003.

it took on a slightly different form. In this case it claimed to draw inspiration from other international ideological projects that were attempting to redefine radical politics in a period of historic retreat for the left.[116] These projects developed new conceptions of democracy and empowerment that could be realized in the form of a 'politics from below', which hollowed out and thus transformed established structures of power.[117]

In Provisionalism's 'great experiment', the structural changes created by the Good Friday Agreement opened up the opportunity for these forms of 'politics from below' because:

> the Republican project is not just about votes – that can't and won't provide us with a united Ireland of equals. We have to build a community that demands its rights ... *we have to build a community for reunification* ... using the 'democratic' framework within which the transitional model of the Good Friday Agreement derives – we can build a revolutionary project and the Ireland of equals that all of us are charged to create. [Emphasis added][118]

In practice, this 'revolutionary project' became a practical strategy based on little more than a series of localized EU-funded initiatives, such as integrated area plans and cross-border corridor groups.[119] The rationale for what was essentially an evolutionary process was that the border might wither away through a combination of its irrelevance to these newly-empowered communities and the pressure of wider socioeconomic dynamics. Senior Sinn Féin politicians believed that the integration of these groups and the cross-border bodies into existing systems could transform the local and national administration and government on both sides of the border.[120]

However, as even its supporters recognized, these structures failed to produce the optimistic results expected of them by the Provisionals' all-Ireland agenda. One left Republican strategist set this failure in the broader context of new forms of 'post-conflict politics' when he argued that 'much of this work, particularly that involving local government, cross-border development and European-funded, has become opaque, technocratic and detached from the lives of ordinary people.'[121]

116 Wainwright, 2003.
117 R. de Rosa, 'United Ireland starts in your community', *An Phoblacht/Republican News*, 12 February 2004.
118 A. M. Anderson, 'The great experiment', *An Phoblacht/Republican News*, 16 October 2003.
119 'Building the community for Irish unity', *An Phoblacht/Republican News*, 23 October 2003.
120 M. McLaughlin, 'Free-statism needs to be tackled', *An Phoblacht*, 3 August 2006.
121 E. Ó Broin, 'Sinn Féin and post-conflict politics', *An Phoblacht*, 3 April 2007.

'Whistling in the green twilight'

The strategic weaknesses in the Provisionals' 'great experiment' were more fundamental than this critique acknowledged. As we have seen, the core of the Provisionals' position was that the agreement was 'clearly transitional' in creating a new political space which 'allows us [Republicans] to move our struggle into a new and potentially more productive phase.'[122] One line of argument was rooted in an assessment of supposed changes to Northern Ireland's legal and constitutional status within the United Kingdom as a result of the Good Friday Agreement. The North–South Ministerial Council established under 'strand two' was said to be a 'partial cession of sovereignty to all-Ireland institutions' and meant 'that the Act of Union has been further diminished because British sovereignty over the six counties is lessened, albeit not eliminated.'[123] In a similar vein, some Republicans suggested that the Union was weakened because of the repeal of Section 75 of the Government of Ireland Act 1920.[124] These analyses were rooted in the assessment that British interests in Ireland were shifting because of the post-Cold War international order and the changing significance of the EU and Dublin in British calculations. As a former senior Sinn Féin strategist explained:

> Although we are at the tail end of English government in Ireland, Britain still has political and strategic interests in Ireland. They're not going in the way traditional Republicans thought: they won't withdraw around a crisis. It's ending with a long-term, easygoing, laid-back strategy of dismantling a piece here and a piece there.[125]

These interpretations were politically and constitutionally inaccurate, arising from wishful thinking rather than close reading. The repeal of Section 75 was legally 'of no significance' because it reconstituted rather than replaced British sovereignty.[126] According to Paul Bew, the underlying principles and implications of both the agreement and the Northern Ireland Act 1998 actually strengthened the Union.[127] As one Unionist critic of this 'whistling in the green twilight' put it:

> The legitimacy of Northern Ireland's position within the UK, by virtue of the will of the majority of its people, is the very first principle affirmed. The impossibility of making any change in that status without majority consent

122 Ard Comhairle motion to 1998 Sinn Féin Ard Fheis, printed as a special supplement in *An Phoblacht/Republican News*, 7 May 1998.
123 Ó Ceallaigh, 2000, 39.
124 Ó Ceallaigh, 2000, 40.
125 Tom Hartley, interview, 12 August 2005.
126 Hadfield, 1998, 615.
127 P. Bew, 'Opinion', *Irish Times*, 13 June 1998, quoted in Ó Ceallaigh, 2000, 41.

is endorsed. The sovereignty of the UK government over Northern Ireland is acknowledged.[128]

Given this entrenchment of the consent principle and the deletion of Articles II and III from Bunreacht na hÉireann, Tony Blair's comments in the months before the Agreement was concluded that British policy was not 'on the slippery slope to a united Ireland' and that his 'government will not be persuaders for unity' proved to be completely accurate.[129] Both the letter of the law and the sprit of British government policy ruled out 'the idea that a transition is possible through accommodating Unionist identities and using the agreement as a stepping stone to a United Ireland.'[130]

If this misreading of British policy and the constitutional thrust behind the agreement was a serious political miscalculation, there were other major weaknesses in New Sinn Féin's transitional strategy. 'The 26 counties' had been a central feature of both the long war and the broad front strategies, either as a key component of the all-Ireland revolution or as an essential element in the Irish nationalist consensus.[131] Whether through revolutionary activism or constitutional politics, for the Provisionals the road to victory in Belfast always lay through Dublin. They believed that the high media profile of the Sinn Féin leadership and its leading position among Northern Ireland's nationalist electorate enhanced their credibility and had a positive electoral impact in the south.[132] The growth in support for Sinn Féin in the 1997 and 2002 general elections and the 2004 European election seemed to confirm the validity of this perspective and to show the political gains to be had from synchronizing electoral politics in the south with the peace process in the north.[133] On the basis of these successes, Sinn Féin's emergence as a factor of sustained importance in southern politics seemed assured.[134]

128 D. Kennedy, 'Dressing up "Brits Out" in a language of legal correctness', *Irish Times*, 9 September 2003.
129 T. Blair, speech at the Royal Ulster Agricultural Show, 16 May 1997, http://www. numberten.gov.uk/output/Page948.asp.
130 D. Kennedy, 'Dressing up "Brits Out" in a language of legal correctness', *Irish Times*, 9 September 2003.
131 For different examples of essentially the same strategic rationale, see J. Drumm, 'Annual Wolfe Tone Commemoration speech', *Republican News*, 25 June 1977, and TUAS document in Moloney, 2002.
132 An example of this thinking was Gerry Adams and Martin McGuinness's prominent roles in the 2007 general election campaign. The Sinn Féin weekly, *An Phoblacht*, gave extensive coverage to their activities during the campaign. See the edition of 17 May 2007 for a typical example of their roles.
133 Appendices 2b, 2c and 2e in Coakley and Gallagher, 2005, 466–467 and 469.
134 Rafter, 2005, 233–243.

Irrespective of the Provisionals' specific political ambitions within the southern state, their overall strategy relied on increased electoral strength and political influence south of the border as an indispensable element in the transitional process. The Provisionals believed that what they regarded as the permanent realignment of northern politics had created a 'strategic beachhead from which to maximize change ... bed down the Good Friday Agreement and advance the all-Ireland agenda.'[135]

The transformative model seemed to be one of a process of 'permanent revolution' that would not be able to limit itself to 'internal' concerns, but would flow over into all areas of the political and social life of the two jurisdictions and 'naturally' draw them together. Such an organic process would combine the grassroots community-based cross-border initiatives outlined earlier with a political dynamic of structural change from above. Thus Sinn Féin called for the appointment of a minister with responsibility for 'driving forward and coordinating the work of the all-Ireland institutions and implementation bodies' alongside other measures to further 'the process of coordinating economic development, service provision and planning on an all-Ireland basis.'[136] Combined with the 'introduction of elected six-county representation to the Oireachtas', Republicans believed these changes would 'aid the evolution of an all-Ireland dynamic, strengthen the integration of the all-Ireland bodies and enable northern nationalist participation in the political life of the nation.'[137] The beauty of this scenario for the Provisional leadership was that the normal operation of the Strand Two structures of the Good Friday Agreement could be presented as the embryonic form of an all-Ireland government with 'a new government in Dublin linking up with a new executive in Belfast for the benefit of all who share this island.'[138] In particular, they highlighted how 'Sinn Féin and DUP ministers ... sitting down with ministers in the new government in the south *taking government decisions on the all-Ireland Ministerial Council* ... will fundamentally change politics on this island' [emphasis added].[139] The real constitutional character of the North–South

135 D. Kearney, 'Sinn Féin must use general election to change political landscape', *An Phoblacht*, 19 April 2007.

136 Sinn Féin, 'Building an Ireland of Equals: Manifesto 2002', http://www.sinnfein.org/releases/02/manifesto.html, and 'Delivering for Ireland's Future', 2007 manifesto, http://www.sinfein.ie/elections/manifesto/49.

137 Sinn Féin, 'Delivering for Ireland's Future', 2007 manifesto, http://www.sinfein.ie/elections/manifesto/49.

138 Caoimhghín Ó Caoláin quoted in 'Sinn Féin enters general election in strongest position ever', *An Phoblacht*, 3 May 2007.

139 Gerry Adams quoted in 'Sinn Féin ready for government after election', *An Phoblacht*, 10 May 2007.

Ministerial Council was further and deliberately obscured by Sinn Féin's description of it as the 'all-Ireland' Ministerial Council.

This superficially plausible schema for a gradual transition was actually an attempt by the Provisionals to ignore rather than transform political reality. Its success relied on a quite narrow and quite unlikely conjuncture. Just as Sinn Féin's strategy ultimately depended to an unrealistic extent on Unionist goodwill to facilitate reunification, so the southern part of the process relied unduly on the political will of Fianna Fáil and the southern political establishment in general to carry out the roles allotted to them by the Provisionals.

Given the attitude of Dublin political parties historically and the contemporary consensus among them that 'the Good Friday Agreement will not lead to a united Ireland', this seemed a rather unlikely scenario.[140] Even when this transitional process was given added momentum by Sinn Féin's presumed ability to mobilize public opinion or exert extra political leverage in a hung Dáil, the possibilities of success still remained extremely remote. Above all, the central conceit of the transitional strategy was of an irreversible political momentum driven by 'the Republican struggle':[141] given this premise, if the forwards movement was not maintained not only would the central dynamics of this strategy be shown to be untenable, but the whole political direction of Provisionalism since the late 1980s would be called into question. If Ireland really was to be reunited by 2016, as Gerry Adams had predicted, there was no room for strategic miscalculations, and little time to waste.[142]

The big picture

In the 1990s, these political dynamics were increasingly linked by the Provisionals to patterns of economic and demographic change to create a new discourse of transformation and historical inevitability. They were right to identify the significance of the rapid changes that had taken place on both sides of the border during the latter part of the twentieth century. Powerful external forces and agencies, such as globalization and the EU, had radically altered the economic and social terrain throughout the whole island. The peace process had developed alongside the emergence of the 'Celtic Tiger' economy in the south and the reshaping of the north by the

140 E. Moloney, 'Mansergh doubts GFA will lead to unity', *Sunday Tribune*, 1 October 2000.

141 'Building the republic', editorial, *An Phoblacht*, 12 April 2007.

142 'Adams predicts United Ireland', 14 January 2000, http://news.bbc.co.uk/1/hi/ northern_ireland/6001115.stm.

ambiguous forms of 'the new economy'.[143]

Republicans focussed, in particular, on the effects of a 'natural' strengthening of trade and investment links between the two economies. They argued that this provided the dynamics for a growing convergence because 'the economy does not recognize any border.'[144] The development of such an all-Ireland economy would thus create a dynamic towards reunification by rendering partition an obsolete barrier to economic development.[145] The argument continued that these economic pressures would inevitably produce political change because 'as sure as night follows day political structures will follow economics.'[146] For some Republicans, this process went even further and would ultimately result in a deeper transformative 'convergence, north and south, of social, cultural, economic and political structures, influences and interests.'[147] As former Sinn Féin General Secretary Tom Hartley argued:

> There are bigger forces and pressures from Europe: two infrastructures for a country of 5.5 million people doesn't make sense. These undercurrents are working away independently of the two governments... Finance and politics are two sides of the same coin and I think that ultimately they want an all-Ireland economy... The Good Friday Agreement fits into that pattern.[148]

The result was that Sinn Féin believed that it had 'certainly won the argument on the all-Ireland economy' by making the pragmatic case that 'Ireland as a single economic region makes sense both in our domestic context and in selling ourselves to other markets', as Gerry Adams told the Northern Ireland Chamber of Commerce in 1998.[149] This economic case for reunification assumed an even greater importance when the devolved institutions and cross-border bodies began to function after May 2007. Riding this tide of economic and social development, the Provisionals hoped to 'sell the benefits of all-Ireland economic and infrastructural integration', arguing that their 'purpose in the coming years must be to progress these institutions to the point of integration of existing systems

---

143 For the contradictory patterns of growth and decline in the new Northern Ireland, see Chapter 1. For recent discussions of this hybrid political economy, see Hogan, 2007, 56–63 and Ó Ruairc, 2007, 14–17.

144 Martin McGuinness quoted in P. Connolly, 'Confident of general election success', *An Phoblacht*, 26 April 2007.

145 Sinn Féin, 1994.

146 D. Ó Cobhthaigh, 'The beginning of the end?', *An Phoblacht*, 13 October 2005.

147 F. Ó hAdhmaill, 'Protestants and Republicanism', *An Phoblacht*, 20 October 2005.

148 Tom Hartley, interview, 12 August 2005.

149 G. Adams, 'Sinn Féin, the Irish economy and the role of business', speech to Northern Ireland Chamber of Commerce, 20 February 1998, .http://www.sinnfein. org/releases/98chamber.html.

... which will *inexorably advance our project'* [emphasis added].[150]

These economic and social changes were considered decisive in the process of transition because of their impact on the outlook and psychology of key political actors and their constituencies. In particular, within Republican assessments of these inevitable patterns of change were two interlinked narratives of nationalist advance and unionist decline.[151] In this perspective the long-term decline of traditional staple industries in the north, combined with the emergence of the nationalist middle class and the Celtic Tiger, further undermined the Unionist community's self-confidence and understanding of its place in the world. For the Unionist working class in particular, the old economic certainties no longer existed, and this was reflected in a sense of political alienation and a collective identity crisis.[152]

These arguments were used to explain how the fragmentation of 'the old Unionist monolith' had produced political division and existential doubt. Some Republicans believed the shift to be so fundamental that they argued that 'it is no longer the case that Unionists ... can clearly identify their interests as being wrapped up in a six-county state based on sectarian privilege and propped up by Britain... It is increasingly unclear to many northern Protestants that their economic interests lie in such separation.'[153] This corresponded to heightened political and social divisions within the Unionist community and reflected a new 'economic reality [which] means that increasingly many middle- and higher-class Protestants will see their economic interests lying in an all-Ireland environment.'[154] These perspectives of crisis and change seemed to open up the possibility of political engagement between Republicans and Unionists. Now that simple economic self-interest was no longer seen as the key to Unionist ideology, the focus was increasingly placed on 'the social and cultural aspects of Unionism which prevents [sic] most Protestants nowadays from embracing the concept of a united Ireland.'[155]

For Republicans, these assumptions were good politics because they boosted the morale of their own supporters and played on Unionism's

---

150 M. McLaughlin, 'Promotion of all-Ireland institutions must continue', *An Phoblacht*, 7 June 2007.

151 J. Nixon, 'Perturbing perceptions', *The Other View*, Spring 2002.

152 For a further discussion on changing Provisional assessments of unionism, see Chapter 6.

153 F. Ó hAdhmaill, 'Protestants and Republicanism', *An Phoblacht/Republican News*, 20 October 2005.

154 F. O'Hamill, 'Republicans must win Protestant support', *Irish Democrat*, August/ September 2005.

155 F. Ó hAdhmaill, 'Protestants and Republicanism', *An Phoblacht/Republican News*, 20 October 2005.

already deeply-rooted sense of pessimism and beleaguered isolation.[156] Typical of this approach were leading Sinn Féin strategist Mitchel McLaughlin's arguments that reunification could be taken as given; in the 2000s, it was now a matter of *when* rather than *if* it took place. The debate was essentially about the form of the new arrangements and the best way to manage the transition, rather than whether such a process was possible.

> *The reunification of Ireland is now the big picture. It is going to happen* although parties will come at it from different perspectives as to how it will come about or how long it will take. I believe that there is a general acceptance that it will happen. Even from Unionists.The parties will react: some of them in a positive way, some in a half-hearted way; Unionists will come at it quite negatively, but they are all coming at it... Nobody could ignore the realpolitik of the peace process emerging, just as *they will not now be able to ignore the realpolitik of the reunification of Ireland emerging.* [Emphasis added][157]

It was not only Unionist politicians who had a different sense of *realpolitik* and doubted Sinn Féin's arguments about the impact of economic change on the collective psychology and political structures of the region. Similar arguments had been advanced since the late 1960s about the impact of multinational capitalism on Northern Irish politics and Britain's neo-imperialist strategy to reintegrate both Irish economies.[158] However, at decisive moments in the history of the Troubles the superstructural factors of politics and ideology in the broadest sense had proved to be more powerful engines of events than the economic base.

The decline of the bastions of Protestant economic and social power had indeed helped to shatter the Unionist cross-class alliance, but the results were the opposite of those predicted by such an economically reductive analysis. By the early twenty-first century, long-term economic and social change had simply contributed to the electoral dominance of the DUP, rather than the terminal collapse of Unionism as such. Consequently, linking processes of economic and social change to specific political developments in this way was to remain problematic for Sinn Féin's analysis of the fundamental character of the Unionist crisis.

If this model of change was inadequate as an explanation for political change and a predictor of the future of the Unionist community, it also had other strategic limitations. For example, Republican arguments about the political impact of the increasing confidence of the nationalist

---

156 Walker, 2004, 284–287.
157 M. McLaughlin, 'SF focus on full and faithful implementation of agreement', *An Phoblacht/Republican News*, 30 January 2003.
158 Woods, 2005, 82–83: Farrell, 1980, 328–334.

community and its advancement could be used *against* their transitional strategy. Far from continuing to push against an even higher glass ceiling, the Catholic middle class might be permanently reconciled to the hybrid form of the new Northern Ireland, provided that its economic interests continued to be protected and its cultural identity recognized under the new dispensation.[159]

Thus, rather than economic and social change increasing the tempo of political change, the converse might be true. Greater economic integration need not automatically result in political reunification. The British and Irish governments both rejected the idea that the all-Ireland economy was a stepping-stone towards a united Ireland.[160] The Secretary of State for Northern Ireland, Peter Hain, was described as being 'these days more inclined to talk up economics and play down politics... The north ... had to now see itself as being part of a fiercely competitive global economy. The "old battles" ... simply did not have a place in this new world.'[161] Constitutional and economic issues would remain separate, so that Peter Hain argued that:

> the interpretation that this is a kind of Trojan horse for a united Ireland is 100 per cent wrong. It has nothing to do with the constitutional future, that's entirely separate and dependent on the votes of the people ... *the border exists constitutionally, but in economic terms it doesn't*: in economic terms it's about cooperating across the border and making best use of friends either side ... *the constitutional separation will remain unless otherwise decided by the people.* [Emphasis added][162]

The economic integration of the Nordic and Benelux countries shows that without a conscious political project, even 'natural' and very close *economic* ties between countries do not inevitably and naturally abolish *political* borders between states. Drawing on his intimate experience of the peace process and the negotiation of the Good Friday Agreement, Martin Mansergh has convincingly argued that the development of the EU and the continuing salience of the concept of national sovereignty shows 'there is no evidence, let alone inevitability, from international experience, that limited cross-border cooperation necessarily leads to political unification.'[163] It was a view of 'good neighbourly' economic

159 See Chapter 2 for a further discussion of the possibility of this development.

160 O. Bowcott, 'Ireland pledges to pour millions into reviving north', *Guardian*, 24 January 2007.

161 R. O' Hanlon, 'Hain fellow well met: North's Secretary brings colourful past to controversial place', *Irish Echo*, 20–26 June 2007.

162 L. Clarke, 'Peter Hain: man with a north–south plan', *Sunday Times*, 15 January 2006.

163 Quoted in E. Moloney, 'Mansergh doubts GFA will lead to unity', *Sunday Tribune*, 1 October 2000.

cooperation that pragmatic Unionists shared: for example, in 2007 DUP ministers welcomed Irish government plans to fund infrastructure projects in Northern Ireland as a 'contribution to helping us ... make Northern Ireland more competitive', and praised the commitment of southern-based companies to investing in and developing the economy in the north.[164] These evolving economic relationships were based on mutual self-interest rather than any ideological commitment to reunification, and showed that Unionists did not share Sinn Féin's view that the constitutional position of Northern Ireland could be undermined by investment or eroded by economic influence.

Perhaps the real nature of economic power and the limited scope for an economically-driven transition beyond the framework of the Good Friday Agreement was best illustrated by Ian Paisley's and Gerry Adams's lobbying of the British government for changes to corporation tax rates and increases in the peace dividend in 2007.[165] When it came to a major issue that determined the real framework of economic life in the region, it was to London and the Chancellor of the Exchequer rather than to the North–South Ministerial Council or any nebulous conception of cross-border cooperation that Sinn Féin turned for effective action.

Demographic time-bombs

An important, if largely unspoken, assumption underpinning Sinn Féin's politics was that the tide of demographic change was flowing in favour of the nationalist community in Northern Ireland. Communal headcounts and shifts in the relative balance between the nationalist and Unionist electorates had been central issues in Northern Irish politics since the foundation of the state. Demography and territoriality were intimately connected and formed an increasingly significant aspect of the new dispensation.[166] As such, they reflected a wider tendency towards increased segregation and the communalization of social life and politics following the Belfast Agreement.[167]

In this dominant communal commonsense, a demographic shift in favour of nationalists would have a corresponding political and psychological

---

164 S. Harrison, 'Republic unveils cash plan for NI', BBC News, 23 January 2007, http://news.bbc.co.uk/1/hi/northern_ireland/6289065.stm, and 'Dodds praises Kerry Group commitment to Northern Ireland', 22 June 2007, http://www.northernireland.gov.uk/news/news-deti-220607-dodds-praises-kerry.

165 J. Murray Brown, 'Finance issues will face N. Ireland', *Financial Times*, 26 March 2007.

166 For a summary of these issues, see Shirlow and Murtagh, 2006, 171–181.

167 Shirlow, 2001, 67–74.

impact on Unionism. This 'evidence' could be use politically to reinforce a sense of historical advance or secular retreat. For example, as the electoral map turned increasingly green west of the Bann and Unionists 'retreated' to their *laager* in Antrim and Down, it was possible to produce a narrative of a Unionist community under siege from an advancing tide of nationalism.[168] Likewise, demography was connected to a sense of political decline and dispossession within particular cities and districts, such as the Fountain in Derry and areas of North Belfast.[169] Some feared that these trends were strong evidence that a *de facto* re-partition of the Northern Irish state was underway.[170] Commentators discussed the political implications of an emerging nationalist majority in Belfast and the impact this might have on Unionist attitudes:

> In a normal society, such sectarian statistics would be meaningless, but they continue to constitute the north's political looking-glass. The era of Unionist majorities is ending and – with the educational, economic and cultural indices for the newly emergent population rising all the time – Unionism appears trapped in the headlights.[171]

Republicans claimed to stand for a universalist ideology that aimed to transcend the old ethnic divisions and replace them with the common name of 'Irish citizen'.[172] Their political arguments rarely referred to shifts in population; if they did, it was to warn of the dangers of sectarianism and Republicanism 'being indelibly linked to just one ethnic group'.[173] However, while crude demographic determinism and ethnic triumphalism were rarely expressed publicly, occasionally Republicans did reflect some of the underlying currents present within nationalist discourse. For example, Mitchel McLaughlin's assumption that there was a process of 'steady *demographic*, political, social and economic change, undeniably pointing in one direction towards support for a united Ireland' [emphasis added] seems rooted in these rarely-articulated assumptions.[174]

This evidence suppported the view that Catholics would be a majority

---

168 S. McKay, 'Sectarian tensions continue to poison the North', *Irish Times*, 11 July 2006.

169 Shirlow and Murtagh, 2006, 57–80.

170 T. McKearney, 'New supercouncils can be models of Irish democracy', *Irish Democrat*, January–February 2007.

171 T. McGurk, 'Power-sharing in north must not be stopped by minority', *Sunday Business Post*, 25 February 2007.

172 F. Ó hAdhmaill, 'Protestants and Republicanism', *An Phoblacht*, 20 October 2005.

173 O'Hamill, 'Republicans must win Protestant support', *Irish Democrat*, August/September 2005.

174 Mitchel McLaughlin quoted in R. Cowan, 'Census hits Republican hopes', *Guardian*, 20 December 2002.

in Northern Ireland within the foreseeable future and would vote for a united Ireland at the earliest opportunity.[175] So, literally by an accident of birth and without much effort, the future belonged to Republicans and nationalists. Demography of this type reduced politics to communal headcounts and a crude out-breeding of the opposition. Debates over the future structure of local government, for example, were conducted with more than half an eye on the communal implications of boundary changes.[176] This emphasis on birth and communal identity reinforced the view that politics in the region was essentially a competition for supremacy and resources between two sectarian blocs.

This primitive communalism strengthened the existing particularist elements within Provisionalism and strongly rejected the universal values that Republicans claimed to stand for.[177] For many, such communal calculations were increasingly the looking-glass through which their politics of 'electoral tribalism' were constituted.[178] In *this* strategy for transition, the object of politics was not to engage in political struggle or to win people over to a political position, but to outnumber the 'other' community in order to impose your will on them.

These communal assumptions ran counter to the view that if 'Republicans are to be successful in achieving a united Ireland … it will need the support or at least the acquiescence of a majority of Protestants in the north.'[179] They also rested on the doubtful electoral equation of 'Catholic' with 'nationalist'. In fact, survey and other evidence consistently indicated that up to one-third of Catholics might not vote for reunification in a referendum. In 2006, a 'Northern Ireland Life and Times' survey found that while 56 per cent of Catholics favoured Irish unity, some 22 per cent supported remaining within the UK.[180] Furthermore, this figure might be expected to grow if the new dispensation successfully consolidated itself and increased social and economic opportunities for Catholics, recognized the legitimacy of their cultural identity within the public sphere and made

175 E. Moloney, 'Nationalists advance inexorably, making love not war', *Sunday Tribune*, 12 April 1998.

176 L. Friel, 'Local government blueprint a "major step forward"', *An Phoblacht/Republican News*, 1 December 2005.

177 See, for example, Sinn Féin MLA Francie Molloy's criticism of the party's support for local government reforms, which he reportedly argued would 'make reconciliation between the two political traditions in the North harder', in 'Molloy speaks against local government reforms', *Irish Democrat*, January–February 2006.

178 P. Shirlow, 'Why it's going to take two to tango', *Belfast Telegraph*, 14 March 2007.

179 O'Hamill, 'Republicans must win Protestant support', *Irish Democrat*, August/September 2005.

180 2006 Northern Ireland Life and Times Survey: http://www.ark.ac.uk/nilt/2006/Political_Attitudes/

the Northern Ireland entity a much warmer house for Catholics.[181]

The demographic intricacies of birth-rates, fecundity and fertility became part of everyday politics in the region in the 1990s. Discussions about rates of emigration and higher education destinations were routinely factored into predictions about Northern Ireland's political future; the 2001 census results were eagerly awaited far beyond the confines of university geography departments to see how quickly Catholics were advancing towards the magic 51 per cent that would activate political change.[182]

The census results undermined these demographic assumptions, producing a population breakdown of 53 per cent Protestant compared with 44 per cent Catholic.[183] Although this represented a 5 per cent reduction in the Protestant population since the early 1990s, the 2 per cent increase in the Catholic population was less than expected. Even the most optimistic projections (from a sectarian nationalist view) predict that the Catholic population will have risen to only 46 per cent by 2021, and many believe that converging birth-rates mean that there will never be a Catholic majority. Given recent social and economic changes, the long-term trends point to a stabilization of the religious balance within the population, with Protestants continuing to constitute a majority in the region, albeit one that is smaller and with a different geographical distribution than in the past.[184] Following these results, demographic arguments lost much of their appeal: they were, as one critic put it, 'another plank gone, dealing a blow to one of the main assumptions underpinning Sinn Féin strategy.'[185]

The transforming power of equality?

The discourse of equality became increasingly important in Provisional politics during the 1990s and 2000s. Gerry Adams, for example, wrote in 2003 that 'equality is the most important aspect of Republicanism', and argued that, along with democracy, the concept has been a key theme in progressive politics in Ireland throughout the twentieth century.[186] Sinn Féin's 2007 Assembly election manifesto linked 'diversity, equality and respect' as a central ideological triad to be 'delivered by rights-based governance'.[187] Similar language was used in the May 2007 Irish

181 L. Ó Ruairc, 'Book review: *Irish Freedom: The History of Nationalism in Ireland* by Richard English', *Sovereign Nation*, January–February 2007.

182 M. O'Doherty, 'Breeding schemes', *Guardian*, 13 April 2001.

183 R. Cowan, 'Census hits Republican hopes', *Guardian*, 20 December 2002.

184 J. M. Thorn, 'Another plank gone', *Fourthwrite*, Spring 2003.

185 Ibid.

186 Adams, 2003, 310.

187 Sinn Féin, *Delivering for Ireland's Future-Saoirse/Ceart agus Síocháin* (Assembly election manifesto 2007), www.sinnfein.ie.

general election, where the party campaigned for 'an Ireland of equals where everyone's rights are guaranteed'; during the campaign, Sinn Féin Chairperson Mary Lou McDonald argued that 'equality is at the heart of Sinn Féin's agenda for government.'[188] For left Republicans, the power of this performative discourse of equality lies in its 'powerful challenge to the status quo', formed from linking 'the demand for deeper democracy and greater equality, *infusing each theme with the full force of the other*, combining both into a single ideological and organizational force' [emphasis added].[189]

Others, however, argue that the emergence of this discourse of equality within Republicanism is a recent development. According to Smythe, it 'arrived from nowhere' and is just one example of the ideological shift that has been undertaken by the Provisionals since the late 1980s. For him, the replacement of the demand for a thirty-two-county socialist republic with a call for an 'Ireland of equals' means that ideas of justice and democracy that had 'revolutionary' connotations while the British state denied them have now been replaced by an essentially 'reformist' conception of equality. His explanation for this development is that 'by engaging in constitutional politics, Republicanism accepted what it has previously denied: that justice and democracy were possible within the British state.'[190]

Whether such a possibility can indeed exist remains a central feature of the equality agenda for Republicans. This agenda has been presented as an essential dynamic of the transitional process, not only extending the existing political, economic and social rights of nationalists but also creating new forms of political and cultural space that facilitated revolutionary change. Typical of this position was the argument that:

> The Good Friday Agreement promised an opening for a peaceful struggle towards a new beginning. Each aspect of Unionist hegemony was challenged… Each strut that provided stability is being attacked by equality-and that's the beauty of it – that *the demand for equality is sufficient to undermine the basis of partition.*' [Emphasis added][191]

This strategic framework had a coherence for Republicans because of their longstanding equation of Unionism with inequality and discrimination. In the 1980s for the Provisionals it was an article of faith and a reflection of the experience of the nationalist community that 'the six-county

188 'The only real alternative', *An Phoblacht*, 17 May 2007.
189 E. Ó Broin, 'Sinn Féin and post-conflict politics', *An Phoblacht*, 3 April 2007.
190 Smyth, 2005, 155.
191 D. Ó Cobhthaigh, 'The beginning of the end?', *An Phoblacht/Republican News*, 13 October 2005.

state was founded on inequality' and that 'as equality cannot be achieved for all citizens within [that state], the otherwise admirable objective of reconciliation becomes meaningless as a result.'[192] Thus the argument that 'Unionism cannot live with equality' had a familiar resonance for Republicans.[193] However, the possibilities that equality would be a way of undermining Unionism and transforming the state would have been seen in this period as an impossibly and impractically reformist schema more suited to the gradualism of the SDLP than the revolutionary struggle of Provisional Republicanism.

Smyth's argument that the Provisionals' discourse of equality came from nowhere is not entirely accurate. The emergence of the idea of 'the equality agenda' as a form of transitional struggle can be charted from the late 1980s. Partly through the developing dialogue with the SDLP and partly as a response to British initiatives in fair employment and anti-discrimination policy following the 1985 Anglo–Irish Agreement, some Republicans began to see the possibilities of using the equality agenda to test the limits of these policy frameworks.[194] This was explicitly justified as a form of revolutionary struggle, since demands for equality and democracy were deemed incompatible with the existence of the Northern Irish state: the expectations raised by Hillsborough could not be met, and so any accommodation with the status quo would be exposed as a reformist compromise.[195] Such an exposure would carry the struggle forwards beyond these reformist limits to a higher revolutionary plane. However, if the reasoning was revolutionary, the practice was reformist. As we have seen in the case of local government and fair employment from 1988, Republicans largely worked within the legislative and policy frameworks established by the state and used a mixture of conventional electoral politics, lobbying and recourse to the courts to advance nationalist interests.[196]

Consequently, by the 1990s Republicans had a great deal of experience in using the structures and institutions of the state to implement their policies. They were also aware of the structural and political limitations that such a strategy could impose as they sought to carry out their equality agenda.[197] They drew on this experience, as well as a wider international

---

192 Art Rooney, 'Analysis of the SDLP position re. Hillsborough', *Iris Bheag*, 9, 1988.
193 D. Ó Cobhthaigh, 'The beginning of the end?', *An Phoblacht/Republican News*, 13 October 2005.
194 Art Rooney, 'Analysis of the SDLP position re. Hillsborough', *Iris Bheag*, 9, 1988.
195 'POWs H5, a pan-nationalist alliance?', *Iris Bheag*, 11, 1988.
196 See Chapter 2 for examples of this increasing engagement between the Provisionals and the state.
197 L. Friel, 'Lisburn Council and the equality duty', *An Phoblacht/Republican News*, 29 March 2001.

body of practice based on the politics of difference and recognition, when they came to operate in the post-Belfast Agreement polity. What resulted was a strategy for transition that rhetorically combined two distinct processes of empowerment: one based on utilizing the structures of the agreement, the other a revolutionary struggle for equality. As Sinn Féin's Director of Unionist Outreach Martina Anderson explained, the two forms of struggle were intertwined because 'discrimination is an historical reality, which can only be overcome through the contest for equality and human rights, within a legislative framework that enshrines human rights and equality.'[198]

This strategy shared a common ideological framework with earlier anti-discriminatory policy, such as the MacBride Principles, and the community activism of the 1980s and 1990s in its belief that because the agreement's legislative frameworks enshrined human rights and equality, they could be utilized to highlight discrimination and disadvantage.[199] Republican understanding of how these frameworks could operate was also influenced by the transition to majority rule in South Africa and the black economic empowerment legislation introduced to reverse the effects of apartheid on economic and social life.[200]

The model expressed great confidence in the transformative potential of the 'progressive elements' contained within the agreement. Structures such as the Consultative Civic Forum and the Charter on Human Rights, along with initiatives such as targeting social need and equality impact assessments, could provide (it was argued) a new ideological framework for change throughout Ireland.[201] One leading Sinn Féin strategist argued that this was 'amazing stuff: you can't miss the revolutionary potential of all of this if you set it in the context of what we have today.'[202]

It also relied on the revolutionary potential of the people to be enthused by this agenda and to become empowered 'to speak for themselves, to claim the rights that should be theirs ... and build a community that demands its rights in an Ireland of Equals.'[203] These models drew quite consciously on the new forms of radical politics that had developed internationally in the 1990s and 2000s, and which replaced the old leftist models of the

---

198 A. M. Anderson, 'The great experiment', *An Phoblacht/Republican News*, 16 October 2003.
199 Ibid.
200 Jim Gibney, interview, 23 July 2005.
201 V. Wood, 'Building on the agreement', Mála Poist, *An Phoblacht/Republican News*, 23 October 2003.
202 A. M. Anderson, 'The great experiment', *An Phoblacht/Republican News*, 16 October 2003.
203 Ibid.

party as a revolutionary leadership from above with decentralized and autonomous struggles inspired from below.

However, like the broad front before it, the equality agenda failed to mobilize such a revolutionary movement. As a strategy for transition it was largely stillborn. The predicted 'groundswell of nationalist expectation at a time of increasing nationalist political power' did not open up the 'new and potentially dynamic arena of struggle around equality'.[204] The reasons for this failure are more fundamental than an underdeveloped understanding among Sinn Féin activists of the radical potential of the strategy.[205] They pointed instead to a major flaw in Republican understanding of the state and how far it could be an instrument for the type of transition that they envisaged.

The structures that Sinn Féin believed would facilitate this form of reunification from below were actually part of a civil society that had been increasingly bound to the state since the 1980s. The peace process had strengthened this co-option, producing hybrid forms of partnership firmly located within the flexible architecture of the post-Good Friday Agreement polity. Far from being 'sites of struggle', the community sector was structurally part of the new dispensation with no real potential for autonomous activity, let alone the type of transition envisaged by the Provisionals.[206] Contrary to Martina Anderson's claims that the equality provisions of the Good Friday Agreement had revolutionary potential, they were in fact quite circumscribed ideologically and structurally from a Republican point of view. It was impossible that they could have acted as either a platform or a framework for the type of empowerment that the 'great experiment' required.[207] This political miscalculation was just one of many weaknesses in the rationale for the equality agenda that pointed to deeper flaws in the Provisionals' strategy for transition.

While the discourse of struggle could still be used rhetorically to argue that it was only the 'pressure of nationalist Ireland and international community' that forced Britain to slowly remove the 'props of Unionist power and supremacy', in practice the main emphasis after 1998 was on using the structures and ideological framework of the Agreement to further the equality agenda.[208]

Far from extra-parliamentary politics, Sinn Féin's equality agenda

---

204 L. Friel, 'Lisburn Council and the equality duty', *An Phoblacht*, 29 March 2001.
205 E. Ó Broin, 'Sinn Féin and post-conflict politics', *An Phoblacht*, 3 April 2007.
206 'Building the community for Irish unity', *An Phoblacht/Republican News*, 23 October 2003.
207 A. M. Anderson, 'The great experiment', *An Phoblacht/Republican News*, 16 October 2003.
208 F. Ó hAdhmaill, 'Protestants and Republicanism', *An Phoblacht*, 20 October 2005.

operated as part of the mainstream politics of the new dispensation. Provisional politicians campaigned for more resources for their constituency and made a critique of British government initiatives, which, they argued, had failed to meet the equality provisions of the Good Friday Agreement.[209] They were increasingly drawn into detailed debates on policy implementation and the contrasting merits of the equality agenda versus the British government's policy for 'good relations'.[210] In this sense, Republicans had become constructive critics of the *status quo*, pointing out its limitations and suggesting improvement, rather than radicals creating a new space for completing their revolutionary project.[211]

Partitionism in practice?

At the beginning of 2007, Gerry Adams, speaking at a rally to commemorate Feargal Ó hAnnluain and Seán South, encapsulated the central strategic problem that the Provisionals had faced since the 1970s. In words that repeated almost verbatim the arguments of the TUAS document made some thirteen years earlier, the Sinn Féin leader realistically explained that ' despite major advances in recent years, Sinn Féin does not yet command sufficient political strength to realize our primary and ultimate aims.'[212] This speech was a rare public acknowledgement of the limitation of the Provisional movement and pointed towards the strategic void at the heart of their project.

The flaws and inconsistencies in the Provisionals' strategy of transition were usually concealed by a language of momentum and historical inevitability. As we have seen, Republicans wrongly placed their faith in powerful social and economic forces and the positive dynamics of the equality agenda to work in their favour. In this respect, their strategy amounted to little more than wishful thinking.

This unfounded optimism and language of progress had historical parallels with an earlier generation of 'Free State' politicians who 'developed a rhetoric designed to hide the contradictions of the irredentism-in-theory and partitionism-in-practice which characterized their attitude to Northern Ireland.'[213] In particular, these inconsistencies were

---

209 L. Friel, 'There's still only one rabbit', *An Phoblacht*, 7 June 2007.

210 U. Gillespie, 'Fighting for equality or drowning in bureaucracy?', *An Phoblacht/ Republican News*, 21 August 2003, and 'Delivering on the equality agenda?', *An Phoblacht/Republican News*, 28 August 2003.

211 A. M. Anderson, 'The great experiment', *An Phoblacht/Republican News*, 16 October 2003.

212 G. Adams, 'Time to show courage and take risks', *An Phoblacht*, 4 January 2007.

213 O'Halloran, 1987, 157.

said to have been especially strong historically in Fianna Fáil's northern policy, which meant that 'given how fundamental the expectation of unity was to Fianna Fáil supporters, it is not surprising that, with so little progress to report, De Valéra placed such emphasis on *the inevitability of unity.'* [Emphasis added][214]

If so many of the basic assumptions of its strategy for transition were flawed, then Sinn Féin's policy was now effectively reduced to 'partitionism-in-practice' too. Stripped of its rhetoric of 'great experiments' and 'structural dynamics', all that appeared to be left was a hopeful belief in the power of dialogue to achieve an historic compromise between Unionism and nationalism. In form, this was the same constitutional nationalist project that John Hume and others had been arguing for since the 1960s. However, while SDLP and Sinn Féin strategies shared a common language and were both designed to operate on the same political terrain *within* a reconstituted Northern Irish state, there were some clear differences between them.

Within Sinn Fein's new discourse of invitation and dialogue was another older theme that aimed to divide Unionism and thus secure an advantage for the nationalist community. Given Northern Ireland's politics of 'electoral tribalism' and communal segregation, this strand began to assume an even greater importance in Republican strategy following the Belfast Agreement and the operation of its devolved institutions in 2007.[215] These structural dynamics, combined with the failure of the transitional strategy, ensured that forms of communal politics rather than the ideal of civic Republicanism would predominate within Provisionalism for the foreseeable future.

---

214 Bowman, 1982, 313–314, quoted in O' Halloran, 1987, 158. Significantly, arguments that economic development in the south and the artificial nature of the northern economy would make reunification inevitable were widespread amongst nationalists in the 1920s and 1930s. See O' Halloran, 1987, 159–163.

215 P. Shirlow, 'Why it's going to take two to tango', *Belfast Telegraph*, 14 March 2007.

Chapter 6

The Historic Compromise?

We cannot, and we should not ever tolerate, or compromise with (by govern-
ment structures or any other means), loyalism [Unionism]. Loyalism is a major
obstacle to democracy in Ireland, and to Irish independence. [Emphasis
added][1]

The [Good Friday] Agreement was an *historic compromise* between Irish
nationalism and Irish Unionism. As such it can only work with the willing
participation of *both political traditions...* Cherished positions have been
reworked and remoulded to facilitate changed political realities... Such
realities require ... a Unionism which takes ownership – co-ownership with
nationalists – of the agreement and its institutions. [Emphasis added][2]

'We need to reach out to each other'[3]

Provisional strategy after 1998 appeared ultimately to rest upon nothing
more substantial than a faith in the dynamics of the Belfast Agreement
and an optimistic belief in the inevitability of demographic and economic
change. As a result, the role of dialogue and the power of persuasion
assumed even greater significance in the Republican rhetoric of transition
during this period. This new language perfectly accorded with the tenor
of the times: the theme of the 'historic compromise', with its implications
of a new beginning and a unique opportunity to bring peace, has become
the dominant political discourse in Northern Ireland.[4] The descriptions

1 'Report of Sinn Féin Ard Fheis', *An Phoblacht/Republican News,* November 10 1981. It is
important to note that the term 'loyalist' as used by Republicans in this period referred
to the Unionist population *as a whole.* Adams's criticism of compromise arose during a
debate about amending the federal structure of the Provisionals' proposed constitution
for an independent Ireland, Éire Nua. This structure meant that 'the Unionist-oriented
people of Ulster would have a working majority within the Province and would therefore have considerable power over their own affairs': Sinn Féin, 1972, 56; Ruairí Ó
Brádaigh, former President, Provisional Sinn Féin, interview, 20 April 2003.

2 Martin McGuinness speaking at the 2003 Sinn Féin Ard Fheis, reported in *Irish Republican News and Information,* 28 March 2003.

3 Gerry Adams quoted in R. McAuley, 'Adams says Republicans and Unionists need to
"reach out to each other"', *An Phoblacht,* 5 October 2006.

4 P. McGuigan, 'Healing needed to build the peace', *An Phoblacht,* 20 April 2006.

of the new Sinn Féin–DUP government in May 2007, for example, drew heavily on these tropes of healing and reconciliation by suggesting that a process of normalization was underway that gave the region a 'chance to shake off those heavy chains of history' and become 'a place of peace and promise.'[5] Sinn Féin joined in this narrative of transformation by arguing that this compromise had occurred because ancient enemies had come together to make 'history rather than hype … [in] one of the mightiest leaps forward' for the whole island.[6] Typical of this new Republican discourse were Gerry Adams's frequent calls for a:

> genuine enlightened dialogue between all of us who share this island. The big question for Unionist leaders is the one provided by the example of the Good Samaritan: 'Who will have the courage to cross to the other side?'… For too long we have each kept a distrustful distance from each other… Now we need to cross the road and address one another's injuries and pain. Now we need to comfort and restore one another.[7]

For many, these appeals for dialogue were further evidence of the significant shift that had taken place within Republicanism during the last twenty years.[8] The changes in both style and substance provided evidence for some that this transformation was so dramatic as to constitute a qualitatively distinct, *post-Republican* ideological form.[9] However, not everyone accepted this rhetorical change at face value or believed that the new style truly reflected the political reality; the result was that debating the sincerity of Provisionalism's conversion to constitutional politics has been the central issue of Northern Irish politics for the last seventeen years.[10]

Many Unionists, for example, regarded the language of empathy and conflict resolution as window-dressing to camouflage the real intentions of Republicans. They were sceptical of the politics of the historic compromise, claiming that 'Republicanism has not changed its spots and that it … is still committed to the ultimate aim of the destruction of Northern Ireland as a separate entity.'[11] Until the St Andrews Agreement, the DUP's public position was that 'to enter into government with the terrorists

---

5   Tony Blair and Bertie Ahern quoted in D. McKittrick, 'The Miracle of Belfast', *Independent*, 9 May 2007.

6   Martin McGuinness quoted in McKittrick, 'The Miracle of Belfast'.

7   R. McAuley, 'Adams says Republicans and Unionists need to "reach out to each other"', *An Phoblacht*, 5 October 2006.

8   S. O'Hagan, 'The day I thought would never come', *Observer*, 6 May 2007.

9   Murray and Tonge, 2005, 263–267.

10 D. Godson, 'Warning for Britain as Irish voters snub Adams', *Daily Telegraph*, 28 May 2007.

11 Smyth, 2005.

of IRA/Sinn Féin would be treason', and they remained 'unequivocally clear' that they would never do any such thing.[12] By simply repeating that argument at election time, Ian Paisley and the DUP became the dominant voice of Unionism at the expense of David Trimble and the UUP.

Even those Unionists of a more charitable disposition were initially unsure how far this change in language and political style really reflected a transformation in the Republican discourse, or whether 'it was simply a repackaging for public consumption or, most importantly, by the British and Irish governments.'[13] Unionist scepticism was understandable, given Republican theory as historically constituted and Provisional practice as developed during the Troubles. For most of their history, the Provisionals explicitly repudiated any suggestion of legitimacy for Unionism, either as a cultural identity or as a political category.

The movement's focus was clearly elsewhere: according to one commentator, for Republicans historically 'the British were the problem, their presence was malign [and] they remained in the North for strategic imperialist and economic reasons.'[14] Republicans had traditionally relegated Unionists to a lesser role by making them adjuncts to the central conflict between Britain and Ireland. At best misguided and at worst active collaborators with British imperialism, Unionism was considered as a purely *political* entity and as such was the antithesis of the Republican *political* project. They were rarely defined as an autonomous group with their own interests and identity: the result was, according to one former leading Provisional, that Republicans had ignored the complexities of Unionism and treated the Unionist population as a 'non-people'.[15] Thus, a Republican critic of New Sinn Féin could argue that:

> if there is one coherent thread in Republicanism it is the need for self-determination and so *there can be no accommodation between Irish Republicanism and Unionism*... I never had any problems with Unionists' cultural rights ... and, at one level, I didn't feel any great sense of difference because we spoke the same language and supported the same football teams... *It is the political contradiction*... the two cannot be reconciled. [Emphasis added][16]

Indeed, Republicans could *only* describe Unionism in such political terms. The language of cultural identity would have taken them on to the political territory of the SDLP, thus giving Unionists a degree of legitimacy that they previously lacked in Republican discourse. It was exactly because

12 I. Paisley, 'Election platform', *News Letter*, 4 May 2005.
13 David Adams, former loyalist prisoner and commentator, interview, 27 July 2005.
14 Feeney, 2002, 249.
15 Tom Hartley, former Sinn Féin General Secretary, quoted in English, 2003, 312.
16 Tommy McKearney, former Republican prisoner, interview, 17 May 1998.

it conferred a form of authenticity that implicitly challenged many of the underlying assumptions of Republicanism that this new language of historic compromise and Unionist outreach seemed such a radically different departure for the Provisionals.

Setting the right Tone

However, while in some senses the novel language of the historic compromise did point towards a different Republican understanding of the nature of Unionism, many contradictions and ambiguities remained within Sinn Féin's position. These were not simply the echoes of older forms of Republican politics or the inevitable remnants of a difficult and long-drawn-out transitional process. The paradox was that the consociational framework of the Belfast Agreement that shaped Northern Ireland's 'new politics' also acted to strengthen the particularist elements within Provisionalism.

This occurred because the politics of the new dispensation were ultimately designed not to transcend communal divisions, but to represent and manage them. In one sense, this 'new' pattern was simply a continuation and a regulation of the 'old' conflict on a different institutional battleground.[17] It was 'an essentially managerial approach ' in which 'communal elites were encouraged to arrive at a rapprochement that did not so much dismantle ... divisions as renegotiate their meaning.'[18] The result was that the electoral successes of both Sinn Féin and the DUP in 2003 and 2007 rested on communal mobilization rather than genuine outreach and real engagement. Behind the smiles and the photo opportunities was a form of cold war rather than an authentic reconciliation of 'the two traditions'. As one commentator concluded, even after the much-heralded historic compromises of 1998 and 2007, 'what we are facing is a culture war and a political struggle between two antagonistic communities, rather than any harmony between them.'[19]

Viewed in this light, the Provisional rhetoric of the historical compromise takes on a number of different political functions in the new dispensation: it aimed to consolidate Sinn Féin's dominance *within* the nationalist community just as much as it attempted to disorientate and divide the Unionists outside it. In the polarized politics and segregated society of Northern Ireland, the Provisionals' new language of reconciliation was just another way of strengthening their electoral support and pursuing

17 For some common criticisms of the impact of these consociational structures see Tonge, 2005, Chapter 2; and Dixon, 2001, 277–280 and 304–307.

18 McGovern, 2000, 142.

19 R. English, 'Sinn Féin's hundredth birthday', Open Democracy, http://www. opendemocracy.net/democracy-protest/sinnfein-3068.jsp.

the old struggle for communal advantage. This discourse could also be connected to the tropes of victimhood in Irish Republicanism and give the Provisionals the opportunity to seize the high moral ground in their dealings with Unionist politicians.[20] It might also offer a similar negotiating advantage for Republicans in their contacts with the British government as well as being helpful in securing international support for their cause.[21]

If these new Republican politics referred back to the older communal forms of representational nationalism, they also looked forward to what have become the prevailing currents of identity politics. As we have seen, the underlying assumptions of New Sinn Féin's ideology are broadly cognate with these contemporary forms of particularist politics embodied in the hegemonic discourse of the 'two traditions' which defines communal identity as the predominant feature of the region's political terrain.

Not only was Provisionalism's eclectic theoretical tradition affected by these changes, but the historical strength of particularist elements within Republicanism also meant that these influences could be easily absorbed and utilized by the movement. Thus, in one sense, New Sinn Féin was not new at all. In this way, the politics of the historic compromise could be understood as a reworking of established themes in a contemporary political idiom.

One of the best ways to understand this contradictory ideological pattern and how far it constitutes a new post-Republican project is to trace the evolution of the Provisionals' assessment of the politics of Unionism and its characterization of the Unionist community. Because of Unionism's central strategic and symbolic place in the new politics of Sinn Féin, these changes are inextricably interlinked with the development of other major ideological themes, such as the evaluation of British policy and a confident narrative of nationalist progress as 'the trajectory ... set for the future'.[22] By understanding the degree of change within this 'new' orientation towards Unionism, we thus can come closer to understanding what constitutes Irish Republicanism both as a contemporary political project and as an historical force.

These processes of change can also be understood by reference to a tension present within the founding myths of Republicanism.[23] The

---

20 Mitchell, 2003, 51–71.
21 Cox et al., 2006, 430–432.
22 G. Adams, 'There is no going back to the old days', *An Phoblacht*, 12 October 2006.
23 The term 'myth', as used here, describes a narrative that encapsulates significant meanings and messages as part of the structure of a given ideology. It is not meant to imply falsehood or an historically distorted 'invented tradition' as such. Understanding Republican myths concerning 1798 in this way helps us to define their contemporary ideology and explain their political position. See Hobsbawm and Ranger, 1983.

ideology of Irish Republicanism has long been a site of contestation between conceptions of the universal and the particular.[24] The result is that Republicans have interpreted the ambiguous legacy of the 1798 rising in quite different ways; every generation has had its own mythological reading of the United Irishmen, ranging from Catholic nationalism through to Enlightenment universalism, which reflects the changing patterns of Republicanism during the last two hundred years.[25]

In the same way, the twenty-first-century Republicanism of New Sinn Féin reinvents its own tradition by stressing its non-sectarian nature, its social radicalism, and democratic credentials drawn from the historical tradition of Protestant radicalism exemplified by Wolfe Tone.[26] Contemporary Republicans define the ideas of Tone and 1798 as a living tradition that had:

> Challenged the conservative and established order of [its] day by embracing new and revolutionary ideas, which centred around the international notions of liberating the oppressed, in Ireland's case Catholic peasants, Presbyterian tenant farmers and women. [Tone's] actions and his written legacy force us to examine our actions and our beliefs.[27]

However, while Republicans have theoretically distinguished between their radical-universalist project of self-determination and the ethnic-particularist forms of nationalism, in practice this distinction has been much less clear-cut.[28] This has posed acute political problems historically when Republicans have attempted to address the place of the Protestant population in Ireland.[29]

Republicans had long been aware that Protestants 'perceived their campaign as inherently sectarian and genocidal' and that their theorization of the Unionist community increasingly did not match political reality.[30] These weaknesses arose from the movement's 'almost exclusive identification with the Catholic community ... [its] embodiments of Catholic

---

24 For the contemporary importance of this distinction, see L. Ó Ruairc, 'Belfast Agreement continues to deepen sectarian division', *Sovereign Nation*, October/November 2005; and McGovern, 2004.

25 For example, see the differing interpretations of 1798 and United Irish ideology in Cullen, 1998.

26 Danny Morrison, former senior Republican strategist, interview, 5 January 2004.

27 J. Gibney, 'It is our job to develop the struggle for freedom', *An Phoblacht/Republican News*, 25 June 1992.

28 For examples of this tension see McGovern, 2000.

29 For a discussion of how socialist Republicans dealt with this issue in the 1920s and 1930s, and how their analyses resonated in later Republican politics, see English, 1994, 2003.

30 J. Hope, 'Protestants and Republicans – Grasping The Nettle', *Iris Bheag* 12, 1988.

culture' and the failure of Republicans to develop a socialist appeal that would encourage Protestants to 'recognise the mutual class interests which outweigh their marginal class privileges'.[31] Working-class Unionists, for example, have continued to see Republicanism as 'deeply sectarian and the antithesis of everything we stood for'.[32] As one perceptive Republican commented in 2005, 'is it ... possible to promote a universal as opposed to an ethnocentric concept of citizenship while being indelibly linked to just one ethnic community?'[33]

The central political problem for Republicans is still succinctly encapsulated in Wolfe Tone's famous statement of his objects and means: 'to break the connection with England ... and to substitute the common name of Irishman in place of the denominations of Protestant, Catholic and Dissenter.'[34] The shifting relationship between these *aims* (breaking the connection with England) and *means* (uniting all with the common name of Irishman) within Republican ideology has historically been an indicator of the deeper silences within the movement's politics.[35]

In this context, Sinn Féin's renewed focus on *means* seems to point to a radical strategic shift. The belief that the transformation of Protestant consciousness is a necessary precondition for change restores Tone's schema for 'breaking the connection with England' to its original form. Determining whether this new discourse really represents a victory for universal values or is simply a repackaging of older forms of particularism will not only clarify contemporary Provisionalism's relationship to its own past, but, more importantly, will help us understand its future place within the new politics of Northern Ireland.

'Celtic supporters with Armalites'?[36]

These tensions were present within Provisionalism from its founding moment and they continued to be a recurring theme throughout its

---

31 Ibid.
32 David Adams, former loyalist prisoner and commentator, interview, 27 July 2005.
33 F. Ó hAdhmaill, 'Republicans must win Protestant support', *Irish Democrat*, August/September 2005.
34 The full text reads 'To subvert the tyranny of our execrable Government, to break the connection with England, the never-failing source of all our political woes, and to assert the independence of my country – these were my objects. To unite the whole people of Ireland, to abolish the memory of all past dissensions, and to substitute the common name of Irishman in place of the denominations of Protestant, Catholic and Dissenter – these were my means': Tone, 1988. See also Elliott, 1989, 134–151 for the eighteenth-century context and significance of the statement.
35 Stewart, 1993.
36 McDonald, 2004, 26.

history.[37] While its dominant discourse emphasized normative universal values, these often sat uneasily alongside strong currents of communal essentialism.[38] A combination of a particular Catholic sensibility and these ethno-cultural definitions of nationality weakened this supposedly civic political project.[39] This sense of communal identity, frequently confirmed by personal experience, could be translated into a 'defenderist' consciousness that might shape attitudes and actions more powerfully than universalist values.[40]

Although explicitly sectarian attitudes rarely surfaced in the public statements of the Provisional movement, these elements provided a fertile subsoil for a particularist analysis of the Unionist community.[41] These elements were given free rein during the initial development of the armed struggle, which, according to some Republicans, 'derailed the whole thrust of the Republican movement so that in many cases it became sectarianized, a purely Catholic versus Protestant conflict'.[42] This closely reflected the heightened communal polarization of the period, when, as one radical civil rights activist put it:

> Everyone applauds loudly when one says in a speech that we are not sectarian, we are fighting for the rights of all Irish workers, but that's really because they see this as the new way of getting at the Protestants... [W]e failed absolutely to change the consciousness of the people. The consciousness of the people who are fighting in the streets at the moment is sectarian and bigoted.[43]

37 For example, the place of Catholic religious practice in Republican commemorations was a recurring issue that symbolized on a small scale these tensions between secular ideology and unspoken communal assumptions. See, for example, the arguments advanced by 'Secular Republican' in 'Rosary at Commemorations', Mala Poist, *An Phoblacht/Republican News*, 12 April 2007.

38 Bourke, 2003, 1–20.

39 This potent combination was said to be an important factor in popular mobilization during the 1980–1981 hunger strikes. See O'Malley, 1990.

40 For discussions on the historical nature of Defenderism, see Elliott, 1989, 244–249. Cronin, 1980, 209 makes contemporary links between Defenderism, the nature of northern Catholicism and the traditional role of the IRA.

41 Mickey McMullen, former Northern Editor, *An Phoblacht*, interview, 13 April 1998; Brendan Hughes, former OC, Belfast Brigade IRA, interview, 10 August 1998; and Tony Catney, former member Sinn Féin Ard Comhairle, interview, 15 April 1998 refer to degrees of sectarianism within the Belfast Provisionals in the 1970s. For their explicitly anti-sectarian definitions of Republicanism, see Bean and Hayes, 2001.

42 John Kelly, former member of Sinn Féin, MLA and founding member of the Provisionals, interview, 24 July 2005.

43 Eamonn McCann, quoted in Barnett, 1969, 5.

Many Provisionals were aware of these communal influences and considered them a danger to the unifying aims of the Republican project. Sectarianism was a product of British imperialism and the structural divisions of northern society, not a core element of Republicanism. While Catholicism was a powerful cultural influence on *Republicans,* the Provisionals argued that their *political* project itself was non-sectarian.[44] Republican socialists, in particular, distinguished between particularist nationalism and Republicanism, which they regarded as incompatible, whereas Republicanism and socialism were both rooted in the universalist ideal of democracy.[45]

Critics of Republicanism, especially those within the nationalist community, dismissed these claims to non-sectarian civic Republicanism. They argued that Provisionalism was merely a communal movement that cloaked its Hibernian particularism in a language of democracy. One commentator, for example, described the Provisionals as 'Celtic supporters with Armalites, Catholic avengers rather than real Republicans'.[46] Thus, one correspondent writing to *An Phoblacht,* in the early 1980s might have revealed some of the deeper silences of Provisionalism when he questioned the Irishness of the Protestant population by arguing that:

> If we find a section giving allegiance to an external power ... as they have been doing down through the centuries, then I propose that we should debate our acceptance of them as children of the nation... Is it good enough to take nationality as a reflection of where you and your direct relatives were born or should it be based on political allegiance? Even if you are born on Irish soil, you still have to choose your country of allegiance. *If your loyalty lies outside the national interest then you should leave for the country of your allegiance*... Free-Stateism and loyalism travel a similar road: they subvert the national status as a unitary body and perpetuate sectarianism and injustice to maintain their own sectional ... interests... You can't sectionalize democracy: it must be power to the people as a whole. You can't be Irish and serve the forces which perpetuate division, be they Free-Stateism or loyalism. [Emphasis added][47]

The Provisionals largely understood Unionism within this colonial context. Initially it was considered to have no objectively independent existence, either politically or as a social force, separate from British Imperialism. The two were inextricably linked because the Unionist population either formed a relatively privileged labour aristocratic stratum or were colonists

---

44 Danny Morrison, interview, 5 January 5 2004.
45 L. Ó Ruairc, 'Why do we commemorate 1916? Why do we think Republicanism is still relevant?', *Starry Plough/An Camcheachta*, April–May 2003.
46 See P. Murphy, 'PIRA has failed Wolfe Tone test', *Irish News,* 6 August 2005; McDonald, 2004, 26.
47 'Nationality' (letter), *An Phoblacht*, 28 October 1982.

comparable to the Algerian *pied noirs*.[48] Ultimately, these relationships were deemed both unstable and indissoluble, historically-based and determined by their function of:

> dividing the working class and maintaining British rule ... loyalism [Unionism] and its sectarian divisions sustain British power, the British presence perpetuates sectarianism. Each feeds off the other — *sinister parasites in our land.* [Emphasis added][49]

As the central pillar of this relationship between Unionism and British imperialism, the northern state was irreformable and the armed struggle justifiable as the only means to remove it. Britain could not structurally confront Unionism for the pragmatic reasons that the northern state acted to 'safeguard British economic and political interests within the six counties', while Unionism was seen as 'the decisive divisive instrument in [Britain's] control of the whole of Ireland. For propaganda purposes they mainly justify their presence through its presence; to smash it would be to jeopardize their own continued rule and interests.'[50]

These patterns of thought were illustrated by a polemical exchange in the mid-1970s that prefigured contemporary debates on the nature of the conflict in Northern Ireland. An argument by a Dublin intellectual that the northern Republican struggle was essentially concerned with 'freedom from English rule, *recognition of nationality ... the right to cultivate and display Irishness'* and the demand for 'substantial control of those parts of the north-east where Catholics are in a clear majority' [emphasis added] was dismissed as 'sectional' by a leading Belfast Provisional.[51] A similar dismissive approach was taken towards other proposed 'reformist' changes to the constitution, laws courts and local government system, which recognized that 'Northern Ireland contains people of Irish nationality' and that any future political settlement would be dependent on the *'political will and behaviour of the Ulster British majority'* [emphasis added].[52]

Proposals that the answer to the conflict could be guarantees of *'equality of treatment for Catholic communities* within Protestant communities' [my

---

48   M. Farrell's *Northern Ireland: The Orange State* (1980) was influential in popularizing this terminology within Provisionalism. See, for example, R. McAuley, 'The Orange State', *An Phoblacht/Republican News*, 19 July 1980.

49   M. McClelland, 'Bodenstown Commemoration', *An Phoblacht/Republican News*, 28 June 1980.

50   P. Dowling, 'Preserving privilege', *An Phoblacht/Republican News*, 17 February 1979.

51   The original article by 'Freeman' (identified as Desmond Fennell) in *An Phoblacht* drew a sharp response from the editor of *Republican News*, Danny Morrison. See 'Freeman', 'Talk of an independent North', *An Phoblacht*, 25 June 1976; and 'Freeman hasn't a clue', *Republican News*, 31 July 1976.

52   'Freeman', 'Talk of an independent North', *An Phoblacht*, 25 June 1976.

emphasis] were similarly denounced as a partitionist parroting of the SDLP and British interpretations of the conflict.[53] In contrast, reunification was posed in democratic terms that were not dependent on either the political goodwill of the Unionist majority or the recognition of Irish cultural identity. It was argued that 'the socialist Republic ... will be achieved through class struggle. This is *a contestation for political power* and its justification lies *not in the sectional ill-treatment of the northern nationalist population*, but in the illegitimacy of partition and British imperialist control' [emphasis added].[54]

The issue of the degree of Unionist autonomy and the appropriate methods to change Unionist consciousness would continue to remain the central analytical and political dilemma for Republicans. It was conceptually difficult for Republicans to define Unionism in terms of identity politics in the 1970s and 1980s. This was impossible revisionism because defining Unionism as a cultural identity would be tantamount to accepting an 'internal conflict' model and thus denying the political basis of Republicanism. Such as analysis would undermine the whole rationale of the Republican war in the north, rendering it a purely sectarian struggle that deliberately misrepresented the nature of the Unionist community. As one Republican was to argue perceptively during an internal debate in the 1980s on 'the thorny question of the Republican movement's relationship with Protestantism', the Provisionals 'had avoided objective, clinical analysis of our relationship to the Protestants ... because in some respects, their existence challenges our struggle'.[55]

Cuckoos in the nest

In practice, Republicans did recognize a considerable potential for independent action by Unionists: their analysis of Unionism was more sophisticated than some of their balder comments would suggest. Certainly, they had recognized that the Republican movement could politically and militarily exploit tensions in the relationship between the Unionists and Britain: from its inception, the IRA's campaign had a political dimension based on exacerbating differences within Unionism to heighten the sense of crisis and deepen political division.

To Unionists there was an essential continuity between these strategic assumptions and the political tactics employed by the Provisionals during the 1990s and 2000s concerning issues such as decommissioning and the

---

53 'Freeman', 'Talk of an independent North', *An Phoblacht*, 25 June 1976; 'Freeman hasn't a clue', *Republican News*, 31 July 1976.
54 'Freeman hasn't a clue', *Republican News*, 31 July 1976.
55 J. Hope, 'Protestants and Republicans-Grasping The Nettle', *Iris Bheag 12*, 1988.

future of the IRA; the only real differences lay in the weapons employed and the terrain on which the battle was fought.[56] In their different ways, 'the long war' and the long negotiating strategy of the peace process were both designed to undermine Unionist resolve and weaken the credibility of its political leadership to the advantage of Republicans.

There was a similar continuity in some of the other unspoken assumptions of the Provisionals' strategy. For example, during the late 1970s and the 1980s, the Provisionals increasingly considered how the Unionist population would react in the event of a British withdrawal, given that they believed the British presence was the main prop for Unionism.[57] In this strategy, Britain remained the key to changing Unionist consciousness. By inverting Tone's dictum, the Provisionals produced a schematic formula where British withdrawal was to be the *means* of uniting Catholic, Protestant and Dissenter.

The Provisional analysis stated that colonial structures of power had historically promoted division and created a sectarianized consciousness that must be removed before conflict could be resolved. Republicans argued that the 'breaking of the union with Britain will be a necessary step on the path to breaking them from their supremacism, their loyalism.'[58] The position that was most identified with the Adams leadership was one of *realpolitik* that anticipated significant Unionist opposition. The implied perspective of civil war was justified and explained as an inevitable stage on the road to the socialist republic. The perspective was of strong Unionist resistance to a united Ireland, with the possibility of a 'nationalist–loyalist [Unionist] civil war in the north in the event of a British withdrawal... There can be no ducking the ... fact of political life ... that the loyalists will become increasingly enraged as they see their Orange statelet ... being destroyed by Republican successes.'[59]

Unlike these Republicans who had previously 'appealed to the Protestants of Ulster to reject the evil and bigotry of Ian Paisley to emerge from the centuries of sectarian rule and to march forward together', this analysis took a harder view of the Unionist population, both in the present and in the future.[60] It argued implicitly that Unionism would act for itself in its own interests: 'loyalism is like a *hungry fat cuckoo in a nest*. Its appetite can

56 Godson, 2004, 445–48.
57 'Brownie', 'Scenario for establishing a socialist Republic', *An Phoblacht/Republican News*, 19 April 1980. 'Brownie' has been identified as Gerry Adams.
58 P. Dowling, 'The British presence, partition and Protestant privilege', *An Phoblacht/ Republican News*, 22 October 1981.
59 Dowling, 'The British presence'.
60 D. Ó Conaill, 'The seeds of victory', *An Phoblacht/Republican News*, 18 August 1979.

never be satisfied. The more it gets the more it wants' [emphasis added].[61] Thus, for Gerry Adams and other opponents of the 'federalism' of Sinn Féin's Éire Nua policy in the early 1980s, the argument was clear:

> We must recognize that loyalists are a national political minority whose basis is economic and whose philosophy is neo-fascist, anti-nationalist and anti-democratic. *We cannot, and we should not ever tolerate, or compromise with (by government structures or any other means), loyalism.* Loyalism is a major obstacle to democracy in Ireland, and to Irish independence. Federalism, by giving loyalism a privileged position, becomes an obstacle. [Emphasis added][62]

The accepted view among Republicans in this period was that the struggle was a chance to start afresh in building a new Ireland, a transformative process of mutual liberation in which 'the nationalist people must liberate themselves and in doing so they will liberate also the loyalist people who are *caught in a trap of history* and are unable to liberate themselves.' [Emphasis added][63] The nationalist population were thus given the central role as the agency of transformation in Irish society, while the Unionists are cast in a passive and illegitimate role and can only be liberated by an external force.[64]

The continuing impact of this strand of thinking was revealed in the first Provisional responses to the new pluralistic discourse of identity emerging within both the northern nationalist community and southern political class in the 1980s.[65] These new understandings of Unionism were perhaps best exemplified by the *New Ireland Forum Report 1984*, which argued that:

> The validity of both the nationalist and Unionist identities in Ireland and the democratic rights of every citizen in this island must be accepted; both of these identities must have equally satisfactory, secure and durable, political, administrative and symbolic expression and protection.[66]

---

61 'Disastrous approach', *An Phoblacht/Republican News*, 3 May 1980. The use of the cuckoo image, with its implication of illegitimacy, is revealing. Compare it to M. McClelland's '*sinister parasites in our land*' (my emphasis), used at Bodenstown in 1980 ('Bodenstown Commemoration', *An Phoblacht/Republican News*, 28 June 1980).

62 'Report of Sinn Féin Ard Fheis', *An Phoblacht/Republican News*, 10 November 1981.

63 R. Ó Brádaigh, 'Ag labhairt leis an Uachtaran', *IRIS*, April 1981.

64 Note that this vanguard's liberating role also extends to freeing 'the ordinary people of England from a centuries-old imperialism which is exercised in their name by the ruling classes of England'. Ó Brádaigh, 'Ag labhairt leis an Uachtaran'.

65 For example, see Bishop Cahal Daly's speech in St Anne's Cathedral, Belfast: 'Bishop Daly urges acceptance of two identities in North', *Irish Times*, 23 March 1983.

66 *New Ireland Forum Report*, 1984.

Similar arguments advanced by Garret FitzGerald about the complexities of identity and the need for a political accommodation between nationalism and Unionism were dismissed by the Provisionals as 'pseudo-intellectual claptrap' and 'the product of a slave mentality'.[67] Unionism continued to be interpreted in political terms as a 'racist and imperialist ideology, which sets British above Irish … and [justifies the] … oppression of half a million nationalists'. Attempts to understand the 'Unionist ethos' and to define the conflict as one grounded in 'different heritages and different identities' were regarded as ludicrous and a product of self-delusion.[68] Cahal Daly's definition of Unionism in cultural terms and his recognition of it as an 'intrinsic, rightful and legitimate component of Northern Ireland and Irish reality' were likewise sweepingly dismissed as an expression of 'double standards which lacked any sense of engagement with political reality'.[69]

The Provisionals continued to oppose these constitutional nationalist analyses during their initial public contacts with the SDLP in the late 1980s. They argued that constitutional nationalism's focus on peripheral cultural issues ignored:

> the substantial and ongoing contribution which British domination has made in creating and sustaining our political crisis. Your concentration on the symptoms of the problem leads you [the SDLP] to blame the attitudes held by nationalists and loyalists as its cause.[70]

In this Republican reading, constitutional nationalism was identified with the essentially passive politics of identity which had been 'channelled into relatively harmless agitation for a few minor social/cultural changes. Coupled with *the nonsense of unity by consent*, the national demand has become an aspiration to be achieved in some far-distant future' [emphasis added].[71]

The rhetoric of reconciliation

From the mid-1990s onwards, a similar critique was being made of the Provisionals' own politics by their Republican critics. This criticism reflected the major rhetorical and ideological changes that had occurred

---

67 P. Dowling, 'Distorted vision', *An Phoblacht/Republican News*, 27 May 1982.
68 'Constitutional manoeuvres in the dark', *An Phoblacht/Republican News*, 25 August 1983.
69 'Bishop defends Unionism', *An Phoblacht/Republican News*, 7 July 1983.
70 'Sinn Féin/SDLP talks: review and analysis', *An Phoblacht/Republican News*, 22 September 1988.
71 K. Currie, 'Strengthening partition: the development of constitutional nationalism', *An Phoblacht/Republican News*, 17 June 1986.

in Republican politics in the relatively short period between 1989 and 1993.[72] During these years, the foundations of a new form of constitutional Republican politics were laid. These politics would ultimately reverse the Provisionals' fundamental hostility to the state and see Sinn Féin participating in its government following the Belfast and St Andrews' Agreements. However, long before these symbolic public events could occur there had to be an internal transformation in the patterns of thought and the structures of meaning that underpinned Republican politics.[73] In whatever way this occurred, whether through the use of organizational power or the self-deception of 'lies, noble and ignoble', there was no doubt that a radical ideological and strategic change had taken place within Provisionalism.[74]

In 1989, this revisionist future would have seemed literally fantastic to IRA volunteers and Sinn Féin activists. Publicly, Sinn Féin still remained *'totally opposed to a power-sharing Stormont assembly ... there cannot be a partitionist solution. Stormont is not a stepping stone to Irish unity.'* [Emphasis added][75] The IRA likewise maintained an unchanged anti-imperialist focus by declaring that:

> at some point in the future due to the pressure of the continuing and sustained armed struggle, the will of the British government to remain in this country will be broken. That is the objective of the armed struggle ... we can confidently state today that there will be no ceasefire and no truces until Britain declares its intent to withdraw and leave our people in peace.[76]

For most Republicans, identity politics and the theorization of Unionism as a cultural form were contradictions in terms because they focussed on the symptoms rather than the causes of conflict.[77] Unionism was still primarily identified as a political ideology defined by its connection with 'English government in Ireland'. For the Provisionals this meant that:

> *theoretically ... the day English government ends in Ireland there is no reason to be Unionist...* For Unionists to negotiate is to negotiate themselves out of existence, since why would you want to be a Unionist in an Ireland where there is no political link with Britain? [Emphasis added][78]

72 For an example of this change compare the different analyses of Unionist politics and the Unionist community outlined in Sinn Féin, 1988 and Sinn Féin, 1992.

73 Bean, 1994.

74 Aughey, 2002, 5.

75 'The Sinn Féin–SDLP talks: Sinn Féin statement', *An Phoblacht/Republican News*, 8 September 1988.

76 'We will break Britain's will – IRA', *An Phoblacht*, 17 August 1989.

77 K. Currie, 'Strengthening partition: the development of constitutional nationalism', *An Phoblacht/Republican News*, 17 June 1986.

78 Tom Hartley, interview, 23 August 2005.

For many contemporary observers, the first indications of a significant revision of the Republican project were a new rhetoric of compromise and reconciliation directed towards the Unionist community in the early 1990s. Even political opponents and critics of Provisionalism were struck by this change of tone. The SDLP'S Alex Attwood, for example, argued that 'there is a real change in [Sinn Féin's] ... political culture', while Cardinal Cahal Daly saw an ideological transformation from 'absolutist and dogmatic statements ... to new themes of consent, respect for diversity and agreement'.[79] Others were also struck by how far Sinn Féin's 'rhetoric of cultural diversity [was] more attuned to the European conflicts of the 1990s', and how its calls for a 'vibrant discourse' with the Protestant community indicated the distance the Provisionals had travelled in such a short time.[80]

The style of this 'vibrant discourse' was indicative of the substantial changes taking place in the movement's structures of thought. A notable feature was the increasing use of a language of empathy influenced by contemporary ideas of politics as a therapeutic activity. This combined a distancing from violence with the idea that dialogue and a mutual search with the Protestant community could end the causes of conflict. These strategies for conflict resolution and transformation figured prominently from an early stage in 'Republican outreach' to Unionists, especially in contacts with churches and community groups.[81] Along with admissions that Sinn Féin's appeals to the Protestant community 'cannot be heard above the deadly sound of gunfire and a recognition of the hurt and pain inflicted by the Republican campaign', this language of engagement and healing appeared to show a genuinely different face of Provisionalism to Unionists.[82]

These themes of reconciliation reflected what was to become one of the dominant narratives of the peace process.[83] Indeed, violence became increasingly defined within Republican discourse as a symptom of a deeper conflict and a barrier to political progress rather than a political instrument. Political violence perpetuated division and sectarian hostility, and was a sign of political failure. This approach suggested that the causes of the conflict were located in identities and cultures so deeply rooted that

---

79 Quoted in Bean, 1994, 1.
80 R. Wilson, 'Beyond ideology', *Fortnight*, October 1992.
81 For references to the importance of dialogue with Protestant Church leaders, see G. Adams, 'The Republican struggle is the force for change', *An Phoblacht/Republican News*, 15 October 1992.
82 J. Gibney, 'It is our job to develop the struggle for freedom', *An Phoblacht/Republican News*, 25 June 1992.
83 L. Friel, 'Former combatants meet as Reconciliation Network launched', *An Phoblacht*, 24 May 2007.

violence was not only ineffective and counter-productive: it was directed at the wrong targets, and was akin to putting out a fire using petrol. Thus, a leading Provisional political strategist could argue:

> We cannot and should not ever try to coerce the Protestant people... We *understand* why there is conflict in our society ... not only do we *understand* the IRA's use of armed struggle; we also *understand* why loyalists use violence and we *understand* why Britain uses violence. [Emphasis added][84]

This new language was more than an aping of the latest linguistic fashions of contemporary politics. It revealed a very different conception of politics and political subjectivity from that traditionally expressed in IRA Easter statements or at Hunger Strike commemorations. It was also rooted in a very different set of explanations for the causes, and thus the solutions, of conflict in Northern Ireland. That these implications were largely uncon-sidered by most Republicans at the time is not only a reflection of the movement's limited theoretical traditions and organizational structures of power: it also points towards a much deeper ideological crisis and profound sense of uncertainty within Provisional Republicanism.

The politics of persuasion

One way to understand this pattern is to consider a number of linked concepts within the new politics of Sinn Féin. The essence of this perfor-mative discourse was encapsulated in the recurring tropes of dialogue, persuasion, consent and identity. This new language was highly ambig-uous, reflecting the uncertainties of an organization cautiously feeling its way into new ideological territory and only abandoning its old positions with great reluctance.

These characteristics were by no means unique to the Provisionals or to Northern Irish politics in general. They reflected a much wider change in the patterns and sensibility of contemporary politics as long estab-lished ideologies and political structures collapsed in the post-Cold War world. Constructive ambiguity and the elision of obvious contradictions were not just tactical sleight-of-hand, the necessary nonsense that kept the Northern Irish peace process going: both as a political art form and as a structure of thought, these ideological inconsistencies were the very essence of 'the postmodern condition'. In the case of the Provisionals, they were also the very public expression of an existential crisis that undermined the fundamental structures and ideological legitimation of their politics.

---

84 Mitchel McLaughlin, Sinn Féin Ard Comhairle member, quoted in R. Wilson, 'Beyond Ideology', *Fortnight*, October 1992.

As we have seen, it was this 'vibrant discourse' of reconciliation that appeared to be the most significant political innovation to contemporary commentators. Although primarily directed towards securing Unionist consent and exploring the contradictions in Unionist identity, this new political framework also changed the way that Republicans understood the politics of the nationalist community as well. By drawing on the therapeutic terminology of identity politics, the Provisionals argued that both communities were affected and defined by the Other, and that any solution to the conflict had to start from that premise.[85]

The emergence of these new themes of persuasion and consent within Provisional politics can be traced through its contacts and dialogue with constitutional nationalism from the late 1980s. During this period, Republicans began to define Unionism and the Unionist community in a startlingly different way. As one former Provisional prisoner described it, 'there was a realization that Unionism, while it is essentially pro-British, has its own agenda, which has to be dealt with. And we had to ask ourselves: what if the British really have no selfish strategic or economic interest? If we take that seriously, then we really should look at the nature of Unionism as the problem.'[86] Most significant for the development of future strategy was an assessment that Unionism was heterogeneous and that its different identities and allegiances reflected deeper social and political divisions.[87]

Republicans increasingly looked at the wider significance of the ideological divisions within Unionism.[88] In particular, there was a focus on the fragmentation of the 'cross-class alliance within the body politic of political Unionism' and the antagonisms that these 'internal contradictions' would produce within its politics.[89] These assessments superseded 'a very simplistic view straight out of the textbooks that Unionism represented a *comprador* class ... and it's just not true because it's so varied. Unionism is an ideology that harks back to the past but it is not static ... it can adapt just like any other ideology, and it has done.'[90]

What emerged from this reassessment of the nature of Unionism appeared to mark a radical departure for Republicans, because their 'understanding of Unionism ... really is now a world away from where it

---

85 Danny Morrison, interview, 5 January 2004.

86 Eamonn Mac Dermott, former Republican prisoner, interview, 14 August 1997.

87 Eoin Ó Broin, Sinn Féin Director of European Affairs, interview, 30 June 2005.

88 H. MacThomas, 'A strong draft of Porter', *An Phoblacht/Republican News*, 28 November 1996.

89 D. Ó Cobhthaigh, 'The beginning of the end?', *An Phoblacht/Republican News*, 13 October 2005.

90 Tony Catney, former Sinn Féin Ard Comhairle member, interview, 13 April 1998.

was twenty years ago'.[91] The novelty of this discourse lay in its apparent authentication of the historical position of the Unionist community and the degree of legitimacy it conferred on Unionism as an ideology. This produced a new realism that neither damned Unionists as a 'counter-revolutionary scourge', nor was unduly optimistic about their radical potential as the heirs of 1798.[92] Unionists were now regarded as a historically formed community and a real force with which Republicans had to engage. Republicans believed this changing understanding of Unionism, as both an ideology and as a community, encapsulated the dramatic scale of their ideological evolution towards new forms of pluralistic politics.

However, this position was to remain only partially developed and implicit throughout most of the peace process, representing a grudging acceptance of political reality rather than a conversion that repudiated past sins. Nevertheless, as political opponents and commentators recognized, the use of such language was a highly significant development. While it is fruitless to look into the souls of Provisional politicians to assess the sincerity of their commitment to these new types of politics, these strategic and ideological changes were crucial in drawing Republicans into a working accommodation with the *status quo* in Northern Ireland.

While the Provisionals explicitly rejected the 'Unionist veto', the objectives of Republican political strategy were now 'to *persuade* Unionists that their future lies ... [in a united Ireland] and to persuade the British government that it has a responsibility to so influence Unionist attitudes' [emphasis added]. One of the means of achieving this was a broad-based campaign directed at Britain alongside 'a debate leading to *dialogue* ... with northern Protestants and northern Protestant opinion on the democratic principle of national self determination' [emphasis added].[93]

In one sense, this new emphasis on Britain acting as a persuader for Irish unity reflected the long-established Republican position that the conflict was a product of Britain's historical and contemporary role in Ireland.[94] This stress would continue throughout the peace process, since Republicans believed that 'theoretically the key to politics in the North is the British government; Unionists won't move as long as the Brits don't move, and the key to get Unionists to move is to get the Brits to move.'[95] However, in practice the Provisionals were moving away from this focus

91 Eoin Ó Broin, interview, 30 June 2005.
92 A. Maskey, 'Reaching out', *An Phoblacht/Republican News*, 15 December 2005.
93 'The Sinn Féin–SDLP talks: Sinn Féin statement', *An Phoblacht/Republican News*, 8 September 1988.
94 M. McLaughlin, 'The tenacity of the oppressed', *An Phoblacht/Republican News*, 10 May 1990.
95 Tom Hartley, interview, 23 August 2005.

on British withdrawal as a key strategic aim. A statement issued following talks between the Provisionals and the SDLP in 1988 shows how quickly they had occupied this new political terrain. They now argued that it was:

> *desirable* that Unionists or a significant proportion of them give their support to the means of achieving Irish reunification and promoting *reconciliation* between Irish people of all *traditions*. It is obviously desirable that everything reasonable should be done to obtain the *consent* of a *majority* in the north to the constitutional, political and financial steps necessary for bringing about the end of partition. [Emphasis added][96]

In the early 1990s, this focus on Unionist consent and agreement became an even stronger element in Provisional politics, making what had been previously defined as *desirable* now an increasingly *essential* precondition for political change. This position was explicitly stated in the 1992 Sinn Féin document *Towards a Lasting Peace in Ireland*, which marked 'a significant evolution of Republican thinking' by clearly acknowledging in cultural and political terms that 'a settlement of the longstanding conflict between Irish nationalism and Irish unionism' was at the heart of the peace process.[97] Republicans now argued that the 'traditional position that a resolution to the problems with the Unionists would have to await the removal of the British government's involvement in Ireland was wrong.'[98] While this schema theoretically still saw the 'de facto veto conferred on the Unionists by the British government' as the main obstacle to reunification, engagement with the Unionist community began to move centre-stage as a necessary precondition for political change.[99] The ideological framework and strategic analysis of *Towards A Lasting Peace in Ireland* became the master-narrative for the Provisionals' strategy in the 1990s and 2000s by explicitly recognizing that the consent and allegiance of Unionists were essential to secure a lasting peace

This new focus on Unionism fundamentally redefined Republican politics. The Hume/Adams statements in 1993, for example, replaced the traditional Republican objective of a British declaration of intent to withdraw with a new formulation of self-determination expressed in an ambiguous language of consent. The Provisionals now agreed that 'the exercise of self-determination is a matter for agreement between the people

---

96 'Sinn Féin–SDLP Talks', *An Phoblacht/Republican News*, 15 September 1988.
97 G. Adams, 'Presidential Address: Sinn Féin Ard Fheis', *An Phoblacht/Republican News*, 27 February 1992; 'Sinn Féin maps road to peace', *An Phoblacht/Republican News*, 20 February 1992.
98 J. Gibney, *An Phoblacht/Republican News*, 2 March 1995.
99 Eoin Ó Broin, interview, 30 June 2005.
100 'Joint statement from Gerry Adams and John Hume', Sinn Féin, 2005, 217.

of Ireland. It is the search for that agreement and the means of achieving it on which we will be concentrating.'[100] This was a significant departure because it 'acknowledged the political imperative ... that any constitutional change would have to earn and enjoy the allegiance of the different traditions on the island', meaning that any political settlement could only take place on terms acceptable to the Unionist community.[101]

This emphasis effectively shifted the focus of Republican politics away from the 'external' intervention of British imperialism in Irish affairs towards a new focus on the 'internal' dynamics of conflict between identities within Northern Ireland.[102] In essence, Provisional politics from the early 1990s onwards was largely an amplification and an elaboration of these themes. In many cases this was quite literally so: a Provisional spokesperson in 2007 could argue that 'our job is to persuade Unionists that their best interests lie within an all-Ireland structure. Within an all-Ireland context, Unionism can have major political role in Ireland.'[103] In doing so, he used exactly the same words that had appeared almost twenty years earlier in a 1988 Sinn Féin statement following talks with the SDLP.[104] However, the real difference in 2007 was that rather than this theoretical 'all-Ireland context', Provisional strategy in practice now focussed on a process of conflict resolution *within* Northern Ireland as a 'way of dealing with the reality of Unionists who do not want a Republic'.[105]

'In the doing rather than the saying'[106]

Following Sinn Féin's acceptance of the Belfast Agreement, the language of 'the historic compromise' and the discourse of constitutional nationalism triumphed over more 'traditional' themes in Provisional politics. The core of contemporary Republicanism was now said to be its commitment 'to a process of national reconciliation ... and a long-term dialogue with representatives of Unionism in our country'.[107] Senior Sinn Féin politicians argued that the agreement's principles of 'equality and parity of esteem for both traditions', which stated that all sections of society should enjoy

101 V. Browne, 'This is a good time for Ireland', *Irish Times*, 31 January 2007.
102 This explanation of the nature of the conflict mirrored that advanced by John Hume since the 1960s. See Murray and Tonge, 2005, 259.
103 Sinn Féin MLA Francie Molloy, quoted in E. O'Dwyer, 'Bringing home the harvest', *An Phoblacht*, 14 June 2007.
104 See note 75.
105 Tom Hartley, interview, 23 August 2005.
106 Sinn Féin Lord Mayor of Belfast Alex Maskey, quoted in 'A mayor for all the people', *An Phoblacht*, 13 June 2002.
107 G. Adams, 'Completing the unfinished business of 1916', *An Phoblacht/Republican News*, 13 April 2006.

'religious and civil liberty, equal rights and opportunities', emulated 'perhaps unwittingly' the sentiments of the 1916 Proclamation.[108]

Republicans stressed that they were 'genuinely committed to building an understanding and establishing a consensus for a shared future based on respect for each other's differences'.[109] According to Martin McGuinness, the peace process had meant that 'cherished positions ... [had been] reworked and remoulded to facilitate changed political realities', offering the possibility of a final settlement, the historic compromise between ancient enemies.[110] Speeches from senior Provisionals were liberally peppered with such references to the necessity of reaching out to Unionism and engaging with the Unionist community, in an attempt to:

> demonstrate that when we say we want to build an Ireland of equals, that means equality ... for every individual regardless of religion, race, sexual orientation or political persuasion. When we pledge to 'cherish all the children of the nation equally', it doesn't mean only Republican or nationalist children.[111]

The language of engagement and reconciliation was everywhere. As Sinn Féin's Director of Unionist Outreach, Martina Anderson, put it:

> engagement based upon equality and respect affords us the opportunity to discuss the past in order to learn from it, to discuss the present, to manage it and to discuss the future to plan it... We want this dialogue to be inclusive and open, without limits, a dialogue that would dispel fears, cast away myths and misconceptions and establish trust.[112]

This 'reaching out' to the Unionist community was exemplified by Belfast Sinn Féin councillor Alex Maskey's term as Lord Mayor in 2002–2003, during which he projected himself as 'a mayor for all the people'.[113] Maskey's term was portrayed as symbolic of a wider tide of change breaking through the undemocratic barriers preventing Republicans from participating in government. His term in office was marked by a carefully thought-out and conscious symbolism of engagement, illustrated by the laying of a wreath during the Somme commemoration, his hosting of a civic reception for the Royal British Legion and a mayoral visit to the

108 M. McLaughlin, 'A Proclamation for all', *An Phoblacht/Republican News*, 13 April 2006.
109 L. Friel, 'Historic initiative heralds new political era', *An Phoblacht*, 31 May 2007.
110 Martin McGuinness speaking at the 2003 Sinn Féin Ard Fheis, reported in *Irish Republican News and Information*, 28 March 2003.
111 M. McLaughlin, 'A Proclamation for all', *An Phoblacht/Republican News*, 13 April 2006.
112 L. Friel, 'Historic initiative heralds new political era', *An Phoblacht*,, 31 May 2007.
113 'A mayor for all the people', *An Phoblacht*, 13 June 2002; A. Maskey, 'Reaching out', *An Phoblacht/Republican News*, 15 December 2005.

opening of the Presbyterian General Assembly.[114]

Likewise, power-sharing in local government and the cooperative spirit evident in the early days of the restored Assembly were cited by Republicans as harbingers of a positive future. These experiences only served to confirm for Republicans the impression that there had been a sea-change in their attitudes towards Unionism; Alex Maskey believed in 'small, symbolic acts of toleration and accommodation... [which] send a clearer message than endless verbal assurances. It's sometimes in the doing rather than the saying.'[115] Mitchel McLaughlin's appeal for a degree of political tolerance in the new Assembly was argued in a similar way:

> it behoves us all to recognize the fact that our community is shared. There is a diversity, which is quite legitimate and has significant and sizable support in the community. If members [of the assembly] are to make politics work, they must strike a balance between all those clashing and competing issues.[116]

The narrative of the peace process, encapsulated in this rhetoric of reconciliation, was the story of Provisionalism's ideological journey from the extremist margins to the political mainstream. Sinn Féin's participation in government with DUP (like their previous 'compromise' with the UUP) appeared to be the logical conclusion of their desire to be 'generous and magnanimous in ... [their] outreach to Unionism'.[117] The pictures of Ian Paisley and Martin McGuinness taking their oaths of office for a new executive in May 2007 – 'a moment that most of us who lived through the Troubles thought we would never see' – only seemed to confirm the dramatic and fundamental revolution that had taken place.[118]

In these new Provisional politics, engagement replaced confrontation. Republicans now argued that through dialogue with Unionism it was possible that an historic compromise might emerge. Such an engagement was 'not about hoodwinking Unionists into a united Ireland ... or assuring Unionists that they can be Republicans too'. The transition on offer appeared not to be the radical transformation that Republicans had traditionally envisaged; instead, it was described as 'a narrative with

---

114 'Maskey rues opportunity lost', *Belfast News*, 29 May 2003.

115 A. Maskey, 'Reaching out', *An Phoblacht/Republican News*, 15 December 2005.

116 McLaughlin was describing Sinn Féin's decision not to vote against a motion for the Assembly to rejoin the Commonwealth Parliamentary Association or 'cause difficulties for members who feel that the motion reflects their cultural, political and social affinities'. See 'McLaughlin acknowledges political differences', *An Phoblacht*, 17 May 2007.

117 Gerry Adams quoted in A. Foley, 'Campaign gears up to challenge direct rule', *An Phoblacht/Republican News*, 5 October 2006.

118 S. O'Hagan, 'The day I thought would never come', *Observer*, 6 May 2007.

which Republicans aren't completely happy, a narrative that finds a place for the Orange Order and other symbols and traditions of Unionism'.[119]

The structures of conflict were no longer solely defined in *political* terms, but were increasingly located within the *cultural traditions* of Unionism and Nationalism. This elision of the differences between politics and culture, expressed in the therapeutic language of identity politics, attempted to sidestep the fundamental *political* contradiction between the Union and the Republic. The idea of the historic compromise, in particular, implied an acceptance of the *authenticity* of the opposing identity and invalidated previous assessments of Unionists as 'Irish people who were confused about their cultural identity and political allegiance or were victims of a false consciousness orchestrated by the British state'.[120]

Thus, while *politically* Unionism and Republicanism remained the antithesis of each other, as *cultural* forms some type of accommodation or even reconciliation might be possible between them.[121] This was an attempt to transcend 'the old ethnic divisions' by 'recognizing that there is a difference between an ethnic identity ... and a political philosophy... Unionism is a political idea, nothing more. There is no historical imperative which prevents Protestants from being non-Unionists.'[122]

Despite this optimism, there were a number of contradictions within this discourse of historical compromise and its suggestions of a 'final settlement' to the conflict. Unionists and the Provisionals still had different understandings of the 'final' direction of Northern Ireland's new political dispensation. Unionists correctly argued that Sinn Féin's participation in the government of Northern Ireland was 'the final settlement' because Republicans 'are trapped and hobbled in an internal settlement, with unification further away than it has ever been ... the reality is that they have reached the end of the road and lost the only battle that ever really mattered to them.'[123] For the Provisionals, however, the process was still incomplete and has yet to be concluded:

> this arrangement [between Sinn Féin and the DUP], worked out and agreed in the Good Friday Agreement negotiations, is a *necessary milestone on the road to national reconciliation...* Republicans are now exercising real political power, impacting on the lives of people throughout the north... If any

119 All quotations from A. Maskey, 'Reaching out', *An Phoblacht/Republican News*, 15 December 2005.
120 Eoin Ó Broin, interview, 30 June 2005.
121 For a discussion of the process by which political aspirations were transformed into cultural categories in Northern Ireland, see Ryan, 1994, 135.
122 F. O'Hamill, 'Republicans must win Protestant support', *Irish Democrat*, August–September 2005.
123 A. Kane, 'Adams's day of unity isn't coming', *News Letter*, 25 June 2007.

Republican was ever in doubt it is clear that we have entered *a new phase of our struggle*. [Emphasis added][124]

It would be easy to dismiss these assessments as either point-scoring triumphalism or mere attempts to maintain flagging Republican morale following Sinn Féin's electoral setbacks in the south in 2007. However, the contradictions between the two positions are useful in shedding light on the unspoken assumption of contemporary Provisionalism and illustrating some of the underlying weaknesses in their strategies of dialogue and transition.

Open and closed dialogue

Republicans used two distinct and mutually-exclusive conceptions of dialogue as part of their discourse of transition. To Sinn Féin, dialogue was either an open-ended engagement between Unionists and nationalists or a narrowly circumscribed process with a predetermined outcome.

The dominant rhetorical form in the 1990s and 2000s was that of open dialogue. This was described in the vague language of transition and national reconciliation as a process that would eventually produce the equally indeterminate 'Ireland of equals'. The other strategy for transition had a more clearly defined outcome – the 32-county socialist republic – but was much less frequently referred to. The process of dialogue by which this objective would be achieved remained unclear.

The idea of open dialogue assumes some common ground between political parties, and it was rooted in a new acceptance by Republicans of the necessity for Unionist consent for any future political arrangements. This definition is closest to the underlying assumptions of liberal democratic polities, where contending parties work within a given political consensus and accept the framework of the state as legitimate. Adopting this consensus model of dialogue and conflict resolution through 'national reconciliation' meant that the Republican political project had ceased to be a transformative challenge to the existence of the Northern Irish state.

Given the clearly expressed preferences of a majority of Unionists, an open dialogue of this type based on the consent principle could reach no other conclusion than the continuation of the Union. As the Provisionals had acknowledged as early as 1993, open negotiations with the Unionists were likely to have a very closed outcome.[125] Furthermore, if the issues at stake could now be resolved through discussion, this posed several questions for Republicans about their analysis of the nature of the

124 '"We have entered a new phase of our struggle" – Adams', *An Phoblacht*, 28 June 2007.
125 See note 101.

conflict and the legitimacy of the armed struggle as a means to achieve their historical aims.

This form of transitional dialogue was heavily influenced by the particularist categories of identity politics and marked the Provisionals' movement away from the universalist discourse of national self-determination. Political subjectivity was now constituted by the component 'identities' or 'traditions' that comprised the nation, rather than by an exercise in democratic self-determination by the nation itself acting as an indivisible whole. Given this context, open dialogue, based as it was on the fixed categories and communal identities of Nationalism and Unionism, was simply an agreement to disagree and to reconfigure the Union on the basis of peaceful coexistence between the 'two traditions'. These forms of politics were essentially concerned with the management and regulation of difference, rather than with its transcendence and transformation. The conflict was not resolved; rather, it was transmuted into new forms of political competition and social polarization.

The other understanding of dialogue had its origins in a transformative conception of politics. This form of politics had clear historical goals and a sense of victory and defeat; in this worldview, there were recognizable winners and losers. Instead of a theoretically indeterminate outcome, this form of Republican politics had the clear objectives of ending the Union and establishing a republic. Traditionally, the measurement of strategic success would have been a British declaration to withdraw and victory sealed by the creation of a politically independent thirty-two county Socialist republic. Throughout the peace process the Provisional leadership argued that New Sinn Féin's constitutional politics continued this war by other means and that Republican objectives could now be pursued by forms of dialogue and persuasion.

However, these closed forms of dialogue were conceptually less a mutual exploration of possible future political arrangements and more (optimistically) a discussion of surrender. Because Republicans understood that Unionists would not 'negotiate themselves out of existence', these models of dialogue either incorporated an element of strong persuasion or identified external forces that would aid their project.[126] For example, the Provisionals in 1992 considered that an important agency for bringing about political change was no longer the subjectivity of the Republican struggle acting *against* the British state, but was instead that same state acting *on* the Unionists as a persuader for change.[127]

In this context, the South African experience of transitional dialogue

126 Tom Hartley, interview, 23 August 2005.
127 Sinn Féin, 1991, 12.

was a model that the Provisionals found attractive. However, the obvious differences between the political strength and negotiating position of Sinn Féin and the ANC only serves to highlight the limitations of this strategy as a means of securing Republican objectives. The ANC was the representative of the majority of South Africans, and was negotiating with the representatives of a small minority to ensure an orderly transition to majority rule. The negotiations confirmed a victory won through wide support and a mass movement against apartheid, whereas Sinn Féin was the representative of a minority seeking to gain from negotiations and 'dialogue' what it had not won through armed struggle or electoral politics.

The political power that supported the 'dialogue ' between the ANC and the National Party, and which enabled the ANC to substantially impose its will, was quite obviously lacking in Sinn Féin's case. Sinn Féin's closed dialogue with Unionism would not be able to 'transform' the consciousness of the Protestant population and 'persuade' Unionists in a way similar to that of the white minority in South Africa. It is doubtful whether the Provisional leadership ever really thought that it would be in such a position, but rhetorically it remained a key theme in Provisional politics. In 1993, Gerry Adams described this process of transformation in a language that would become familiar during the peace process:

> a real peace settlement ... will create a revitalization of national morale and an *irreversible thrust* which will swamp the sectarian begrudgers and permit the merging of Catholic and Protestant working-class interests, *freeing* in the process the Protestant tradition from its association with Unionism. [Emphasis added][128]

In this schema, the force that will shift Protestant consciousness is not armed struggle, socialist revolution or British withdrawal, but the 'irreversible thrust' of the peace process itself. Initially, Republicans argued that this 'thrust' would be found in a structured dialogue between Unionism and nationalism facilitated and encouraged by the British government. However, by the time of the Belfast Agreement New Sinn Féin had ceased to believe in the possibilities of such a transformation. The process of change was now the subject agent of change itself; the means had become the ends.

'A dual identity that must be accommodated'[129]

The circular form of this 'transitional' process was further strengthened by the increasing importance of identity politics within Provisionalism.

128 G. Adams, 'Protestants' future lies with the rest of us', *An Phoblacht/Republican News*, 20 May 1993.
129 J. Gibney, *An Phoblacht*, 2 March 1995.

These new elements produced a contradictory discourse that intertwined engagement and 'Unionist outreach' with a narrative of Unionism as an ideology and a community in crisis. Understanding this 'crisis' became a central task of Provisional strategy; exploiting it became the central aim of Republican politics.

The dominant narrative of the historical compromise accepted 'that there are divided political allegiances within the nation and that the Unionists have a *dual identity* that must be accommodated' [emphasis added].[130] Using a 'language of invitation', leading Provisionals argued that in their 'vision of a united and independent Ireland there must be a place for those who consider themselves British and those who wish to *stay British*' [emphasis added].[131] This definition of Unionism and Britishness as cultural categories that could be accommodated within an independent Ireland was in marked contrast with earlier assessments. As we have seen, these positions described Unionism solely in political terms and questioned 'why would you want to be a Unionist in an Ireland where there is no political link with Britain?'[132]

These new formulations of Unionism as a cultural form raised the possibility that it could be detached from its political essence and identification with the Union of Great Britain and Northern Ireland and converted into a mere identity of rituals and 'harmless' spectacle.[133] Although framed polemically, the argument that 'if Unionists expect nationalists to be Irish within a "British Northern Ireland", why couldn't' Unionists remain British within an "Irish Northern Ireland"' seems to suggest that some Republicans thought this a realistic possibility.[134] A Protestant Republican 'following in the path of Tone and McCracken' argued a similar case when he suggested that:

> we are not going to turn lots of Protestants into Republicans, but at least we can reduce the fear that Protestants have of Republicans and of the Republican agenda and therefore an independent Ireland... We have to do all we can to basically tell the truth about what we want.[135]

130 Ibid.
131 J. Gibney, *An Phoblacht*, 2 March 1995.
132 Tom Hartley, former Sinn Féin General Secretary, interview, 23 August 2005.
133 Interestingly, this possibility reflects the arguments of some Unionists that Orange marches, for example, could become 'simply' cultural events and tourist attractions comparable to the Notting Hill Carnival, rather than points of communal contention. See O. Bowcott, 'Ulster's Orange parades "could become carnivals"', *Guardian*, 23 June 2006.
134 H. MacThomas, 'A strong draft of Porter', *An Phoblacht/Republican News*, 28 November 1996.
135 Protestant Republican activist Sam Porter quoted in 'Following in the path of Tone and McCracken', *North Belfast Sinn Féin News*, undated (summer 2006).

For some Republican socialists, the truth was that these cultural definitions of Unionism represented an accommodation with a reactionary and
backward-looking identity. To them, the dominant forms of identity
politics in Northern Ireland represented the triumph of particularist
essentialism over universal values. In what was very much a minority
position within the 'Republican family', they argued that Republicanism
was still a universal ideology capable of transcending and overcoming
particularist forms of identity, whether these be Unionist or nationalist.
From this point of view, these forms of identity politics only acted to
deepen communal division and entrench sectarianism:

> Everyone in Ireland has the right to hold on to his or her own identity,
> culture and perceived nationality. Republicans accept the right of the 'Protes-
> tants' and the British to define themselves as they want... Many Protestants
> who consider themselves to be British only hold on to one aspect/expres-
> sion of British identity: the monarchy, nostalgia for the Empire... Repub-
> licans would point out that there other ways of being British, why don't
> you explore and appropriate for themselves all that which is progressive in
> British heritage? What about being British Republicans like the Levellers and
> the Chartists?[136]

However, for the Provisionals these issues of dual identity and divided
allegiance found expression in a willingness to explore the interplay of
different political structures and identities as a basis for a historic compromise. Increasingly, cultural identity was elevated to a central category of
political discourse: for many, paradoxically, it was portrayed as a cultural
realm almost beyond politics: a type of local fifth province in which reconciliation could take place.[137] For New Sinn Féin, this space seems, however,
to have been a meeting place for the *accommodation* of existing identities
rather than a site of *transformation* and the creation of new forms.

These formulations implied a *de facto* recognition of Unionism by
Republicans, initially as a legitimate cultural identity but ultimately as
a political position, through their acceptance of the consent principle in
the Belfast Agreement. Leading Sinn Féin strategist Mitchel McLaughlin
illustrated the importance of this form of identity politics when he argued
before the Good Friday Agreement that a political settlement:

136 L. Ó Ruairc, 'Belfast Agreement continues to deepen sectarian division', *Sovereign
      Nation*, October–November 2005.
137 A reference to the Field Day project's ideal of a cultural space as point of meeting for
      the diverse traditions in Ireland. See Kearney, 1997, 99–107.
138 M. McLaughlin, 'The Republican ideal' in Porter, 1998, 81.
139 Eoin Ó Broin, interview, 30 June 2005.
140 Danny Morrison, interview, 5 January 2004.

can only be achieved by negotiations that examine and *provide for all the elements of a community's identity*. The assertion of an absolute and unconditional right to a political Union will not produce an agreed Ireland. It is only by *focussing on all the Unions* and on a multiplicity of connecting factors that a compromise can be achieved between nationalists and Unionists that will stand the test of time. [Emphasis added][138]

However, there were other less positive strands within these forms of identity politics. For Republicans, the Unionist community faced a fundamental crisis inherent in its historical development and contradictory position within both the United Kingdom and Ireland. Drawing from both British and Irish sources, it was a hybrid that appeared ill-at-ease with itself and uncertain of its place in the world. One feature of this fusion was 'Unionism's failure to construct an identity that was rooted in the actual cultural fabric of the people, or invent a tradition that means real things to real people in real moments of history'.[139] For Republicans, this reflected the essentially incoherent nature of Unionist identity and the failure of Unionists to successfully interrogate their own tradition.[140] One symptom of the resulting crisis was a sense of 'Unionist alienation', illustrated by the lack of political leadership shown by Unionist politicians and the social disintegration of the loyalist working class.[141]

Unionists were portrayed as 'the victims of a history made behind their backs' who consequently reacted to change like any rejected and betrayed members of an imperial outpost.[142] Continuing this theme, some Republicans saw Unionism as 'an aberration of history, a politic [sic] that is used and abused by the British state' whose ambiguous present and uncertain political future could be exploited to further the Provisionals' political project.[143] This sense of abandonment produced a crisis of identity that was reflected in the collective psyche and in the politics of the Unionist community, because:

> it is the British government which will decide the future of the Union. Unionists know this and ... rarely have had confidence in the British government... Unionists are the human face of this very negative connection with Britain. At times my heart goes out to them. I know working–class loyalist areas are leaderless. They were able to live too long in the shadow of the Empire and the shadow of the Orange Hall.[144]

These contradictions were further heightened by political developments

141 D. Morrison, 'Destroying Ulster, not loving it', *Daily Ireland*, 14 September 2005.
142 M. McLaughlin, 'Protestantism, Unionism and loyalism', *An Camcheachta/Starry Plough*, November 1991.
143 Tom Hartley, former Sinn Féin General Secretary, interview, 23 August 2005.
144 Gerry Adams interview in *Irish Times*, 2 October 1993.

within the British state, the process of devolution in Scotland and Wales and the wider debates about the nature of Britishness, all of which seem to find no place for the values and traditions identified by Ulster Unionists as 'British'.[145] According to Republicans, the result was a 'desperate identity crisis' with Unionists rejecting a 'very rich Irish culture' and agonizing 'over whether they are Ulster-Scotch, Picts, English or British'.[146] The Provisional analysis argued that, paradoxically:

> it is the very nature of that Britishness which makes Unionists most Irish because it is particular to the specific historical cultural and geographical location of Unionism, emerging out of nineteenth- and twentieth-century history. This means that *the history of Unionism in Ireland is an Irish tradition*, especially when compared to what people in Scotland, Wales and England define as Britishness. [Emphasis added][147]

According to Republicans, the resulting self-doubt and crisis of identity gave Unionists and nationalists alike a common historical and contemporary sense of victimhood at the hands of British imperialism. They were able to play on Unionism's cultural pessimism and sense of besiegement, threatened by a circle of enemies both within and without. This sense of a garrison under siege was further reinforced throughout the peace process by Republican comparisons with South Africa and the failure of Unionist leadership to 'take them into the twentieth century: [they have] no De Klerk'.[148]

The Provisionals' response to this perceived crisis was to pursue two distinct but intimately connected political strategies of recognition and confrontation. Using the differing forms of cultural engagement and the politics of tension, the common aim was to exploit and exacerbate the divisions within Unionism. Although rarely expressed in these terms, this had been an important strategic aim throughout the peace process and was central to what the Provisionals defined as the transitional process. By weakening it ideologically and politically, it was argued that these new strategies would ultimately secure some support, or at least acquiescence, from within the Unionist community for the transitional process towards

145 M. Derrig, 'Signs of an emerging English separatism?', *An Phoblacht/Republican News*, 29 June 2006. For recent debates on Britishness and identity politics, see 'Britain rediscovered', *Prospect*, April 2005. For the political implications of constitutional change in Scotland for Northern Ireland, see M. Devenport, 'Intriguing parallels of Scots poll', BBC News, 28 April 2007, http;//news.bbc.co.uk/1/ki/northern_ireland/6603033.stm

146 Gerry Adams quoted in D. Rose, 'Chalk and cheese', *The Other View*, spring 2002.

147 Eoin Ó Broin, interview, 30 June 2005

148 G. Adams, 'Protestants' future lies with the rest of us', *An Phoblacht/Republican News*, 20 May 1993.

an Ireland of equals.[149] In defining the crisis as one of cultural identity, it took on an existential character and challenged Unionism at a much more fundamental level than that of a mere political ideology.

In this context, Unionism was optimistically defined by some Republicans as a much more fluid and potentially malleable identity now open to the possibilities of transformation through dialogue. Echoing the dominant discourse of the peace process, this form of political engagement was conceived as having a therapeutic character, because it would:

> enable Unionists to carve out for themselves a contemporary identity that takes into account everything that shapes them. Unionists are affected by the nationalist community just as we are affected by their presence. This new understanding and recognition would transform *their uncreative identity* and the siege mentality that has refused to share power with nationalists or to be positive or generous towards the nationalist community. [Emphasis added][150]

Provisional politics used a familiar language in tune with the contemporary sensibilities of identity politics, but whose particularist forms and political practice also echoed the older narratives of Irish nationalism. Unionist disorientation and confusion was contrasted with the coherence and pluralism of contemporary nationalism: as one Republican described it, 'nationalists have no problem with their identity: they know who they are. The identity issue becomes a problem because Unionists try to impose a "British" identity that doesn't work at all.'[151]

Identity politics were thus a continuation of war by other means, used to score points and politically undermine Unionism. They also acted to consolidate the nationalist communal identity in opposition to a perceived fractured and inauthentic Unionist culture. Unionists recognized the importance of Republican cultural politics in what they defined as a strategy of 'cultural imperialism', which promotes a 'nationalist programme of expansion, assimilation and cultural cleansing'.[152] It is not necessary to agree with that strongly-worded assessment to see how central the politics of cultural identity had become to the new dispensation in general and to Provisional strategy in particular.

---

149 F. Ó hAdhmaill, 'Republicans must win Protestant support', *Irish Democrat*, August/ September 2005.
150 Danny Morrison, interview, 5 January 2004.
151 Ibid.
152 D. Rose, 'Chalk and cheese', *The Other View*, spring 2002. David Rose is a leading member of the Progressive Unionist Party (PUP).

Conclusion:
The End of a Song?

With the thundering of cannons, the Irish ghost which, since the eighteenth century, has constantly kept the rulers of England on the trot, has been ceremoniously buried. The Irish question, a question that could endanger England's position towards the outside, has come to an end... After the great agrarian reform, the Catholic population of Ireland no longer consists of malcontent hungry people but of small farmers with peaceful conservative leanings... The Irish peasantry abandoned the banner of the fight for independence, when its economic interests were no longer in conflict with the English government. It contented itself with the fight for self-government. Tragically enough, the Sinn Féiners – being petty bourgeois – didn't understand that but lulled themselves to sleep with nationalistic dreams...[1]

The men in suits

By the summer of 2007 many of the questions that had been central to Northern Irish politics since at least the late 1980s appeared to have been resolved. The formation of a new executive headed by formerly irreconcilable opponents Ian Paisley and Martin McGuinness marked the lifting of the last taboo and finally signified the Provisionals' acceptance as a legitimate political party. Like the Good Friday Agreement in 1998 or the IRA's commitment in 2005 to 'purely political and democratic programmes through exclusively peaceful means' before it, the new executive was taken as yet another powerful symbol of the apparent transformation of Northern Irish society and politics.[2] The conversion of Provisional Republicans from fanatical terrorists into mainstream politicians was central to this 'new normality', if only because the main focus of British state strategy for nearly forty years had been on defeating Republicanism's military and political challenge to the constitutional *status quo*. Now the IRA is quickly passing into history and is thought sufficiently harmless to

1 K. Radek (trans. A. Probst) , 'The End of a Song', *Berner Tagewacht*, 9 May 1916: http://www.marxists.org/archive/radek/1916/05/1916rising.htm
2 'Full text of the IRA statement issued on July 28, 2005', *Timesonline*, http://www.timesonline.co.uk/tol/news/uk/article548962.ece.

be re-packaged as heritage for Troubles tourism and theme bars.[3] The boys in balaclavas have been being replaced by the men in suits, giving this New Sinn Féin a significant role in the narratives of successful normalization. The second IRA ceasefire is now over ten years old as is the new political dispensation ushered in by the Belfast Agreement: despite a series of crises around issues such as IRA decommissioning and suspensions of the Executive, the main institutional features and underlying forms of the new polity have proven to be remarkably durable. It may well have been 'Sunningdale for slow learners', but, in general, even the most reluctant and sceptical among Northern Ireland's political class have seen the Good Friday Agreement as a vehicle to further their different political agenda.[4]

The description 'New Sinn Féin' was originally coined by journalists in the 1990s as a way of comparing the changes taking place within the Provisional movement to those initiated by Tony Blair in the British Labour Party. This characterization initially focussed on matters of political style rather than substance, but it accurately reflected the dramatic ideological transformation taking place within the Provisional movement in this period.[5] Unionist politicians, for their own understandable electoral reasons (along with many other sections of the Unionist population), remained sceptical about the *bona fides* of the Provisionals and doubted the sincerity of their conversion to constitutional politics while the IRA remained in existence. This scepticism was further strengthened by the political gymnastics displayed by both the IRA and Sinn Féin leadership as they tried to minimize internal opposition to the new departure by insisting that the historic goals of Republicanism remained unaltered and that there would be no decommissioning of weapons.[6]

3 W. Scholes, 'Vodka and bitterness at Moscow IRA themed bar', *Irish News*, 6 April 2007. R. Sheeran, 'Northern Ireland: Troubled waters', *BBC News Northern Ireland*, 15 July 2005, http://news.bbc.co.uk/go/pr/fr/-/1/hi/programmes/politics_show/4681789. stm. For a more politically engaged form of Troubles tourism see the Republican prisoners' group Coiste na nIarchimí website, coiste.com

4 The phrase 'Sunningdale for slow learners' has been widely attributed to Seamus Mallon of the SDLP. See T. Kelly, 'The necessary evil of democracy is upon us', *Irish News*, 26 April 2005.

5 Much of the early discussion of 'New Sinn Féin' quite literally focussed on matters of style and presentation. Many journalists and Republican opponents of the new departure, for example, commented on the slickness of the Provisionals' media relations and the cut of their suits as evidence of a political shift. See, for example, comments by former Provisionals in S. Breen, 'Decommissioned: provos [sic]on scrap heap of history', *Sunday Tribune*, 16 April 2006 and online discussions on The Blanket website: http://www.lark/phoblacht.net

6 H. McDonald, 'Militant behind Provo's [sic] offer', *The Observer*, 14 May 2000; for examples of these deliberate obfuscations see Geraghty 2000, xxix on the role of leading IRA member Brian Keenan, who stated in May 1996 that 'the only thing to

These duplicities and ideological evasions were not simply 'noble lies' dictated by the necessities of an internal power struggle. Although Republican opponents suggested that the New Sinn Féin project was a deep-laid plot contrived by the Adams leadership, its hesitant evolution from the 1980s reveals instead a much more inchoate ideological direction, reflective of the political culture and theoretical limitations of Irish Republicanism as a whole.[7] Rather than being an alien growth, the constituent elements of the New Sinn Féin project were present within Provisionalism from its founding moment. This only appears to be a contradiction if Provisionalism is simply equated with a static, historically determined ideology that acts as a touchstone of Republican purity.[8] The determining characteristics of Provisionalism's trajectory were discontinuity and contingency rather than adherence to Republican tradition.

The Provisionals were the product of a specific conjuncture: the founding moment that has continued to define them was the fundamental crisis that the Northern Irish state faced in the late 1960s and early 1970s. Provisional Republicanism was present at its own birth. Its political and ideological development was shaped by many influences and creative reactions to the world around it: it was not simply an unsophisticated replication of traditional Republicanism.[9] As such, it was an ideological hybrid formed from the tension between the universalist, democratic framework of the nation and the particularist elements of communal identity and sectarian essentialism. The defining characteristic of its political practice was a stress on political subjectivity and agency expressed through Provisionalism's belief that its armed struggle would provide the vanguard to challenge imperialism and secure national liberation. From the beginning Provisionalism invented its own tradition rooted in this distinctive Northern experience and imagined its own community based within that same nationalist working class and rural poor.[10] The complexities of this relationship between the Provisionals and the nationalist community are a crucial element in shaping their political development.

Their current political containment within the new dispensation not only returns Sinn Féin to these origins: it also reveals that the underlying

---

be decommissioned in Ireland is the British state' and yet in 2005 was the IRA's representative during the final decommissioning process.

7 'Eternal hostility to British forces in Ireland', *Saoirse*, August 2007.

8 This conception of a republican tradition is perhaps best exemplified by Republican Sinn Féin and its attacks on 'the Provisionals' collaboration with British imperialism'. See 'Republican ideal still burns bright', *Saoirse*, November 2007.

9 For an example of this definition of early Provisionalism see Maillot, 2005, 18.

10 A. McIntyre, 'A Structural Analysis of Modern Irish Republicanism 1969–73' (unpublished PhD thesis, Queens' University Belfast, 1999).

dynamics for their armed struggle were not those of traditional Republicanism, which had been historically weak within Northern Ireland.[11]
Thus the IRA's campaign was not sustained 'by nationalist resentment at
the British state presence but rather by widespread resentment at British
administered structural inequality within the northern state...'[12] The
corollary of this argument is that once these inequalities were addressed
support for the armed struggle would evaporate because 'the removal
of structural discrimination within the six-county state represented the
apex of northern nationalist aspirations'.[13] If the Provisional movement is
understood in this context its political trajectory and ideological evolution into the form of New Sinn Féin becomes not simply explicable but
perhaps almost inevitable.

The forward march of Sinn Féin halted?

The contradictions at the heart of contemporary Provisionalism are
perfectly illustrated by two different sets of election results in 2007. The
first, held in March of that year, was for the Northern Ireland Assembly
and confirmed the electoral trends that had first become apparent in the
late 1990s. Sinn Féin consolidated its position as the largest nationalist
party, winning 26.2 per cent of the poll and 28 seats compared to the
SDLP's 15.2 per cent and 16 seats.[14] On the basis of this electoral mandate
the Provisionals were able to enter government as the representatives of
the nationalist community and create a stable partnership with what had
been formerly Republicanism's most implacable opponents in the DUP.
Variously described as a *danse macabre* between Ian Paisley and Martin
McGuinness or a 'Molotov–Ribbentrop pact by the Lagan', this historically unlikely turn of events, which had resulted from the St Andrews
Agreement, was presented as proof by the Sinn Féin leadership that their
strategy was working and that the process of transition using the structures of the Good Friday Agreement to implement the 'all-Ireland Agenda'
was now back on course.[15]

   The second set of results for the Dáil in May 2007 told a less positive
story from the Provisionals' perspective. In the Irish General Election Sinn
Féin failed to make any gains and instead lost a seat, leaving them with
four TDs. Although there was an increase in the party's share of the vote

11   Staunton, 2001, 263–312.
12   P. Maguire, 'Revising the Uprising?', *New Republican Forum*, April 2007.
13   Ibid.
14   Election data from ARK Northern Ireland Elections: http://www.ark.uk/elections
15   D. Godson, 'The real lessons of Ulster', *Prospect*, November 2007; 'A good day for
     Ireland', *An Phoblacht*, 10 May 2007.

from 6.5 per cent in 2002 to 6.9 per cent in 2007 this was of little comfort to Sinn Féin given the high expectations that had been expressed during the campaign.[16] It was reported that the Provisionals had been expected to double their representation in the Dáil and thus become a significant force in parliamentary politics south of the border.[17] It was clear that Sinn Féin were seriously prepared to consider a coalition with Fianna Fáil: they talked about being 'ready for government North and South' and saw this potential electoral advance as an essential part of their strategy of transition towards an 'Ireland of Equals'.[18]

These results were greeted with a predictable degree of *schadenfreude* by political commentators and opponents alike. The initial journalistic assessments of this electoral setback described Sinn Féin's march coming to 'an unceremonious halt' or of brakes being applied to a previously unstoppable bandwagon.[19] Although it was a new experience for the 'Peace Process generation' of younger Republicans, this setback was not unprecedented.[20] The late 1980s and early 1990s were a period of electoral stagnation on both sides of the border following the spectacular surge in support following the development of the Armalite and ballot paper strategy.[21] The decision to end abstentionism in 1986 had not resulted in a dramatic breakthrough and Sinn Féin had to wait until 1997 for the first election of a TD to Leinster House.[22] The long-awaited electoral gains finally occurred in 2002 with the election of five TDs to seal what had been accurately described as 'the rise and rise of Sinn Féin'.[23] In the North, Sinn Féin's renewed advance resulted from the IRA ceasefire in 1994 and continued concurrently with the peace process: they only emerged as the largest nationalist party at the 2001 Westminster elections.[24] Given this twenty-five-year history of erratic development, could these results

16 Election data from ARK Northern Ireland Elections: http://www.ark.uk/election/gdala.htm
17 D. McKittrick, 'Sinn Féin makes inroads south of border', *The Independent*, 18 May 2007.
18 D. Sharrock, 'Sinn Féin eyes power south of the border', *The Times*, 17 May 2007; 'Ready for Government North and South', editorial, *An Phoblacht*, 3 May 2007.
19 C.Byrne, 'Sinn Féin's march comes to an unceremonious halt', *Irish Independent* , 28 May 2007; 'Brakes applied to SF bandwagon', *News Letter*, 31 May 2007.
20 C. Donnelly, 'Taking it on the chin', *Irish Republican News*, 22 May–28 May 2007: htpp//republican-news.org
21 O'Brien, 1993, 198–99.
22 R. Smyth, 'Clear path for local election gains as Sinn Féin polls 143,410 votes', *An Phoblacht*, 31 May 2007.
23 Election data from ARK Northern Ireland Elections: http://www.ark.uk/election/gdala.htm; L. Walsh, D. Corless, K. Smyth and M. Lehane, 'Looking Up – The Rise and Rise of Sinn Féin', *Magill*, March 2000.
24 Election data from http://cain.ulst.ac.uk/issues/politics/election/electsum.htm

not simply be regarded as a temporary aberration in an otherwise clearly rising curve of political success?[25]

Even in the immediate aftermath of the election campaign Sinn Féin recognized that the deeper significance of this electoral hiatus went beyond the details of first preference votes or the need to 'refresh' particular aspects of policy.[26] The specific electoral dynamics where smaller parties were 'squeezed' by the two larger blocs around Fianna Fáil and Fine Gael or the campaign performance of Gerry Adams (whose failure to grasp the details of southern politics was clearly evident during a televised debate with other party leaders) were not the *causes* of Sinn Féin's relative failure, but they were indicative of major flaws in the party's strategy.[27]

These election results challenged the fundamental strategic assumptions that had been at the heart of the Provisional project since the late 1970s. This strategy was in turn rooted in what had been the core Republican belief since 1922 that the nation was indivisible: Republicans argued that despite the existence of two polities on the island, which had grown further apart since partition, it was both possible and indeed necessary to mobilize the whole nation on both sides of the border to reunite the country and thus complete the national revolution. Whether through the Long War or the Peace strategy, Republican advance in the South was an essential precondition for success: the road to victory in Belfast lay through Dublin. In the 1970s and 1980s the Republican project was conceived in revolutionary terms linking 'the advanced forces of Irish national liberation' and 'its other half – the struggling mass of workers and small farmers in the 26-Counties [both]... at the mercy of British Imperialism'.[28] In the 1990s and 2000s the strategy was an electoral one, initially aiming to apply pressure on Dublin governments and then to secure cabinet seats on both sides of the border to advance the reunification project.[29]

In both cases these strategies tied the fortunes of Provisionalism to political developments in the South and their ability to secure a either a mass revolutionary base or the elusive electoral breakthrough, as the case may be. Without this support Republicanism would remain isolated in the North and, as the IRA statement ending the 1956–62 campaign put it, would be doomed to defeat given 'the attitude of the general public whose

25 M. Mac Donncha, 'Serious analysis needed to plan the way forward', *An Phoblacht*, 31 May 2007.

26 Gerry Adams, 'Take stock, move forward', *An Phoblacht*, 31 May 2007.

27 L. Clarke, 'Sinn Féin loses its appeal', *Sunday Times*, 27 May 2007; K. Rafter, 'Stars up North, but down here, their stars have dimmed', *Sunday Tribune*, 27 May 2007.

28 'The Tasks Ahead', *Republican News*, 25 June 1977.

29 E. Moloney, 'SF leaders too slick for the party's own good', *The Irish Times*, 31 May 2007.

minds have been deliberately distracted from the supreme issue facing the Irish people – the unity and freedom of Ireland'.[30] Thus changing the 'attitude of the general public' and 'becoming champions of a new commonsense' had been both Republicanism's central political task and its central political failure in the 26 counties since partition.[31]

As Republicans had long recognized in their attacks on the gombeen politics of the Free State, a form of 26-county nationalism had sunk deep roots in southern society since partition leaving the resolution of 'the national question' for the southern political class as either a pious aspiration or an empty electoral slogan, according to political taste.[32] Periods of intense political mobilization during the Troubles, such as the protests following Bloody Sunday in 1972 and the election of two prisoners as TDs during the Hunger Strike in 1981, appeared to challenge this view and were used to justify the Republican assessment that there was widespread latent support in the South for their cause. However, these were relatively isolated movements: if anything the Troubles accentuated the tendencies towards partitionism and strengthened a distinct form of Irish national identity centred on the South which increasingly defined the North as a troubled 'place apart'.[33] The economic and social transformation ushered in by the Celtic Tiger in the 1990s and 2000s merely acted to consolidate these political and cultural currents, producing 'deeply rooted partitionist attitudes' that were reflected electorally in the radically different priorities between the two jurisdictions.[34]

In practice, Republican politics had long recognized this problem. When the Republican movement had faced isolation and strategic setbacks it had adapted and developed new forms of politics. In 1962 the solution was a verbal commitment to socialism and the development of what became 'Official Republicanism'.[35] In the 1980s the Provisionals demonstrated considerable strategic skill and political pragmatism by drawing on their experience of translating community politics into

---

30 'IRA Statement', *United Irishman*, March 1962.

31 D. Kearney, 'Sinn Féin must use General Election to change political landscape', *An Phoblacht*, 19 April 2007.

32 For examples of this rhetoric and its impact on Irish politics in the 1980s see O'Halloran, 1987, 181–210

33 For the development of a 26-county 'national identity' and its causes and consequences see Bew, 2007, Chapter 10; Brown, 2004; Foster, 2007; McWilliams, 2006; and Patterson, 2006, Chapter 9. For changing patterns of Irish identity in relation to Britain, the USA and the rest of Europe see British Council, 2003.

34 Paul Bew quoted in H.McDonald, 'Goodbye Mary Lou as Adams fails', *The Observer*, 27 May 2007.

35 For the development of Official Republicanism in the 1960s and 1970s see Swan, 2007.

electoral success in the North as they attempted to develop a political base in the South.[36] However, despite effective campaigning and a programme that emphasized social and economic issues rather than simple appeals to nationalist fervour, the results were disappointing.[37] Expectations that the peace process and the IRA ceasefire would yield electoral dividends and that '[i]n the absence of violence many voters who otherwise would never have supported the party would possibly be more open to voting for Sinn Féin' failed to materialize.[38] Even at their peak in the 2002 Dáil elections Sinn Féin support was largely confined to 'traditional' Republican areas in the Border region, Kerry and the working-class constituencies of Greater Dublin.[39] Apart from a core vote around 'the national question' Sinn Féin's constituency seemed similar to that of other 'left-wing' parties: its principal function within southern politics was as a marginal form of protest party and a vehicle for passing discontent in the mould of Official Sinn Féin and the Workers' Party in the 1980s.[40]

The electoral containment of Sinn Féin in the South posed a number of strategic and psychological difficulties for Provisional activists. Since the early 1980s the Adams leadership had built a deserved reputation among Republicans for delivering political success. This accumulated political capital combined with brilliant organizational manoeuvres had proved invaluable throughout the peace process in isolating internal opposition and maintaining the leadership's control within the Provisional movement.[41] Given that the electoral strategy in general and the 2007 campaign in particular was strongly identified with Gerry Adams this reputation might have been weakened by the disappointing outcome.[42] Sinn Féin election posters in many Dublin constituencies, for example, combined pictures of the candidate and the Sinn Féin leader. His image loomed large – quite literally – over the campaign.[43]

---

36 For a critique of this tendency from a republican socialist perspective, see J. Martin, 'The United Irishmen: Republicans, Socialists and Bodenstown', *The Starry Plough*, August/September 2003.

37 Rafter, 2005, 139–69.

38 Ibid, 154.

39 Gallagher, Marsh and Mitchell, 2003, 92–94 and 100–02

40 For evidence of this pattern see the findings on electoral behaviour and party support in the Irish National Election Study 2002 quoted in Coakley and Gallagher, 2005, 181–209. For examples of these tendencies in specific constituencies in the early 2000s see Walsh, Corless, Smyth and Lehane, 'Looking Up – The Rise and Rise of Sinn Féin'.

41 Moloney, 2006, 445–57.

42 M. Hennessy, 'Party gets wake-up call as outcome upsets expectations', *The Irish Times*, 26 May 2007.

43 The calculation seemed to be that Gerry Adams 'superstar' status in Northern Ireland would produce electoral rewards in the South. As party leader, Adams was prominent

While the Adams leadership remained internally secure, albeit with a somewhat diminished reputation, the results did call into question a number of the assumptions underpinning the New Sinn Féin project.[44] One critical commentator argued that such was their disarray that 'Sinn Féin is now more directionless than at any point since the peace process began'.[45] This was because Sinn Féin's strategy rested on a dynamic of momentum and a sense of inevitability pushing the Provisionals on to victory. This thrust was not only important for the political psychology of Republicanism, but was regarded by Republicans as the key factor in political change. Electoral success and increased political influence in Dublin would give added impetus to 'the all-Ireland agenda'. Sinn Féin ministers in the Northern Ireland Executive working with their southern colleagues, either in government or as a strong bloc in the Dáil, would further this strategy through the operation of the Good Friday Agreement's implementation and cross-border structures.[46] A successful presidential campaign in 2011 putting Gerry Adams in Áras an Uachtaráin would be yet another tangible symbol that an inevitable process of fundamental change was under way.[47] Taken as a whole these developments could thus be presented by the Provisionals as increasing the tempo of reunification and vindicating their long-term strategy of transition through electoral politics by 2016.

However, without such a political beachhead or other clear evidence of success, the strategy would remain simply aspirational and be exposed as a utopian dream. This was the political difficulty that Sinn Féin faced in 2007 as it considered its position and how it could implement its strategy with only the northern half of the dynamics in place. Having gambled on an inevitable momentum sustained by its own activist *élan* and a propitious conjuncture, the Provisional project was now becalmed. Even in its moderate New Sinn Féin incarnation the all-Ireland 'revolution' had failed, leaving the Provisionals as the sectional representatives of the northern nationalist community rather than the vanguard of the nation as a whole.

Their forward march was halted; reunification using the mechanisms of the Agreement and by building political strength in the South was impossible; the wishful thinking and strategic limitations at the heart of the Provisional project were exposed. The *de facto* partitionism that

---

at press conferences, in media interviews and in the pages of *An Phoblacht* during the campaign. See, for example, *An Phoblacht*, 24 May 2007

44 E. Moloney, 'President Adams is parked', *The Irish Times*, 10 October 2007.

45 Moloney, 'President Adams is parked'.

46 'Sinn Féin ready for government after election', *An Phoblacht*, 10 May 2007.

47 Moloney, 'President Adams is parked'.

had underpinned Irish nationalist politics on both sides of the border was further strengthened by this electoral setback. In drawing lessons from the elections, leading Provisionals seemed to support this assessment by arguing that the long-term failure of the Republican project had been compounded by the partitionist fragmentation of the country and the creation of 'two distinct and separate political realities'.[48] Thus while Gerry Adams continued to proclaim that 'the front line' of the struggle 'is now clearly shifting south', Unionists correctly understood that Sinn Féin's real focus would now be on consolidating and preserving its power base in the North: as one DUP MLA commented, 'Sinn Féin has nothing left now except Stormont so they would be foolish to threaten it in any way'.[49] Sinn Féin would remain isolated in its northern electoral strongholds, imprisoned within an executive administering British rule and 'facing the unpalatable situation of being part of the British establishment' for the foreseeable future.[50]

Governing Her Majesty's territory

The 2007 election results in the two jurisdictions illustrate what will be the real dynamics behind the New Sinn Féin project. The disparity between the Provisionals' political and electoral success in Northern Ireland (which exceeded their wildest dreams) and the setback they have suffered in the South (which deflated their most optimistic hopes) means that for the foreseeable future the movement's political trajectory will be largely determined by the nature of the new dispensation. Circumscribed by the consent principle and its embodiment in the institutional structures of the Belfast Agreement, the very conditions under which they are in government mean that the Provisionals cannot function as Irish Republicans. Their politics must therefore be, perforce, those of constitutional nationalism. As one perceptive Unionist commentator put it: 'how republican is a party which governs part of Her Majesty's territory?... Sinn Féin has shredded the sheet music of a "A Nation Once Again" while their ministers and MLAs get on with the business of governing this part of the United Kingdom.'[51]

Despite claims that the party offers a radical alternative to establishment politics and remains committed to the two main goals of national

48 J. Gibney, 'SF must learn quickly from election results', *The Irish News*, 31 May 2007.
49 Gerry Adams, 'We have entered a new phase of our struggle', *An Phoblacht*, 28 June 2007; DUP sources quoted in Moloney, 'President Adams is parked'.
50 DUP MP William McCrea quoted in 'SF is "part of the establishment"', *News Letter*, 30 May 2007.
51 A. Kane, 'Adams' day of unity isn't coming', *News Letter*, 25 June 2007.

independence and democratic socialism, Sinn Féin's future role in Northern Ireland's governance will reflect its past performance.[52] For example, in the previous executive Sinn Féin ministers who controlled the largest spending departments of health and education operated within the conventional frameworks and budgetary disciplines of contemporary politics using Private Finance Initiatives and making the necessary 'difficult' decisions on expenditure and the allocations of scarce resources.[53] For some critics, 'crawl[ing] up the steps of Stormont under the jurisdiction of the Queen' marked 'the death of radical republicanism' as an historical force in Irish politics.[54] New Sinn Féin had demonstrated its willingness to compromise with capitalism and collaborate with imperialism: it was now taking the path of other revolutionary nationalist movements which would result in the Provisionals becoming the neutered left populist version of Fianna Fáil.[55]

In practice the operation of devolved government in Northern Ireland would bring Sinn Féin ideologically much closer to those forms of 'new nationalism' operating in the various regional governments in Western Europe. The flexible architecture of the Good Friday Agreement and the changing relationships within the United Kingdom that have developed as a result of new devolved institutions in Scotland and Wales will further act to strengthen this tendency: the growing links between the Scottish government and Parliament and its equivalents in Northern Ireland show the potential importance of these constitutional structures and their consequent impact on New Sinn Féin.[56]

Just as Sinn Fein's involvement in local government and the community sector in the 1980s and 1990s drew Republicans and their constituency into a closer relationship with the state and its agencies, so the day-to-day participation of Sinn Féin Ministers and MLAs in the governance and administration will act in a similar way to strengthen the working relationship between the Provisionals and the state. As the joint lobbying by Ian Paisley and Martin McGuinness for reduced corporation tax rates and increased public expenditure in the early days of the new executive showed, the everyday business of practical politics will become

52 E. Ó Broin, 'Sinn Féin, Socialism and the 21st Century Challenge', *Irish Democrat*, January /February 2006.

53 E. Moloney, 'McGuinness moves to reassure Unionists with new policy on school building', *Sunday Tribune*, 17 September 2000.

54 McCrea quoted in 'SF is "part of the establishment"'; K. Allen, 'The death of radical Republicanism', *International Socialism*, 114 Spring 2007, 53.

55 Allen, 'The death of radical Republicanism', 53.

56 'Salmond calls for closer NI ties', BBC News, 18 June 2007, http://news.bbc.co.uk/go/ pr/fr/-/1/hi/northern_ireland/6761769.stm

increasingly important in shifting Sinn Féin's attention away from transformation and onto administration.[57] As one commentator noted during the talks between the DUP and Sinn Féin to establish the new executive, 'The Rev. Paisley and Mr. McGuinness will find little difficulty making common cause in asking for even larger public spending to be showered [by the British Treasury], equitably, on their constituencies.'[58]

Despite these narratives of normalization (exemplified by the positive PR spin applied to the good working relationship enjoyed by the 'Chuckle Brothers' Ian Paisley and Martin McGuinness as First and Deputy First Minister), the institutional structures of the new dispensation reflected the political and communal divisions that were the basis of conflict in Northern Ireland.[59] These structures were designed to manage and regulate conflict: the result was a form of 'electoral tribalism', because 'Sinn Féin and the DUP are not political parties, but political movements that seek to develop broad electorates around popular and uncomplicated ideas... Ultimately, they are intertwined until the end, whatever that may be.'[60]

Given this structured form of conflict, Sinn Féin's function as the largest nationalist party will continue to be representational rather than transformative. Arguments that the Union could be hollowed out from within or that the dynamics and facilitating structures for the transition towards a united Ireland were present in the institutions were far from convincing.[61] In contrast to the active agency of the ballot paper and Armalite campaign, this transitional strategy was largely passive and relied upon dynamics and contingent forces of social and economic change external to the Republican movement.

Since the Belfast Agreement had ruled out fundamental political and constitutional change, political conflict increasingly has taken the form of symbolic battles and sham fights around cultural and identity politics, such as the Irish language and other expressions of cultural difference.[62] This type of politics reflected the growing importance of the particularist politics of recognition and difference within Provisional ideology. These tendencies were strengthened by Sinn Féin's representational function

---

57   B. Purcell, 'Old political foes join in bid to secure funding for the North', *Irish Independent*, 23 April 2007.

58   T. Hames, 'Don't swap your guns for begging bowls', *The Times*, 29 January 2007.

59   For examples of the heightened communal divisions and segregation that has developed since 1994 see D. McCarney, 'Behind those walls, thoughts of the future', *Andersonstown News*, 22 February 2007.

60   P. Shirlow, 'Why it's going to take two to tango', *Belfast Telegraph*, 14 March 2007.

61   B. Feeney, 'Stormont leaders need to take the lead', *Irish News*, 11October 2007.

62   'Language Act will be enacted says Sinn Féin leader', *Andersonstown News*, 19 October 2007.

in making claims to the state for resources on behalf of the nationalist community using a discourse of victimhood and passive supplication.

The Provisional movement has proven to be a significant partner for the state in the successful operation and long-term stability of the new dispensation not just because it had a strong electoral base, but because it was a form of social power that could act as a mediator between the nationalist population and the British state. These networks and structures of social power had deep roots in the nationalist population and had been strengthened by the developing links between the nationalist community and the state in the 1980s and 1990s. This process of integration was accelerated by the political de-mobilization of the Provisional movement and the developing partnership between the leadership and the British during the peace process and the establishment of the new political dispensation after 1998. Despite the radical rhetoric, these social networks and community organizations were intimately connected to the state by a myriad of funding streams, training contracts and partnership arrangements: the nationalist community's pseudo-state form mirrored and partnered the official form at every level. The former insurgents and militant activists were now integrated into the very structures of power that they had once sought to overthrow. As a result Hobsbawm's description of another ambiguous group of social rebels moving into mainstream politics and social power could equally apply to these activists:

> He is 'one of us' who is constantly in the process of becoming associated with 'them'. The more successful he is... the more he is both a representative and champion of the poor and a part of the system of the rich... His equivalent in the... city, the local... political boss... is much less the rebel and outlaw, much more the boss. His connection with the centres of official wealth and power... are much more evident – they may indeed be the most evident thing about him.[63]

'The archaic banner'?

The Troubles are fading from memory into history. The political, social and ideological terrain that Provisionalism inhabits has radically altered in the last twenty-five years. The context in which it operates is so fundamentally different that even comparisons with its own past are problematic. For many of the younger generation living in the Provisional heartlands, 'the struggle' is not something contemporary. Northern Ireland's population is one of the youngest in Europe and there is an increasing generation gap between those who were adults at the start of the Troubles and those

63 Hobsbawm, 1985, 88.

now reaching voting age who were ten years old at the time of the Belfast Agreement.

The region's economy and social life has changed dramatically since 1998. News reports are dominated by Northern Ireland's economic success story. Editorials comment on the 'optimism and realism... that is dissolving ancient prejudices and boosting business confidence... Belfast and Londonderry have been transformed by peace...'[64] The nationalist population has shared in this economic growth and social advancement with many commentators pointing to the emergence of new social elites fuelled by new nationalist money made during the peace process. In this period nationalist communal interests were advanced by the Good Friday Agreement which both copperfastened partition *and* guaranteed the social position of the new nationalist middle class.[65]

The politics of Provisionalism have been decisively shaped by these forces of social and economic change. Ideologically New Sinn Féin reflects the political patterns of the post-Cold War world: its transition from radical challengers to partners in government follows a familiar scenario for a wide range of former revolutionary and nationalist movements. This process of incorporation is by no means unusual historically, in Ireland as elsewhere, and it might be objected that this is nothing more than the 'natural' process of institutionalization of political movements by liberal capitalism. What makes contemporary processes of incorporation so different is that they spring not merely from a fundamental political disillusion and exhaustion with radical and transformative politics, but with the very idea of the political itself. The New Sinn Féin project shows all of the symptoms of the postmodern condition: its rhetoric is stale and unconvincing, its ambitions are scaled down to the routine of electoral politics and its historical goals postponed to an indefinite future. It apes the style of conventional politics and politicians with its post-Provo candidates and celebrity leadership, and in the 2007 Dáil elections it was judged accordingly by the Irish electorate.[66]

This process of transition and incorporation has been widely regarded as a model for conflict management and resolution. Not only has Northern Ireland's experience of the peace process been drawn on internationally, but many of the Republicans who took part in it have lent their expertise to programmes of conflict resolution from Iraq to Sri Lanka.[67] As one

---

64 'Ulster moves forward', editorial, *The Times*, 5 October 2006.
65 S. Breen, 'On the One Road', *Fortnight*, September 2000.
66 Rafter, 'Stars up North, but down here, their lights have dimmed'.
67 See, for example, R. Faligot, 'De l'IRA a l'Irak: l'étonnante mediation de McGuinness', *Rue 89*, 17 September 2007, http://www.rue89.com/2007/09/17/de-lira-a-liral-letonnante-mediation-de-mcguinness; 'McGuinness in Iraqi peace negotiations', *An*

commentator has put it 'this squalid little war... which seemed utterly *sui generis* for much of the time after the start of the Troubles in 1969... has suddenly become a trendy template for conflict resolution across the world. There is now something of an "international ideology of Northern Ireland."'[68] Central to this 'international ideology' is 'the development of dialogue at every level, a dialogue delivering the most obdurate constituencies [and] focusing on key leaders [to develop] unconditional dialogue with the most intransigent', a process which has been likened to 'dancing with wolves'.[69] While this 'authorized version' propagated by British politicians and military leaders has become the dominant consensus about counter-insurgency and peace-making in Northern Ireland, the truth is somewhat more complex. These narratives of normalization which see 'one time bitter enemies... embracing a new prosperity' and 'vast amounts of British taxpayer and EU money' allowing the region to revert 'into its complacent, parochial, per-Troubles self' raise more questions than they answer about exactly what type of 'normality' the new political dispensation can deliver.[70]

What the peace process has delivered is New Sinn Féin: as a constitutional party and the voice of a majority of the nationalist population it will continue to be assured of seats at Northern Ireland's cabinet table for as long as the new political dispensation lasts. Although the political, social and economic forces that brought about this result can be identified, it is perhaps still too soon to write the obituary of Irish Republicanism. Radek's obituary for militant Irish nationalism after the defeat of the Easter Rising has an uncannily contemporary feel to it. To Marxists such as Radek the future belonged instead to a new social force – the Irish proletariat – whose 'historical role' was only just beginning and whose final victory was assured. In practice, however, Radek's initial reactions to 1916 proved to be unreliable guides to the later development of Irish politics: his obituary was premature because, whatever its 'historical basis', revolutionary nationalism continued to be a major force for

---

Phoblacht, 6 September 2007 and, for references to the British state's experience of the 'obvious idea [that] you reconcile with your enemies', see R. Norton-Taylor and I. Black, 'US agrees further British withdrawal from Iraq', *The Guardian*, 19 September 2007.

68 D. Godson, 'The real lessons of Ulster', *Prospect*, November 2007.

69 Former Ulster Unionist leader David Trimble quoting former Secretary of State for Northern Ireland Peter Hain's assessment of the peace process in D. Trimble, 'Ulster's lesson for the Middle East: don't indulge extremists', *The Guardian*, 25 October 2007.

70 D. McKittrick, 'From the gun to the school run – the new Belfast', *Independent on Sunday*, 4 March 2007; D. Godson, 'The real lessons of Ulster', *Prospect*, November 2007.

political change in twentieth-century Ireland. The proletariat continued to be shaped 'in an atmosphere saturated with the heroic recollections of national rebellions' and continued to fight under what Trotsky described as the 'archaic banner' of 'national revolution'.[71]

Despite the very different historical period in which they were written and the inaccuracy of their predictions, these first drafts of history do have some resonance for our own times. While we do not share their certainty and confidence, the questions that these early twentieth-century Marxists posed about the character of revolutionary nationalism and its future political trajectory are still relevant to our understanding of the ideological and organizational evolution of Republicanism in the early twenty-first century. In 1916 Radek was trying to peer into the future and discern how the Marxist schema of historical development would unfold in Ireland. His perspective was one of revolutionary change and the disintegration of the old order internationally: his narrative of historical progress, in Ireland and elsewhere, was at its beginning. In contrast, our narratives seem to have run their course; we appear to be at the end looking back to understand, to explain and perhaps to learn from what happened.

71 L. Trotsky (trans. A. Clinton), 'On the Events in Dublin', *Nashe Slovo*, 4 July 1916: http://www.maxists.org/archive/trotsky/1916/07/dublin.htm

Bibliography

Primary Sources

Archives
Northern Ireland Political Collection
Linen Hall Library, Belfast
Tom Hartley Collection
Northern Ireland Office Press Cuttings Collection
Republican Boxes
SDLP Boxes
Community Groups Boxes
Peace Process Boxes
Miscellaneous Boxes

Printed Primary: Newspapers and Magazines
Andersonstown News
Atlantic Monthly
Belfast Telegraph
Blanket
An Camcheachta/Starry Plough
Congress '86
Daily Ireland
Daily Telegraph
Fight Racism! Fight Imperialism!
Fortnight
Fourthwrite
An Glor Gafa/Captive Voice
Guardian
Hands Off Ireland!
Hibernia
Hibernian
Independent
International Herald Tribune
International Socialism
IRIS
Iris Bheag
Irish Democrat
Irish Dissent

Irish Echo
Irish Freedom
Irish Independent
Irish News
Irish Political Review
Irish Post
Irish Press
Irish Reporter
Irish Times
Left Republican Review
Le Monde
Living Marxism
Magill
Marie Claire
News Letter
Observer
Other View
Parliamentary Brief
An Phoblacht
An Phoblacht/Republican News
Prospect
Red Banner
Republican Forum
Republican News
Resource
An Rheabhloid
Saoirse
Socialist Republic
Sovereign Nation
Starry Plough (IRSP)
Sunday Times
Sunday Tribune
Times
Tiocfaidh ar la
Troops Out
Vacuum
Variant
Village
Weekly Worker
United Irishman

Websites
http://www.ark.ac.uk
http://news.bbc.co.uk
http://www .cain.ulst.ac.uk
http://www.feilebelfast.com/aboutus/
http://www.marxists.org

http://www.opendemocracy.net
http://lark.phoblacht.net
http://www.sinnfein.ie
http://www.spiked-online.com

Interviews

Patricia Campbell, former member of Sinn Fein Ard Comhairle and Tyrone Anti-H Blocks Committee. Interviewed and recorded in Belfast, 6 January 2004

Tony Catney, former IRA member and former Sinn Fein Ard Comhairle member. Interviewed and recorded in Belfast, 15 April 1998

Sir David Goodall, Deputy Secretary, Cabinet Office 1982–84. Interviewed and recorded 28 July 2005.

Tommy Gorman, former Operations Officer, First Battalion, Belfast IRA, and community worker, Upper Springfield Development Trust. Interviewed and recorded in Belfast, 12 August 1998

Clare Hackett, former Projects Manager, Upper Springfield Development Trust, and oral history project, Falls Community Council. Interviewed in Belfast, 27 August 2004

Pauline Hadaway, former Community Arts Development Manager, Upper Springfield Development Trust. Interviewed in Belfast, 15 August 2004

Tom Hartley, Sinn Fein Councillor and former General Secretary, Sinn Fein. Interviewed in Belfast, 11 February 1999

Brendan Hughes, former OC, Belfast Brigade, IRA and OC, IRA prisoners, Long Kesh. Interviewed and recorded in Belfast, 10 August 1998

John Kelly, former Sinn Féin MLA and Provisional activist. Interviewed and recorded in Maghera 15 August 2005

Sir Gerard Loughran, former Permanent Secretary in the Department for Economic Development (Northern Ireland) 1991–2000 Interviewed 16 August 2005.

Bernadette McAliskey, former civil rights activist and H-Block campaigner. Interviewed in Coalisland, 28 August 2001

John MacAnulty, former People's Democracy Councillor, Belfast City Council. Interviewed and recorded in Belfast, 10 August 2002

Eamonn MacDermott, former IRA member and IRA staff, Long Kesh. Interviewed and recorded in Derry, 15 October 1998

Anthony McIntyre, former OC, IRA Lower Ormeau area, and prisoner, Long Kesh. Interviewed and recorded in Belfast, 30 May 1999

Tommy McKearney, former OC, Tyrone Brigade, IRA and GHQ staff. Interviewed and recorded in Monaghan, 30 May 1998

Mickey McMullan, former IRA member, former Vice-OC, IRA prisoners, Long Kesh, and former Northern Editor, *An Phoblacht/Republican News*. Interviewed and recorded in Belfast, 13 April 1998

Donnachda Mac Nellis, former Republican prisoner and Bogside Residents Group. Interviewed in Derry, 19 August 1998

Kevin McQuillan, former General Secretary, Irish Republican Socialist Party. Interviewed in Belfast, 3 August 2003

Danny Morrison, former Sinn Fein Publicity Director and Editor, *Republican News* and *An Phoblacht/Republican News*. Interviewed and recorded in Belfast, 5 January 2004

Sir Richard Needham, former Parliamentary Under Secretary of State (Northern Ireland Office) 1985–92 Interviewed and recorded in London, 25 July 2005.

Ruairi Ó Bradaigh, former President, Sinn Fein. Interviewed and recorded in Dublin, 20 April 2003

Eoin Ó Broin, Director of European Affairs, Sinn Féin. Interviewed and recorded in Belfast, 23 August 2005

Liam O Ruairc, Ard Comhairle IRSP. Interviewed 9 April 2004

Glen Phillips, West Belfast Festival Community Outreach Officer. Interviewed 9 April 2004

Gerard Rice, former Republican prisoner and Lower Ormeau Residents Group. Interviewed and recorded in Belfast, 7 April 2003

Matt Tracey, former IRA member, Dublin Brigade, and prisoner, Portlaoise. Interviewed in Dublin, 12 December 1998

Secondary Sources

Adams, G., 1986, *The Politics of Irish Freedom*, Dingle

Adams, G., 1988, *A Pathway to Peace*, Cork

Adams, G., 1992, *The Street and Other Stories*, Dingle

Adams, G., 1996, *Before The Dawn: An Autobiography*, London

Adams, G., 2001, *An Irish Journal*, Dingle

Adams, G., 2003, *Hope and History*, Dingle

Adams, G., 2007, *An Irish Eye*, Dingle

Adams, J., Morgan, R., and Bambridge, A., 1988, *Ambush: The War between the SAS and the IRA*, London

Agnew, J., 1987, *Place and Politics*, Boston

Alexander, Y., and O'Day, A. (eds), 1984, *Terrorism in Ireland*, London

Ali, T., and Watkins, S., 1998, *1968: Marching In The Streets*, London

Allen, K., 1997, *Fianna Fáil and Irish Labour: 1926 to the Present*, London

Allen, N., and Kelly, A. (eds), 2003, *The Cities of Belfast*, Dublin

Alonso, R., 2007, *The IRA and Armed Struggle*, London

Anderson, B., 1991, *Imagined Communities: Reflections on the Origin and Spread of Nationalism*, London

Anderson, P., 2005, *Spectrum: From Right to Left in the World of Ideas*, London

Ardoyne Commemoration Project, 2002, *Ardoyne: The Untold Truth*, Belfast

Arthur, P., 2002, 'Conflict, Memory and Reconciliation', in M. Elliott (ed.), *The Long Road to Peace in Northern Ireland*, Liverpool

Aughey, A., 2003, 'The Art and Effect of Political Lying in Northern Ireland', *Irish Political Studies*, Vol. 17 No. 2

Aughey, A., 2005, *The Politics of Northern Ireland: Beyond the Belfast Agreement*, Abingdon

Augusteijn, J., 2003, 'Political Violence and Democracy: An Analysis of the

Tensions within Irish Republican Strategy 1914–2002', *Irish Political Studies*, Vol. 18 No. 1

Bamberg, C., 1987, *Ireland's Permanent Revolution*, London

Bardon, J., 1992, *A History of Ulster*, Belfast

Barker, C., 2001, 'Robert Michels and "the Cruel Game"', in C. Barker et al. (eds), *Leadership and Social Movements*, Manchester

Barnett, A., 1969, 'People's Democracy; a discussion on strategy', *New Left Review*, May–June, 3–19

Barry, B., 2001, *Culture and Equality*, Cambridge

Baudrillard, J., 1988, *Selected Writings*, Cambridge

Bauman, Z., 1992, *Intimations of Postmodernity*, London

Bean, K., 1994, *The New Departure: Recent Developments in Irish Republican Ideology and Strategy*, Liverpool

Bean, K., 2002, 'Defining Republicanism: Shifting Discourses of New Nationalism and Post-Republicanism', in M. Elliott (ed.), *The Long Road to Peace in Northern Ireland*, Liverpool

Bean, K., 2005, 'Roads Not Taken', in P. Hadaway (ed.), *Portraits from a 50s Archive*, Belfast

Bean, K., and Hayes, M. (eds), 2001, *Republican Voices*, Monaghan

Bell, J.B., 1989, *The Secret Army: The IRA 1916–1979*, Dublin (1st edn, London 1970)

Bell, J.B., 1990, *IRA Tactics and Targets*, Dublin

Bell, J.B., 1993, *The Irish Troubles: A Generation of Violence, 1967–1992*, Dublin

Bell, J.B., 2000, *The IRA 1968–2000: Analysis of a Secret Army*, London

Bennett, A., 2006, *The History Boys: The Screenplay*, London

Beresford, D., 1987, *Ten Men Dead: The Story of the 1981 Irish Hunger Strike*, London

Bertramsen, R.B., Frolund, J.P., Thomsen, B., and Torfing, J., 1991, *State, Economy and Society*, London

Bew, P., 2005, *The Making and Remaking of the Good Friday Agreement*, Dublin

Bew, P., 2007, *Ireland: The Politics of Enmity 1789–2006*, Oxford

Bew, P., Gibbon, P., and Patterson, H., 1995, *Northern Ireland 1921–1994: Political Forces and Social Classes*, London

Bew, P., and Gillespie, G., 1999, *Northern Ireland: A Chronology of the Troubles 1968–1999*, Dublin

Bew, P., and Patterson, H., 1985, *The British State and the Ulster Crisis: From Wilson to Thatcher*, London

Bew, P., Patterson, H., and Teague, P., 1997, *Between War and Peace: The Political Future of Northern Ireland*, London

Bhabha, H. (ed.), 1990, *Nation and Narration*, London

Bishop, P., and Mallie, E., 1988, *The Provisional IRA*, London

Boal, F., 1995, *Shaping A City: Belfast in the Late Twentieth Century*, Belfast

Boggs, C., 2000, *The End of Politics: Corporate Power and the Decline of the Public Sphere*, New York

Bourke, R., 2003, *Peace in Ireland: The War of Ideas*, London

Bowman, J., 1982, *De Valera and the Ulster Question 1917–1973*, Oxford

Boyce, D.G., 1995, *Nationalism in Ireland*, London

Boyce, D.G., Eccleshall, R., and Geoghegan, V. (eds), 1993, *Political Thought in Ireland since the Seventeenth Century*, London

Brady, C. (ed.), 1994, *Interpreting Irish History: The Debate on Historical Revisionism 1938–1994*, Dublin

Breuilly, J., 1993, *Nationalism and the State*, Manchester

British Council, 2003, *Through Irish Eyes*, Dublin

British Council, 2006, *Britain and Ireland: Lives Entwined II*, Dublin

Brown, T., 2004, *Ireland: A Social and Cultural History 1922–2002*, London

Bryan, B., 2000, *Orange Parades: The Politics of Ritual, Tradition and Control*, London

Buckland, P., 1981, *A History of Northern Ireland*, Dublin

Burton, F., 1978, *The Politics of Legitimacy: Struggles in a Belfast Community*, London

Byrne, S., and Irvin, C., 2001, 'Economic Aid and Policy Making: Building the Peace Dividend in Northern Ireland', *Policy and Politics*, Vol. 29 No. 4

Callinicos, A., 1989, *Against Postmodernism: A Marxist Critique*, Cambridge

Campbell, A., and Stott, R., 2007, *The Blair Years: Extracts from the Alastair Campbell Diaries*, London

Campbell, B., McKeown, L., and O'Hagan, F. (eds), 1994, *Nor Meekly Serve My Time: The H-Block Struggle 1976–1981*, Belfast

Campbell, F., 1991, *The Dissenting Voice: Protestant Democracy in Ulster from Plantation to Partition*, Belfast

Carr, E.H., 1987, *What Is History?*, London

Carruthers, M., Douds, S., and Loane, T. (eds), 2003, *Re-imagining Belfast: A Manifesto for the Arts*, Belfast

Casquette, J., 2001, 'Review of C.L.Irvin, *Militant Nationalism: Between Movement and Party in Ireland and the Basque Country* (Minneapolis 1999)', *Mobilization*, Vol. 6 No. 2

Casquette, J., 1996, 'The Sociopolitical Context of Mobilization: The Case of the Anti-military Movement in the Basque Country', *Mobilization*, Vol. 1 No. 2

Catterall, P., and McDougall, S., 1996, *The Northern Ireland Question in British Politics*, Basingstoke

Chaliand, G., 1976, *Mythes révolutionnaires du Très Monde*, Paris

Chandler, D., 1999, *Bosnia: Faking Democracy after Dayton*, London

Clarke, L., 1987, *Broadening the Battlefield: The H-Blocks and the Rise of Sinn Fein*, Dublin

Clarke, L., and Johnston, K., 2001, *Martin McGuinness: From Guns To Government*, Edinburgh

Coakley, J., 2002 , 'Conclusion: New Strains of Unionism and Nationalism', in J. Coakley (ed.), *Changing Shades of Orange and Green*, Dublin

Coakley, J., and Gallagher, M., 2005, *Politics in the Republic of Ireland*, London

Cochrane, F., 2002, *People Power? The Role of the Voluntary and Community Sector in the Northern Ireland Conflict*, Cork

Cohen, J., Cohen, M., and Cohen, M.J., 1995, *The Penguin Dictionary of Twentieth Century Quotations*, London

Collins, E., 1997, *Killing Rage*, London

Collins, M. (ed.), 1989, *Ireland After Britain*, London

Comerford, R.V., 1998, *The Fenians in Context: Irish Politics and Society 1848–82*, Dublin

Comerford, R.V., 2003, 'Republicans and Democracy in Modern Irish Politics', in F. McGarry (ed.), *Republicanism in Modern Ireland*, Dublin

Connolly, J., 1910, *Labour in Irish History*, Dublin

Connolly, J., 1910, *Labour, Nationality and Religion*, Dublin

Conrad, J., 1988, *The Heart of Darkness*, New York

Conroy, J., 1988, *War as a Way of Life: A Belfast Diary*, London

Conversi, D., 1997, *The Basques, the Catalans and Spain: Alternative Routes to Nationalist Mobilisation*, London

Coogan, T.P., 1980, *On the Blanket: The H-Block Story*, Dublin

Coogan, T.P., 1980, *The IRA*, London

Coogan, T.P., 1995, *The Troubles: Ireland's Ordeal 1966–1995 and the Search for Peace*, London

Cooper, R., 2003, *The Breaking of Nations: Order and Chaos in the Twenty-First Century*, London

Coulter, C., 1990, *Ireland: Between the First and the Third Worlds*, Dublin

Coulter, C., 1999, *Contemporary Northern Irish Society: An Introduction*, London

Coulter, C., and Coleman, S., 2003, *The End of Irish History? Critical Reflections on the Celtic Tiger*, Manchester

Cox, M., 2006, 'Rethinking the International and Northern Ireland: A Defence', in M. Cox, A. Guelke and F. Stephen (eds), *A Farewell to Arms? Beyond the Good Friday Agreement*, 2nd edn, Manchester

Cox, M., Guelke, A., and Stephen, F. (eds), 2006, *A Farewell to Arms? Beyond the Good Friday Agreement*, 2nd edn, Manchester

Craig, G., 1981, *Germany 1866–1945*, Oxford

Craig, J., McAnulty, J., and Flannagan, P., 1998, *The Real Irish Peace Process*, Belfast

Crawford, C., 2003, *Inside the UDA*, London

Cronin, S., 1980, *Irish Nationalism: A History of its Roots and Ideology*, Dublin

Cullen, M. (ed.), 1998, *1798: 200 Years of Resonance: Essays and Contributions on the History and Relevance of the United Irishmen and the 1798 Revolution*, Dublin

Cunningham, S., 1997, 'The Political Language of John Hume', *Irish Political Studies*, Vol. 12

Cunningham, S., 2001, *British Government Policy in Northern Ireland 1969–2000*, Manchester

Currie, A., 2004, *All Hell Will Break Loose*, Dublin

Dalton, D., and Hayden, J., 2006, *One Hundred Years of Revolution: A Proud History Gives Confidence of Victory*, Dublin

Darby, J., and McGinty, R. (eds), 2003, *Contemporary Peace Making: Conflict, Violence and Peace Processes*, Basingstoke

Davidson, N., 2006, 'Enlightenment and Anti-Capitalism', *International Socialism*, 110, Spring

Deane, S. (ed.), 1983, *Civilians and Barbarians*, Derry

Deane, S. (ed.), 1991, *The Field Day Anthology of Irish Writing*, Derry

Deane, S., 1991, 'Revivals', in S. Deane (ed.), *The Field Day Anthology of Irish Writing*, Derry

de Baroid, C., 1999, *Ballymurphy and the Irish War*, London

de Breadun, D., 2001, *The Far Side of Revenge: Making Peace in Northern Ireland*, Cork

della Porta, D., and Diani, M., 1999, *Social Movements: An Introduction*, Oxford

della Porta, D., Kriesi, H., and Rucht, D., 1999, *Social Movements in a Globalising World*, Basingstoke

de Paor, L., 1997, *On The Easter Proclamation and Other Declarations*, Dublin

Devenport, M., 2000, *Flash Frames: Twelve Years Reporting Belfast*, Belfast

Devlin, B., 1969, *The Price of My Soul*, London

Devlin, P., 1993, *Straight Left: An Autobiography*, Belfast

Dixon, P., 2001, *Northern Ireland: The Politics of Peace and War*, Basingstoke

Docherty, T., 1994, *Postmodernism: A Reader*, London

Dolan, A., 2003, 'An Army of Our Fenian Dead: Republicanism, Monuments and Commemorations', in F. McGarry (ed.), *Republicanism in Modern Ireland*, Dublin

Dudley Edwards, R., and Pearse, P., 1977, *The Triumph of Failure*, Dublin

Duncan, J., 2003, *Trees from Germany*, Belfast

Dunphy, R., 1997, 'The Contradictory Politics of the Official Republican Movement 1969–1992', in R. Deutsch (ed.), *Le Républicanisme Irlandais*, Rennes

Duverger, M., 1962, *Political Parties: Their Organisation and Activity in the Modern State*, London

Eagleton, T., 1991, *Ideology: An Introduction*, London

Eagleton, T., 1996, *The Illusions of Postmodernism*, Oxford

Eagleton, T., 1999, 'Nationalism and the Case of Ireland', *New Left Review*, Vol. 234, April/May

Eagleton, T., 2003, *After Theory*, London

Eccleshall, R., Geoghegan, V., Jay, R., Kenny, M., MacKenzie, I., and Wilford, R., 1994, *Political Ideologies: An Introduction*, London

Edwards, R.D., 1977, *Patrick Pearse: The Triumph of Failure*, Dublin

Elliott, M., 1989, *Wolfe Tone: Prophet of Irish Independence*, New Haven

Elliott, M., 2000, *The Catholics of Ulster: A History*, London

Elliott, M., 2002, 'Religion and Identity in Northern Ireland', in M. Elliott (ed.), *The Long Road to Peace in Northern Ireland*, Liverpool

Elliott, M. (ed.), 2002, *The Long Road to Peace in Northern Ireland*, Liverpool

Elliott, S., 1973, *Northern Ireland Parliamentary Election Results 1921–1972*, Chichester

Ellis, P.B. (ed.), 1988, *James Connolly: Selected Writings*, London

Ellis, P.B., 1989, *A History of the Irish Working Class*, London

English, R., 1994, *Radicals and the Republic: Socialist Republicanism in the Irish Free State 1925–1937*, Oxford

English, R., 1998, *Ernie O'Malley: IRA Intellectual*, Oxford

English, R., 2003, *Armed Struggle: A History of the IRA*, Basingstoke

English, R., 2006, *Irish Freedom: The History of Nationalism in Ireland*, Basingstoke

Etzioni, A., 1995, *The Spirit of Community: Rights, Responsibilities and the Communitarian Agenda*, London

European Union, 1995, *European Union Special Support Programme for Peace and Reconciliation in Northern Ireland and the Border Counties of Ireland 1995–1999*, Brussels

Fairweather, E., McDonough, R., and McFadyean, M., 1984, *Only the Rivers Run Free: Northern Ireland – The Women's War*, London

Falls Community Council, 1987, *West Belfast: Some of the Facts Behind the Issues*, Belfast

Farrell, M., 1973, *The Battle for Algiers*, Belfast

Farrell, M., 1976, *The Orange State*, London

Farrell, M., 1980, *Northern Ireland: The Orange State*, London

Farrell, M. (ed.), 1988, *Twenty Years On*, Dingle

Feehan, J.M., 1983, *Bobby Sands and the Tragedy of Northern Ireland*, Cork

Feeney, B., 2002, *Sinn Fein: A Hundred Turbulent Years*, Dublin

Feile an Phobail, 1994, *Feile An Phobail Development Plan 1994*, Belfast

Fennell, D., 1983, *The State of the Nation*, Swords

Fennell, D., 1986, *Nice People and Rednecks*, Dublin

Fennell, D., 1989, *The Revision of Irish Nationalism*, Dublin

Fennell, D., 1993, *Heresy: The Battle of Ideas in Modern Ireland*, Belfast

Ferriter, D., 2004, *The Transformation of Ireland 1900–2000*, London

FitzGerald, G., 1991, *All in a Life: An Autobiography*, Dublin

FitzGerald, G., 2003, *Reflections on the Irish State*, Dublin

Foley, C., 1992, *Legion of the Rearguard: The IRA and the Modern Irish State*, London

Foot, P., 1989, *Ireland: Why Britain Must Get Out*, London

Foster, R., 1988, *Modern Ireland 1600–1972*, London

Foster, R., 1993, *Paddy and Mr Punch: Connections in Irish and English History*, London

Foster, R., 2001, *The Irish Story: Telling Tales and Making it Up in Ireland*, London

Foster, R., 2007, *Luck and the Irish: A Brief History of Change. 1970–2000*, London.

Fox, R. (ed.), 1940, *Marx, Engels and Lenin on Ireland*, New York

Freire, P., 1972, *Cultural Freedom for Action*, Harmondsworth

Freire, P., 1972, *Pedagogy of the Oppressed*, Harmondsworth

Frost, C., 2006, 'Is Post-Nationalism or Liberal-Culturalism Behind the Transformation of Irish Nationalism?', *Irish Political Studies*, Vol. 21 No. 3

Fukuyama, F., 1992, *The End of History and The Last Man*, London

Furedi, F., 1992, *Mythical Past, Elusive Future: History and Society in an Anxious Age*, London

Furedi, F., 2004, *Therapy Culture*, London

Gaffkin, F., and Morrissey, M., in.P. Teague (ed.), 1987, *Beyond the Rhetoric: Politics, the Economy and Social Policy in Northern Ireland*, London

Gaffkin, F., and Morrissey, M., 1990, *Northern Ireland: The Thatcher Years*, London

Gallagher, E., 1994, 'Northern Ireland: Towards a New Paradigm', *Fortnight*, March

Gallagher, M., Marsh, M. and Mitchell, P., 2003, *How Ireland Voted 2002*, Basingstoke

Garvin, T., 1983, *The Evolution of Irish Nationalist Politics*, Dublin

Garvin, T., 1987, *Nationalist and Revolutionaries in Ireland 1858–1928*, Oxford

Gellner, E., 1983, *Nations and Nationalism*, Oxford

Geraghty, T., 1998, *The Irish War: The Military History of a Domestic Conflict*, London

Giddens, A., 1994, *Beyond Left and Right: The Future of Radical Politics*, Cambridge

Giddens, A., 1995, *New Thinking for New Times*, Belfast

Gilligan, C., and Tonge, J., 1997, *Peace or War? Understanding the Peace Process in Northern Ireland*, Aldershot

Gilmore, G., 1966a, *Labour and the Republican Movement*, Dublin

Gilmore, G., 1966b, *The Relevance of James Connolly in Ireland Today*, Dublin

Gilmore, G., 1978, *The Irish Republican Congress*, Cork

Godson, D., 2004, *Himself Alone: David Trimble and the Ordeal of Unionism*, London

Godson, D., 2007, 'The Real Lessons of Ulster', *Prospect*, November

Goldring, M., 1987, *Faith of our Fathers: The Formation of Irish Nationalist Ideology 1890–1920*, Dublin

Goodall, D., 2002, 'Hillsborough to Belfast: Is it the Final Lap', in M. Elliott, (ed.), *The Long Road to Peace in Northern Ireland*, Liverpool

Goodhart, D., 2006, 'National Anxieties', *Prospect*, June

Graham, B., and Shirlow, P., 1998, 'An Elusive Agenda: The Development of the Middle Ground in Northern Ireland', *Area*, Vol. 30 No. 3

Graham, B.D., 1993, *Representation and Party Politics: A Comparative Perspective*, Oxford

Gramsci, A., 1971, *Selections from the Prison Notebooks*, London

Gray, J., 1995, *Enlightenment's Wake: Politics and Culture at the Close of the Modern Age*, London

Gray, J., 1997, *End Games: Questions in Late Modern Political Thought*, Cambridge

Gray, J., 2003, *Al Qaeda and What It Means to be Modern*, London

Greater London Council, 1986, *Terence MacSwiney Memorial Lectures 1986*, London

Greaves, C.D., 1971, *Liam Mellows and the Irish Revolution*, London

Greaves, C.D., 1972, *The Life and Times of James Connolly*, London

Guelke, A., 2003, 'Civil Society and the Northern Irish Peace Process', *Voluntas: International Journal of Voluntary and Nonprofit Organizations*, Vol. 14 No. 1

Gurr, T.R., 1970, *Why Men Rebel*, Princeton

Hadaway, P., 2001, 'Cohesion in Contested Spaces', *Architects' Journal* November

Hadaway, P., 2003, 'Meaning over Form', unpublished MA thesis, University of Ulster

Hadaway, P., n.d., 'Identity Crisis', *The Vacuum*, undated: February (2004?)

Hadaway, P., 2007, 'A Cautionary Tale – The Experience of Belfast Exposed', *Printed Project*, October

Hadfield, B., 1992, *Northern Ireland: Politics and the Constitution*, Buckingham

Hadfield, B., 1998, 'The Belfast Agreement, Sovereignty and the State of the Union', *Public Law*, Vol. 15 Winter

Hall, S., 1990, 'Cultural Identity and Diaspora', in J. Rutherford (ed.), *Identity, Community Culture and Difference*, London

Hall, S., Held, D., and McGrew, A. (eds), 1992, *Modernity and its Futures*, Cambridge

Harnden, T., 1999, *'Bandit Country': The IRA and South Armagh*, London

Harris, M., 1997, 'Catholicism, Nationalism, and the Labour Question in Belfast, 1925–1938', *Bullan3*

Hart, P., 1998, *The IRA and its Enemies: Violence and Community in Cork, 1916–1923*, Oxford

Harvey, D., 1989, *The Condition of Postmodernity: An Enquiry into the Origins of Cultural Change*, Oxford

Hasek, J., 1973, *The Good Soldier Svejk and his Fortunes in the World War*, London

Hayden, T., 1999, 'Foreword', in M. Ó Muilleoir, *Belfast's Dome of Delight: City Hall Politics 1981–2000*, Belfast

Heartfield, J., 2002, *The 'Death of the Subject' Explained*, Sheffield

Hennessey, T., 2000, *The Northern Ireland Peace Process: Ending the Troubles?*, Dublin

Hepburn, A.C., 1996, *A Past Apart: Studies in the History of Catholic Belfast 1850–1950*, Belfast

Hils, C., 2004, *Archive Belfast*, Ostfildern-Ruit

Hobsbawm, E.J., 1985, *Bandits*, Harmondsworth

Hobsbawm, E.J., 1990, *Myth and Reality*, Cambridge

Hobsbawm, E.J., 1994, *The Age of Extremes: The Short Twentieth Century 1914–1991*, Harmondsworth

Hobsbawm, E.J., 2000, *The New Century*, London

Hobsbawm, E.J., 2007, *Globalisation, Democracy and Terrorism*, London

Hobsbawm, E.J., and Ranger, T. (eds), 1983, *The Invention of Tradition*, Cambridge

Hogan, G., 2007, 'Northern Ireland's New Troubles: The Privatization of Peace', *International Socialism*, Vol. 114, Spring

Holland, J., and Mac Donald, H., 1994, *INLA: Deadly Divisions*, Dublin

Holland, J., and Phoenix, S., 1997, *Phoenix: Policing the Shadows*, London

Hollinger, R., 1994, *Post-Modernism and the Social Sciences: A Thematic Approach*, Thousand Oaks,

Howe, S., 2000, *Ireland and Empire: Colonial Legacies in Irish History and Culture*, Oxford

Hume, J., 1996, *Personal View: Politics, Peace and Reconciliation in Ireland*, Dublin

Hutchinson, J., and Smith, A.D. (eds), 1994, *Nationalism*, Oxford

Hutton, W., 1994, *Britain and Northern Ireland: The State We're In – Failure and Opportunity*, Belfast

Ignatieff, M., 1994, *Blood and Belonging: Journeys into the New Nationalism*, London

Irvin, C., 1999, *Militant Nationalism: Between Movement and Party in Ireland and the Basque Country*, Minneapolis

Jessop, B., 1990, *State Theory: Putting Capitalist States in Their Place*, Cambridge

Kearney, O., and Wilson, D., 1988, *West Belfast: The Way Forward?*, Belfast

Kearney, R., 1984, *Myth and Motherland*, Derry

Kearney, R., 1991, 'Transitions', in S. Deane (ed.), *The Field Day Anthology of Irish Writing*, Derry

Kearney, R., 1997, *Postnationalist Ireland: Politics, Culture, Philosophy*, London

Kennedy, F., 2002, 'The 2002 General Election in Ireland', *Irish Political Studies* Vol. 17 No. 2

Kiberd, D., 1995, *Inventing Ireland*, London

Knox, C., and Carmichael, P., 2005, 'Improving the Quality of Public Services?', *Fortnight*, December

Koff, S., 2000, *Italy from the First to the Second Republic*, London

Kriesi, H., and Rucht, D., 1999, *Social Movements in a Globalizing World*, Basingstoke

Kymlicka, W., 2002, *Contemporary Political Philosophy: An Introduction*, Oxford

Laganside Corporation, 2004, *Laganside Corporation Annual Report and Accounts 2003–2004*, Belfast

Lahusen, C., 2004, 'Joining the Cocktail Circuit: Social Movement Organizations at the European Union', *Mobilization: An International Journal*, Vol. 9 No. 1

Lane, J. (ed.), 2006, *Was 1916 A Crime?*, Millstreet

Laqueur, W., 1987, *The Age of Terrorism*, London

Lechte, J., 1994, *Fifty Key Contemporary Thinkers: From Structuralism to Postmodernity*, London

Lee, J.J., 1989, *Ireland 1912–1985: Politics and Society*, Cambridge

Lenin, V.I., 1971, *What Is To Be Done?*, Moscow

Lenin, V.I., 1973, *Imperialism, the Highest Stage of Capitalism*, Peking

Livingstone, K., 1988, *If Voting Changed Anything They'd Abolish It*, London

Livingstone, K., 1989, in M. Collins (ed.), *Ireland After Britain*, London

Lloyd D., 1999, *Ireland After History*, Cork

Loughlin, J., 2004, *The Ulster Question Since 1945*, Basingstoke

Lynn, B., 2003, 'Tactic or Principle? The Evolution of Republican Thinking on Abstentionism in Ireland, 1970–1998', *Irish Political Studies*, Vol. 17 No. 2

McAdam, D., 2003, 'Symposium on the Dynamics of Contention', *Mobilization: An International Journal*, Vol. 8 No. 1

McAdam, D., Tarrow, S., and Tilly, C., 2001, *Dynamics of Contention*, Cambridge

McAuley, J.W., 2003, *An Introduction to Politics, State and Society*, London

McCaffrey, B., 2003, *Alex Maskey: Man and Mayor*, Belfast

McCall, C., 1999, *Identity in Northern Ireland: Communities, Politics and Change*, Basingstoke

McCann, E., 1993, *War and an Irish Town*, London

McCann, E., 1998, *War and Peace in Northern Ireland*, Dublin

McCrone, D., 1998, *The Sociology of Nationalism: Tomorrow's Ancestors*, London

MacDonagh, O., 1983, *States of Mind: A Study of Anglo–Irish Conflict 1780–1980*, London

McDonald, H., 2004, *Colours: Ireland from Bombs to Boom*, Edinburgh

McGarry, F., 2003, *Republicanism in Modern Ireland*, Dublin

McGarry, J., and O'Leary, B., 2004, *The Northern Ireland Conflict: Consociational Engagements*, Oxford

McGeough, G., 1996, *The Ambush and Other Stories*, New York

McGinty, R., 2006, 'Irish Republicanism and the Peace Process: From Revolution to Reform', in M. Cox, A. Guelke and F. Stephen (eds), *A Farewell to Arms? Beyond the Good Friday Agreement*, 2nd edn, Manchester

McGovern, M., 2000, 'Irish Republicanism and the Potential Pitfalls of Pluralism', *Capital and Class*, Vol. 71

McGovern, M., 2004 'The Old Days Are Over: Irish Republicanism, the Peace Process and the Concept of Equality', *Terrorism and Political Violence*, Vol. 16 No. 3

McGovern, M., and Shirlow, P. (eds), 1997, *Who Are 'The People'? Unionism, Loyalism and Protestantism in Northern Ireland*, London

McGrath, C. and O'Malley, E., 2008, *Irish Political Studies: Key Contributions*, Abingdon

McIntyre, A., 1995a, 'Modern Irish Republicanism: The Product of British State Strategies', *Irish Political Studies*, Vol. 10

McIntyre, A., 1995b, 'A Framework That Won't Work', *Report of University of North London Conference*, London

McIntyre, A., 1999, 'A Structural Analysis of Modern Irish Republicanism 1969–1973', unpublished PhD thesis, Queens' University, Belfast

McIntyre, A. , 2001, 'Modern Irish Republicanism and the Belfast Agreement: Chickens Coming Home to Roost, or Turkeys Celebrating Christmas?', in R. Wilford (ed.), *Aspects of the Belfast Agreement*, Oxford

McIntyre, A., 2003, 'Provisional Republicanism; Inequities, Internal Politics and Repression', in F. McGarry (ed.), *Republicanism in Modern Ireland*, Dublin

McKeown, L., 2001, *Out of Time: Irish Republican Prisoners Long Kesh 1972–2000*, Belfast

McKittrick, D., 1989, *Dispatches from Belfast*, Belfast

McKittrick, D., 1996, *The Nervous Peace*, Belfast

McLaughlin, M., 1995, 'Northern Ireland in the Year 2000', *Report of University of North London Conference*, London

MacNamara, J.K., 2006, 'The MacBride Principles', unpublished PhD thesis, University of Liverpool

Mac Swiney, T., 1921 *Principles of Freedom*, Dublin

McVeigh, R., 2002, 'Between Reconciliation and Pacification: The British State and Community Relations in the North of Ireland', *Community Development Journal*, Vol. 37 No. 1

Maillot, A., 2005, *New Sinn Fein: Irish Republicanism in the Twenty-First Century*, London

Malik, K., 1996, *The Meaning of Race: Race, History and Culture in Western Society*, Basingstoke

Malik, K., 2005, 'Born in Bradford', *Prospect*, October

Malik, K., 2006, 'Illusions of Identity', *Prospect*, August

Mallie, E., and McKitterick, D., 1996, *The Fight for Peace: The Secret Story Behind the Irish Peace Process*, London

Mansergh, M., 2003, *The Legacy of History For Making Peace in Ireland*, Cork

Marx, K., and Engels, F., 1970, *Selected Works*, London

Marx, K., and Engels, F., 1971, *Ireland and the Irish Question*, London

Merrifield, A., 1993, 'Place and Space: Lefebvrian Reconciliation', *Transactions of the Institute of British Geographers*, new series, Vol. 18

Meyer, C., 2005, *DC Confidential*, London

Michels, R. (translated by Paul, E. and Paul, C.), 1959, *Political Parties: A Sociological Study of the Oligarchical Tendencies of Modern Democracy*, New York

Miller, D., (ed.), 1998, *Rethinking Northern Ireland: Culture, Ideology and Colonialism*, London

Mitchell, B., 1966, *British Parliamentary Results 1950–1964*, Cambridge

Mitchell, C., 2003, 'From Victims to Equals? Catholic Responses to Political Change in Northern Ireland', *Irish Political Studies*, Vol. 18 No. 1

Moloney, E., 2002, *A Secret History of the IRA*, London

Moloney, E., 2006, 'The Peace Process and Journalism', *Britain and Ireland: Lives Entwined II*, Dublin

Moloney, E., 2007, (2nd edn) *A Secret History of the IRA*, London

Monaghan, R., and McLaughlin, S., 2006, 'Informal Justice in the City', *Space and Polity*, Vol. 10 No. 2

Morrison, D., 1984, *The Good Old IRA*, Dublin

Morrison, D., 1986, *The Hillsborough Agreement*, Belfast

Morrison, D., 1989, *West Belfast*, Cork

Morrison, D., 1999, *Then The Walls Came Down: A Prison Journal*, Cork

Morrow, D., 2005, 'Governing a Divided Society', *Fortnight*, December

Mulgan, G., 1994, *Politics in an Antipolitical Age*, Cambridge

Munck, R., Rolston, B., and Moore, G., 1987, *Belfast in the Thirties: An Oral History*, Belfast

Murphy, Y., Leonard, A., Gillespie, G., and Brown, K. (eds), 2000, *Troubled Images: Posters and Images of the Northern Ireland Conflict from the Linen Hall Library*, Belfast

Murray, C., 1984, *Losing Ground: American Social Policy 1950–1980*, New York

Murray, C., 1990, *The Emerging British Underclass*, London

Murray, G. and Tonge, J., 2004, *Sinn Féin and the SDLP: From Alienation to*

Participation, London

Murtagh, B., 2001 'The URBAN Community Initiative in Northern Ireland', *Policy and Politics*, Vol. 29 No. 4

Nairn, T., 1981, *The Break-up of Britain: Crisis and Neo-Nationalism*, London

Nairn, T., 1997, *Faces of Nationalism: Janus Revisited*, London

Needham, R., 1998, *Battling For Peace*, Belfast

Neill, W., 1995, 'Lipstick on the Gorilla; Conflict Management, Urban Development and Image Making in Belfast', in W. Neill, D. Fitzsimmons and B. Murtagh (eds), *Reimagining the Pariah City: Urban Development in Belfast and Detroit*, Aldershot

Neumann, P., 2003, *Britain's Long War: British Strategy in the Northern Ireland Conflict, 1969–98*, Basingstoke

New Ireland Forum Report, 1984, Dublin

Nic Craith, M., 2003, *Culture and Identity Politics in Northern Ireland*, Basingstoke

Ni Dhonnachadha, M., and Dorgan, T. (eds), 1991, *Revising the Rising*, Derry

Nisbet, R., 1986, *Conservatism*, Milton Keynes

Northern Ireland Annual Abstract of Statistics, 1997, Belfast

Novick, B., 2001, *Conceiving Revolution: Irish Nationalist Propaganda during the First World War*, Dublin

Ó Bradaigh, R., 1997, *Dílseacht: The Story of Comdt. General Tom Maguire and the Second All-Ireland Dáil*, Dublin

O'Brien, B., 1993, *The Long War: The IRA and Sinn Fein 1985 to Today*, Dublin

O'Brien, B., 1997, *A Pocket History of the IRA*, Dublin

O'Brien, C.C., 1972, *States of Ireland*, London

O'Brien, C.C., 1994, *Ancestral Voices: Religion and Nationalism in Ireland*, Dublin

O'Brien, C.C., 1998, *Memoir: My Life and Themes*, Dublin

O'Brien, E., 2003, 'A Nation Once Again: Towards an Epistemology of the Provisional Imaginaire', in F. McGarry (ed.), *Republicanism in Modern Ireland*, Dublin

O'Callaghan, S., 1998, *The Informer*, London

Ó Ceallaigh, D., 1996, *Britain and Ireland: Sovereignty and Nationality*, Dublin

Ó Ceallaigh, D., 2000, *Irish Republicanism: Good Friday and After*, Dublin

O'Connell, S., and Greenfield, J., 2006, 'From joyriders to death drivers: masculinity and car crime in Belfast, 1930–1990', paper given at the University of Liverpool, 23 February

O'Connor, F., 1993, *In Search of a State: Catholics in Northern Ireland*, Belfast

O'Day, A., 1995, *Terrorism's Laboratory: The Case of Northern Ireland*, Aldershot

Ó Dochartaigh, N., 1997, *From Civil Rights to Armalites: Derry and the Birth of the Irish Troubles*, Cork

O'Doherty, M., 1998, *The Trouble with Guns: Republican Strategy and the Provisional IRA*, Belfast

O'Doherty, M., 2003, 'A Bit of a Nuisance', in M. Carruthers, S. Douds and T. Loane (eds), *Re-Imagining Belfast: A Manifesto for the Arts*, Belfast

O'Doherty, S., 1993, *The Volunteer: A Former IRA Man's True Story*, London

O'Donnell, C., 2003, 'Fianna Fáil and Sinn Féin: The 1988 Talks Reappraised', *Irish Political Studies*, Vol. 18 No. 2

O' Donnell, C., 2007, *Fianna Fáil, Irish Republicanism and the Northern Ireland Troubles 1968–2005*, Dublin

O'Hagan, D., 1996, 'Allies or antagonists? Irish Catholicism and Irish Republicanism 1980–1996', unpublished paper given at University of Central Lancashire Irish Studies Conference, June

O'Halloran, C., 1987, *Partition and the Limits of Irish Nationalism*, Dublin

O'Hare, S.P., 2006, '*Fáilte*/Welcome', *Féile Programme*, Belfast

O'Hearn, D., 2006, *Bobby Sands: Nothing but an Unfinished Song*, London

O'Leary, B., and McGarry, J., 1993, *The Politics of Antagonism: Understanding Northern Ireland*, London

O'Leary, B., and McGarry, J., 1995, *Explaining Northern Ireland: Broken Images*, Oxford

Oliver, P.E., and Myers, D.J., 2003, 'The Coevolution of Social Movements', *Mobilization: An International Journal*, Vol. 8 No. 1

O'Mahony, P. and Delanty, G., 1998, *Rethinking Irish History: Nationalism, Identity and Ideology*, Basingstoke

O'Malley, P., 1983, *The Uncivil Wars: Ireland Today*, Belfast

O'Malley, P., 1990, *Biting at the Grave: The Irish Hunger Strikes and the Politics of Despair*, Belfast

Ó Muilleoir, M., 1999, *Belfast's Dome of Delight: City Hall Politics 1981–2000*, Belfast

O'Rawe, R., 2005, *Blanketmen: An Untold Story of the H-Block Hunger Strike*, Dublin

Ormsby, F., 1992, *A Rage for Order: Poetry of the Northern Ireland Troubles*, Belfast

O' Rourke, L., n.d., 'From Alternative Press to Corporate Mainstream: The Case of the Andersonstown News', *The Vacuum* Issue 14, undated (2004?)

Ó Ruairc, L., 2007, 'The Agreed Truth and The Real Truth: the New Northern Ireland', *Variant*, Vol. 39 Spring

Ozkirimli, U., 2000, *Theories of Nationalism*, Basingstoke

Panebianco, A., 1988, *Political Parties: Organisation and Power*, Cambridge

Partridge, H., 1998, *Italian Politics Today*, Manchester

Patsios, D., and Tomlinson, M., 2003, *Bare Necessities; Poverty and Social Exclusion in Northern Ireland*, Belfast

Patterson, H., 1997, *The Politics of Illusion: A Political History of the IRA*, London

Patterson, H., 2007, *Ireland Since 1939*, London

Pearsall, D., and Salter, E. (eds), 1967, *William Langland's Piers Plowman*, London

Pearse, P.H., 1976, *The Murder Machine and Other Essays*, Cork

'People's Democracy: a discussion on strategy', 1969, *New Left Review*, Vol. 55 May–June

Phoenix, E., 1994, *Northern Nationalism: Nationalist Politics, Partition and the Catholic Minority in Northern Ireland 1890–1940*, Belfast

Pierson, C., 1994, *Beyond the Welfare State? The New Political Economy of Welfare*, Cambridge

Pine, R., 1985, 'Reflections on Dependence and Independence', *The Crane Bag*, Vol. IX,

Pollak, A. (ed.), 1993, *A Citizen's Enquiry: The Opsahl Report on Northern Ireland*, Dublin

Porter, N., 1998, *The Republican Ideal: Current Perspectives*, Belfast

Power, M., 2005, 'Building Communities in a Post-Conflict Society: Churches and Peace Building in Northern Ireland since 1994', *The European Legacy*, Vol. 19 No. 1

Przeworski, A., and Wallerstein, M., 1982, 'The Structure of Class Conflict in Democratic Capitalist States', *American Political Science Review*, Vol. 76 No. 2

Purdie, B., 1986, 'The Irish Anti-Partition League, South Armagh and the Abstentionist Tactic 1945–58', *Irish Political Studies*, Vol. I

Puzo, M. and Coppola, F.F., 1972, *The Godfather Part I – Screenplay*, http://www.imsdb.com/scripts/Godfather.html

Quinn, R.J., 1999, *A Rebel Voice: A History of Belfast Republicanism 1925–1972*, Belfast

Rafter, K., 2005, *Sinn Féin 1905–2005: In the Shadow of Gunmen*, Dublin

Reed, D., 1984, *Ireland: The Key to the British Revolution*, London

Robson, T., 2000, *The State and Community Action*, London

Rolston, R., 2003, 'Changing the Political Landscape: Murals and Transition in Northern Ireland,' *Irish Studies Review*, Vol. 11 No. 1

Rolston, B., and Miller, D., 1996, *War and Words: The Northern Ireland Media Reader*, Belfast

Rowan, B., 1995, *Behind the Lines: The Story of the IRA and Loyalist Ceasefires*, Belfast

Rowan, B., 2003, *The Armed Peace: Life and Death after the Ceasefires*, Edinburgh

Rowthorn, B., and Wayne, N., 1988, *Northern Ireland: The Political Economy of Conflict*, Cambridge

Ruane, J., and Todd, J., 1996, *The Dynamics of Conflict in Northern Ireland: Power Conflict and Emancipation*, Cambridge

Ruane, J., and Todd, J. (eds), 1999, *After the Good Friday Agreement: Analysing Political Change in Northern Ireland*, Dublin

Ruane, J., and Todd, J., 2001, 'The Politics of Transition? Explaining Political Crises in the Implementation of the Good Friday Agreement', *Political Studies*, Vol. 49 No. 5

Rucht, D., 1999, 'Linking Organization and Mobilization: Michel's Iron Law of Oligarchy Reconsidered', *Mobilization: An International Journal*, Vol. 4 No. 2

Rutherford, J. (ed.), 1990, *Identity, Community Culture and Difference*, London

Ryan, M., 1994, *War and Peace in Ireland: Britain and the IRA in the New World Order*, London

Ryan, M., 1997, 'From the Centre to the Margins: The Slow Death of Irish Republicanism', in C. Gilligan and J. Tonge (eds), *Peace or War? Understanding the
Peace Process in Northern Ireland*, Aldershot

Said, E., 1993, *Culture and Imperialism*, London

Sands, B., 1981, *The Diary of Bobby Sands*, Dublin

Sands, B., 1998, *Writings from Prison*, Cork

Sharrock, D., and Devenport, M., 1997, *Man of War, Man of Peace: The Unauthor-
ised Biography of Gerry Adams*, London

Sheehan, M., and Tomlinson, M., 1996, 'Long Term Unemployment in West
Belfast', in E. McLaughlin (ed.), *Aspects of Employment Equality Policy in
Northern Ireland*, Belfast

Sheehan, M., and Tomlinson, M., 1999, *The Unequal Unemployed: Discrimination,
Unemployment and State Policy in Northern Ireland*, Aldershot

Shirlow, P., 1997, 'The Economics of the Peace Process', in C. Gilligan and J. Tonge
(eds), *Peace or War? Understanding the Peace Process in Northern Ireland*,
Aldershot

Shirlow, P., 1997, 'Class, Materialism and the Fracturing of Traditional Align-
ments', in B. Graham (ed.), *In Search of Ireland*, London

Shirlow, P., 2001, 'Fear and Ethnic Division in Belfast', *Peace Review*, Vol. 13
Issue 2

Shirlow, P., and Murtagh, B., 2006, *Belfast: Segregation, Violence and the City*,
London

Shirlow, P., and Shuttleworth, I., 1999, 'Who Is Going to Toss the Burgers?',
Capital and Class Special Issue, No. 69

Sinn Féin, 1972, *Éire Nua*, Dublin

Sinn Féin, 1973, *Freedom Struggle*, Dublin

Sinn Féin, 1973, *The Good Old IRA*, Dublin

Sinn Féin, 1986, *The Politics of Revolution: Main Speeches and Debates 1986 Sinn
Fein Ard Fheis*, Dublin

Sinn Féin, 1987, *Setting the Criteria: Tackling Discrimination – Sinn Féin's Analysis
and Proposals*, Dublin

Sinn Féin, 1988, *A Scenario for Peace*, Dublin

Sinn Féin, 1992, *Towards a Lasting Peace in Ireland*, Dublin

Sinn Féin, 1994, *Setting The Record Straight*, Dublin

Sinn Féin, 1994, *The Economics of a United Ireland*, Dublin

Sinn Féin, 2005, *Sinn Fein: A Century of Struggle*, Dublin

Sinn Féin, 2007, *Delivering for Ireland's Future: Saoirse, Ceart agus Síocháin*, Dublin

Sinn Féin, n.d., *Internal Conference on Community Politics*, Belfast (1991?)

Sinn Féin Education Department, 1983, *Election Interventions: Historical and
Contemporary*, Belfast

Sinn Féin Education Department, n.d., *The History of Republicanism: Part 1*,
Dublin (1990?)

Sluka, J.A., 1989, *Hearts and Minds, Water and Fish: Support for the IRA and
INLA in a Northern Irish Ghetto*, Greenwich

Smith, A.D., 1995, *Nations and Nationalism in a Global Era*, Cambridge

Smith, M.L.R., 1995, *Fighting For Ireland? The Military Strategy of the Irish Republican Movement*, London

Smith, S., 1999, 'The Cultural Politics of Difference', in D. Massey, J. Allen and P. Sarre (eds), *Human Geography Today*, Cambridge

Smyth, J., 2005, 'On the Road to God Knows Where: Understanding Irish Republicanism', *Capital and Class*, Vol. 86 Summer

Springfield Inter-Community Development Project, 2003, *Community Development: Socialism in Practice?*, Newtownabbey

Staunton, E., 2001, *The Nationalists of Northern Ireland 1918–1973*, Blackrock

Stevenson, J., 1996, *'We Wrecked the Place': Contemplating an End to the Northern Irish Troubles*, New York

Stewart, A.T.Q., 1977, *The Narrow Ground: The Roots of Conflict in Ulster*, London

Stewart, A.T.Q., 1993, *A Deeper Silence: The Hidden Roots of the United Irish Movement*, London

Stewart, P., and Shirlow, P. (eds), 1999, 'Northern Ireland: Between Peace and War?', *Capital and Class*, Vol. 69

Swan, S., 2007, *Official Irish Republicanism 1962 to 1972* (n.p.)

Tarrow, S., 1998, *Power in Movement: Social Movements and Contentious Politics*, Oxford

Taylor, A., 2005, 'The State', in G. Blakeley and V. Bryson (eds), *Marx and Other Four Letter Words*, London

Taylor, C. (ed.), 1994, *Multiculturalism: Explaining the Politics of Recognition*, Princeton

Taylor, P., 1997, *Provos: The IRA and Sinn Fein*, London

Taylor, P., 2000, *Loyalists*, London

Teague, P. (ed.), 1987, *Beyond the Rhetoric: Politics, the Economy and Social Policy in Northern Ireland*, London

Teague, P. (ed.), 1993, *The Economy of Northern Ireland: Perspectives for Structural Change*, London

Thompson, E.P., 1971, 'The Moral Economy of the English Crowd in the Eighteenth Century', *Past and Present*

Thompson, E.P., 1978, *The Poverty of Theory*, London

Thompson, E.P., 1980, *The Making of the English Working Class*, Harmondsworth

Thompson, E.P., 1991, *Customs in Common*, Harmondsworth

Tilly, C., 1978, *From Mobilisation to Revolution*, Reading

Todd, J., 1990, 'Northern Irish Nationalist Political Culture', *Irish Political Studies*, Vol. V

Tomlinson, M., 1995, 'Can Britain Leave Ireland? The Political Economy of War and Peace', *Race and Class: Ireland New Beginnings*, Vol. 37

Tone, T.W., 1998, *The Life of Theobald Wolfe Tone*, Dublin

Tonge, J., 2002, *Northern Ireland: conflict and change*, Harlow

Tonge, J., 2005, *The New Northern Irish Politics?* Basingstoke

Tonge, J., 2006, *Northern Ireland*, Cambridge

Toolis, K., 1995, *Rebel Hearts: Journeys Within the IRA's Soul*, London

Turner, B.S. (ed.), 1991, *Theories of Modernity and Postmodernity*, London

University of North London, 1995, *Report of University of North London Conference on the Future of Northern Ireland*, London

Upper Springfield Development Trust Annual Report 2004, 2004, Belfast

Wainwright, H., 2003, *Reclaim the State: Experiments in Popular Democracy*, London

Walker, B., 2000, *Past and Present: History, Identity and Politics in Ireland*, Belfast

Walker,G., 2004, *A History of the Ulster Unionist Party: Protest, Pragmatism and Pessimism*, Manchester

Walsh, P., 1994, *Irish Republicanism and Socialism: The Politics of the Republican Movement 1905 to 1994*, Belfast

Walton, S., 2002, *Scared of the Kids? Curfew, Crime and the Regulation of Young People*, Sheffield

Weight, R., 2003, *Patriots: National Identity in Britain 1940–2000*, London

White, A.P., 2000, 'The Role of the Community Sector in the British Government's Inner-City Policy in Northern Ireland', unpublished PhD thesis, Queen's University, Belfast

White, R.W., 1988, 'Commitment, Efficacy, and Personal Sacrifice Among Irish Republicans', *Journal of Political and Military Sociology*, Vol. 16

White, R.W., 1989, 'From Peaceful Protest to Guerrilla War: Micromobilisation of the Provisional Irish Republican Army', *American Journal of Sociology*, Vol. 94

White, R.W., 1991, 'Revolution in the City: On the Resources of Urban Guerrillas', *Terrorism and Political Violence*, Vol. 3

White, R.W., 1992, 'Political Violence By The Nonaggrieved: Explaining The Political Participation Of Those With No Apparent Grievances', *International Social Movement Research*, Vol. 4

White, R.W., 1993, *Provisional Irish Republicans: An Oral and Interpretive History*, Westport

White, R.W., 2006, *Ruairí Ó Brádaigh: The Life and Politics of an Irish Revolutionary*, Bloomington and Indianapolis

Whyte, J., 1990, *Interpreting Northern Ireland*, Oxford

Wichert, S., 1999, *Northern Ireland Since 1945*, New York

Wilford, R., 2001, *Aspects of the Belfast Agreement*, Oxford

Williams, R., 1976, *Keywords*, London

Williams, R., 1977, *Marxism and Literature*, Oxford

Wilson, D., 1988, *West Belfast: Liberation or Oppression*, Belfast

Wilson, R., 1997, *Continentally Challenged*, Belfast

Witoszek, N., and Sheeran, P., 1985, 'From Explanation to Intervention', *The Crane Bag*, Vol. IX

Wolfe, A., and Klausen, J., 2000. 'Other People', *Prospect*, December

Woods, A., 2005, *Ireland: Republicanism and Revolution*, London

Wright, F., 1992, *Northern Ireland: A Comparative Analysis*, Dublin

Index

Page references for footnotes are followed by n

Printed and bound by CPI Group (UK) Ltd, Croydon, CR0 4YY

13/04/2025

14656605-0002